INNOVATION MANAGEMENT
Strategy and Implementation using the Pentathlon Framework
SECOND EDITION

KEITH GOFFIN & RICK MITCHELL

Includes 77 innovation case studies – from the service and manufacturing
sectors and from around the globe

palgrave
macmillan

First edition 2005
Reprinted six times
This edition published 2010 by
PALGRAVE MACMILLAN

Palgrave Macmillan in the UK is an imprint of Macmillan Publishers Limited, registered in England, company number 785998, of Houndmills, Basingstoke, Hampshire RG21 6XS.

Palgrave Macmillan in the US is a division of St Martin's Press LLC, 175 Fifth Avenue, New York, NY 10010.

Palgrave Macmillan is the global academic imprint of the above companies and has companies and representatives throughout the world.

Palgrave® and Macmillan® are registered trademarks in the United States, the United Kingdom, Europe and other countries.

ISBN: 978-0-230-20582-6 hardback

This book is printed on paper suitable for recycling and made from fully managed and sustained forest sources. Logging, pulping and manufacturing processes are expected to conform to the environmental regulations of the country of origin.

A catalogue record for this book is available from the British Library.

A catalog record for this book is available from the Library of Congress.

10 9 8 7 6 5 4 3 2
19 18 17 16 15 14 13 12 11 10

Printed and bound in China

Contents Overview

Table of Contents

Case Studies

Innovation management is a very practical subject and for this reason we have included 77 cases studies in this edition. Each chapter includes five or more mini case studies and one main case study. The main case studies look at themes raised in the chapter and include a set of assignment questions. These are designed to help the reader generalize some of the ideas from the case study. The box cases are linked to the text and give a unique set of examples of innovation management in practice. The majority of the cases are based on material supplemented with interviews with the managers involved. A deliberate international mix of examples from both the service and manufacturing sectors has been chosen.

Service cases	32
Manufacturing cases	37
Manufacturing and service	4
Government cases	2
General cases	2
TOTAL	77

Acknowledgements

To write a book aimed at MBA students and practising managers requires a high level of contact with both of these groups, in order to try to understand their needs. In our teaching and research we are fortunate to come into constant contact with excellent students and managers who are not only very good at what they do but are also reflective on the issues they face. We have benefited enormously from interacting with both these groups, and from their ideas, probing questions and the experiences they have shared with us. This second edition includes many ideas based on feedback from our students and work with executives.

A number of our MBA students have directly helped us with preparing material for the book and in providing comments on drafts: many thanks to Danu Chotikapanich, Micha Dannenhauer, Rodrigo Gamarci, Synthiea Kaldi, Helmut Kraft, Hector Martinez, Alejo Ribalta and David Watsham. Several of our former doctoral students, particularly Ursula Koners and Bertram Lohmüller, helped us with both identifying the key literature on specific aspects of innovation management and through generating new ideas from their own research.

The Pentathlon Framework that provides the backbone for this book was developed from research generously supported by the *Anglo-German Foundation*. Thanks also to the many managers who were interviewed as part of this research and contributed many of the ideas about how a framework for innovation management could be used.

A large number of managers in industry have given up precious time to help us in with the case studies, or have provided material and ideas through being regular guest speakers at our lectures. Thanks to the following: Patty Arellano (Texas Instruments), Jörg Asbrand (time:matters), Stefanie Bartle (Mondial), Mirjam Berle (time:matters), Seth Bishop (Leapfrog), Simon Bradley (Domino Printing Sciences), Mark Chizlett (Britannia), Vorapant Chotikapanich (Cobra International), Dave Cope (Domino Printing Sciences), Martin Cserba (21Torr Agency), Massimo Fumarola (Fiat-Iveco), Klaus Fischer (Fischer GmbH), John Fisher (PA Consultancy), Julian Glyn-Owen (Boxer), Angelique Green (Boxer), Torsten Herzberg (Vodafone), Dr Christiane Hipp (Vodafone), Erik Hoppenbrouwer (Organon), David Humphries (PDD), M. N. Karthik (Wipro Technologies), Dr Armin Khan (Malaysia Airlines), John Lagerling (NTT-DoCoMo), Mr T. Linganatham (Texas Instruments Malaysia), Michael Mallon (Fruit of the Loom), Steve Marriott (Domino Printing Sciences), Bob McKune (Texas Instruments), Liam Mifsud (Equant), Franz-Joseph Miller (time:matters), Dr Edwin Moses (Evotec), Sachin Mulay (Wipro Technologies), Wim Obouter (Micro-mobility), John O'Neill (AXA), Cheryl Perkins (Innovationedge), Dr Mario Polywka (Evotec), Dr Helmut Rapp (Sidler GmbH & Co.), Klaus

Stemig (Mondial Assistance GmbH), Dr Magnus Schoeman (Steria), Klaus Schnurr (PureInsight), Daniel Scuka (Wireless Watch Japan), Chris Towns (Clarks), Katja van der Wal (Philips), Mr A. Vasudevan (Wipro Technologies), Eva Weber (Vodafone), Bob Wheedon (Texas Instruments), Catherine Whelan (AXA), Howard Whitesmith (Domino Printing Sciences), Werner Widmann (Verigy), David Williams (Richardsons, Sheffield) and Michael Yonker (Texas Instruments).

To help keep a practical focus to our work, three managers assisted in reviewing early drafts, providing contacts in industry and in helping with the preparation of case study material. Their help was invaluable and so many thanks to Trudy Lloyd (Synectics), Mike Northcott (Hewlett-Packard) and William Pipkin (Pipkin Associates).

Matching pragmatism with academic rigour is essential and we are fortunate to have supportive colleagues who looked at many drafts and helped us to get our ideas straight. Prof. Dr Harald Hagemann (Hohenheim University), Prof. Dr Cornelius Herstatt (Hamburg-Harburg); and David Probert, Rob Phaal, Pete Fraser, Clare Farrukh and Francis Hunt (all of Cambridge University) all contributed material and gave us useful ideas. Dr Ralph Levene[†] (Cranfield), Prof. Paul Millier (EMLyon), particularly Prof. Dr Rolf Pfeiffer (Reutlingen), Dr Alan Cousens (Cranfield) and Chris van der Hoven (Cranfield) all contributed ideas on how best to present the Pentathlon framework. Particular thanks goes to Dr Fred Lemke (San Diego); Prof. Dr Udo Staber (Canterbury, New Zealand), Dr Marek Szwejczewski (Cranfield) and David Walker (Giraffe Consultants, New Zealand) for reviewing drafts and giving us their insights. Our anonymous academic reviewers also took the time and effort to make many useful and concrete suggestions. And 'last but not least', changes and copyright issues were managed very professionally by Maggie Neale (Cranfield).

Preface

This book is for students and managers who want a practical but academically rigorous guide to Innovation Management. It is based on a framework of innovation management – the Innovation Pentathlon – which was developed from our research and has been used extensively in our work with companies. Our research showed that senior managers felt the need for an overall framework to help them understand the innovation performance of their companies, as well as tools and techniques they need to improve it. At a meeting in 2000, where over twenty European universities presented the results of their research to industrialists, a senior manager from the GlaxoSmithKline pharmaceutical company commented forcibly that he needed integrative tools for innovation management, not the ad hoc collection of, what he called, 'snippets of best practice' given by university researchers. Managers recognize that there are many facets to managing innovation: it involves strategy (for example, whether to be first-to-market, or to be a fast-follower); people management (for example, organizing and motivating teams); good project management (for example, in striving to meet challenging time-to-market goals); and much else. Integrating the many facets of innovation management is the challenge, and managers in the real world need all the help they can get from the academic world.

This book borrows ideas and concepts from a range of disciplines, from economics to organizational behaviour and change management. Throughout the book, we have tried to present a clear outline of the theory relating to each topic together with illustrative examples of how it has played out in practice. There are 67 half-page 'mini cases' and one multi-page case study per chapter; a total of 77 in all. In writing these cases we have deliberately sought to achieve parity between the manufacturing and service sectors – too often the service sector is not done justice in writings about innovation management. In addition, we have tried to provide a truly international mix of cases. The table on pages xii–xv lists both the mini and main cases per chapter. Additional teaching material such as study questions, teaching notes and slides are provided on the associated web site.

There are no 'quick fixes' in the complex field of innovation management. Therefore, the challenge for managers is not just to adopt the ideas in this book but to adapt and blend them to fit the context their organizations face. We wish them every success in meeting that challenge.

About the Authors

KEITH GOFFIN BSC, MSC, PHD

Keith is Professor of Innovation and New Product Development at Cranfield School of Management in the UK.

He graduated from Durham University in 1977 with a degree in Physics and subsequently obtained an MSc in Medical Physics from Aberdeen University. For 14 years he worked for the Medical Products Group of Hewlett-Packard (HP), starting as a support engineer working on new product development. In subsequent management roles he gained extensive experience in international marketing and, for example, took HP's defibrillator products from a 5 per cent market share to market leadership position within a year. Parallel to his management responsibilities, Keith studied part-time for a PhD at Cranfield. The results of his research on customer support have been applied at Ford, NCR and HP. In 1991 he became Product Marketing Manager at HP and focused on developing the intensive care market in Asia/Pacific, before leaving HP in 1994 to join Cranfield.

At Cranfield, Keith lectures on both the MBA and Executive Programmes and has developed a number of new courses on innovation management. Keith regularly lectures at other schools, including Bocconi University, ESSEC in Paris, EM-Lyon, Mannheim Business School, the Technical University of Hamburg-Harburg, Stockholm School of Economics and the Universiti Teknologi Malaysia. From 2002–2004 he worked as Academic Dean at Stuttgart Institute of Management and Technology.

His current research interests are innovation leadership, tacit knowledge in R&D, project-to-project learning and empathic design. He has published two books, eleven reports and over eighty articles in a number of journals and magazines, including the International Journal of Operations & Production Management, the Journal of Product Innovation Management and Journal of Operations Management. In addition to his work at universities, he regularly acts as an innovation management consultant to companies including Agilent Technologies, Bosch, Kellogg's, HSBC Bank, BOC Gases, the Xerox Corporation, Philips, Sony, UPM and Heidelberger Druckmaschinen.

RICK MITCHELL MA PHD CENG FIET

Rick is Visiting Professor of Innovation Management at Cranfield School of Management and a visiting research fellow in the Engineering Department at Cambridge University.

He has a degree in Natural Sciences from Cambridge University and he joined Philips Research Laboratories in 1965 where he worked on thermal imaging, acoustic wave devices and radio system design. He has received 26 patents and published over twenty papers on these developments. Parallel to his work at Philips, Rick studied for a PhD in electrical engineering, which he received from Queen Mary College in London in 1971.

After three years as a Corporate Planner for Philips Electronics, Rick moved to their Pye Telecommunications subsidiary as Radio Systems Division Manager for four years, before becoming International Development Manager for all Philips mobile radio business in 1986.

Joining Domino Printing Sciences, a world leader in coding and marking equipment, in 1985, Rick managed both the R&D and Quality functions and developed the company's expertise in new areas such as laser-based equipment. He joined the main board of the company in 1994 as Technical Director, with responsibilities across 4 R&D sites and 12 subsidiaries. In 1990, he co-authored the book *How to Profit from Innovation*. He has been a guest speaker at many conferences on R&D and manufacturing management, both for the Department of Trade and Industry and Cranfield School of Management.

In February 2001, Rick was appointed as Visiting Professor at Cranfield and he takes an active role in designing and presenting courses on technology and innovation management at Cranfield and Cambridge. These interests have increased since his retirement from Domino in 2003. He has taught on academic courses in France, Malaysia, Germany, Hong Kong, USA and Trinidad.

Copyright Material

1 KEY ASPECTS OF INNOVATION MANAGEMENT

radical / incremental innovation

Innovation – n., introducing something new

Oxford English Dictionary

INTRODUCTION

Innovation: yes, but how? Every year, the latest surveys by government organizations and leading consultancies show the importance of innovation for companies in both the service and manufacturing sectors. The surveys also show that successful innovation management requires 'orchestration from the top'.[1] But in practice, recognizing the need for effective innovation management and achieving it are two vastly different things. Ten years ago Peter Drucker said that how to manage innovation was a largely unanswered question.[2] But in the past decade the tools and techniques for managing innovation have advanced significantly – enough for *The Economist* to recently state that innovation management is no longer an art but is 'becoming a practical science'.[3] So, to get ahead, managers need to quickly develop the range of skills they need to be able to manage innovation effectively.

This book was written to meet the needs of both managers and MBA students. It presents an integrated view of the skills, tools and techniques needed to successfully develop and implement an innovation strategy. The choice of tools and techniques which are presented was based not only on an extensive review of the literature but also on the authors' own experience in industry, teaching, research and consultancy. The book is relevant to organizations in the service, manufacturing and not-for-profit sectors and it gives many company examples.

Managing innovation is complex and so there are no 'quick fixes', 'no universal solutions'.[4] The challenges of managing innovation are also compounded by the fact that many ideas that are effective in one organization cannot be easily transferred; it is not simply a case of *adopting* best practice, managers need to *adapt* ideas to the specific situation their company faces. This book describes the results of management research and it does not try to oversimplify the issues. Where the results of research are ambiguous, or solutions to innovation problems are difficult to manage, these are clearly identified. Similarly, we assume that innovation is a capability to be developed, not necessarily an end in itself – companies consciously need to decide when and where to apply this capability.

Too many companies focus on just one area of innovation management – typically ideas generation – although there are other aspects of innovation management that are equally important. Leading organizations take a broader view and consider a range of issues including idea generation, implementation and business culture (see Mini Case 1.1). In this sense, innovation management is like competing in the Olympic pentathlon; excellent performance in one discipline alone will not guarantee a gold medal. Based on our research, we have characterized the main issues of innovation management by five different elements, which we will refer to as the *Pentathlon Framework*. This framework is presented in this chapter and also forms the structure of the book. The Pentathlon Framework has been used extensively in our teaching and our work with many leading organizations.

This chapter introduces the role and characteristics of innovation, and the emerging science of innovation management. It covers the following:

- The drivers of innovation.
- Characteristics of innovation.
- The Innovation Pentathlon Framework.
- The structure of this book.
- A detailed case study on NTT-DoCoMo, a Japanese company in the service sector, which shows how a broad approach to innovation can lead to successful market segmentation.

INNOVATION DRIVERS

Few markets are stable and four main factors (as shown in Figure 1.1) create the need for innovation: technological advances, changing customers, intensified competition and changing business environment.

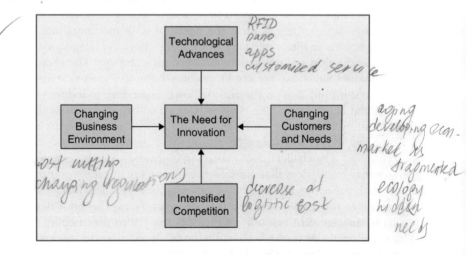

Figure 1.1   Drivers of the Need for Innovation (modified from Sheth and Ram)

Source: Sheth, J. N. and Ram, R., *Bringing Innovation to Market: How to Break Corporate and Customer Barriers* (New York: Wiley, 1987).

Technological Advances

There are numerous examples of new technologies having a major influence on business. For instance, logistics is being revolutionized by RFID technology – radio frequency identification labels – which automatically transmits information about the nature and location of articles. Nano technology is increasingly being used in products, such as 'easy to clean' surfaces. New technologies often create new industries and both biotechnology and multimedia have created significant employment over the past decades.[5] In addition, new applications of established technologies are constantly emerging. For instance, sophisticated electronics are now an important aspect of car design. With the vast array of technological developments, even multinational companies that used to conduct all their own basic research cannot keep abreast of all of the developments, using internal resources alone. This is one of the drivers towards *Open Innovation*, the sourcing of ideas and technology across organizational boundaries. (We will cover Open Innovation in Chapters 4 and 10.) Organizations need to monitor the progress of both the technologies they currently use and also that of potential substitutes.

Technology is equally important for service companies and R&D is increasingly having a major impact on how service companies do business. For example, banks are developing technologies that will allow them to have customized services for specific customer segments. FedEx, the leading courier services company, has always recognized the importance of investing in technology and led much of the development of hand-held bar code readers, which enabled them to provide the first parcel tracking capability. Bank of America and other leading service organizations have created innovation departments to monitor new technology and test it with actual customers (see Mini Case 1.1 on Metro AG).

Mini Case 1.1

Metro AG's 'Future Store' – Prototyping a Supermarket

Technology can help companies in the service sector make it easier for their customers to receive a service and reduce costs. Take the retail trade, where RFID 'smart-tag' technology is poised to make a big impact. Chip manufacturer Intel and supply chain software giant SAP have joined forces with the world's fifth largest retailer, the German company Metro AG, to create a fully running prototype of the supermarket of the future, in the small town of Rheinberg, Germany.[6]

Products in the supermarket are all labelled with RFID in order to automate stock keeping and make shopping easier for customers. Each shopping trolley has a touch-screen computer with a scanner, and as the customer selects each item, it is scanned in. The computer displays a range of useful information. This includes detailed product information on the item scanned, the total amount spent, special offers, the customer's 'standard' shopping list and a map with the customer's position in the store. The biggest advantage is that the items in the trolley do not need to be unloaded at the

▶▶

cashier's desk and this saves time for the customer. The trolley's computer automatically indicates the total amount to be paid and, having paid the cashier, the customer can simply push their trolley to their car. Queuing is virtually eliminated.

Metro has called the project the 'Future Store Initiative' and through the extensive use of technology is looking for major increases in supply chain efficiency. The main limitation is that smart tags are still relatively expensive and so are not viable for every individual item in every supermarket. The cost of tags is falling quickly, though, as they become more widely used.

Manufacturing companies often use prototypes to gain detailed customer feedback on new products. Extending the idea to the testing of a new service concept is a bold approach that few service companies have yet contemplated. Metro's prototype is helping the company to identify 'real advantages for both the retail industry and consumers'.[7] And the rollout of the concept across other locations in Germany is expected soon.

Changing Customers and Needs

The second driver of innovation is the changing characteristics and requirements of customers. Demographics show that many markets will evolve. For instance, the ageing population in the West will change many consumer markets. In contrast, other markets (for example, Southeast Asia) are largely made up of young consumers with different aspirations. The earnings in many newly industrialized countries will soar and demand for particular products and services will develop. The Whirlpool Corporation has recently launched the 'Ideale', the world's cheapest automatic washing machine, which retails at around $150 in countries such as Brazil and China.[8] Similarly, Tata's Nano car will have a big impact.

Changing customers also means that traditional market segments are disappearing or fragmenting and companies will need to adjust their product ranges accordingly – for example, car manufacturers now target over fifteen key segments in the US, as opposed to only five in the late 1960s. Contrast this to the type of market faced by Henry Ford! At the same time, there is the pressure for more environmentally acceptable, better value for money products and services. As basic needs are met, there is an additional challenge to innovation – determining customers' *hidden needs* (see Chapter 5).

Intensified Competition

The third driver shown in Figure 1.1 is growing competition. Logistics costs have plummeted and, consequently, 'safe, home markets' are being threatened by foreign competition. Companies may also face competition from sources normally outside their industries. An example of this is the bicycle industry in Japan where Nippon Bicycle has taken a significant share of the market by offering made-to-order, highly customized mountain bikes with a fast delivery time. Interestingly, Nippon is owned by the consumer electronics company Panasonic, which has made use of its expertise in logistics to become successful in a new market.

Changing Business Environment

Business environments change and are always subject to change – sometimes gradual and sometimes radical.

Gradually markets have become more open as the market economy has been embraced by most governments and through the efforts of trade groupings such as the European Union and North American Free Trade Association. In addition, the regulations affecting specific markets are being relaxed in many Western countries (for example, the de-regulation of transport, post and tele-communications). An example of changing regulations that could drastically change one market is the US Food and Drug Administration's (FDA) planned faster approval of generic drugs.

Many companies have focused on cost cutting. A gradual reduction in the resources required for key business processes has been achieved. A continued focus on efficiency gains will bring only diminishing returns and cost-reduction myopia needs to be replaced by a focus on increasing revenues and profits through new products and services.

Economic cycles have a radical impact and the financial crisis of 2008 will influence innovation for some time to come. Downturns (which are discussed in Chapter 2) drive many companies to cut their investments in innovation but the winners which emerge have continued to invest.[9] In financial services, the crisis will certainly lead to a more stringent risk analysis and higher-risk financial products will probably be regulated.

Responding to the Environment – Strategic Intent

Although the four external forces provide the drivers for innovation, how an organization chooses to respond to them depends on *Strategic Intent*: the aims of the key stakeholders, including senior management. As we observe in Chapter 4, developing an innovation strategy involves comparing how an orga-nization is expected to perform in the future with stakeholders' expectations: any difference points to where innovation is required.

Innovation management is multifaceted; it includes ways to motivate employ-ees, select clear performance measures and create a positive business culture. It also includes an emphasis on R&D in manufacturing firms (or the creation of innovation groups in service organizations), new products, technology and process innovation, see Mini Case 1.2. Overall, this shows the wide range of approaches to stimulating and managing innovation that need to be consid-ered. The main theme of this chapter is to introduce *how* innovation can be managed. But, before we can discuss *managing innovation*, we need to establish the characteristics of *innovation* and the terminology that we will be using in this book.

Mini Case 1.2

Manufacturing and Service – Innovation Initiatives

Many companies are taking initiatives to improve their innovation performance and the 3M Company's highly publicized initiatives have become icons of innovation management. With a portfolio of over 60,000 products, where do you start if you want to increase innovative levels rapidly? 3M has launched a host of initiatives to drive innovation. The cornerstone has been a focus on a clear measure of innovation performance – the percentage of revenues generated by new products. For example, in 1995 the company aimed (and succeeded) in generating 30 per cent of revenues from products less than four years old. In 1997 tougher goals were set including 10 per cent of revenues from products less than one year old. The use of tough, financially based measures is only one aspect of 3M's initiatives. Their approach to stimulating creativity is legendary – employees are allowed 10 per cent of their time to work on ideas and projects that they have themselves devised.

Johnson & Johnson, the health-care products company, has innovation as one of its core values. To support a coherent view of innovation throughout the company, the company has identified three ways in which innovation supports the business: it forges a vision of the future; fuels business growth; and promotes continuous learning. Regular articles in the company's magazine give examples of successful innovation within the company, with process innovation being given as much attention as new products.

Service organizations are increasingly focusing on innovation and using new approaches to improve customer service. For example, American Express and Mastercard are looking at how new 'contactless' technology can avoid credit cards having to be swiped through a reader and thus speed up the process of payment. Others such as HSBC and Bank of America have a broad interest in innovation. For example, HSBC management have strongly communicated to staff the importance of innovation, and used workshops to generate ideas for new or improved customer services. Bank of America generates many ideas for new services and tests these with real customers in a number of 'prototype branches' in the Atlanta area. Hospitals are applying process management concepts, which were originally developed in the manufacturing sector, such as just-in-time management. Health-care providers are looking at all of the factors that influence patient outcomes and are finding that making hospital environments more pleasant can have a positive impact on patients' health. And the organizational culture of hospitals is also being investigated, so that they can be made more open to innovation.

So there are many different ways in which organizations are trying to stimulate innovation.

CHARACTERISTICS OF INNOVATION

Although the need for more innovation is widely recognized, there are different opinions on what innovation means in a business context. Many employees think primarily of innovation as breakthrough products like the iPod but this is a narrow view, as we will see.

The dictionary definition of *innovation* – introducing something new – is clear, but this does not help managers or employees understand the nature of innovation sufficiently. It focuses on newness and can lead us to overlook the fact that innovation can be based on modifying existing ideas. The dictionary definition also fails to give insights into the following questions. What are the most important types of innovation? How can innovation lead to sustainable competitive advantage? What is the most effective way to boost the innovation performance of an organization? This book answers these questions and this section looks at the following:

- Definitions of innovation.
- The different *dimensions* of innovation.
- The different *degrees* of innovation.
- The *phases* of an innovation.
- The functional areas involved.

Definitions of Innovation

Various definitions of innovation have been developed and these will be reviewed, in order to develop our terminology. Managers and employees may have a range of opinions on the real nature of innovation in their business environment. Therefore, establishing a clear understanding of the characteristics of innovation is essential in organizations, where diffuse views on innovation arising from different functional perspectives will hinder the implementation of innovation strategy.

The importance of understanding innovation was first recognized by the Austrian economist Joseph Schumpeter in the 1930s. His work on innovation strongly influenced the field of economics and this will be discussed in Chapter 2. Schumpeter considered five different aspects of innovation and, although developed over 70 years ago, his definition is comprehensive[10]:

1. The introduction of a good (product), which is new to consumers, or one of increased quality than was available in the past;
2. Methods of production, which are new to a particular branch of industry. These are not necessarily based on new scientific discoveries and may have, for example, already been used in other industrial sectors;
3. The opening of new markets;
4. The use of new sources of supply;
5. New forms of competition, which lead to the re-structuring of an industry.

Michael Porter defined innovation 'to include both improvements in technology and better methods or ways of doing things. It can be manifested in product changes, process changes, new approaches to marketing, new forms of distribution, and new concepts of scope…[innovation] results as much from organizational learning as much as from formal R&D'.[11] This definition covers very similar points to Schumpeter's but indicates that the source of innovation can originate from an organization's learning and not just its R&D department.

Both Porter and Schumpeter use the word 'new' in their definitions, but it should not be forgotten that many commercial innovations are not totally original and Everett Rogers, an expert on how innovations spread through markets, reminds us that innovation '... is an idea, practice, or object that is perceived as new by the individual or other unit of adoption'. The perception of newness is important rather than originality as such.

The definition from the Organisation for Economic Co-operation and Development (OECD)[12] is 'innovation consists of all those scientific, technical, commercial and financial steps necessary for the successful development and marketing of new or improved manufactured products, the commercial use of new or improved processes or equipment or the introduction of a new approach to a social service. R&D is only one of these steps'. Similar to Porter's definition, this indicates that R&D is not the only element of innovation, but the OECD definition adds understanding of the steps involved and points out that innovations are also important in social services.

In the service sector, the term innovation can be confusing.[13] A useful definition is, 'innovations in the service sector comprises [*sic*] new services and new ways of producing or delivering services as well as significant changes in services or their production or delivery'.[14]

Psychologists view innovation as a social process, 'the intentional introduction and application within a role, group, or organization of ideas, processes, products or procedures, new to the relevant unit of adoption, designed to significantly benefit the individual, the group, organization or wider society'.[15] This indicates that the emergence of innovative ideas depends on the culture of an organization.

Comparing the various definitions of innovation, it can be seen that there are several common elements *what* is changed (such as product or process changes); *how much* is changed (whether it is completely new or only perceived as such); the *source* of the change (sometimes technology); the *influence* of the change (for example, its social or commercial value).

Dimensions of Innovation

Figure 1.2 shows what we will refer to as the *Dimensions of Innovation*. These also apply to the service sector but we will first discuss how they apply to manufacturing. *Product Innovation* is important and can be thought of as the first dimension of innovation. However, opportunities for sustainable competitive advantage can be missed if an organization focuses solely on product innovation (see Mini Case 1.3 on Gillette). Companies in the manufacturing sector can also create services to help differentiate their products – *Service Innovation* is the second dimension. Improvements can also be made to the manufacturing and delivery process (normally referred to as *Process Innovation*). Companies can also use *Business Process Innovation*; optimizing

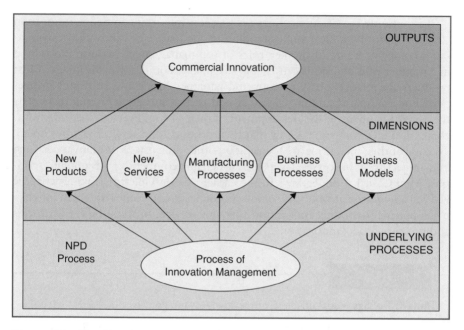

Figure 1.2   The Dimensions of Innovation in the Manufacturing Sector

processes to make it easier for customers to do business with the company (for example, order fulfilment). Finally, *Business Model Innovation* can be a key source of commercial innovation.

Gillette – First-to-Market Risks

Some managers perceive innovation to be inextricably linked to a first-to-market strategy. Breakthrough products such as the iPod have captured the imagination of many people, who now perceive innovation as consisting of radically new products. Unfortunately, this view can lead managers to forget the biggest downside of being first-to-market – competitors may copy your innovation if you do not think of ways to protect it. What is worst, competitors may learn from the limitations of the first-to-market product and the 'copy' can be better than the original!

The Gillette 'Mach 3' razor was a first-to-market product. Gillette developed this advanced razor, with its characteristic three blades set at different very precise angles, at a very high cost. A UK supermarket chain was quickly able to introduce a good copy of the product at a fraction of the development costs. This made Gillette more dependent on expensive television advertising in trying to protect sales of their product. When products are easy to copy, competitors can even 'leapfrog' the original features and the Wilkinson Sword Company introduced a four-blade razor. Now the market even has a five-blade product!

It is not only for academic purposes that it is important to define innovation clearly. Promoting a clear understanding of the nature of innovation throughout a company is one of the key roles of top management because innovating in a number of dimensions can enable sustainable competitive advantage. Most products are relatively easy to copy and patents seldom give sufficient protection. For example, Cannon worked round several hundred patents owned by the Xerox Company in the development of their first and very successful photocopier. Leading companies know that their products and services will be copied. To combat this, such firms are focusing on other dimensions of innovation, such as manufacturing processes, to ensure sustainable competitive advantage[16] (contrast Mini Case 1.4 on Tetley's to the earlier one on Gillette). Taking what we will call a *multidimensional* view of innovation leads companies to search for ways to complement product innovation through service, process, business process and business model innovation.

Mini Case 1.4

Tetley's Teabags – Sustainable Competitive Advantage[17]

Tetley is a market leader in the world teabag market and originator of the round teabag. On the face of it, the round teabag was only an incremental change from the traditional square version. However, through the process innovation required to support the production of the new product, Tetley gained sustainable competitive advantage. When the company developed the round teabag, it knew that with suitable marketing, this new product could capture significant market share. Advertising copy was based around the better cup of tea that would result from bags where the tea could circulate better. Tetley knew that competitors would quickly try to copy this product innovation. So the company decided not to discuss it with its normal supplier of manufacturing equipment. Instead, it hired Cambridge Consultants Ltd to develop a new manufacturing line for round teabags. When the new product was introduced, the competition was unable to obtain similar manufacturing equipment quickly and Tetley maintained its lead.

Tetley became part of Tata Tea in 2000, forming the world's second largest tea company. Tata Tea is itself a subsidiary of the Tata Group, a successful, growing conglomerate with a reputation in India for doing business responsibly. In addition to tea, Tata also has interests in a broader group of beverage companies which includes Eight O'Clock Coffee in the USA and Mount Everest Mineral Water, with its Himalayan brand of mineral water in India.

Andrew Dobson, Director of Global Innovation at Tetley says, 'Innovation is critical. It's really important to continually bring new and fresh things to market which surprise and delight, whether that's simply a new blend or flavour, an entirely new product or a new route to market. It's also vital to stand out from the crowd and consistently communicate what makes the Tetley brand unique and better than its competitors. A good product is one thing but in our competitive environment, it is equally important to be innovative at getting our message over to consumers. The objective of our innovation programme is to be one step ahead of our competitors and develop brands and

▶▶

products that offer consumers both functional and emotional benefits. We've built a reputation as pioneers in the tea industry – we were the first to launch the teabag, the first to "change the shape of the market" by introducing round teabags in 1989 and then the "no-drip" drawstring bags in 1997, and the first big "black tea" brand to really branch out into new and exciting varieties such as green tea and rooibos. We're always looking for new ways to revolutionize the tea industry and our relationship with the Tata Group gives us access to greater resources and exposure to a different culture which is global, acquisitive, fast moving and responsive to change'.

Management need to drive the underlying processes that stimulate innovation within a company (Figure 1.2). Some innovation management processes will be formally defined and documented, such as the new product development (NPD) process. Others will be less tangible, such as idea generation, or the management of company culture. Therefore, managers face a real challenge in managing innovation.

In a modern manufacturing company, the line operators are not simply responsible for manufacturing products. They are also given full responsibility for constantly improving the manufacturing processes (through continuous improvement and other means). Some companies even talk about their operators being 'process owners'. Senior managers need to see themselves as the process owners for innovation management and not simply as managing the outputs of new products and services. With this different perspective, managers should view the innovation processes within their organizations as one of their biggest assets.

Dimensions of Innovation in Services

Typically, the dimensions of innovation are different in the service sector. For example, the human dimension can give opportunities for innovation (see Mini Case 1.5 on Les Concierges).

One insurance company we worked with was concerned that its output of new products was low and decided to examine its overall innovation performance. A group of senior and product managers took part in a workshop to identify all of the dimensions of innovation relevant to their markets. To stimulate the team to come up with ideas, the discussion was based on the parallels to innovation in manufacturing companies (Figure 1.2).

The workshop results are summarized on Figure 1.3. New products – in this case new insurance policies – are important for competitive advantage. However, a range of other dimensions was identified. This included customer profiling to identify and contact customers with a unique value proposition; closer contact with third parties to help them contribute more to innovation (as most of the insurance policies were underwritten by suppliers); use of different sales channels (including banks, the Internet and brokers); and the creation of innovative

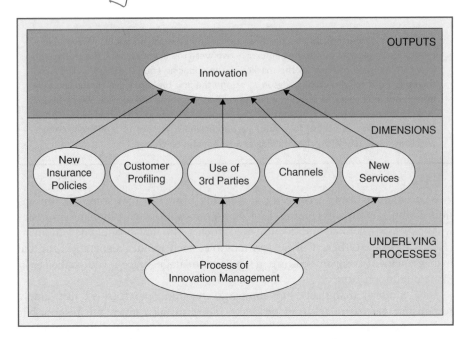

Figure 1.3   The Dimensions of Innovation for an Insurance Company

Source: Based on unpublished research by Goffin.

new services – typically better ways for customers' enquiries to be handled – in order to increase customer loyalty.

As a result of the workshop, the insurance company recognized that they had more possibilities to innovate than they had previously thought. Now, as each new product is developed, the company looks at each of the dimensions shown in Figure 1.3, with the goal of making their new insurance products 'hard to copy'.

Mini Case 1.5

Les Concierges – Serving Indian Professionals[18]

The 'cash rich, time poor' market segment consists of professional people who are top earners but because of their demanding jobs and family commitments have very little spare time. Providing services for this segment in India has allowed founder and CEO of Les Concierges, Dipali Sikand, to build a business of over $1M with over 350 staff. The company was started in Bangalore, the centre of India's software industry, but it is now active in half a dozen Indian cities.

The idea behind Les Concierges is simple and extends the concept of the 'travel desk' operated by travel companies for large employers. Sikand's business targets large employers (rather than individuals) and offers to make their employees' life easier by helping them with some of their personal and family organizing. This means that a company can help its employees focus more on their work and Les Concierges has posted

▶▶

one or two of its staff to 70 companies, mainly in the information technology industry. The host company provides a desk and an intranet connection for Les Concierges and then the 'help desk' can go live, offering four categories of service: shopping, everyday tasks, entertainment and travel. The host company pays a retainer each year based on its number of employees (but it sees the return through increased employee productivity) and a transaction fee is normally paid by the employee (who saves precious time in a busy schedule).

The interaction with customers is highly important and Sikand refers to this as 'high touch'. She has hired almost exclusively women, as she feels that they are more sympathetic to customers' needs. With such empathy, Les Concierges can often delight its end-customers by coming up with original ideas for birthday presents and the like. The importance of the behind-the-scenes organization is also recognized and Sikand has concentrated on making this high-tech – including proprietary software to track each customer transaction and coordinate the many tasks that are each day passed to outside suppliers. The idea behind Les Concierges may be simple but recognizing the need and developing a 'high-touch, high-tech' solution are Sikand's real innovations.

The above discussions on service and manufacturing demonstrate the multidimensional nature of innovation. Recently, the R&D manager of an industrial safety equipment company told the authors 'if I ask five different people at our company what innovation is, I will get at least five different answers'. Many organizations lack a common understanding of the need for innovation. AXA Insurance had a similar experience and their visual 'definition' of innovation will be discussed in the main case study at the end of Chapter 3.

Degrees of Innovation

Innovation can be dramatic. Breakthroughs such as penicillin, the Walkman personal stereo, the ubiquitous Post-It, the iPod and the iPhone are the most common examples that people use when they talk about innovation. However, it is important to recognize that there are different *degrees of innovation*. There can be breakthroughs, which are normally referred to as *radical* innovations. They may create new markets or completely change existing ones. In addition, though, there are *incremental* innovations, small changes to existing products, services or processes that can also be important.

Although radical innovations often capture the imagination of the public, a lower degree of innovation is much more common. Research investigating over 100 companies showed that 84 per cent of product innovations were 'line extensions' (that is, incremental innovation) and that on average 62 per cent of revenues came from such products.[19] As might be expected, though, 38 per cent of revenues (and 61 per cent of profits) came from the radical product innovations.

The degree of innovation – from no change, to incremental, to radical – is an important concept. Consultants Booz-Allen and Hamilton proposed that

Table 1.1   Degrees of Product Innovation

Degree of product innovation	Old/new product development
1. Improvement and revisions of existing products	Old
2. New products that provide similar performance at lower cost	Old
3. Existing products that are targeted to new markets	Old
4. Addition of products to an existing product line	New
5. Creation of new product lines	New
6. New-to-the-world products	New

Source: Booz-Allen and Hamilton, *New Products Management for the 1980s* (New York: Booz-Allen and Hamilton Inc., 1982).

there are six degrees of product innovation (Table 1.1). The first degree is the improvement of existing products to provide improved performance or greater perceived value to customers. Developing new products that provide similar performance at lower cost is the second degree, followed by existing products that are targeted to new markets. New products that supplement a company's established product lines is the fourth degree. Another form of product innovation is the creation of new product lines. The last degree is defined as 'new-to-the-world' products that create entirely new markets. Table 1.1 shows that three categories are related to 'old product development' and three to 'new product development'.

The degree of innovation is somewhat ambiguous; some observers will view certain innovations as radical, whereas others will perceive them as incremental. This discourse is often heard in academia, but the search for an unambiguous definition is probably not a very productive one, since the degree of innovation is context dependent.

Evaluating Dimensions and Degrees

The concepts of the dimensions and degrees of innovation can be used to analyse the competitiveness of individual innovation projects and also a company's portfolio of innovation projects. We will refer to this as *Dimensions & Degrees analysis*. Consider the example of a project to develop an incremental product. This product might not be very competitive, as it is based on previous products and similar to the competition. Table 1.2 shows a typology and the tick in the column 'product' indicates that it is an incremental product innovation ('improvements'). Although the degree of product innovation is low, the new product could be supported by related services, which can be

Table 1.2 Example Analysis of Dimensions and Degrees

Degrees of Innovation	Dimensions of Innovation				
	Product	Service	Process	Business Process	Business Model
1. No innovation				√	
2. Improvements	√				√
3. Similar performance at lower cost		√			
4. Targeting new markets					
5. Addition to an existing product line					
6. Creation of new product line(s)					
7. New-to-the-world			√		

provided at lower cost (see tick under column 'service'). In the manufacturing process, radical innovation is planned in the way the product will be produced, as this will lead to a sustainable advantage in terms of lower costs. Table 1.2 is useful because it forces organizations to think how they can innovate across the various dimensions and become more competitive. For example, the Mars Group, manufacturers of confectionary and other products, always considers where their prowess in manufacturing can be utilized for each new product.

Table 1.2 can also be used as the basis for reviewing the range of innovation projects that a company is in the process of implementing. Each individual project can be analysed and then the overall balance in the portfolio, for instance, the mix between incremental and radical products, can be determined and compared with the goals of the innovation strategy. Organizations are not typically able to develop radical products all the time, as these normally require significant resources, are high risk and need high levels of creativity. Table 1.2 can prompt ideas on how to make less innovative products more competitive.

Innovation and Continuous Improvement

Continuous incremental improvements to manufacturing processes or service operations can lead to higher-quality output at lower cost and may add up over time to significant increases in performance. Many manufacturers have and continue to reap rewards from continuous improvement – *kaizen* in Japanese. The challenge for management is to communicate to employees the potential contribution of continuous improvement to overall innovation.

The service sector is now adopting continuous improvement and other techniques to improve processes. An intimate part of the service delivery process is the interaction between a company's employees and the customer. Although the service delivery process is intimately dependent on people, this does not mean that constant improvements are not possible. On the contrary, continuous improvement is essential in the service sector because even small improvements are quickly recognized by customers and can increase satisfaction levels significantly.

Figure 1.4 summarizes the relationship between incremental improvement and innovation. The dimensions of innovation are plotted on the horizontal axis, in order of the size of the impact they typically make on the running of the organization, from process changes to completely new business models. The degree of innovation is plotted on the vertical axis. Incremental improvements to processes occupy the bottom left corner; this is the domain of *Quality Management* (kaizen etc.), where steady improvements are made to the way the business runs, without significantly changing its nature. In the upper right-hand corner is truly revolutionary change when major alteration is made to the very business model of the firm. Examples would be Virgin's move from a record label into transatlantic travel, or Nokia moving from logging into mobile phones.

In the bottom left-hand corner, the well-established techniques of quality management such as the work of Deming can be used.[20] It should be remembered that if incremental improvements are difficult to copy, then they give sustainable competitive advantage and should be classed as innovation.[21] The area between these two extremes is the realm of innovation management. Here, research and practice now provide many useful tools and insights and a complete and coherent approach is emerging. For this reason, in this book we place

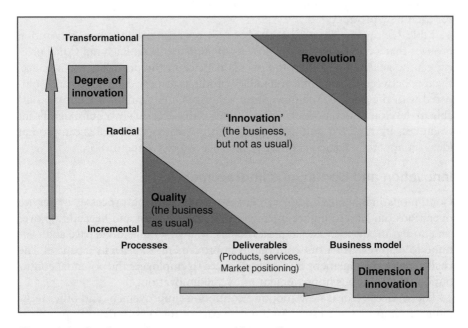

Figure 1.4   Continuous Improvement and Innovation

strong emphasis on a balanced broad approach to managing innovation. Some argue that incremental improvements are not innovation; we believe that there is no value in agonizing over where the boundary between incremental improvement and innovation lies. However, the further one moves up the diagonal on Figure 1.4, the more difficult the management challenge becomes and the more the techniques presented in this book are required.

Phases of Innovation

Any innovation must progress through a number of *phases* before it is commercially viable. This is true, irrespective of the type of innovation – whether it is a new product, a new service, a new process, an improved business process or any combination of these. All innovations begin with the generation of ideas and the road to implementation and commercial success can be a long and difficult one. Many ideas will fall by the wayside. For example, in the pharmaceutical industry, ideas for new drugs are based on novel chemical structures called 'new chemical entities' (NCEs). These take years to develop, test and to introduce to the market. The majority of NCEs are rejected along the way for one reason or another (for example, undesirable side effects) and typically only one NCE in a thousand will be commercially successful.

Figure 1.5 shows the typical phases of innovation, with a funnel of ideas being generated. Some ideas are filtered out immediately whereas others progress further and are developed into *concepts*. Such a concept might be

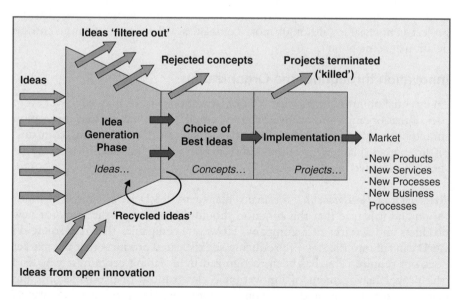

Figure 1.5   The Typical Phases of an Innovation ('The Development Funnel')

Note: The idea to compare the phases of an innovation to a funnel goes back to at least to: Majaro, S., *The Creative Gap* (London: Longman, 1988).

prepared by a small team from different functional areas of the business working together part-time over a few weeks or, for more complex ideas, the process of developing the concept will take longer. At the concept stage, an idea for a new product or new service will have been formalized to the extent that some questions such as the size of the potential market and the best way the product or service can be designed will have been considered (although these questions will not have been answered to a high level of detail). Similarly, each concept will have been analysed as to the investment required and the potential return. Normally, management decides on which concepts will be selected to become *projects* (the implementation phase), and the way in which an organization chooses concepts may not be transparent to many of the employees. Certain concepts may be rejected as currently uninteresting, to emerge later as 'recycled ideas'.

Obviously, the innovations developed will have varying levels of success. The analogy to a funnel used in Figure 1.5 is not new; Simon Majaro of Cranfield School of Management has used it for many years. Kim Clark and Steven Wheelwright from Harvard Business School have also used it as a basis for discussions with managers on the typical phases of innovation.[22] They had managers draw their own versions of the funnel and found that managers perceived that the different phases often overlap, problems are common and so iterations are necessary. Therefore, it must be recognized that Figure 1.5 is a simplification. For example, ideas may well be modified and refined several times as they are turned into useable concepts, so the boundary between the *idea generation phase* and the *choice of best ideas* may not be clear-cut. And a project may be modified or cancelled during *implementation* when new information shows that the project is not viable (although most companies will require a firm go/no go decision at some point).

Innovation throughout the Organization

An essential point to note is that if an organization is to be fully effective, every part of that organization needs to actively contribute to innovation. Innovation should not only originate in the R&D department in a manufacturing company, or the strategic planning group in a service operation. The functional areas that should be involved are:

Research and Development: for many managers, R&D is *the* source of innovation and it is true that this function should drive many of the ideas for new products and services in a company. However, companies that rely solely on R&D can fall into the trap of producing sophisticated products that the market does not require. This has been recognized by a leading economist who said 'the proper management of innovation is much more than establishing and maintaining a research and development laboratory that produces a great deal of technical output'.[23] Service companies may not have an R&D department but leading ones have the equivalent, with titles such as 'service innovation group' (time:matters, Germany) or 'innovation development team' (Bank of America).

Marketing: has a key role to play in innovation. It needs to identify customers' needs, through creative forms of market research. It needs to be involved throughout the whole process of innovation, including product definition, pricing decisions, positioning and the product launch. Good marketing should make the difference between a good idea and a successful product.

Operations: this function, which is often called *production* or simply *manufacturing* in the manufacturing sector, also should contribute to innovation. Unfortunately, many operations managers do not perceive that they have a key role in driving innovation. This limits the ability of a company to obtain longer-term competitive advantage, as process innovations are harder to copy than product innovations. Service sector companies often underestimate the potential of operations to contribute to innovation.

Finance and Accounting: is normally not perceived as being able to make a contribution to innovation. However, it can provide essential support in calculated return on investment for innovation projects.[24] At the high-tech company Verigy, the controlling function plays a key role in determining which projects offer the best combination of low risk, high return and a good match to the available resources. The finance function can also help develop effective pricing packages. An example of this is the 'power by the hour' leasing offered by Rolls-Royce, the aero engine manufacturer.

Human Resource Management: is involved in hiring, developing and motivating good people, the essential and challenging aspects of innovation management. The creative atmosphere of small teams can easily be lost as organizations grow and so the human resource function can and should proactively support the maintenance of culture of innovation in their organization.

Outside Resources: have been recognized as essential for *Open Innovation.*[25] For example, suppliers in the automotive industry conduct significant parts of the product development for car manufacturers. Similarly, universities and research institutes can enable small organizations to economically partake in the development of new technologies, and develop new core competencies.

The task of general management is to stimulate the cross-functional teamwork that is needed for effective innovation. Researchers have identified the friction and lack of understanding that commonly arise between different functions, particularly marketing and R&D.[26] Achieving effective interaction between different functional areas is a key task for management and Akio Morita, the late Chairman of Sony recognized this saying, 'this is the job of top management – to arrange good communications [between functions]'.[27]

Our discussion on the characteristics of innovation has shown its broad nature and next we will discuss the findings of research on how innovation can be managed.

KEY RESEARCH ON INNOVATION

Innovation is an area in which both economists and management researchers have been active. Throughout the chapters of this book, the pertinent research will be presented but here we will give an overview of the field, in order to understand how the different topics interrelate. This will help us develop a framework through which to view and plan the management of innovation.

The three levels at which innovation has been researched are as follows:

- The *macro level:* research on the sources and impact of innovation within economies and industries;
- The *micro* or *company level:* investigations of how companies manage innovation and the advantages that it brings them in terms of revenues and profits;
- The *project level:* which looks at the management of innovation projects, particularly NPD.

It is surprising how many of the articles in the popular management press are based on anecdotal evidence – cursory investigations that have questionable validity because, for example, they looked at a very limited number of companies or companies in very specific business environments. As a result, innovation management is plagued with 'quick fixes' – approaches that have worked at one company and which their proponents claim are universal solutions. There are no panaceas for the management of innovation and the context in which an organization finds itself plays a key role. In assessing how the results of research can be applied in managing innovation, it is important to consider both the internal and external validity of the studies that are being described.

Macro-Level Investigations

For many years economists have researched innovation, and in the 1800s it was recognized that new products impact the economy. Schumpeter realized that process innovations in manufacturing can have a strong impact and can threaten established industries. Economists normally use measures of innovation such as R&D expenditures, the number of major innovations generated in an industry over time, and patent counts.[28] The studies made at the macroeconomic level fall into two categories: research on the factors that influence innovative performance, and the spread and influence of innovation.

Typical of the studies on the factors that influence performance are those looking at the size of companies. Part of Schumpeter's work was the recognition that larger companies are at an advantage when it comes to innovation, because of the economies of scale they have in R&D.[29] Much research has focused on the size of companies and innovation, and it has been shown, for example, that entrants are more likely to develop pioneering products and small firms are important innovators.[30] The effects of educational levels and national culture on product innovation have also been investigated (by looking at the correlations between qualification levels and patent counts), and similarly the success rate of government policies that aim to support innovation.[31] The field of *development economics* is also relevant to the study of innovation. This has looked at the reasons why developing countries remain behind advanced countries. Factors such as infrastructure, human capital (in turn, determined by health and education), and the availability of credit to fund innovation all influence growth.

Studies on the diffusion and impact of innovation are numerous and Everett Rogers has conducted some of the key studies in this area. Innovations are adopted slowly at first, but as they become known and information is more widely communicated, they can be embraced by the market.[32] As an innovation is widely adopted, this stimulates growth through sales of new products and services. It may change the basis of competition or the structure of an industry. Innovation has also been shown to drive long-term business cycles, and to directly influence employment levels.[33] The work of economists on innovation is useful in demonstrating the interaction between the market environment and the firm. It indicates to firms the gravity of conducting a thorough analysis of their business environment and hence Chapter 4 will focus on this topic.

Although the relationship between industry structure, company size and innovation has received considerable attention, economists have seldom investigated the actions of individual companies.[34] Management researchers from a number of disciplines including marketing, strategy, organizational behaviour and operations management have been active in this area and their findings provide many insights.

Micro-Level Investigations

Managing innovation is a challenge because of the wide range of factors influencing its success or failure, including the allocation of resources, the skills of key staff, the generation of ideas and the organization of development teams.[35] As innovation is a process, it is far from clear how companies can best improve their performance,[36] or what the key aspects of innovation management are.

One of the most common forms of research at a company level has been the quest to unearth the characteristics of innovative organizations. The companies chosen for these studies are normally large, have a reputation for being innovative and exhibit high market share and growth. For example, leading companies develop over twice as many new products, develop them faster, use more technologies and compete in more geographical markets.[37] The limitation of such studies has been demonstrated by a meta-study, which showed that over half the key factors identified were unique to specific studies.[38] This strongly demonstrates the need to consider context carefully when attempting to take innovation best practice from one company to another. In this book we will point out the contextual issues and always stress that in innovation management it is not a question of *adopting* best practice but *adapting* it.

It has been recognized that innovation should play a central role within business strategy.[39] Innovation should be fully evaluated during strategic planning and clear processes are needed to manage the development of new products and services. Technology can be a prime component of innovation and therefore it should be given full management attention.[40] The work of Kim Clark of Harvard shows that general managers must investigate the value of technology to their organizations.[41] In manufacturing firms, R&D needs not only to develop new products but it must also give a lead to other departments in becoming a continuously innovating company.[42]

Michael Tushman of Harvard has been a major contributor to the study of organizations and innovation. He and others determined that the organization and the culture of a company strongly influence innovation.[43] Firms need to be good at coordinating the work of different functions and managing the linkages to other organizations. It has been shown that leading companies often change their organizational structure and so executives need to create organizational architectures that are both efficient and adaptive.[44] Company culture is recognized as being fundamental in supporting innovation; however, culture is a concept that can be difficult to manage.[45] Studies have concluded that the innovative companies display certain cultural attributes. These include the propensity to experiment, and the capability to motivate employees to be creative and to develop radical ideas. Successful projects are often discussed within such organizations and these 'stories' help focus the organization on the values of innovation.

Project-Level Investigations

The third level at which researchers have investigated innovation is the project level. Most of the projects studied have been new product development ones but we should bear in mind that the challenges faced are similar for new service products and also in the management of process innovation projects. New services are also essential and process innovation – developing efficient manufacturing – is often a key source of competitive advantage because it is difficult to copy.[46]

Studies of new-product development projects are extremely common. Unfortunately, the success rate for new products has been found to be very low.[47] This is due to the many problems that can occur at every stage of product development: from the creation of ideas, to the introduction of products onto the market.[48] Researchers have looked at these problems and the main findings can be grouped into the following main articles on the benefits of faster NPD, the need for robust NPD processes, teams, techniques for accelerated development and evaluation of product development.

Faster New Product Development

Much has been published on the need for companies to develop new products faster.[49] The time required to develop and introduce a new product to the market is referred to as *time-to-market* or *cycle time*. It has become essential for companies to have short cycle times, and faster NPD has been a key focus in manufacturing for nearly twenty years.[50]

Fast cycle time is considered to have two main advantages. If a product is a totally new concept, then being first-to-market enables a company to define key market requirements before competitors enter the market. In established markets, being faster leads to increased profit and market share. Although the advantages of short cycle times appear clear in the popular business literature, they are not backed by unequivocal evidence and the link between fast cycle time and profitability is weak. To make NPD not only fast but also efficient, there are a number of requirements. These include a clear process, teamwork and leadership.

The NPD Process

Much has been written about the need for a clear new-product development process, which defines the responsibilities of different functions, such as R&D and marketing, at different phases of NPD. Robert Cooper and Elko Kleinschmidt of McMasters University in Canada have published the definitive studies on the NPD process. One investigation looked at companies' practices and led to the well-known *Stage-Gate*™ approach.[51] In this approach, management meets at the end of each stage of product development and has to approve the progression to the next stage. The functional areas within a firm have clearly defined responsibilities at each stage, to ensure that an effective new product or new service product is developed. Most companies in the service and manufacturing sectors have developed formal processes based on Cooper and Kleinschmidt's recommendations. It has been found that companies with formal NPD processes were more satisfied with their performance.[52] However, having a process alone will not necessarily lead to faster NPD. Firms need to collect data on NPD projects, so that companies can learn from the past and improve by, for example, avoiding bottlenecks in the process.[53]

Team Organization and Leadership

The skills and the motivation of people working on product development are crucial and such teams need to be well organized and led.[54] Steven Wheelwright and Kim Clark have investigated many aspects of product development teams. A widely applied approach is to draw members from a number of functions to ensure that all aspects of the business are considered at the design stage. For example, R&D and manufacturing will consider how to make the product easy to manufacture. Although they can be difficult to implement, it has generally been recognized that cross-functional teams have made NPD more efficient.[55] The people chosen to lead NPD teams need particular skills in motivating the team and managing communications both within the team and externally. Research has shown that problems in managing new product teams are also prevalent in the service sector.[56]

Techniques for NPD

After the importance of faster NPD was recognized at the end of the 1980s, there followed a wave of prescriptive articles on the techniques that could be used to achieve it. Many of these articles were based on anecdotal rather than hard evidence.[57] One technique hailed as a major advance in reducing cycle time was *Quality Function Deployment* (QFD) – a Japanese method for ensuring that customer requirements are accurately captured – but this method is not a panacea.[58] (We will discuss QFD in Chapter 7.) There are many techniques for improving NPD but the use of one of these alone or several in combination will not, in itself, guarantee reduced cycle times. Bringing products to market faster is just not that simple – the situation and the way techniques are implemented play a key role.[59]

Overall, the perceived value of tools and techniques for new product development is a contentious area. Whilst many of the articles in the popular management literature have extolled the benefits of certain tools, the evidence on the utility of such tools is thin. Managers need to deal with this by recognizing that there are no 'quick fixes' and the application of any tool or technique to speed NPD will take time and effort to make it effective within the particular situation faced by the organization in question.

Evaluating NPD Projects

If NPD is to be improved, then the efficiency of the process, and not simply the success of the product, needs to be evaluated. Several studies have found that many companies do not evaluate their projects effectively because suitable measures are unavailable. Few companies capture accurately the time-to-market and this type of measurement is essential because, without it, valid comparisons are impossible. Abbie Griffin of the University of Illinois has studied the topic of NPD measures extensively and recommends that metrics should cover the outcomes and characteristics of the project (inputs) and the process of NPD itself.[60] However, it has been recognized that 'the performance of individual projects can be influenced by idiosyncratic factors ... that may be difficult to duplicate from project to project'.[61]

Service Innovation Research

We lament the fact that most of the research on innovation has focused on products and not services.[62] Although from a historical perspective this is understandable – most economies were manufacturing-driven when innovation research first started – today, the developed economies are mainly service-driven. Fortunately, researchers are slowly catching up and our knowledge of the impacts and management of service innovation is improving.

A major issue in the macro-level studies of the service sector is that the categories of innovation used in manufacturing studies (product, process and service innovation) are difficult to apply in services. Often innovations in the service sector do not neatly fit into these categories as, for example, a service product is often difficult to differentiate from the way it is delivered.[63] Measures of 'innovation' in services are also more difficult than in the manufacturing sector; for example, the spending on innovation related activities is difficult to ascertain.[64]

Studies in the service sector have looked at the nature of innovation (and how it is different from the manufacturing sector). Such research has concluded that in addition to new service development, ways to improve quality and delivery, to lower costs and to make innovations harder to copy are all important aspects of service innovation (see Mini Case 1.6 on Singapore Airlines). Because of the intangible nature of service products, service innovation can be challenging to manage and it is recommended that managers adopt formal process management to increase service innovation levels.[65] In Chapter 3, we will focus on the contrast between innovation in the service and manufacturing sectors.

Mini Case 1.6

Singapore Airlines – Sustainable Competitive Advantage[66]

Singapore International Airlines (SIA) has regularly been voted the world's best airline in surveys by travel magazines such as *Condé Nast Traveler* and the quality of its services is legendary. Its business strategy is based on a solid service product and attention to every detail of the way it is delivered. A first-to-market innovation strategy has been an important part of SIA's approach for years.

The SIA product itself – air travel – is reliable and the range of routes offered has been extended through alliances with other airlines. The way the service is delivered by SIA is designed to achieve maximum customer satisfaction and includes both people and technology related ideas. Cabin staff are renowned for being friendly and helpful and this has been strongly promoted through the *Singapore Girl* advertising. Staff receive longer and more detailed training than that offered by other airlines. For example, all cabin trainees spend time in homes for the aged in order to understand the problems faced by older travellers (a growing segment worldwide). Technology is also constantly updated and the aircraft fleet is one of the most modern in the industry. Having more modern aircraft has helped SIA differentiate their service product; passenger areas have larger than average seating, and a French fashion house designed the décor and all of the service ware (including the tableware). In-flight services have been constantly enhanced and the list of firsts here is long: first in-flight telephones; first in-flight fax machines; first Dolby surround sound and personal video screens in coach class; first to introduce electronic tickets but the company still allowed flexibility in allowing flight confirmations by telephone, fax or email.

It is interesting to note that competitors have quickly copied the technology-based innovations, whereas the quality of the service provided by staff has been harder for competitors to follow. In managing service innovation, a key question is how can service operations be made hard to copy?

MANAGING INNOVATION – THE CHALLENGE

Research has demonstrated the complexity of managing innovation at both the company and project level. Many aspects need to be considered, as do different functional areas. So, can an integrated approach be achieved? How can the recommendations from the different fields of research be related to the situation facing an organization?

Need for a Framework

Innovation management often requires managers to match 'technical' expertise, in areas such as technology, project management and finance, with 'soft' skills in managing people and creativity. The skills needed for technology management relate closely to engineering and the physical sciences, whereas the soft skills are closer to the social sciences, and finance is covered in business education. Few managers have been educated in all of these areas. In addition, developing new products, services and processes is inherently uncertain and this requires managers to be aware of techniques for dealing with risk. Due to its complexity, the management of innovation requires a mix of skills which makes it a fascinating challenge.

In many ways innovation management is in its infancy. Although there are tools, theories and approaches, there is not yet a clear methodology to help managers improve innovation performance. A similar situation existed in the 1980s in the area of quality management, where even the meaning of 'quality' was being debated (for example, should an 'internal' or 'customer' viewpoint be adopted?).[67] Quality management tools, such as Statistical Process Control (SPC) and cause and effect figures were emerging, as were approaches to people management such as quality circles (groups of manufacturing employees meeting on a regular basis to discuss how their work could be made more efficient). Today, this collection of tools and techniques has been combined into the widely recommended methodology of 'Six Sigma' quality management.[68] The Motorola Company was largely responsible for creating this integrated approach. Currently, innovation management has not reached this level of maturity and probably never will. Therefore, no integrated methodology is available and managers are faced with the challenge of having to select and combine ideas from different areas of thinking.

In our own research, it emerged that managers identify many facets to managing innovation: they cite strategy (for example, whether to be first-to-market, or to follow); people management (for example, motivating teams); and good project management (for example, in striving to meet challenging time-to-market goals).[69] Integrating these facets of innovation management is difficult, and the director of one manufacturing company said he really needed a 'systematic way to encourage and manage innovation'. Taking the main areas of the research literature at the company and project level, a framework has been developed to illustrate the main elements of innovation management and their relationships.

The Innovation Pentathlon Framework

Figure 1.5 gave a simple representation of the way a business generates and implements innovation: the process of innovation within an organization or, as Wheelwright and Clark termed it, the *development funnel*. The funnel illustrates the process of idea generation, selection and implementation, but it does not show the link to a firm's strategic intent (the importance of which emerged from our discussion of the research literature), or the link to a company's culture.

Building on the development funnel work, two extra elements – *innovation strategy* and *people and organization* – needed to be added. This is because senior managers perceive the importance of linking the portfolio of projects to their overall strategy and supporting the innovation levels of their organizations through effective people management. As its name suggests, the *Innovation Pentathlon* framework identifies five, what we will term, *areas* or *elements* of innovation management, as shown in Figure 1.6. In each of the five areas, there are a number of key topics to be managed:

Innovation strategy: developing and implementing an innovation strategy requires top management to focus on a number of issues. Assessing market trends and determining how these drive the need for innovation in the company's chosen sector(s) is the first step. The role of technology, the opportunities it can open and how to acquire expertise in the relevant technologies need to be considered. Management needs to communicate the role of innovation within

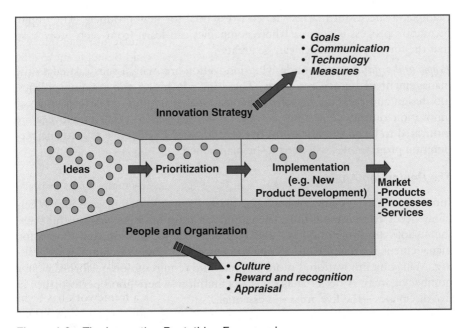

Figure 1.6 The Innovation Pentathlon Framework

a company – product, service, process and business process innovation – and match the resources to the strategy. For example, first-to-market approaches require particular capabilities in R&D and market development. Lastly, gauging innovation performance through the use of appropriate measures is essential.

Ideas: are the raw material for innovation and managers need to create an environment that supports creativity at both the individual and team level, and makes use of creativity techniques. Creativity should harness the knowledge both within and outside the organization. A large number of ideas need to be generated, which address customer requirements for products, services and streamlined processes. Good ideas blend technical, customer and market requirements. As innovation includes new products, services and new or improved processes, the scope for idea generation needs to be kept wide and should involve external sources.

Prioritization: an efficient process is required to ensure that the best ideas are chosen for development into new products, services and process innovations. This requires suitable tools to analyse the risk and return of individual projects. The finite resources available for innovation projects need to be carefully assigned. Managers need to collate the information across the range of projects, to check that the portfolio of innovation projects is balanced and matched to the company's innovation strategy. Collecting information on portfolio decisions, so that in the future management teams can review and learn from their previous decisions.

Implementation: this phase should focus on quickly and efficiently developing new products, services or processes, or a combination of these. Faster development times can be achieved through effective cross-functional teams, prototyping and testing. Commercialization is the last step in implementation and, for example, a successful market launch is essential for new products. The implementation process is an area where companies can learn from each project, so that the future performance can be greater.

People and organization: underlying innovation are many issues related to the management of human resources. These include hiring and training policies, job design and creating effective organizational structures, which will increase innovation outputs. Creating a *culture of innovation* in which employees are motivated to be constantly innovative is fundamental. Effective reward and recognition programmes will need to be maintained.

The Pentathlon Analogy

Innovation management has been previously compared to a marathon.[70] It certainly needs constant and long-term attention from managers and in this sense the analogy to a marathon is valid. However, the implication that innovation management is a matter of high performance in a single discipline is misleading. Managing innovation is more complex and requires good performance in a number of areas. A better analogy is a pentathlon, where good performance in five disciplines – the five areas – is essential.

There are two key points to note about the Pentathlon Framework. First, each of the five elements is, in itself, a complex area and so it is not surprising

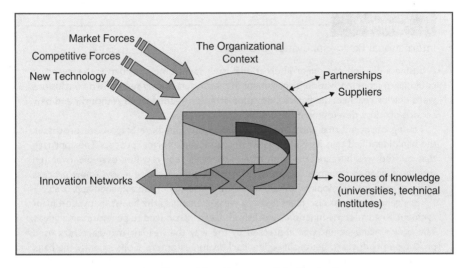

Figure 1.7   The Innovation Pentathlon Framework in Context

that innovation management – which is made up of these interrelated factors – is hugely challenging. Second, top performance in one area alone will not lead to long-term competitiveness. Similarly, many companies confuse innovation with creativity and so focus on generating more ideas, without considering how the best ideas can be selected, resources allocated and implementation quickly achieved. Overall, the framework allows us to split a large topic into more understandable and manageable parts.

The Pentathlon essentially represents the innovation processes within one organization. The context – the business situation – strongly influences innovation management and this is shown in Figure 1.7, where the market and other forces directly impact how an organization should manage its innovation. The figure also indicates that an organization must look outside its boundaries to increase innovation levels and the concept of *Open Innovation* has become very popular over the past few years. For example, links to suppliers and technical institutes are increasingly important (the main case study at the end of this chapter on NTT-DoCoMo looks at partnerships and alliances).

Applying the Framework

The Pentathlon Framework can be applied to identify the areas of innovation management in which an organization is both strong and weak. To demonstrate this, two short examples will be given, one from the service sector and one from manufacturing. Each of these has been disguised to ensure confidentiality and Figures 1.8 and 1.9 indicate the areas of innovation management where the companies were weaker. (In Chapter 9 we will also describe an *innovation audit* – a detailed method for identifying strengths and weaknesses using the Pentathlon Framework.)

Example I

International Bank – Innovation Processes

A business division of a major international bank spent time considering the lessons it could learn from innovation management in the manufacturing sector. Two conclusions were quickly reached: the bank's innovation strategy needed to be rethought and new service-product development needed a better process.

Having observed that most manufacturing companies have Stage-Gate processes, the bank identified that its NPD was weak and lacked a formal process. The approach that existed was bureaucratic, with many approvals required (for example, over ten managers needed to agree to a new advertising copy). Consequently, a new process was designed for developing new service products, including streamlined approvals.

Idea generation was also identified as a weak element in the bank's innovation management. Regular cross-functional workshops were introduced to generate initial ideas. The bank's management was impressed by the way that leading manufacturers used prototype products to get qualified feedback from customers. Consequently, the bank focused on turning ideas as quickly as possible into 'service prototypes' (with, for example, material on explaining the new service to customers and proposed advertising).

The improvements at the bank were also closely linked to the overall innovation strategy, which was then clearly communicated to all staff.

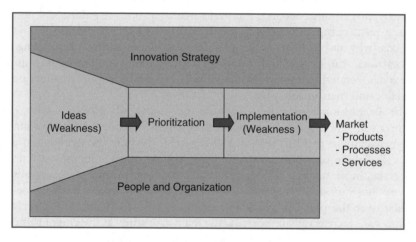

Figure 1.8 Innovation Management at an International Bank

Example 2

VehicleCo – Cross-Functional Creativity

Setting the right atmosphere for creativity is essential and the physical environment, the people and the business culture can all play a role. At a UK specialist vehicle manufacturer, which we will refer to as *VehicleCo*, much is the legacy of the charismatic

▶▶

founder who still takes an active role in generating technical ideas and ensuring that they are commercially feasible. By asking critical questions about new products – acting in some ways as a devil's advocate – he has created a culture that blends three distinct elements. A focus on developing first-to-market technical solutions is blended with a strong commercial awareness in R&D, and an emphasis on constant 'prototyping'. Prototypes are used as the basis for both internal discussions on new concepts and for making discussions with customer groups more concrete.

The factory has an ideal physical environment for creativity; it is an open plan with marketing and R&D sitting together, separated from production by a glass wall. Similarly, only a glass wall separates the workshop used for producing prototypes and so its work is visible for all to see.

At VehicleCo cross-functional teams are used to develop all ideas. For example, although most companies use continuous improvement teams, these are normally only staffed by manufacturing employees. Marketing and other functions are represented in kaizen projects, to bring a commercial focus and 'outside ideas' to brainstorming sessions. Similarly, production people are present in new product-development discussions. Brainstorming has become synonymous within the company with mixing different functional perspectives. With such a strong cross-functional orientation, it is not surprising that the functional R&D organization has gone – replaced by business teams where R&D and marketing are combined in small groups with clear target markets. Over the past decade, the organization has been changed several times and is expected to change again. Employees see this as inevitable and not negative; it means the organization is flexible enough to react to market changes.

It would be wrong to leave the impression that VehicleCo have no issues with innovation management. They have only recently introduced an NPD process to solve problems with the quality of new products and transfer to production. Similarly, they have no review process to determine what can be improved from one project to the next.

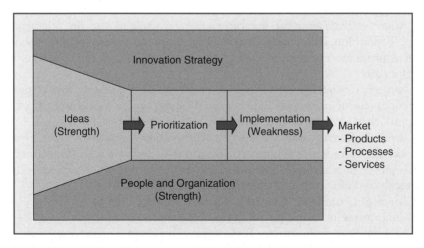

Figure 1.9 Innovation Management at VehicleCo

Limitations of the Framework

The Pentathlon Framework has limitations that we need to consider. First, it is a categorization of the main elements of innovation management and not a predictive model of innovation performance. The framework provides a visual means of visualizing and assessing all aspects of innovation management within an organization and can be used as a diagnostic tool. However, the five different elements of the Pentathlon are difficult to assess quantitatively and so care must be taken in concluding whether performance in one area is sufficient. Also, the interaction between the elements of the Pentathlon, for example, how changes in a company culture will influence the generation of ideas, are hard to predict and context-specific. Within these limitations, the framework enables clearer discussions on the nature of innovation (just as the development funnel enabled managers to better understand how ideas are developed into products). It can also be used as a communication tool, to explain to employees why, where and how improvements in innovation management are to be made.

THE STRUCTURE OF THIS BOOK

The structure of this book is based around the Pentathlon Framework with chapters as follows:

- *Chapter 2: Innovation and Economics* explains the economic impact of innovation.
- *Chapter 3: Contrasting Services with Manufacturing* discusses the innovation management issues in the service industries, compared with those in manufacturing. It also introduces much of the terminology of innovation management.
- *Chapter 4: Developing an Innovation Strategy* explains the first element of the Pentathlon Framework. It covers the importance of companies setting an appropriate innovation strategy based on analysis of their markets and resources.
- *Chapter 5: Generating Creative Customer-Focused Ideas* discusses how to generate ideas for new products, new service products and new processes. It covers approaches to improve both individual and organizational creativity.
- *Chapter 6: Selecting and Managing an Innovation Portfolio* discusses how to select the best ideas for commercialization and achieve a balance portfolio.
- *Chapter 7: Implementing Innovations* explains how innovation projects can be quickly and efficiently implemented and commercialized.
- *Chapter 8: Creating an Innovative Culture* discusses how to achieve a culture of innovation including the role of people management.
- *Chapter 9: Boosting Innovation Performance.* This chapter on innovation change management first discusses how to audit innovation performance. It then indicates how improvements can be made to increase overall performance

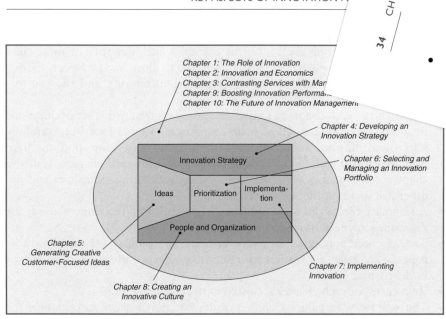

Chapter 1: The Role of Innovation
Chapter 2: Innovation and Economics
Chapter 3: Contrasting Services with Man
Chapter 9: Boosting Innovation Performa...
Chapter 10: The Future of Innovation Management

Chapter 4: Developing an
Innovation Strategy

Innovation Strategy

Chapter 6: Selecting and
Managing an Innovation
Portfolio

Ideas | Prioritization | Implementation

People and Organization

Chapter 5:
Generating Creative
Customer-Focused Ideas

Chapter 7: Implementing
Innovation

Chapter 8: Creating an
Innovative Culture

Figure 1.10   Chapter Structure and the Pentathlon Framework

since – as just like in a pentathlon – good performance in one area alone is not enough. Performance measures are also discussed.

- *Chapter 10: The Future of Innovation Management* concludes with directions for the future. As companies are becoming more effective at managing innovation, where will the leaders derive competitive advantage? This and other key trends are covered.

Figure 1.10 illustrates the structure of this book, showing that the five Chapters 4, 5, 6, 7 and 8 as being directly related to specific elements of the Pentathlon. The outer circle indicates that Chapters 1, 2, 3, 9 and 10 discuss topics that are related to the whole topic of innovation management.

Format of the Chapters

Each chapter follows a similar style:

- The relevant theory is discussed, in order to provide a solid theoretical understanding of the issues involved and insights into the latest research.
- The most relevant management tools and concepts are explained. These have been selected through an extensive review of the literature, and are based on our own experience of managing innovation and our consultancy work with organizations.
- Important terms related to innovation management are first shown in italics and then their meanings are explained.

The theory and tools are backed by examples, including five or more 'box cases' (mini case studies) per chapter, selected to illustrate key aspects of how companies manage innovation in service, manufacturing and the not-for-profit sector.

- At the end of each chapter a longer case study is given with a set of questions for readers to consider. These main chapter case studies have been carefully selected to illustrate the challenges facing companies, how solutions have been developed and the main learning points from each chapter. Half the chapters have main case studies based on manufacturing companies and the other half focus on the service sector.
- A summary recaps the main points and gives practical recommendations for the management of innovation.
- Two or three annotated recommendations for readings – either books or papers – are given, for readers who want to go deeper into the topics covered in the chapter.
- References for each chapter are listed at the end of the book.
- The website www.palgrave.com provides additional notes and material for each chapter.

For this introductory chapter, our main case looks at the innovation management challenges facing a Japanese mobile telephony service provider, NTT-DoCoMo.

SUMMARY

Many reports and articles continue to be published on innovation management. However, improving performance of a company is still a real challenge for managers. Therefore, the aim of this book is to present ways to improve innovation performance through the development and successful implementation of an innovation strategy. This chapter showed the following:

- The need for innovation is increasing and is being driven by technology, customers, new forms of competition and the business environment.
- There are five main dimensions of innovation – product, service, process, business process and business model innovation. Companies need to identify which dimensions are important for them.
- Innovation has different degrees. It consists of not only breakthroughs (radical innovations) but also incremental improvements, which are equally important to companies in both the manufacturing and service sectors.
- Extensive research has shown that innovation management is complex and multifaceted. Its scope is wide, ranging from business strategy, managing technology and new product development to organization and people management. The Innovation Pentathlon Framework is a diagnostic framework for managing innovation.

> ### MANAGEMENT RECOMMENDATIONS
>
> - Determine the intended role of innovation in your organization and clearly communicate this to employees.
> - Consider how innovation can be enhanced from contributions throughout the organization.
> - Use analysis of Dimension & Degrees to identify whether your products or service products can be made more competitive.
> - Use the Pentathlon Framework to pinpoint the areas of innovation management that your organization needs to improve.

RECOMMENDED READING

1. Anonymous, 'Something New Under the Sun: A Special Report on Innovation', *The Economist*, 13 October 2007. [Excellent overview of key issues in managing innovation and technology. Written in the characteristic style of the *Economist* – clear and to the point.]

2. Chan Kim, W. and Mauborgne, R., 'Value Innovation: The Strategic Logic of High Growth', *Harvard Business Review*, Vol. 75, No. 1 (January–February 1997), pp. 103–112. [Presents how product innovation needs to be complemented by service and other forms of innovation.]

CASE STUDY
NTT-DoCoMo, Japan – Partnerships for Innovation[71]

Before reading this case, consider the following generic innovation management issues:

- How can partnerships and alliances help a company in the service sector achieve its innovation strategy?
- How can service and product strategies of different companies be aligned to target specific customers segments?
- How can a service provider make it harder for competitors to copy innovations?

Today, NTT-DoCoMo is the top Japanese mobile telephone service provider with an enviable 60 per cent market share. The company was formed in 1992 when the Japanese government broke up the monopoly of Nippon Telephone and Telegraph (NTT) and the name comes from both an abbreviation of '<u>Do</u> <u>Co</u>mmunications over the <u>Mo</u>bile Network', and a play on 'dokomo', the Japanese word for 'anywhere'. Although now the market leader, ten years ago the company was facing a serious situation. The Japanese economic situation was poor, handsets were heavy, subscriptions and call charges exorbitantly high, transmission quality was infamously bad and, to cap it all, DoCoMo was losing money.

TECHNICAL QUALITY UP, PRICE DOWN

Some managers might have decided to try and manage the crisis through cost cutting alone but CEO Kouji Ohboshi made heavy investments to develop both the transmission quality and DoCoMo's total coverage in Japan. Parallel to this, a pricing strategy was adopted with the aim of making mobile telephone services affordable for everyone. DoCoMo slashed prices and, although competitors followed, raised the number of its subscribers significantly – to the point where it has 44 million today. This growth was at the expense of what the industry refers to as ARPUs (average revenues per user) and so, from an early stage, it was clear to management that a strategy based solely on increasing call quality, market penetration and cutting prices was not sustainable.

One of the unusual characteristics of the Japanese mobile telephone market is that there is no direct channel by which mobile telephone ('handset') manufacturers can market their products. Every handset in Japan is provided as part of a service contract. In addition, Japanese law prevents DoCoMo from manufacturing equipment for retail sale.[72] Maybe this is what caused DoCoMo to take a broader view of innovation than many of the other service providers around the world and, in particular, not only to develop new services but also to take steps to strongly influence the design of manufacturers' handsets. Fortunately, through its history as part of NTT, external links to handset manufacturers such as NEC and Fujitsu were strong and this enabled DoCoMo to push for handsets with special features for specific market segments.

MATCHING SERVICES, SEGMENTS AND PRODUCTS

With ageing populations worldwide, many companies are trying to target what is often called the 'silver [haired] market' or 'silver segment' but DoCoMo has been particularly successful. Millions of new senior subscribers in recent years have adopted the Raku Raku ('easy-easy') range of mobile telephones, which have a set of features aimed at the particular needs of this segment. Today, 22 per cent of Japanese owners of mobile phones are over 50 years of age. The handsets were developed for DoCoMo by Fujitsu and have the following features:

- Larger keyboards;
- Larger text on the display and simpler user interfaces than most cell phones. In addition, a synthesized voice explanation can be enabled, for each key pressed;
- Colours available include 'traditional silver' and 'eternal pink'. The handset comes with a set of standard ringtone options to match users' tastes including the Japanese song 'Kawa no Nagare no Yoni', 'Raindrops keep falling on my head', and 'When the Saints go marching in';
- The latest version of the Raku Raku includes a pedometer function that measures how far the person carrying the phone walks, and sends daily emails to subscribers telling them how far they walked and how many calories they burned. According to the press release, this 'is particularly relevant to users wishing to regularly update their doctors with this data'.

In marketing the Raku Raku, DoCoMo has trodden a careful path. The company 'highlights its technical features but in its advertising always cleverly links these to

▶▶

emotional benefits', says industry watcher Daniel Scuka of Wireless Watch Japan. 'For example, their adverts show grandparents operating the handsets easily and keeping in easy contact with their families...and, of course, "age" is never directly mentioned in their marketing'. The deep understanding of older consumers has put DoCoMo and its suppliers in a strong position. A stream of new features with real benefits for silver segment customers is planned in 2009, such as advanced signal processing. This enables reduced background noise and can even slow down the speed at which someone's speech is heard on a handset.

It is not just for the silver segment that specific products have been deemed necessary. Japan has extensive mountains and many of its population enjoy outdoor activities, such as hill-walking and mountaineering. This is a segment that DoCoMo is also addressing with a corresponding handset, the 'Geofree II'. This has a set of features designed to appeal to those with an interest in outdoor activities:

- It is lightweight;
- It floats, is water resistant and shock-proof;
- It has a large (1.8 inch) liquid crystal display;
- It supports 'i-Area', a function that gives local information based on the unique base-station in which the handset is located;
- Matching its usage, the handset is marketed in colours such as 'active red' and 'dynamic blue'.

To understand its target segments, DoCoMo undertakes regular market research. Recent studies have looked at urban usage of mobile phones by 1000 adults,[73] how adolescents use wireless services and the particular functions they most want in their handsets – 600 young people were interviewed.[74] John Lagerling, a manager in the DoCoMo strategy team, says that the company is careful to make sure that its approach to market research is broad. 'We regularly conduct research outside the mobile telephone market, as we are interested to see how "lifestyle" changes affect customers' needs. Take for example the Geofree. Users' ideas provided the inspiration for the handset, supplemented with by research looking at the developments in the digital watch industry, where rugged designs combined with 'outdoor' features had been very successful. Combining a range of features in a handset offers outdoor sportspeople added safety – easy access to weather, local information and emergency services. You do not get these sort of insights for new products if you only research your own industry'.

Although the robust Geofree II, the handy Raku Raku, and handsets aimed at young people increase market penetration, this is not enough. 'Voice-based revenues' from these segments will not generate growth, as the Japanese market has matured and call rates remain an area of strong price competition. So non-voice services are also being developed.

NON-VOICE AND THE PORTFOLIO OF SERVICES

'Non-voice services have become a fundamental part of DoCoMo's strategy', says Scuka. Initially, these services were simple ones – such as downloadable, changeable ringtones (these have become a success story worldwide for service providers, generating

▶▶

surprisingly high revenues). Once the downloadable ringtone feature had been strongly marketed and the market educated, further downloadable services were added such as '30K Applications', relatively small Java games, paid for on a one-off download fee. DoCoMo introduced their most prominent non-voice service in February 1999. This is 'i-mode' (Internet mode), a service that is generating significant revenues.

The idea behind i-mode involved making Internet access mobile and easy and now it is the world's largest mobile Internet service with 38 million subscribers. Handsets with an 'i' button and special menus were developed to meet DoCoMo's requirements for fast and efficient Internet usage. Not only the handsets have been optimized but also the websites that are available have been coordinated – including those 'authorized by DoCoMo' – and a new business model created. Internet access is priced on the amount of information downloaded rather than the access time and this, combined with the low basic rate of 300 yen ($2.4) a month for i-mode service, and one yen for a typical email, mean that it is good value for money.

Four categories of i-mode service are provided:

- 'Transaction' (e-commerce, banking and ticket booking through the websites of Amazon.com, Northwest Airlines and Citibank);
- 'Information' (for example, CNN news, Bloomberg market updates);
- 'Entertainment' (for example, Pokemon games, Hallmark e-greeting cards and hit songs);
- 'Databases' (for example, telephone directories, restaurant guides, etc.).

Each of these categories has a number of websites providing what the industry refers to as 'content'. DoCoMo has carefully selected content partners for the quality of their services, a willingness to optimize their websites for i-mode access, a willingness to accept site development risk and an interest in forming a partnership (in which DoCoMo brings more traffic to the content provider in return for a commission on the information charges levied).

Fast and easy access has been achieved by reprogramming websites using a subset of the programming language HTML, which increases access speed. The version of HTML used also allows new websites to be quickly created and this focus on keeping it simple has allowed independent programmers to create a wealth of unofficial i-mode content. Although 'unofficial' sites do not generate content commission for DoCoMo, the availability of extra content has been well received by customers and does generate a great deal of data traffic revenue for the carrier.

STIMULATING AND COORDINATING INNOVATION

Over 1100 engineers are employed in DoCoMo's R&D and spending on development has increased by four times since 1998. This investment pays for a very wide range of projects, from improvements to handsets to better networks to support the uninterrupted availability of services. DoCoMo's R&D has adopted a central coordinating role – including stimulating innovation – between the equipment manufacturers, content providers (websites) and platform vendors (network providers) as shown in Figure 1.11. In his role in the i-mode strategy department, Lagerling is responsible for

▸▸

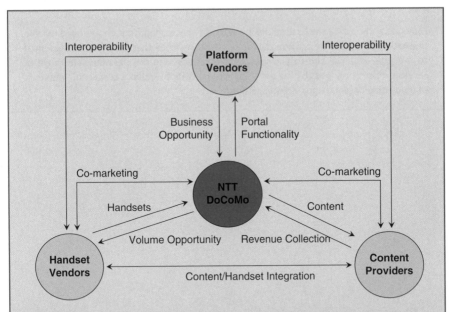

Figure 1.11 DoCoMo's i-mode Collaboration Concept – The 'Ecosystem'
Source: Adapted from: www.nttdocomo.com/corebiz/imode/why/strategy.html, used with permission.

managing some of these international collaborations. 'Our strategy is to view the value chain as an "ecosystem", in which all of the partners need to have a fair margin. If we as a company are too greedy, the system will not function well and relationships will suffer. Therefore, we share both risk and gain'.

From the figure it can be seen that handset vendors receive information from DoCoMo on specific product requirements and the potential sales volumes. This encourages close collaboration on handset NPD and often DoCoMo makes direct investments in such work, to ensure that new handsets are developed on time and these are 'integrated to the content' available. Close links with the content providers include joint work on website operability and co-marketing. The platform vendors are the third set of partners with which DoCoMo R&D has constant contact, as networks determine the availability and reliability of services. Availability is a key concern for Japanese users, as the country suffers from earth tremors and following these there is extreme usage of mobile telephones, as people check whether their relatives are alright. Therefore, network capacity needs to be planned to match these 'spikes' in usage. Overall, Lagerling says that 'subscribers judge the value of mobile Internet services on the basis of the quality of content'.

Mobile telephone service providers worldwide are looking for what they term 'killer applications' – services that mobile telephone users will use extensively and that will generate significant revenue growth for providers. DoCoMo is somewhat different in that it is not searching for one solution. Instead, it is looking to be the coordinator that

▶▶

can constantly create the best mix of innovative services, handsets, content and reliable network platforms that provide customers with services that they will find essential to everyday life. 'We aim to provide our customers with the best possible range of services. That's only possible by developing our position within a sustainable network of innovative organizations', says Lagerling.

2 INNOVATION AND ECONOMICS

> He that will not apply new remedies must expect new evils; for time is the greatest innovator.
>
> Francis Bacon

INTRODUCTION

Most of this book concentrates on innovation at the level of the organization or company, because it is here that most of us work and where our actions can have some effect. But it is also worthwhile to step back and consider the economic considerations that shape our working environment and influence the need and the scope for innovative activity within organizations. Most studies of innovation by economists have focused at this macro level in order to develop theories that are applicable to whole industries or nations. This approach has acknowledged limitations because, 'when we look at technological change in the aggregate – as a socioeconomic process – we are obviously forced to simplify an enormously complicated set of activities'.[1] Nevertheless, the insights are vital for framing policy at the industry, government or supra-government context. Every manager should understand this background, though the links to action at the level of the individual firm are indirect.

There is a long history of innovation research by economists. A major influence has been what became known as the Austrian school of economic thought. The earliest work was by A. F. Riedel in 1839, who first recognized that new products have a significant impact on the economy. Surprisingly, he did not identify the importance of process innovation even though the Industrial Revolution had included process innovations which made a big impact, such as the power loom and the Spinning Jenny. The most significant work on innovation from the Austrian school came a century later with Joseph A. Schumpeter, who later moved from Vienna to become a professor at Harvard University.[2] His work, which was already mentioned in Chapter 1, laid the foundations for our understanding of both the nature and impact of innovation, and his book *The Theory of Economic Development*[3] is one of the classic texts of economics. It discusses the importance not only of product innovation but also of process innovation, such as new manufacturing techniques that can drastically alter the cost structures of an industry. Our main case for this chapter, Aravind Hospitals, gives a dramatic example of this.

This chapter covers the following:

- The factors which appear to influence innovation levels in organizations.
- Links between innovation and economic performance, including a discussion on long-term business cycles.
- The findings of research on how individual innovations are adopted and the typical changes that they bring to a market.
- A Main Case Study on Aravind Eye Hospitals.

ECONOMIC MEASURES OF INNOVATION

Research into the causes and consequences of innovation has been hindered by the problems of measuring 'innovation' itself. Economists have used various measures, such as patent counts, R&D expenditure or the number of new products launched, because these data are readily available for many companies and industries. These measures can give insight into innovation performance but they also have significant limitations.[4] Certainly, they are not the ones typically used by companies themselves to assess their performance. These, according to a survey of 1075 companies by McKinsey[5] are, in order of priority: revenue growth from new products and services; customer satisfaction with new products and services; number of ideas or concepts in the pipeline; R&D as a percentage of sales; and percentage of sales from new products or services in a given period. Clearly, many of these measures are not generally made available to outsiders, which may be why the survey found that only about half the companies benchmarked their innovation performance against others. The majority of companies chose their investment levels on the opportunities they perceived, not on more global comparisons.

Table 2.1 summarizes the three main measures of innovation performance used by economists with their advantages and limitations. It will be seen that they are generally not very satisfactory. As Marco Iansiti of Harvard Business School has pointed out, 'after all, what a company gets for the money it spends on R&D is what ultimately matters'.[6] Moreover, the trend towards Open Innovation means that many companies are acquiring new products through partnerships with others, or by acquisition, so purely internal R&D is a less complete measure of innovative activity than it used to be.

The issue of measuring innovation performance is not just of concern to economists; it is also often a worry for managers. How can you manage something that you can't properly measure? Our answer at the management level is that there is no generally applicable measure of innovation because innovation is

Table 2.1   Economic Measures of Innovation

Measure	Advantages of the Measure	Limitations of the Measure	Implications for Managers
Number of patents, per employee, or over time	• Data are readily available and can be analysed by industrial sector, country, etc. • Useful (but not complete) measure of performance in research laboratories.	• Patents are a measure of invention, not of innovation. • Some companies chose not to apply for patents, as it is time-consuming and does not always offer good protection. • Patents are of not of equal value. Many are effectively worthless.	• It is useful to monitor the contents of patents filed by competitors. • Patent counts are used as an indication of a knowledge base in mergers and acquisitions.
R&D expenditure as a percentage of sales	• Data on investment levels are normally published in company annual reports. • Widely used	• An 'input'measure, rather than a measure of results.	• R&D spend of comparable competitors is a useful benchmark.
Number of new products	• Is a measure of the output of R&D (but not strictly of innovation, unless product success is considered). • Can include innovations sourced externally.	• The meaning of 'new product' is equivocal (for example six different degrees of product innovation – see Chapter 1). • Seldom available externally so comparisons with others are not easy.	• Need to carefully define what counts as a new product. • Few companies use this measure to check the performance of their competitors.

a capability rather than an end in itself. Each company needs and uses innovation in a different way and to a different extent. There is some benefit in making comparisons with competitors but the individual needs and capabilities of the firm concerned are the dominant issue. It is more useful to give attention to improving how well the organization is able to perform on each part of the Pentathlon separately; just as an army assesses its preparedness for battle not by some overall measure but by reviewing its separate capabilities: men, guns, communications, transport and so on.

Despite the difficulties in trying to study innovation at the macro level, the findings of this type of research have strongly influenced our understanding of the subject and give some general pointers to managers. The research at the macro level can be classified into studies looking at the factors that mediate innovation levels and further studies on the impact of innovation on both companies and markets.

FACTORS MEDIATING INNOVATION

Economists have looked at the precursors of innovation. *Development Economics* is the study of the factors that are necessary for economic growth, such as infrastructure, the health of the workforce, education levels and economic aid. The development economics viewpoint is important in that it indicates some of the factors that must be present to develop economies, but we shall concentrate on the macroeconomics of innovation itself. Most of the macroeconomic studies of innovation have taken product innovation as their focus rather than process or service innovation. Product innovation levels have been found to be related to

- Company size.
- Market sector.
- Education levels and traits of national culture.
- Government policies to support innovation.

Company Size and Innovation

There is a significant body of research on the influence of company size on innovation performance. Once again, the work of Schumpeter is important. In one of the earliest studies, he pointed out that larger companies are at an advantage when it comes to innovation, because of the economies of scale that they have in R&D.[7] Indeed, several later studies found that R&D expenditures increased almost in proportion to firm size.[8] Similarly, an investigation of nearly 600 companies in the USA showed that both the size and age of companies are determinants of the number of new products produced per dollar of sales.[9] Yet another study determined that in larger companies both R&D expenditures and the number of patents awarded are higher than in small ones.[10] The conclusion that larger organizations are more innovative than smaller ones is not universally accepted, however. Other studies have found no differences between the innovation performance of large and small companies, apparently because although larger companies can have higher R&D expenditures, small companies may have more innovative employees (for example, young graduate scientists bringing with them the latest scientific knowledge and ideas).[11] Research by the London Business School concluded that small firms are the most important innovators.[12] Another study showed that the number of new products developed in smaller companies tends to be proportionally higher.[13] Of course the findings depend on the business sectors studied and the measures of innovation used. But overall, economists themselves have construed that the research investigating the influence of company size on innovation is inconclusive.[14] Large companies should have lots of advantages: resources, slack time to develop ideas, readily available funding, knowledge of markets and technologies, management experience and so on. So, why is it not overwhelmingly clear that large companies are the main source of innovation? Specific barriers to innovation certainly arise within large and well-established organizations and management has the challenge of recognizing and dealing with them.

What is clearer is the role of start-ups in new industries. High-technology start-up companies are well known for their innovations and there are many examples where such firms, rather than the market leaders, have been responsible for the breakthroughs. One case is the bag-less vacuum cleaner, which was developed by an entrepreneur-innovator, James Dyson, rather than a market leader such as Hoover. One study showed that small companies backed by venture capital are disproportionately successful. Of the nearly one million companies formed in the USA each year, only a few hundred are successful at obtaining backing from venture capitalists[15]; yet these make up over a third of companies that eventually go public. A partial explanation of the high success rate of such start-ups is that they have to go through a very demanding approval process to obtain venture capital. This has helped companies to recognize the importance of tough approval processes for innovation; and Texas Instruments, Philips and others have mimicked the approaches used by venture capitalists, in their internal new venture approval process.

Market Sectors and Innovation

Although the research on the influence of company size is inconclusive, data on worldwide R&D investment levels give interesting comparisons between market sectors. Table 2.2 shows the spending, both in absolute terms and as a percentage of sales, of the five companies that invest most in R&D in each of six important market sectors, worldwide. The figures are for 2007. As would be expected, different sectors require and support very different levels of R & D expenditure, reflecting the state of their markets and technologies. What is more surprising is the diversity within the sectors themselves. This reflects the different histories and ambitions of the companies, and the fact that the sectors themselves are very broad groupings and may include companies with quite different markets and business models. Clearly, Microsoft and IBM are not really comparable businesses although they are both in the same sector; nor are BAe systems, who are primarily a defence contractor and EADS, whose activities are mostly civil.

Certainly, any company should carefully compare its own investment on innovation with what its competitors are spending. If they are significantly different, alarm bells should ring; but the real meaning must be sought at a level of detail far below the gross figures for expenditure.

The service sector is of vital importance to developed economies. Most European economies generate well over 60 per cent of their gross domestic

Table 2.2   R&D Investment in Different Industries

Top Five Companies in sector by R&D investment	R&D Spend (£ Billions)	R&D Intensity (% of sales)
Aerospace and defence sector	10.8	4.9
1) EADS	1.9	7.3
2) Boeing	1.7	5.3
3) Finmeccanica	1.3	16.1
4) BAe Systems	1.3	10.1
5) United Technologies	0.8	3.2
Automobiles & parts sector	41.0	4.1
1) Ford Motor	3.7	4.5
2) DaimlerChrysler	3.5	3.4
3) Toyota Motor	3.5	3.9
4) General Motors	3.4	3.2
5) Volkswagen	2.8	4.0
Banks	1.6	4.1
1) Royal Bank of Scotland	0.38	1.4
2) HSBC	0.30	0.8
3) Societe Generale	0.14	1.0
4) Rabobank	0.12	1.9
5) Banca Intesa	0.10	1.5
Fixed Telecommunications	4.9	1.6
1) NTT	1.3	2.9
2) BT	1.1	5.5
3) France Telecom	0.57	1.6
4) Telefonica	0.40	1.1
5) Deutsche Telekom	0.33	0.8
Software and Computing	17.5	10.1
1) Microsoft	3.6	13.9
2) IBM	2.9	6.2
3) Oracle	1.1	12.2
4) Fujitsu	1.0	5.0
5) SAP	0.875	13.8

Continued

Table 2.2   Continued

Top Five Companies in sector by R&D investment	R&D Spend (£ Billions)	R&D Intensity (% of sales)
Pharmaceuticals and Biotech	**47.4**	**15.9**
1) Pfizer	3.9	14.5
2) Johnson and Johnson	3.6	13.4
3) GlaxoSmithKline	3.5	14.9
4) Sanofi-Avensis	3.0	15.5
5) Roche	2.8	15.7

Source: *UK Department for Innovation, Universities and Skills 2007 R&D Scoreboard. www.innovation. gov.uk.*

product (GDP) from services; in the USA the figure is 80 per cent, whereas in China it is still only 33 per cent. Moving from an agricultural-led economy to a manufacturing-led one, and then to a service one is a natural progression. As services become dominant, the investments of this sector in R&D also increase. It is now estimated that 24 per cent of the total spent on R&D in the USA is in the service sector, compared with only 5 per cent in 1983.[16] (It should be noted that the 24 per cent figure is probably an underestimate of the true investment, as it is difficult to obtain accurate figures on R&D and innovation spending in services[17]).

Education Levels, National Culture and Innovation

Economists stress the importance of technological capability for economic growth. This, in turn, is strongly influenced by national culture and educational levels. For example, the number of new products developed and the number of high-tech and start-ups within a country appear to be dependent on these factors.[18]

Several studies have found not only that high investment in education makes it possible for countries to create more innovative products[19] but that the availability of skilled staff aids the spread of innovations. For example, the shortage of IT skills is currently a major problem in most countries and this is disrupting their ability to take full advantage of such technologies. Employees' qualifications at the time they enter the workforce is not the only factor. Investments in maintaining and increasing employees' skill levels and motivating them to personally take responsibility for honing their skills – *lifelong learning* – are crucial. Transfer of know-how from science into industry can be an important source of ideas for new products, services and processes.

Certain characteristics of a national culture also play a key role. Many studies have found that entrepreneurial thinking and personal autonomy are related to the national cultures and strongly influence innovation levels.[20] Examples of the entrepreneurial spirit of particular groups abound in history. For example, several

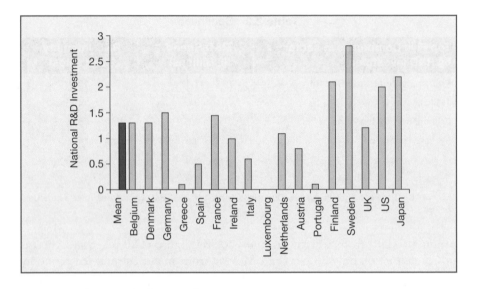

Figure 2.1   National R&D expenditures

Source: ESN, Brussels, *European Trend Chart on Innovation* (Brussels: European Commission, ESN, 2000).

studies have identified the positive impact of the work ethic of Asian entrepreneurs on the US economy. More recently, it has been argued that the secret of US economic success continues to be its innovative and entrepreneurial culture.[21] It is widely recognized that innovation needs a supportive social and political climate. Governments can take a lead in influencing culture, particularly within the public sector, as is shown in Mini Case 2.1 on Australian Medical care.

Some countries focus more on R&D and innovation than others. For example, Figure 2.1 shows the percentage of gross national product that is invested in R&D by business in European Union countries, the USA and Japan. This averages 1.3 per cent, but some countries such as Sweden and Finland invest significantly more (2.8 and 2.1 per cent respectively). The effect of these high levels of investment by companies in these countries is very visible around the world – the ubiquitous IKEA furniture and Nokia mobile telephones are the best-known but by no means the only examples of successful Scandinavian-designed products. In contrast, countries such as Italy and Greece do not have a strong R&D tradition and both local companies and multinationals conduct very little R&D there. The generation of knowledge is generally seen as a fundamental precursor to national innovation levels, with the strength of the links between universities, industrial R&D laboratories, marketing specialists and consumers being the key factor.[22]

Although the influence of education systems and national cultures on innovation activities appears clear, it is difficult to make specific recommendations for managers, except to find ways to take advantage of the national cultures and different laws that apply in the countries in which they operate. National cultures can have very direct influence on innovation and, for instance, Japanese engineers are far more open to taking and adopting existing ideas than engineers from some other countries.[23]

Mini Case 2.1

Australian Medical Care – Changing the Culture[24]

Medical care is a major part of the service sector, with both public and private hospitals in most countries. Hospitals have been relatively slow to adopt management techniques, such as process flow analysis (which can be used to optimize the speed at which a patient receives treatment) and quality management. The use of quality management techniques boomed in manufacturing in the 1980s and approaches such as *zero defects* (analysing product manufacturing problems with the aim of eliminating them) were widely and successfully used. Only now is formal quality management becoming widespread in the health-care industry.

The Australian Resource Centre for Healthcare Innovation supports the implementation of effective and quality improvements in healthcare. It does this through seminars, publishing reports, producing case studies and communicating new ideas to health-care professionals. The Centre's website offers some interesting insights into the reasons that quality management has been slow to be adopted in healthcare. Reports speak of a culture in the medical profession that was reluctant to recognize mistakes; 'adverse events' were kept quiet, and learning from mistakes was impossible without 'greater openness'.

Fortunately, the culture of the medical profession is now changing and, worldwide, the quality of treatment is being improved not only by improved drugs and medical technology but also through suitable use of quality management techniques. Innovation is not possible without a culture of openness. This chapter's main case, Aravind Hospitals, demonstrates the impact that new processes can have in healthcare.

Government Policies and Innovation

Ever since economists identified the link between innovation and economic growth, national governments have taken steps to stimulate technological developments and innovation. In the past 15 years particularly, technology and innovation policy have become an integral part of government support for business and developed countries invest a considerable portion of their budgets in supporting research and technology in science and industry.[25] For example, since 1996 there has been an action plan with measures to speed the transfer of ideas from research establishments into industry in the European Union.[26] Typically government programmes fit into the following three main categories:

- Programmes to optimize the interface between science and industry. These include measures to strengthen the links between industry and universities and, for example, allow scientists to move between academia and industry more easily.

- Political measures to support the foundation and growth of more innovative companies. These include the creation of a favourable financial climate for companies needing start-up capital. Such measures are often focused on *new technology-based firms* (NTBF) and sometimes on a particular range of technologies or innovations. Key technologies supported by governments in Europe, North America and Japan include biotechnology and aerospace. China is also investing significantly in biotechnology. Studies have shown that government support for specific areas can be particularly effective.
- The creation of new public bodies with a focus on innovation. For example, Spain formed a new ministry for science and technology in 2000 and a national R&D strategy was developed for the first time in 2000 in Italy, as investment in research had been comparatively low for many years (as shown by Figure 2.1).

Government policies can have a positive influence on product innovation. An investigation of the support for research and technology development in the USA, Japan, Sweden and the Netherlands concluded that this has helped increase the number of new products developed by industry.[27] The role of non-university research establishments, focusing on knowledge transfer is also seen as important and, for example, the Fraunhofer Institutes has helped to close Germany's technological gap with North America.

Empirical studies have identified that the availability of credit can affect innovation and because of this, many governments are moving to encourage the improvement of credit mechanisms.[28,29] Generally, governments are attempting to encourage entrepreneurial innovative companies by making capital available for technology-based ventures to be launched (often called 'pre-seed capital'), and supporting a climate in which venture capitalists are active. The influence of venture capitalists has been found to be positive in that they not only provide capital but also impose a demanding set of selection criteria as well as often providing direct management support.

Politicians and policy-makers regularly try to support innovation directly through, for example, grants for relocation, lower taxes for start-up companies and changes in education. The Dutch government's use of taxation policy to stimulate R&D in small and medium enterprises (SMEs) is highlighted in Mini Case 2.2. A key factor in the success of such schemes is how easy it is for small companies to apply for financial support. However, despite the actions of governments to support innovation, it is still individual organizations that are at the sharp end of managing it. If political changes support companies in their drive towards innovation, then this is positive. However, it is better for managers to focus on the areas of innovation management that they themselves can influence.

> **Mini Case 2.2**
>
> Dutch government policy and R&D[30]
>
> Many governments have used taxation, or rather its relaxation, as a means to stimulate innovation. There are various mechanisms but for these to be effective, especially for SMEs, a key factor is that they should be easy for companies to operate. In Holland, where companies must deduct income tax and social security payments directly, this has been achieved by allowing organizations to pay lower tax amounts on behalf of their R&D staff. It has proved popular with SMEs – who receive 60 per cent of the budget allocated to the scheme – and a total of approximately 15,000 organizations benefited in 1999. Research conducted on behalf of the Dutch government has shown that both R&D expenditures and the number of R&D employees have increased.

IMPACTS OF INNOVATION

Four main topics have been studied related to the impacts of innovation. These are

- Innovation and business cycles.
- Innovation and employment.
- Innovation and company performance.
- Product innovation and growth.

Innovation and Business Cycles

The relationship between business cycles and innovation is complex. Schumpeter believed that in addition to the underlying slow and continuous increase in economic performance, innovation also drives long-term cyclical patterns of economic performance. Innovation drives economic development, and often implies irreversible changes in the way things are done. Schumpeter introduced the term *creative destruction*, which accentuates both the novel ideas behind innovations and their power to disrupt markets and industries.[31]

To understand the impact of innovation on economic performance requires a historical perspective. Table 2.3 summarizes the characteristics of the 'long waves' of economic cycles, which are also called Kondratieff cycles, after the Russian economist.

The table shows the groups of innovations that stimulated industrial revolutions and their approximate dates. The Industrial Revolution started in Britain and lasted from about 1780 to 1845 and was the result of the innovations based on steam technology, which influenced a number of industries; and the power loom, which affected the textile industry.[32] The disruption in the textile industry

Table 2.3   The Kondratieff Cycles: Waves of Industrial Innovation

Long Waves	Important Innovations	Schumpeter's First Phase of Innovation	Schumpeter's Second Phase of Innovation		
		Prosperity	Recession	Depression	Recovery
1.	The Industrial Revolution (Division of labour, steam engine, loom)	1782–1802	1803–1825	1826–1836	1837–1845
2.	Railroads, Steel, Mechanization	1845–1866	1867–1872	1873–1883	1884–1892
3.	Electricity, Automobiles, Chemical Industry, Water Supply	1892–1913	1914–1929	1930–1937	1938–1948
4.	Atomic Energy, Computer, Robots, Electronics, Civil Aviation	1948–1966	1967–1973	1974–1982	1983–1995
5.	Information and Communication Technologies, Biotechnologies	1995–2000	2008–	?	?

Source: Based on teaching material prepared by Professor Dr Harald Hagemann, University of Hohenheim, Germany (2001). Used with permission.

was stark – the loss of jobs caused by the loom led to riots in Lancashire, England, which was at the time a centre of textile production. Strong protests were also seen in Europe, with textile workers desperate to retain their jobs and willing to destroy the looms. (In fact the word *sabotage* is derived from *sabot* – the name of the wooden clogs commonly worn by workers in Benelux countries.) The prosperity resulting from the innovations of the Industrial Revolution was seen between 1782–1802 and, as Schumpeter identified, innovations spread and in doing so led to recession (1802–25), depression (1825–36), followed by a recovery phase.

The second industrial revolution was the result of what is referred to as the 'Group of Five' innovations: electricity, internal combustion engines, chemical processing, communications (including the influence of the telegraph, the telephone and the phonograph), and the widespread availability of clean water. As shown in Table 2.3, these innovations were responsible for two long waves with years of prosperity in 1845–66 and 1892–1913. Since the Second World War, the main innovations have been atomic energy, the computer, robots, microelectronics and commercial aviation.

The innovations since the 1990s have been seen as creating the 'Information Age' and recently the Internet has been portrayed as creating the much-hyped 'New Economy'. Its impact, however, is debatable; economists view the Internet as having significantly less effect on people's lives than, for example, the availability of running water.[33] Similarly, economists believe medical treatment and technology have made far less of an impact on longevity than the refrigerator, which has drastically reduced serious illness caused through eating food stored in unhygienic conditions. Long waves, 'constitute an interesting interpretation, but one that cannot be taken as a well-established fact; there haven't been enough of them to serve as convincing evidence'.[34]

Schumpeter's explanation of the impacts of innovation fits closely with the cycles of growth and recession discussed above. He observed that there is often a time lag between an invention and its widespread adoption (for example, the lag between the invention of steam technology and its diffusion during the Industrial Revolution, mentioned earlier). In addition, he pointed out that the number of discoveries and inventions is high and information about them is relatively easily available, while in contrast, useful innovations are limited in number and normally very few individuals are able to capitalize on them. These individuals are the *entrepreneur-innovators*, who apply the ideas from inventions and drive them to commercial success. This requires a particular type of leadership, which Schumpeter believed is seldom found in management or amongst the owners of existing firms. Consequently, he believed that incumbent organizations are more likely to be followers rather than leaders of innovation.

An innovation founded on entrepreneurship is followed by two main phases. First, the diffusion phase in which the innovation leads to new products with higher utility and often reduced production costs. This disrupts the pricing structure and employment in the existing market and radically changes customers' expectations. Successful innovation in one field often enables faster innovation in other fields, as the ideas are copied. Entrepreneurs are able to generate higher profit levels through the enhanced value that innovations offer and this stimulates economic growth. As others follow, the diffusion path becomes easier as barriers are broken and experience is accumulated. The *market equilibrium*, as economists refer to it, is disturbed and this triggers a process of market adaptation with many new products being developed and competition intensifying.

Innovations do not last forever and the second phase is recession (column 4 in Table 2.3). Once innovations have diffused throughout an economic system they lose their power as a source of growth. This leads to depression and a form of equilibrium is reached in which the value of products and their pricing are largely stable. This market stagnation continues until new technologies emerge and are applied as innovations. Entrepreneurs who invest in innovation at times when the economy is slow can help to break this stagnation. The rate of technological change is broadly recognized by economists as the single most important determinant of the economic growth rate of countries.[35]

A number of points are noteworthy for managers:

- In times of low growth and increased competition, investments in R&D are likely to be lower as companies strive to maintain their profitability.
- Being first-to-market with an innovation may bring increased profits[36] (though not always, see Chapter 4). The improved product utility or significantly reduced process costs disrupt the pricing structure of markets and allow the innovating companies to earn higher profits.
- The increased profits achieved by the entrepreneurial organizations will quickly attract interest and innovations will be copied. Therefore, there is an argument for making it as difficult as possible for a competitor to copy an innovation. As discussed in Chapter 1, there is a need to create multidimensional innovations where the essence of a product innovation is embedded in the manufacturing or service delivery process (see mini case on Tetley's teabags in Chapter 1).
- As innovations diffuse to more companies, competition increases and prices are forced down. In this phase the overall business competence of companies (*their Complementary Assets* – see Chapter 4) rather than their innovative ability often determines who will benefit most from the innovation in the longer run.

Innovation and Employment

New products and services have been shown to have a positive influence on employment. However, improvements in processes in either the manufacturing or the service sector can also significantly reduce labour requirements in the industries concerned.[37] In Schumpeterian terms, this creative destruction is irreversible and so actions to try and save industries based on old technologies may meet with limited success. Of course, the reduced costs and prices release spending power that can provide employment in other industries. The question, and often the problem, is that those new opportunities may be in another region, or even another country. It is well established that SMEs contribute significantly to employment.[38] Such small firms that are generally founded to promote new technologies are important generators of new employment[39] and consequently the policies of many governments are aimed to be particularly supportive towards SMEs, especially in regions where older industries are in decline.

Innovation and Company Performance

In view of the evident importance of innovation in the long run it is frustrating that efforts to establish a clear link between measures of innovation and the performance of individual companies have not been very successful. For example, in 2007 the UK government did an analysis to examine whether there is evidence of a statistical relationship between investment in R&D and business performance in the 850 UK firms and 1250 worldwide covered by their

R&D scoreboard (the source of the data in Table 2.2). The analysis focused on considering whether changes in business performance over the previous five years – as measured by sales growth, profitability and stock market capitalization – could be explained in terms of changes in investment in R&D over the same period, and related factors. Despite extensive analysis, no statistically significant relationships were found. However, 'Our current conclusion here is that the relationship between R&D and firm performance is complex rather than non-existent... there may be long lags between changes in investment in R&D and subsequent company performance, and the effects work at levels within companies that cannot be isolated at whole firm level.'

Product Innovation and Growth

Product innovation appears to be closely linked to market share. A comprehensive mail survey of over 3000 companies showed that the main objectives of manufacturers' product innovations were to increase market share and improve product quality. Innovating companies were also found to have faster growth, and on average companies earned approximately 23 per cent of their revenues from products less than four years old.[40] Several other studies have confirmed these points. For example, one study found that on average, new products generated approximately 30 per cent of manufacturing companies' revenues.[41] In the service sector, new products were found to generate approximately 50 per cent of revenues.[42] The reliance of companies on innovation, particularly product innovation, is clear from research: they 'are increasingly relying on new products for profitability'.[43] Mini Case 2.3 on Extricom is an example. However, the profits that can be generated from new products do appear to be highly dependent on the particular market sector.[44]

Mini Case 2.3

Extricom GmbH – Small but Innovative[45]

Extricom, based in Lauffen am Neckar near Stuttgart in Germany, is a small company competing in the 'twin-screw extruder' market. Twin-screw extruders are large machines used to mix and form a wide variety of materials, such as plastics, chemicals, pharmaceuticals and foods. The manufacturing process for such products is normally continuous, and the twin-screws are often exposed to high temperatures and abrasive or corrosive materials, which means that replacement parts are required regularly.

   The original twin-screw extruder was developed in the 1950s. Patents protected the technology and the monopoly this provided allowed high margins on both the machines and the replacement parts. When the patents expired, further players entered the market and several of them copied the original technology (with small variations), or produced replacement parts that fitted the market leaders' machines. Today, there are over 100 companies worldwide offering twin-screw extruder technology and this competition forced the prices down by 70 per cent. The technology has largely become a commodity, margins are relatively narrow and this has led the market leaders to also produce replacement parts for their competitors' machines.

With intense competition, innovation can be a differentiator. Extricom has developed the latest technology – 12-screw extruders – which allows materials to be processed more efficiently through improved flow dynamics. Micha Dannenhauer, Sales and Operations Manager at Extricom says, 'we are only a small company with about 50 employees and do not have the R&D resources of the big players. However, we do have a great deal of process know-how, which has enabled us to quickly develop the 12-screw technology. Our challenge is to continue to be faster than our competitors at making innovations that make our customers' processes more efficient'.

DIFFUSION OF INNOVATIONS

The last area of research in innovation at the macro level that we will consider concerns *diffusion*: the way in which innovations spread through populations. Our concern in this book is mostly with how new products and services spread through markets but many of the most influential studies have been done at the social level: the spread of farming practices in South America, or of contraceptive methods in India, for example. The original and most influential study concerned the spread of hybrid seed corn in Iowa in the 1930s.[46] A particularly active researcher in diffusion studies has been Everett Rogers at the University of New Mexico, whose book *Diffusion of Innovations* is a classic text.[47] It is highly relevant for managers, as it gives indications on how product and process innovations can be planned so that they are adopted more quickly.

The way an innovation spreads through a population depends on several factors: the characteristics of the innovation itself; the personal characteristics of the adopters, or customers; the communication channels through which they learn about and evaluate the innovation; and *Change Agents* – people such as teachers, consultants, public health workers and sales people, who help adopters to get to grips with the innovation.

The Influence of Product Features

The characteristics of innovations themselves have a powerful effect on how quickly and readily they are adopted. These insights are useful in designing the scope of innovations, particularly new products or services. Everitt Rogers[48] identifies five such characteristics:

- Relative advantage – the extent to which the innovation is perceived as being better than what preceded it. This, of course, is where attention normally goes when designing a new product.

- Compatibility – how well the innovation fits with existing habits or expectations. Innovations that require a significant change of behaviour or attitude tend to be resisted, however great their other benefits may be. Medical innovations (contraceptive methods, for example) are an obvious case where cultural norms have a big influence. The demand for telephony grew very slowly partly because it required new social habits; whereas mobile telephony took on quickly because it built on existing practices.
- Complexity – innovations that are perceived as complicated or difficult to use are adopted slowly. Major simplifications to an existing idea often spur adoption (see Mini Case 2.4 on Repsol).
- Trialability – new products are more readily adopted if there is an easy way for customers to try them out before purchasing. Radio stations provide this service for pop music; and most software is now available in free trial versions. Products where trial is not possible (or is difficult or prolonged) face more resistance.
- Observability – the degree to which the results of an innovation are observable to others. Preventative innovations are notoriously problematic because the adopter can never know whether the risk was there to start with. One of the reasons given for the success of the rat poison Warfarin is that the rats typically come out in the open to die, so the effects of the poison are made clear.

Although these attributes are conceptually distinct they may overlap somewhat in practice, as Rogers concedes. But they have been tested empirically and certainly emphasize the importance of factors other than the apparent advantage in determining how readily an innovation will spread. The Dvorak keyboard (Mini Case 2.5) is a good example of an innovation that has great functional advantages but has never caught on for other reasons.

Mini Case 2.4

Repsol YPF – Offering Full Service in Argentina[49]

Economic downturns create an environment where innovations that save money are particularly attractive to consumers. Argentina had already been in recession since 1998, when in December 2001 it suffered an economic crisis and the currency plummeted by 45 per cent. The affect for the 'man in the street' was drastic: real salaries for workers fell by 25 per cent and the cost of living soared by 75 per cent. The cost of petrol became prohibitive and car sales fell by half within one year. Natural gas was a cheaper and locally available alternative to petrol – Argentina is the third largest producer in Latin America – but although a conversion kit had been on the market for some time it had not been widely adopted. This was mainly because the modifications that had to be made to the engine were too complicated for someone who was not a mechanic and, in addition, the conversion required a time-consuming re-registration of the car with the relevant authorities (the Argentine Chamber of Natural Compressed Gas).

Enter Repsol YPF, a Spanish-Argentinian oil company which also distributes natural gas to more than 9 million clients in Spain and Latin America. In 2002, Repsol, working in partnership with Volkswagen (VW), introduced the Polo CNG which worked on compressed natural gas. The car is ready to drive, registration documents are included and there is a one-year guarantee regardless of the kilometres driven. With the Polo CNG, the popularity of gas-powered cars has rocketed and there are now nearly a million on the roads. So, too, has the number of petrol stations offering gas. There are now over a 1100 such stations in Argentina making LPG available to the majority of the population.

For a family driving an average of 1000 kilometres a month, the annual saving is the equivalent an average earner's monthly salary. No wonder that the Polo CNG has become a top seller in Argentina. Repsol YPF and VW have met customers' needs not only by providing a new and more cost-effective product but also in overcoming the installation and registration issues that stood in the way.

The Adoption Life Cycle

The effects of the other factors are conveniently summarized by discussing the Adoption Life Lycle, which is shown in Figure 2.2. The basis of this is that potential users have different attitudes and motivations with regard to innovation and so adopt it at different times.[50]

The first adopters are the *Innovators*. They are interested in novelty for its own sake and will often be technicians, with the knowledge and interest to experiment and to overcome teething problems. The next adopters are the *Early Adopters*. These typically are not technologists: they are more interested in the new opportunities that the innovation presents. As individuals they will be financially and socially secure and so able to accept mistakes and failures. As companies they will be technically competent and will aim to use the innovation for competitive advantage – to get a step ahead of their rivals. The third group, the *Early Majority*, is particularly important because they are numerous and represent the start of the mainstream market. They are typically more practically minded and will adopt only when they have clear proof that the idea really works. Unlike the early adopters, who will rely on their own judgement, the early majority will move only when they can see that others like them are using the innovation successfully. The fourth group, the *Late Majority* are typically more cautious and less confident in dealing with novelty so they need plenty of support and often the security of buying from a large company or well-known brand. Finally the *Laggards* will adopt only when they absolutely have to, and then with ill grace.

The adoption life cycle curve has been found usually to be bell-shaped in practice and this has led to the easy assumption that it is 'really' a normal distribution

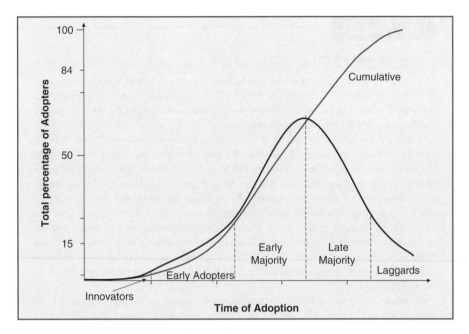

Figure 2.2   Adopter categories for innovations

with the boundaries between the adopter categories falling at the standard devia-
tion points, so that the Early and Late Majority 'should' each be 34 per cent of
the total, with Early adopters 13.5 per cent and Innovators 2.5 per cent. There
is no justification for this; in practice the proportions are bound to vary substantially from case to case.

The adoption life cycle has had a major influence on marketing theory and
practice, and companies will adapt their marketing and sales strategies according
to their estimate of the state of the cycle. A recent addition to the theory has
been Geoffrey Moore's recognition that the transition from one adopter category to another can be problematic, particularly in technology-based market.[51]
He particularly emphasizes the difficulty of the transition (now often known
as 'Moore's Chasm') between the Early Adopters and the Early Majority. The
problem is that the Early Adopters are interested in innovations that will give
them serious competitive advantage. The Early Majority, on the other hand,
will be seeking to make an improvement in their business, not a revolution; and
being practical they will demand hard proof that an innovation can deliver it.
The problem is that the experience of the Early Adopters often will not provide
the proof that members of the Early Majority look for; and anyway they may
want to keep it to themselves. The result is that the sales of radically new products often start well but then stall or even collapse at the end of the Innovator/
Early Adopter phase. Companies may have to make special efforts to cross the
chasm into the mainstream markets.[52]

> ## Mini Case 2.5
>
> ### Dvorak versus QWERTY[53]
>
> The most common type of computer keyboard is the QWERTY layout. However, it is not the most efficient design. A faster alternative, the Dvorak keyboard, was developed years ago but it is still virtually unknown, demonstrating the uncertainty involved in the diffusion of innovations.
>
> Consider the difference in how the two keyboards were designed. The QWERTY version was actually designed to slow the rate at which you can type! This was because it was developed for mechanical typewriters, where there was a problem of the levers catching together and jamming. People who have used typewriters will remember the annoying problem of two levers jamming, and the need to flip the levers back (which nearly always resulted in you getting ink on your fingers). To minimize the chances of two levers jamming, designers looked at the most common sequences of letters in words and deliberately moved letters that commonly come in sequence (for example, 'e' and 'r') close together on the keyboard where they will not be pushed simultaneously. The sequence of keys on the keyboard led to its name, QWERTY.
>
> Professor Dvorak, an American, analysed the process of typing with the aim of maximizing the speed of typing. To do this he considered how the letters could be distributed on the keyboard to take advantage of the fact that most people are right-handed. Therefore, approximately 55 per cent of the work is allocated to the normally stronger right hand, by locating more of the common letters on right-hand side of the keyboard. The central row of keys was reserved for the most common letters, with the less common letters allocated to keys further away from the strongest fingers. Despite the clever ideas behind the Dvorak keyboard, it has not been widely adopted although a number of computer manufacturers offer it as an option.
>
> Diffusion theory can be used to understand the failure of the Dvorak innovation. Although once trained, a touch typist is faster on the Dvorak keyboard, the *relative advantage* of the device is too low – it will not make them twice as fast. In addition, potential users are aware of the effort that they must make to learn the keyboard. Similarly, the *observability* of the innovation is low, that is potential users cannot perceive the advantage that the keyboard can bring to them until they have taken the time to learn to use the keyboard. *Trialability* is good and it is easy for users to try the keyboard but the compatibility does not allow the keyboard to be tried by users with their own computers. Superficially, the *complexity* of the keyboard is the same as a QWERTY one but to a user the *compatibility* with their current modus operandi is low. It is perceived as too high for the return in terms of increased typing speed.

SUMMARY

The literature on the impacts of innovation has been reviewed, including the precursors of innovation, and its influence on markets and industries. This

chapter has showed that

- Innovation has a major impact on the economy, it drives business cycles and employment levels.
- Economic cycles can make business conditions harder, but lead to opportunities for particular innovations.
- Large or small companies may equally be innovative. For managers in existing organizations, the challenge is to maintain or increase innovation levels. For entrepreneurial managers in start-ups, the challenge is to generate an innovative idea that can dislodge the incumbents.
- Most studies have focused on the manufacturing sector, and only in recent years has innovation research started to look at the service sector in detail.
- The way innovations diffuse through a population or market depends strongly on the characteristics of the innovation itself and also on the adopters (customers). Different types of people adopt at different stages of the market and marketing efforts must adapt accordingly.

MANAGEMENT RECOMMENDATIONS

- Measure the actual growth and profitability benefits arising from your innovation investments. Don't rely on input measures alone to assess your innovativeness.
- Compare your expenditure on innovation with your immediate competitors, and understand the effects the differences may have on your competitive position.
- Apply the insights provided by diffusion theory to individual innovation projects.

RECOMMENDED READING

1. Rogers, E.M., *Diffusion of Innovations* (New York: The Free Press, 1995). [This is one of the classic texts on innovation, with a wealth of fascinating examples of innovations in both the manufacturing and service sectors.]

CASE STUDY
Aravind Eye Hospitals: Process Innovation in Healthcare[54]

Before reading this case, consider the following generic innovation management issues:

- What advantages do developing countries have in innovation, particularly in processes and services?
- What kinds of innovation most require inspiring (rather than effective) leadership?
- While reading it, consider the following:
  - Why has an equivalent of Aravind not yet arisen in the West?

○ If one were to attempt to found an equivalent in your own country how would it be different?

○ What risks might lie ahead for Aravind as India's economy develops?

Aravind Eye Care was founded in 1976 by Dr G Venkataswami with the mission to eliminate needless blindness in India. 'Dr V' was inspired by two things. The first was the knowledge that 5–10 million people in India, and 45 million worldwide, suffer blindness, much of which is avoidable. The second, surprisingly, was the McDonalds Hamburger chain. In this, Dr V saw an example of how good science and disciplined processes could turn a variable, skill-based service into a product that could be delivered with high quality and low cost in any culture. Today, the Aravind Eye Care system is the largest eye care facility in the world with 5 hospitals treating 2.4 million outpatients and doing 285,000 operations a year (2008–9). The company runs at a profit, generating all the surplus funds it needs to finance expansion; and yet the price for an operation to fit an intraocular lens is as little as $300 (in 2005). The money received from each paying patient subsidizes two more who cannot afford to pay. The clinical results are at least as good as those achieved in the Western hospitals.[55]

To make all this possible Dr Venkataswami had to take a radically different approach to the eye care process. The success of Aravind is based on three principles: workflow management, good use of technology, and above all, a culture that emphasizes service, humility, kindness and equality. The underlying business model is one of the oldest: increase volume, build efficiencies and reduce costs. All employees know that every rupee saved helps in treating more patients.

Recognizing that the doctors', and especially the surgeons', time is the key constraint in a specialist hospital, Aravind sets out to maximize the efficiency with which it is used. As many as possible of the subsidiary tasks, such as refraction testing and counselling, are done by paramedical staff (there are six nurses to every doctor), leaving the doctors free for medical advising and operations. Recruiting and training the right calibre of paramedical staff is vital for Aravind. In the words of Dr Natchair, who is in charge of training paramedical staff, 'We recruit girls from a rural background...with the right attitudes. Knowledge and skills are important, but not so much as the right attitude. After recruitment we give them two years training. The training is excellent and is recognized in the USA, and the government of India is considering adopting our syllabus.'

Much of the initial diagnosis, scanning and counselling is done in camps in the countryside. Aravind is also pioneering the use of broadband radio and webcams in remote rural areas allowing doctors to assess and diagnose eye conditions remotely. Patients are bussed into hospital on the day of their appointment. On arrival it takes 2 minutes to book a patient in thanks to a very efficient IT system. They then see a doctor for a definitive diagnosis and a paramedical counsellor to help them decide what action is best for them. The outpatient department sees 1000 patients a day, 6 days a week. Those that need surgery usually have their operation on the same day, unless they prefer not to. Those that need spectacles can have them made and fitted on site within 4 hours.

The operating theatres have four tables on which two surgeons work, aided by a team of nurses. While the surgeon is operating on one patient, the next is being made

▶▶

ready by the theatre staff on an adjacent operating table. As soon as one operation is complete, the surgeon can move straight to the other table where he will find the patient fully prepared and sedated, the surgical instruments laid out and the magnifying microscope focused on the eye. The next patient, who has been waiting on a chair, then takes up the vacant table. In ordinary hospitals multiple use of an operating theatre would be considered hazardous because of cross-contamination but it is possible in the special circumstances of Aravind thanks to excellent procedures and because the patients are otherwise entirely healthy. Surgeons at Aravind conduct an average of over 2000 operations a year (ten times the national average), yet they operate only in the mornings, leaving the afternoons for outpatients and research. The high throughput of patients also means that doctors get more clinical experience in a month at Aravind than they would in a year elsewhere. As one said, 'In Delhi, where I studied, we did not have so many cases of varied nature. There we did one or two cases of surgery a month; here we do some 30 cases a day!'

Follow-up counselling is provided by specially trained paramedical staff, keeping doctors free for medical work.

Although doctors and nurses are paid at about the national rates, the efficiency and very high throughput of patients keeps costs low. The large number of patients also gives doctors far more experience of diverse eye conditions than they would normally obtain as Dr V says 'Doctors are not paid more because they do more operations but ours is a teaching institution and the more patients we have the better the training can be.'

In the developing world up to 50 per cent of blindness comes from cataracts, which can be cured by replacing the affected lens with an artificial one. This procedure accounts for 70 per cent of all Aravind's surgical work. In the 1980s the cost of these lenses was around $100 which made the cost of surgery quite high, so in 1991 Aravind set up a separate activity called Aurolab to make them at lower cost. This, too, was highly successful and today Aurolab manufactures a million intraocular lenses a year for $5–10 each. The surplus is sold internationally.

Prahalad, in his book 'The fortune at the bottom of the Pyramid[56]' points out that in providing products and services for the very poor, companies have to reverse the usual operational logic. The usual approach is 'Work out the cost, add the necessary margin and that determines the minimum price that must be charged. Now go and find somebody who will pay it.' In these markets the opposite applies: 'Work out the maximum that customers can afford to pay, subtract the necessary margin and that determines the maximum cost. Now go and find a way to do it.' Aravind Eye Care is a dramatic and inspiring example of where this logic can lead. Another is the Jaipur foot (see Mini Case 10.5).

3 CONTRASTING SERVICES WITH MANUFACTURING

Addressing the challenge of service innovation requires a clear understanding of its concepts and dimensions.[1]

INTRODUCTION

The contrast between services and manufacturing warrants a chapter for several reasons. First, the service sector is of increasing importance in many countries and often accounts for 60–70 per cent of gross national product. Second, services can also be used to differentiate manufactured products – for example, research has shown that manufacturers' services play a key role in the achievement of high customer satisfaction levels.[2] So manufacturers need to concentrate on developing high-quality services, such as product maintenance and customer support. Third, the distinct characteristics of services mean that there are significant differences to managing innovation in the service arena, such as the intangible nature of services and the challenges of ensuring consistent quality. Finally and importantly, the study of service innovation still lags behind research into manufacturing companies' innovation,[3] therefore the most effective ways to manage service innovation are still emerging.

So this chapter has a strong focus on how to manage innovation in the service sector. In addition, it will discuss managing innovation in sectors such as education, and not-for-profit sector. The main sections are

- The role of services in the economy.
- The terminology of services and manufacturing and describe the characteristics of services.
- The challenges of managing quality for services.[4]
- Key issues to be addressed in developing new service products.
- Other sectors, such as education.
- A case study of the management of innovation at a service company – AXA Insurance in Ireland.

THE IMPORTANCE OF SERVICES

The service sector is dominant in many countries, as can be seen by looking at its contribution to GDP, its role in providing employment, and the increasing levels of investment in R&D in the sector. The importance is demonstrated by the fact that several governments have recently commissioned major reports on how to stimulate the service sector.[5] Services are also essential for companies in the manufacturing sector because of the competitive advantage they can bring and the differentiation they allow in commodity markets.

Service and the Economy

Table 3.1 indicates the contribution of services to the economy in 22 selected countries in the Americas, Asia Pacific, Europe and Africa. It can be seen that in the US the service sector contributes 79 per cent of GDP, whereas in Japan it is 72 per cent. In contrast, the service sector is currently of less importance in countries such as Nigeria (29 per cent) and Indonesia (39 per cent). Economic studies show that as economies mature, the proportions of the GDP that are generated by agriculture, *industry* and services change significantly.[6] (The term industry refers to manufacturing, mining, construction, electricity, water and gas.) Developing countries are dependent on agriculture and it typically generates in the order of 20 per cent of GDP (18 per cent in India, for example). As countries develop, they first *industrialize*, as the demand for food is satisfied and demand for industrialized goods rises. In parallel, agricultural labour productivity rises and consequently agricultural products become less expensive and account for a lower proportion of GDP. Later, *post-industrialization* sees a shift, as the demand for tangible products saturates and people start to focus on services, such as healthcare, education and entertainment. Since services are labour intensive, their cost can be relatively high and they can provide employment for a high proportion of the workforce. The shift to the service sector is accelerated by technological advances, which reduce labour requirements in manufacturing and agriculture. Mature economies have service sectors that contribute more than 60 per cent of GDP.

The term *services* covers a wide range of offerings, as is illustrated by Table 3.2. This table summarizes the main types of services and the levels of employment in the service sector in Europe. Note that the research that generated these figures looked only at what were termed 'market services' (52 per cent of the EU economy), which excludes healthcare and education, two fields that provide significant employment. It can be seen that the retail sector provides over 25 per cent of the employment in market services, followed by approximately 12 per cent provided by hotels and restaurants and approximately 13 per cent by wholesalers.

R&D in Services

Research and development used to be associated only with the manufacturing sector. But the amount spent on R&D by service companies has increased

Table 3.1   Selected International Economic Comparisons (2007)

	Country	Total GDP ($)	Population (millions)	Agriculture (%GDP)	Industry (%GDP)	Service sector (%GDP)
Africa	Egypt	258 (billion)	81.7	14	38	48
	South Africa	467 (billion)	48.7	3	31	66
	Nigeria	296 (billion)	146.2	18	53	29
	Kenya	61 (billion)	137.9	24	17	59
Americas	USA	13.78 (trillion)	303.8	1	20	79
	Brazil	1.849 (trillion)	196.3	5	29	66
	Canada	1.271 (trillion)	33.2	2	29	69
	Mexico	1.353 (trillion)	109.9	4	27	69
	Argentina	526 (billion)	40.5	10	34	56
Asia Pacific	China	7.09 (trillion)	1,330.4	11	49	40
	Japan	4.27 (trillion)	127.2	1	27	72
	India	2.96 (trillion)	1,147.9	18	29	53
	Indonesia	844 (billion)	237.5	14	47	39
	Australia	773 (billion)	20.0	3	26	71
	Hong Kong	293 (billion)	7.0	0.1	8	92
Europe	Germany	2.8 (trillion)	82.3	1	30	69
	France	2.1 (trillion)	64.1	2	21	77
	UK	2.13 (trillion)	60.9	1	23	76
	Italy	1.8 (trillion)	58.1	2	27	71
	Nether-lands	645 (billion)	16.6	4	24	72
	Finland	188 (billion)	5.2	3	33	64
	Russia	2.1 (trillion)	140.7	5	39	56

Source: Based on the *CIA World Factbook 2008*, accessed under http:/www.cia.gov/cia/publications/factbook/index.html (June 2009). The statistics are mainly for 2007 (refer to website for the latest estimates).

Table 3.2   Employment in the Service Sector in Europe (2005)

Sectors	% Total Employment
Other business activities	23.8
Retail trade (exc. motor vehicles), repair of personal goods	22.5
Wholesale/commission trade, exc. for motor (-cycles)	12.8
Hotels and restaurants	11.6
Land transport, transport via pipelines	7.2
Sale, maintenance/repair of motor vehicles	5.4
Post and telecommunications	4.0
Real estate activities	3.5
Computer and related activities	3.5
Supporting transport activities, travel agencies	3.4
Renting of machinery, and of personal and household goods	0.8
Air transport	0.5
Research and development	0.5
Water transport	0.3

Note: Differences between components and total are due to rounding.

Source: Based on Alajääskö, P., *Eurostat Statistics in Focus*. European Communities Catalogue Number KS-SF-08-078-EN-N (2008).

significantly in the past 20 years. In the US it is now estimated that 24 per cent of the total spent on R&D is in the service sector, compared with only 5 per cent in 1983.[7]

Table 3.3 lists the 12 international companies from different service sectors that are spending the most on R&D. The high level of investment by the large telecommunications companies is clear. In many service sectors, investments are low but there are exceptions such as Amazon which invests 6.4 per cent of revenues in R&D. Banks had started to invest in R&D and it can be seen that Royal Bank of Scotland invested 1.4 per cent of its revenues in 2007, largely in the development of information technology. (With the 2008/09 economic recession and banking crisis, investments in innovation by banks are sure to decrease for a time.) In the service sector, it should be noted that the revenues invested in R&D (termed R&D intensity) are not always easy to identify, as formal R&D departments with separate budgets seldom exist in the service sector. With increasing competition in the sector, it is likely that forward-looking companies will use R&D and innovation as a means of developing services that can be differentiated from their competitors and that are harder to copy. In point, the construction industry is now looking at how it can be more innovative in the management of the key stages of typical construction projects.[8] R&D in the service sector is more

Table 3.3   Top Investors in R&D in Different Service Sectors in 2007

	Sector	Company	R&D spend (€ millions)	R&D intensity	Employees
1.	Telecommunications	BT, UK	1,339.6	6.0	108,500
2.	Telecommunications	NTT, Japan	1,309.0	2.5	199,733
3.	Telecommunications	France Telecom, France	702.6	1.7	183,799
4.	Telecommunications	Telstra, Australia	661.7	5.9	47,840
5.	Telecommunications	AT&T, USA	529.5	0.8	310,000
6.	Banking	Royal Bank of Scotland	514.7	1.5	170,000
7.	Retail	Amazon.com	509.0	6.4	17,000
8.	Telecommunications	Telefonica, Spain	466.8	1.1	244,052
9.	Electricity	AREVA, France	447.9	4.8	65,583
10.	Telecommunications	Deutsche Telekom, Germany	430.2	0.9	243,736
11.	Retail	eBay, USA	392.6	9.5	15,500
12.	Electricity	Korea Electric Power	346.1	2.1	37,490

Source: Based on data from Anonymous, *The 2008 R&D Scoreboard*. (UK: Department of Trade and Industry, January 2009).

difficult to manage than in manufacturing because few companies know how to apply technology effectively to services and due to a lack of personnel who understand both technology and business opportunities in the service environment.[9]

Manufacturers Need Services

Few manufacturers sell only a product; most must offer services to support the use of their products.[10] For example, car manufacturers offer leasing and other financial services, and repair and maintenance. Increasingly, food manufacturers offer nutritional advice services to support their products. Services that help the customer derive maximum value from their purchase are normally referred to as *after-sales service*, whereas services to support sales are called *customer service*. Service has a major impact on customer satisfaction and can also make a significant contribution to revenue.[11] Services are not only important for achieving customer satisfaction; they also make a significant contribution to revenue. Profit margins on after-sales service are normally higher than those on the products themselves and, for example, after-sales accounts for 13 per cent of revenues in electronic systems but 39 per cent of contribution.[12] Manufacturers need to become more efficient at matching services to their products to remain competitive (see Mini Case 3.1). Such services are best designed in parallel to new product development.[13] Many manufacturers fail to adequately consider services during the development of their (tangible) products.

Mini Case 3.1

Jura – Exclusive Coffee Machines and More[14]

Do you like cappuccino? The Swiss company Jura specializes in premium coffee machines, with a range of models for both private and professional use. For example, the top selling 'Impressa Z5' was the first machine to offer single-button operation to produce a cup of really frothy cappuccino.

With its headquarters in Niederbuchsiten in Switzerland, the Jura company was founded in the 1930s and its first product was a special electrical iron for use in manufacturing shoes. In 1937 Jura designed its first coffee machine and it is this line of products that has grown into an international business. In 2008 Jura, which employs 335 people worldwide, generated revenues of 405 million Swiss Francs (268 million euro).

The Impressa Z5 was developed to make top-tasting coffee and Jura's R&D has expertise in coffee grinding, brewing and in producing excellent frothy milk – this requires expert knowledge in a number of technical disciplines, from mechanical engineering, to the physics of foams, to control software. In addition, though, Jura places high emphasis on the aesthetics of their machines and their designers took inspiration from the shape of a coffee bean in defining the unique lines of the Z5. However, Jura has not just concentrated on the design of the product; it also offers a carefully designed premium service to match the product.

First, the Z5 is designed for easy operation and maintenance. For example, in contrast to many other products on the market, the grinder does not need to be removed, as it is self-cleaning. The Z5 also has an array of sensors that enables it to prompt owners to refill the coffee beans, or change the water filter, or initiate the cleaning cycle. Should owners have a problem, then a hotline number provides first-line advice on how to solve problems. Should the machine experience a fault that the hotline operator will advise on fast dispatch and repair. In Switzerland owners often drive to Jura's state-of-the-art 'service factory' (a servicescape in itself), where they can personally watch while the problems with their machine are diagnosed and the repair costs estimated. Fast maintenance and repair are foremost in Jura's service strategy but they are also careful to work on customer contact. Many manufacturers send advertising and other material to owners registered through warranty schemes. Often such marketing can be intrusive and so Jura have focused on just one communication a year – Z5 owners receive a Christmas card with new coffee recipes.

To support luxury products, manufacturers increasingly need to be just as careful in designing their services as the products themselves. Few do it as well as Jura.

CHARACTERISTICS OF SERVICES

The United Nations has recognized the diversity of what is commonly referred to as the *service sector*. It describes services as being 'a heterogeneous range of

Table 3.4   GATT Classification of Services

	Categories
1.	Business Services
2.	Communication Services
3.	Construction and Related Engineering Services
4.	Distribution Services
5.	Educational Services
6.	Environmental Services
7.	Financial Services
8.	Health-related and Social Services
9.	Tourism and Travel-related Services
10.	Recreational, Cultural and Sporting Services
11.	Transport Services
12.	Other Services

Source: United Nations, *Manual on Statistics of International Trade in Services* (New York: United Nations Publications, 2002), p. 12.

intangible products and activities that are difficult to encapsulate within a simple definition'.[15] In 1991, the General Agreement on Tariffs and Trade (GATT) produced a classification of the 12 major categories of service, as shown in Table 3.4. Considering the variety in this list, it might be concluded that there is little that can be said about services that apply across the board. Nevertheless, some generic characteristics can be identified and these allow services to be better understood. Before we discuss these generic characteristics, it is important to establish the vocabulary that we will be using to discuss services and manufacturing in this chapter and throughout the rest of this book.

Terminology of Services and Manufacturing

Most service companies refer to their *products*, which are produced and delivered to the customer. These are best referred to as *service products*. Service products cannot be stored and the customer's perception of the quality and utility of a service product is dependent on what is termed the *service augmentation* – the production and delivery mechanisms for the service product. Research shows that the competitive advantage is often gained from the service augmentation and not the service product itself.[16] The total package, consisting of the service product and the service augmentation, is called the *augmented service offering*, which is what customers focus on when making their judgements on the quality of the service (as a whole), as illustrated by Figure 3.1.

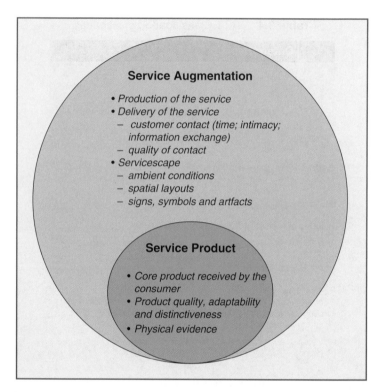

Figure 3.1   The Augmented Service Offering (Service Product and Service Augmentation)

Service Delivery

In the service sector, we refer normally to *consumers* as the end-persons receiving the service (the equivalent of end-users for manufactured goods). Not all of the employees in a service operation have contact with consumers and therefore the terms *front office* (contact with consumers) and *back office* (supporting functions that do not have direct customer or consumer contact) are often used. Some service companies base their organizational structures on this distinction. Front-office staff are normally responsible for most aspects of the production and delivery of service products (this is often called the *operations* function). Their attitude and behaviour is crucial as it directly influences how consumers perceive the service. Innovation is normally one of the responsibilities of the back-office function. In the service sector, innovations consist of *new service products*, and *new service augmentations*, as well as significant changes in service products, or their production and delivery.[17] The term *new service development* (NSD) will be used in this book, to differentiate from new product development for tangible products (though some companies use the term *new product development* when referring to the development of new service products and service

Table 3.5 Terminology for Innovation in Manufacturing and Services

Term	Usage in manufacturing	Usage in service
Product innovation or *products*	Refers to tangible products developed by R&D departments.	When used in the service sector, this term is synonymous with service innovation.
Process innovation	New or improved ways of manufacturing products.	New or improved ways of producing and delivering service products.
Service innovation or *service products*	New or improved services associated with the manufacturer's products.	New or improved service products (including enhanced *service augmentations*).
New product development (NPD)	The process of developing new or improved (tangible) products.	Sometimes used to refer to as the development of new or improved service products.
New service development (NSD)	The process of developing services to support customers gaining maximum value from products (for example, *after-sales*). Often overlooked by manufacturers.	The process of developing new or improved service products. The *augmented service offering* consists of both the *service product* itself and the *service augmentation*.
R&D	The organization that conducts basic research (for example, to develop technology) and product development.	Relatively seldom used in the service sector. Groups conducting research and new service development may be termed *innovation departments*.
Manufacturing	Production facilities and organizations for the preparation of products.	Not applied to services in the past but the term is now being used by some UK banks.
Operations	Normally only used as the term *manufacturing operations*, which is synonymous with manufacturing.	The facilities and organizations used to produce and deliver a service. Includes the human resources required. Normally, only the *front-office* is part of *service delivery*.
Supply chain	The network of organizations that supply materials and components to the manufacturer, plus the distribution channels that deliver the products to customers.	The network of organizations that supply materials and components to the manufacturer, plus the distribution channels that deliver the products to customers.

augmentations). Table 3.5 summarizes the key terms, contrasted between the manufacturing and service sectors.

The Servicescape

A key concept in the management of services is the *servicescape*.[18] This is the environment in which the consumer receives the service. It is important in many ways, as psychologists have identified that all of our social interactions are influenced by the environment in which they occur.[19] The physical environment gives the consumer clues as to the quality of the service and influences customer satisfaction. A functional and pleasant environment can increase the satisfaction of service employees and boost their performance, which in turn can mediate further increases in consumer satisfaction.

The servicescape has three dimensions: (1) ambient conditions such as odours, air quality and temperature; (2) spatial layout of the facilities and their suitability for delivering the service; (3) signs/symbols and artefacts, such as the quality of the signage provided to travellers at an airport and the uniforms and appearance of staff. These three dimensions generate physiological responses in the consumer (in response to the sounds and odours related to a service environment); cognitive responses (consumers' perceptions of a service); and emotional responses (leading to satisfaction or dissatisfaction). For example, supermarket design will take account of the ambient conditions (as appropriate background music and the smell of freshly baked bread can influence our willingness to purchase); the spatial layout to make finding goods easy (the French chain Carrefour has researched the order in which customers prefer to buy food and arranged their stores accordingly); and the signs and symbols (the appearance of staff at the meat counter strongly influences our perception of how fresh the produce is). The servicescape is an aspect of service management that is often overlooked but should be considered during new service development (see Mini Case 3.2 on Boeing and Airbus).

Mini Case 3.2

Boeing and Airbus – Competing on (the Feeling of) Space[20]

Sometimes attributes of manufactured products can have a major impact on the servicescape of service providers. An example is passenger aircraft design. Airlines want well-designed aircraft passenger cabins and manufacturers Boeing and Airbus are being challenged to provide more innovative cabin designs, within the limitations of costs and the space available. The ambient conditions, such as air quality and temperature need careful control but the main focus in recent years has been on the spatial layout, more comfortable seating and cabins that give the impression of being spacious. Innovations such as luggage bins that lift out of the way provide extra space. Perception plays a key role and so the subtle use of décor, mirrors, dividing walls and lighting can give the impression of more space (through reducing shadows and other effects that make passengers feel more cramped). The size of windows also has been found by psychologists to have a strong influence on passenger well-being and so aircraft interior design is developing into an area of strong competition between Airbus and Boeing.[21] The latest move in this competitive battle is the increased usage of composite materials by Boeing. Light, strong composites have allowed fuselages to be developed that withstand higher cabin pressure. Long-haul passengers will now be able to look forward to a higher cabin pressure (the equivalent of 1800 metres altitude instead of 2400), higher humidity and larger windows – all of which will help make flights less tiring.

Manufacturers may also need to manage servicescapes. For example, a large number of European Mercedes customers personally collect their new cars from the factory at Sindelfingen in Germany. The Sindelfingen customer centre has been carefully designed not only to make the collection process easy but also to be a pleasant environment. The building supports the overall impression of Mercedes quality and customers are encouraged to take a trip around the factory. In this sense, both the customer centre and the factory itself are part of the servicescape and they influence customers' perceptions. Similarly, the Swiss luxury coffee machine manufacturer, Jura, has an impressive 'repair factory' where customers can bring their machines for maintenance and repair.

Service Characteristics and Innovation

Many researchers have identified the generic characteristics of services and it is useful to recognize their implications for the management of innovation. Five characteristics of services have the greatest influence over how they can be managed[22]:

- *Intangibility.* Service products are normally intangible: they do not have components that can be perceived by touch (in contrast to manufactured products). Banks provide the service to their customers of being able to collect cash from anywhere in a network of automatic teller machines (ATMs). The ability to collect cash is intangible although some aspects of the service delivery, for example, the ATM itself and the printed receipt, are tangible. Intangibility means that the perception of the quality of a service is more subjective than that of a tangible product. It also means that the customer may find it difficult to judge the quality of a service in advance. Customers may be forced to take their cues about the quality of a service product from the tangible aspects (the *physical evidence* of the service product as shown in Figure 3.1) and the servicescape. For example, the appearance of the ATM itself can act as a surrogate for the quality of the banking service itself. More directly, we assess the style and appearance of a restaurant, its staff and menu when considering eating there for the first time.
- *Customer contact.* Contacts with the customer are critical as they have a strong influence on the customer's perception of the service provided. To stress the importance of points of contact the terms *moments of truth,* or *touch* points are sometimes used. The level of customer contact in the consumption of a service is an important characteristic and it is normally divided into three categories: *interpersonal service, remote service* and *self-service.* On the one hand, many service products require a high degree of contact between the customer and the employees responsible for the delivery. For example, a business consultancy project will require regular contact between consultants and the employees and managers of the client company. On the other hand, some services are designed for low contact, such as the telephone help lines for answering customers' questions on computer

problems. In self-service, customers cooperate in delivering most of the service themselves and contact with the service provider's staff is minimal, perhaps only with the checkout operator. Managing the level and nature of customer contact is important as it impacts the perceived quality of the service. Recent research has shown that the customer contact can be better understood as consisting of three dimensions: the contact *time*, the *intimacy* of the contact and the *information exchanged*.[23] This is also indicated on Figure 3.1. Internet retailers may have no direct contact with the customer but they still need to manage the contact. For example, Amazon.com tries to develop a level of intimacy with its customers by monitoring previous purchases and making helpful suggestions on books and music that the individual customer will probably enjoy. Managing remote contact professionally is dependent on good staff training (see Mini Cases 3.3 on Career Launcher and 3.4 on DialA Flight).

Mini Case 3.3

Career Launcher – Expertise Online 24/7[24]

In many Western countries there is a shortage of qualified mathematics teachers. Enter Career Launcher India Ltd., which offers an online tutoring service for US students. In live one-to-one sessions, students can ask their tutors questions about the mathematics topics they have not adequately understood at school. In an age when call centres based in India have acquired a negative image in many countries, Career Launcher has been careful to manage its service product effectively, especially the customer's perception of contact. Discussions on mathematics problems are made easier by specially designed software that controls webcams and a tablet PC. These enable discussions to be more effective, as diagrams and formulae can be easily drawn and written. The India-based tutors are carefully selected, all have degrees in mathematics or physics, and are well briefed on the curricula in US schools (to ensure that they show the right level of knowledge and empathy).

- *Inhomogenity* (that is service products are *heterogeneous* but we will use the US term inhomogeneous). The output from service providers is often variable because the augmented service offering is dependent on both the employees responsible for delivery and the consumer. There can be differences in the service delivered from one employee to another, or from the combination of the employees and the consumer. This can have positive aspects, as leading service companies give their front-office staff some discretion to be flexible in the service provided to the consumer. Inhomogenity can influence service quality positively or negatively and so it must be managed carefully. Another aspect of inhomogenity is that different services have very different characteristics. Therefore, the contrast between managing, say, financial services and recreational services is greater than the contrast between managing innovation in an electronics and a food company.
- *Services are perishable.* Since services cannot be stored, the location and timing of the delivery are crucial. This means that the delivery mechanism must

provide geographical availability to match the distribution of consumers and a clear example of this is the franchised chains of fast-food restaurants around the globe. The rapid advances in the past 20 years in transport, computing and telecommunications have also enabled services to be globally more available. The production, delivery and consumption of a service are essentially simultaneous; this is one reason why the consumer does not differentiate between the service product and the augmented service. In the eye of the consumer, they are inseparable and if the quality of either one does not meet expectations, then disappointment or dissatisfaction will result.

- *Service quality is multifaceted.* Quality for manufactured products is a simpler concept, largely because customers are able to base their opinions on a tangible product. For services, as mentioned above, the intangibility has a direct impact in that the customer will indirectly form a view of a service based on the tangible aspects. In addition, the delivery mechanism and in particular the employee working with the customer influences the overall quality. Managing service quality has a number of facets that need to be considered simultaneously and will be discussed in the next section.

Mini Case 3.4

DialA Flight – Managing Customer Contact

DialA Flight is a successful European Internet retailer of travel and tourism services. They have succeeded in a competitive, low-margin sector through a strategy that includes a conscious attempt to improve customer contact (intimacy) and provide a degree of customization. Similar to other Internet travel retailers, the company has a fast search engine to identify locations, flights and other information. For confirmation, however, the customer telephones the company and is connected to a call centre employee, who clearly identifies him or herself by name. In the process of the discussions with the customer, DialA Flight employees are skilled, personable and enthusiastic about offering advice on travel destinations, flights and budget packages. In the event of further questions, it is the original employee who phones back and, similarly, repeat customers are encouraged to return to 'their representative'. Although based on a simple idea, the DialA Flight approach is very well implemented and leaves the customer with a very different impression to that left by many (anonymous) call centres. DialA Flight now even advertises how quickly you will be connected within seconds to a 'real' person who will answer your travel questions professionally.[25]

Managing Quality in Services

Research shows that one of the main goals of innovation in the service sector is to improve service quality.[26] Managing service quality includes recognizing that customers' and consumers' *expectations* and *perceptions* of a service depend on both the quality of the service product and the augmentation. One of the leading researchers in this area Christian Gronroos, from the Swedish School of Economics in Finland, uses the term *perceived service quality* (PSQ) to stress that it is the customer's or consumer's perception that counts and not an organization's internal view of how good their services are. PSQ is dependent on both the quality of the service product and the augmentation.

The Gap Model of Service Quality

In order to design and deliver high-quality services, it is necessary to understand how a consumer's expectations are derived. The team of 'Parsu' Parasuraman, Valerie Zeithaml and Leonard Berry (often referred to as PZB), from the universities of Miami, North Carolina and Texas A&M respectively, developed a widely used approach, which builds on the ideas of Gronroos. This is called the *Gap Model* and it can be applied to analyse the quality of service products. The model covers the differences – termed *Gaps* – that may exist between an organization's view of their service products and customers' perceptions. The intuitive idea behind this model is that managers must accurately understand their customers' requirements, if customer satisfaction is to be achieved.

The Gap Model (Figure 3.2) is a useful diagnosis tool. There are several key things to note. First, the domains of both the customer (top of diagram) and the organization (bottom) are shown as shaded areas. In the customer's domain, the customer's expectations of a service product are based on previous experiences, communications and the image of the service product. These expectations lead a customer to form his or her own informal 'specification' of the quality of service he or she expects. A central point of the Model is that if the customers' perceptions of what they receive do not match or exceed their expectations, this will lead to customer dissatisfaction – Gap 5. To identify the root causes of Gap 5, the Model identifies four contributing gaps. These are

- *Gap 1*: the differences between the customer's (informal) specification of the quality they expect and the actual specification of quality in the organization.
- *Gap 2*: the difference between management's concept of what customers expect and the organization's internal quality specifications. Managers' views on what customers expect and what is actually specified by an organization can be very different.
- *Gap 3*: the difference between service-quality specifications and the service product actually delivered (this is determined by how the service product is implemented, including the service augmentation). Too often the product delivered differs considerably from the intention.
- *Gap 4*: the difference between service delivered and the image of the service that is communicated.

The Gap Model provides a logical process by which service organizations can check whether customers' expectations are being met and it has been used extensively to diagnose service quality problems in a wide range of industries, including both pure services and services provided to support manufacturing products. The size of the gaps can be estimated using the *SERVQUAL* questionnaire, also developed by PZB.[27] Once problems have been identified, management can take actions to close the gaps.

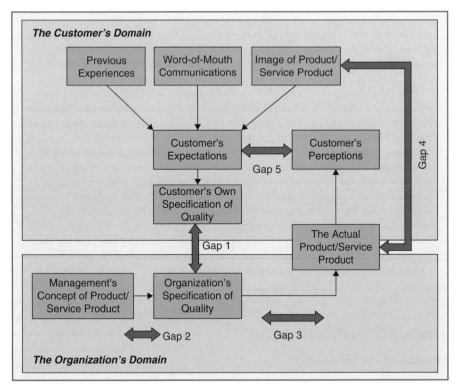

Figure 3.2   The Gap Model

Source: Adapted from Slack, N., Chambers, S. and Johnston, B., *Operations Management*, 2nd edition (London: Pitman, 2003), p. 640

Researchers have tested the validity of the Gap Model. The main limitations have been found to lie in the ambiguity of terms such as 'expectations', from a customer's perspective. This can result in inaccurate estimations of the gaps when these are measured via the questionnaire.[28] However, the basic idea of the Model – the relationship between what the customer expected and the service they received – has been successfully applied in a wide range of service industries (see Mini Case 3.5 on Malaysia Airlines).

Mini Case 3.5

Malaysia Airlines – Airfreight Service Quality[29]

Airfreight is a significant business. Currently one-third of the dollar value of all goods shipped globally is airfreight and the growth rate of this market is estimated to remain at over 6 per cent for the next 20 years. The competitive Asian market is currently

▶▶

estimated at approximately 50 per cent of the world market and is growing. Typical shipments from Asia include high-value electronics and perishables such as seafood for top restaurants. The region is particularly dependent on airfreight because of the distances to markets and the, as yet, underdeveloped infrastructure in many countries.

What are the most important factors when shipping airfreight? How can these be addressed in new service offerings? Management at Malaysian Airlines had their own opinions on the key factors but rather than rely on an internal view, and prompted by the Gap Model, they decided to conduct interviews. An innovative market research technique was used to unearth customers' true needs, and in-depth discussions with 19 airfreight managers revealed a total of 44 attributes of airfreight. Many of these were previously unknown and were related to the service augmentation. Next a subset of attributes was used to identify how shipping managers make trade-offs between price and other service attributes when choosing between different airlines. This information allowed Malaysia Airlines to decide on how to enhance service augmentation and also how it should be priced. Finally, as prompted by the Gap Model, the enhancements to the service augmentation were clearly communicated to customers, in order to set expectations realistically and gain a competitive lead.

INNOVATION IN SERVICES

The Need for Innovation

The need for innovation in the service sector is widely recognized and so are the challenges. For example, many new products fail in the market and so it is with new services. Also, competitors can easily copy new service products, and the speed with which new service products can be introduced to the market can create an over-supply (which in turn leads to more failures).[30] Service augmentation should be fully considered during new service development to make the innovation harder to copy (as patent protection is different for services).

A study of innovation at over 150 companies in the financial services sector looked at the development of new services.[31] The research found that new service products can open new opportunities but such products are perceived by managers to have only a modest impact on sales and profit. It is only the new service products that have distinct attributes and are difficult to copy that bring a sustainable competitive advantage. Conversely, innovations in the service augmentation are perceived by managers to have a big impact on both sales and profit (and also to positively impact the success of other products from the same service provider). The aspects of service augmentation that managers perceived to have the most potential for innovation included distribution channels, effective communications about the new service product, improving the interaction between customers and service employees and enhancing the overall customer experience.

Research in Germany has shown that the majority of service companies make innovative changes not only to their service products but also to their

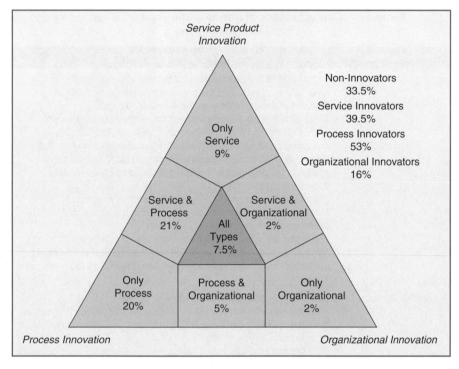

Figure 3.3   Innovation in the German Service Sector (after Hipp, Tether and Miles)

operations (the processes and organizations that deliver services).[32] It can be seen from Figure 3.3 that 9 per cent of innovating companies focus only on the service product, whereas others combine service product innovations with either process or organizational changes. However, only 7.5 per cent of companies are innovating in all three possible dimensions – this is a missed opportunity, as combining innovation in the core product with, for example, innovation in the augmentation, can lead to sustainable competitive advantage.

Managing Service Innovation

The characteristics of services, particularly their intangibility and temporal nature, have a big impact on innovation management. Table 3.6 shows how intangibility and three other factors influence innovation.

Service intangibility has four main implications. First, it means that the design of a service product should be considered inseparable from the design of the production and delivery system – the intangible nature of a service product means that customers' perceptions are strongly influenced by the delivery process. Second, particular care must be taken in designing the servicescape, as this is often the most tangible aspect of a service. Third, the intangible nature of

Table 3.6   Characteristics of Services and Their Implications for Innovation Management

Characteristics	Implications for Innovation Management
Intangibility	• The design of the production and delivery mechanisms (augmentation including the servicescape) must be carefully planned at the same time as the service product. • Tangible and intangible aspects of the service concept must be both identified and managed appropriately. The tangible components of services (physical evidence) need to be carefully managed to give customers a positive perception of the service product. Tangible elements should be used to give a positive impression of the intangible. • Intangible products can easily lead to informal processes. Managers in the service sector need good processes for the development of new services. • The intangible nature of services can make it more difficult to conduct effective market research than for physical products, as customers may find it harder to articulate their ideas for improved services.*
Customer contact	• Deciding on the appropriate degree of customer contact is essential. What is the current level of contact and does this match the expectations? Consider timing, intimacy and information exchanged. • New service products may change the nature of customer contacts and so staff retraining may be necessary. • Innovations in the way the customer contact is managed can give opportunities to improve the perceived quality of the service product. • New service prototypes can only be tested with customers; 'laboratory testing' is not possible.
Inhomogenity	• Service innovation must take account of the dependency of the service offering on both the consumer and (often) the main persons in the delivery chain. Either consistency or customization can be a valid aim. • Different customer segments can require both changes to the service product and the service augmentation. It is important to identify the main market segments.
Services are perishable (simultaneous production and delivery)	• The production and delivery mechanisms must ensure easy access for consumers. Both front and back-office staff need to be involved in new product development. • Capacity issues need to be considered at the design stage. • To achieve high customer satisfaction, the quality of the augmented service must be high.
Service quality is multifaceted	• Expectations and perceptions need to be managed. Internal perceptions need to be matched to those of the customer and/or consumer. • Managing service quality requires good cross-functional interaction between the front and back office.

Note: *Magnusson, P. R., Matthing, J. and Kristensson, P., 'Involvement in Service Innovation: Experiments with Innovating End Users', *Journal of Service Research*, Vol. 6, No. 2 (November 2003), pp. 111–124.

services can trap companies into not having well-defined new service-development processes. Good NSD processes define the responsibilities of all departments (including both front and back offices). Fourth, market research is more challenging for intangible products.

Customer contact can be the deciding factor in achieving customer satisfaction. Therefore, managers need to make decisions on the appropriate level of customer contact at the design stage of new service products. This can be a trade-off as, although customers generally perceive high levels of contact positively, the provision may be labour intensive and expensive. It is important that customer expectations are set realistically. Customer contact itself is also an area where there are opportunities for innovation: in the timing, intimacy, information exchanged and servicescape (see Mini Case 3.6 on healthcare).

Services involve different consumers and different people in the service delivery chain and so they may be inhomogeneous. Normally, service consistency is a goal but companies may use the interaction between their employees and customers to deliberately provide heterogeneous (customized) service offerings. These may also be required to reach certain customer segments. Potentially, each segment will require not only a variation on the service product but also a modified service augmentation to increase perceived quality. Prototyping and experimentation can help perceived quality to be better understood. As innovations are introduced to the market, service staff will require product training.

Services cannot be stored and so the access provided by the delivery channel (locations) and its capacity is important. For many services, the capacity is directly related to the number of service outlets. Therefore, a mantra for many managers in the service sector is 'location, location, location' (attributed to the founder of the UK retail chain, Selfridges). The staff members who are regularly involved in service delivery (the front office) have knowledge that is vital in developing new service products. The Internet has now altered our understanding of location, as some successful companies have achieved a considerable 'presence' via the web ('clicks and mortar', to use the jargon), without resorting to physical outlets ('bricks and mortar'). Products where the physical experience of the product is essential in the buying decision (such as clothes, furnishings, etc.) cannot be effectively marketed via the Internet.[33] Many innovations in services are aimed at improving quality levels. Therefore, the development of new service products and augmentations require an analysis of how service quality is influenced by expectations and perceptions. The Gap Model is a useful tool during new service development. In particular, the Model forces organizations to compare their internal views of service products with their customers' expectations and perceptions, to ensure that discrepancies do not occur. The back and front offices need to be closely coordinated as, 'the interface between these functions becomes critical for a successful service offering'.[34] Teamwork leads not only to an enhanced augmented service offering (consisting of both the service product and service augmentation) but also speeds development and improves quality.

Mini Case 3.6

Innovating in Healthcare – Not Just Treatment[35]

The importance of customer perception in the service sector is paramount and never more so than in healthcare. Healthcare is more than diagnosis and treatment although these have traditionally been the focus of health-care managers. For example, the waiting times in many health-care systems are long; staff members are overworked and may have too little time to spend with patients (assuring them and informing them about the diagnosis and treatment); and drab décor is found in many hospitals and clinics. However, the role of the augmented service and, in particular the servicescape, has been linked directly to the 'bottom-line'. In recent research in the US, patients in certain hospitals were found to require less medication. Hospital departments that had been redecorated in pastel shades and where attractive artwork was hung on the walls were found to generate patient well-being. Perhaps it is not surprising that in more pleasant surroundings patients perceived the service more positively. What is enlightening is that these same departments discovered that the amount of painkiller requested was up to 45 per cent lower and this led to significant savings.

New Service Development Processes

NSD is often less well organized than product development in the manufacturing sector. Research, including the work of Dick Chase, a leading authority on services from the University of Southern California, has identified three enablers of effective NSD: information technology, cross-functional teamwork and formal processes.[36] Using information technology, for example, databases, to stimulate ideas for new service products and improved delivery, can be very important. Cross-functional teamwork is essential to NSD and this requires managers to coordinate the front-/back-office boundary between marketing and operations. A well-defined development process is less common in service companies but just as important as in manufacturing. There are normally four stages in the development of a new service product: generation of a concept; business analysis and planning; development; and market launch[37] (see Mini Case 3.7 on the Halifax Building Society).

In generating a concept for a new augmented service offering, ideas can come from a number of sources. An EU survey of the service sector found that more than 80 per cent of organizations gained most of their ideas from customers.[38] This indicates that companies are talking to their customers but raises the question of whether they are doing so effectively. High-quality market research is needed to gain insights into what sort of service products and what type of service augmentation is needed. Often internal ideas based on anecdotal evidence are used rather than decisions about service innovations being appropriately based on facts gathered from the marketplace.[39] It should be noted that service consumers, just as product users, might not be able to clearly articulate their future product needs, particularly due to the intangible nature of service products. (How to identify the *hidden needs* of both manufacturing and service

---

Mini Case 3.7

Halifax Building Society – New Service Development

The Halifax Building Society in the UK focuses on the fast development of new service products. These include new lending packages for house purchasers, which for instance allow borrowers to customize repayment levels to their needs over a number of years. With the financial crisis of 2008–9, such packages which reduce risks for both borrowers and the lender are essential. Halifax has reduced the time to develop and introduce new mortgage packages from six months to a matter of a few weeks. There are four main steps to their development process and in each of these the responsibilities of each department are clearly defined:

1. *Concept development.* This takes account of previous products, competitive products and perceived customer requirements. The concept will be refined, taking particular account of the views of marketing and operations. An initial check is made on whether the concept can be delivered with existing systems or whether it will require changes at the operational level.
2. *Trial.* Customers (in focus groups) are asked their opinions of the new service. This market research largely replaces the market piloting of new mortgage packages, which was common in the industry a few years ago.
3. *Delivery system definition.* The delivery of a new service requires that a suitable system is set up. The *system* means all resources involved in the delivery, which typically will include computer resources (for tracking payment level, etc.) and human resources (for marketing and administering the service).
4. *Introduction.* Once the delivery system has been defined, the introduction of the new service largely involves the implementation of training programmes to explain it to staff, preparation of necessary software to run systems, and so on.

---

customers is discussed in Chapter 5.) New services can easily be designed on paper[40] but it can be difficult to imagine how the customer will perceive them. To counter this, HSBC Bank make discussions about concepts for new service products more tangible by using role-plays to show how the new product will be presented to the customer. Using these 'service prototypes' has been found to be particularly useful at the concept stage.

Most NSD researchers have recommended that NSD processes be based on those used in NPD.[41] However, we think there is a real need for a different approach. Our work with service companies leads us to think that simply applying NPD thinking is not enough. Service companies must consider their unique situation and build their NSD process appropriately. Chapter 7 describes NPD in detail and our recommended approach to NSD.

SERVICES AND INNOVATION MANAGEMENT

This chapter has shown how the management of innovation for service products differs from that for manufactured products. In reading the next chapters on the elements of the Innovation Pentathlon, the main points about service

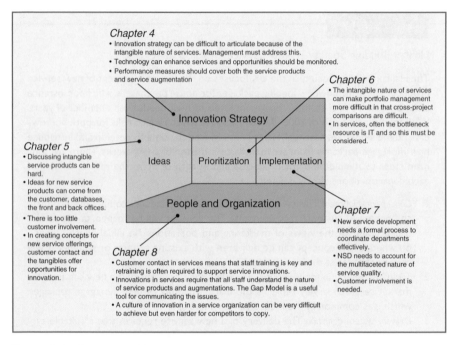

Figure 3.4 Summary of Service Issues to Consider in the Next Five Chapters

organizations that should be kept in mind are summarized in Figure 3.4. This shows that an innovation strategy can be more difficult to articulate in a service organization because of the intangible nature of service innovation and normally the lack of a single department such as R&D, which is seen as having the main responsibility for innovation. Similarly, technology increasingly impacts the service sector and so technological advances and their potential impacts need to be monitored. Other differences that are highlighted in the figure are the difficulty of discussing intangible service products and the range of sources for ideas (including the front and back offices); the difficulty of choosing the best projects as service projects is intangible and therefore hard to imagine; the need for a formal NSD process, which ensures that different service departments are coordinated; and the challenge of creating a service culture of innovation.

SUMMARY

Managing service innovation involves particular challenges that are relevant to both manufacturers (facing the need to provide more services) and the service sector. This chapter showed:

- The leading role of the service sector in developed economies and the increasing importance of services for manufacturers.

- That service products are inextricably linked to their production and delivery – the service augmentation. Service augmentation, including the environment in which the service is delivered, has a strong influence on customer satisfaction.
- The intangibility, customer contact, inhomogenity, non-storability and the multifaceted quality of services all have implications for the management of innovation.
- Managing service quality requires an awareness of the customer's perception plus management of the core service product and the service augmentation. The Gap Model is a useful tool for this.
- New service development is challenging because of the nature of services. A suitable management process is required and this must consider not only the product itself but also the augmented service offering. The process also needs to ensure good teamwork, spanning the front- and back-office boundary.

In the next five chapters, each of the elements of the Pentathlon Framework will be considered.

MANAGEMENT RECOMMENDATIONS

- Irrespective of whether your organization is in the manufacturing, service, public, or not-for-profit sector, identify the role of services in your business. Consider which customer segments require particular services.
- Identify where innovations in both the service product and the augmentations can lead to competitive advantage. Make these improvements as tangible as possible to customers.
- Use the Gap Model to gauge the current quality of your services and identify potential improvements.
- Recognize the need for an efficient new service development process.

RECOMMENDED READING

1. Johnston, R. and Clark, G., *Service Operations Management* (London: Financial Times – Prentice Hall, 2001). [Leading textbook on the management of services, including useful discussions on quality and new service development.]
2. Johne, A. and Storey, C., 'New Service Development: A Review of the Literature and Annotated Bibliography', *European Journal of Marketing*, Vol. 32, No. 3/4 (1998), pp. 84–251. [Key review of the research into new service development.]
3. Tidd, J. and Hull, F.M. (eds), *Service Innovation: Organizational Responses to Technological Opportunities & Market Imperatives* (London: Imperial College Press, 2003). [Useful collection of readings on the latest research on innovation in the service sector.]

CASE STUDY
AXA Insurance – the Innovation Manager[42]

Before reading this case, consider the following generic innovation management issues:

- What sort of ideas lead to the most important innovations? Are they the 'brainwaves' that lead to radical products or are they more pedestrian?
- How can the best ideas be selected?
- How can the nature of innovation be effectively communicated to the employees in a service organization?

INTRODUCTION

The French company AXA is the largest insurance company in the world with approximately 150,000 employees. Their Irish subsidiary was formerly part of the Guardian Insurance Group and today it has high market shares in the motor and household insurance sectors and distributes its service products through a network of branch offices, insurance brokers and telesales operations. Although the insurance sector is not normally known for its innovativeness, the parent company has established innovation as one of its company core 'values' and the Irish operation has created an impressive reputation for creativity. In Ireland the focus on innovation started in January 2000, when AXA created the new role of 'Innovation Manager' (and in doing so became one of the very first companies in the world to conceive the role of innovation manager).

The responsibility of this role was broadly defined as 'to raise the innovation capability of the organization through staff involvement and shared knowledge' and a service manager Catherine Whelan was quickly asked to accept the challenging position. Her task was not simple, especially as there had been no previous incumbent, on whose ideas she could build. Furthermore, the Irish AXA organization did not have a tradition of innovation and colleagues greeted her appointment as the Innovation Manager with some scepticism. In contrast, Catherine had the full support of the Chief Executive Officer, John O'Neill, who had joined the Irish operation in late 1999. He had immediately announced that one of his main business targets was for AXA Ireland to become more innovative, to match the worldwide emphasis that AXA placed on innovation. However, his aim was also strongly influenced by the need to find ways of addressing factors such as the significant inflationary pressures in the Irish economy, cut throat competition, market consolidation in the insurance industry and the urgent need to reduce costs.

THE MADHOUSE

O'Neill had acted quickly to stimulate innovative thinking within AXA Ireland, both through the appointment of an Innovation Manager and, shortly before, through the launch of an initiative which he christened the 'MadHouse Programme'. It was a team-based way of stimulating innovative ideas, with members meeting regularly over a period of two to three months. Typically, it brought together half a dozen employees from different areas of the business and different levels in the organization, on a

▶▶

part-time basis with the stated objective of coming up with innovative business ideas. This activity was carried out in a way that involved both learning and fun and there was a dedicated room for the use of the MadHouse teams. This contained a PC, Internet access, information on creativity techniques, books and magazines, coloured hats hanging from the ceiling as a reminder of Edward de Bono's 'Thinking Hats', and other symbols and decorations from around the AXA organization.

In its first six months the MadHouse Programme generated more than 200 business ideas. These ideas were passed to Catherine, who as Innovation Manager was responsible for choosing the best ideas for further development. She realized that the MadHouse Programme had achieved a lot in a short time and had helped to raise the profile of innovation within the organization. It had generated enthusiasm among staff. It had created an environment of shared learning and was helping to build cross-functional business relationships. It had also generated a significant number of business ideas. Nevertheless, Catherine was worried whether the Programme would continue to be successful for a number of reasons:

- First, given the time and resources allocated to the programme, it was the view of several managers that too few really 'new' ideas had emerged and little contribution had been made to the business.
- The 200 ideas generated were only at the concept stage. They required selection and development but the business units were reluctant to take on this additional work. Catherine knew that achieving some successful implementations was key to the continuing credibility of the programme.
- It was obvious that both the MadHouse and innovation were still viewed as something separate from normal business activity. Catherine perceived her role was to embed innovation activity as part of the way AXA Ireland staff act and think during their day-to-day work. As AXA Ireland was a traditional insurance company, this change looked like being difficult.

LINKING INNOVATION TO THE BUSINESS

In looking for a way to push innovation further, Catherine focused on a number of areas. First, she decided to quickly push the implementation of one of the ideas from the MadHouse. This was the 'TaskMasters' initiative in which every employee at every level in the business would be empowered and encouraged to engage in innovation and continuous improvement on a daily basis, rather than as only part of the MadHouse initiative. TaskMasters encouraged employees to continuously question the value of what they were doing on a daily basis and check if it was supporting the relationship with customers. The focus would be on addressing small problems and issues that could be implemented quickly and at low cost. A reward structure was established to support the initiative and measures were set to gauge the success of this programme.

Second, Catherine actively promoted the awareness of innovation in general and specifically the TaskMasters initiative. Regular communications were sent to all staff and, additionally, an 'Innovation Corridor' was created on the way to the staff restaurant. This created a wider familiarity about the need for innovation, which had previously been restricted to the relatively small number of people involved with the MadHouse.

▸▸

Still, Catherine felt that perhaps too much emphasis was being placed on the generation of new ideas and this kept her thinking about the meaning of innovation in the AXA Ireland business in general.

Third, she realized that the generation of many business ideas was positive but the selection of the best ideas from the 200 concepts already existing would not be easy. To address this problem she worked with management to understand their views on the factors that needed to be considered when choosing projects: such as the potential market impact, the resources available and the urgency. When viewed from this perspective, many of the ideas appeared less viable and so a set of 'filters' was created for MadHouse participants and a selection process that involved management. The filters consisted of a set of questions that participants were encouraged to use to evaluate their own ideas. A selection process was also created where, at the end of a three-month period, MadHouse participants were required to present their ideas to a management panel that, if convinced, would quickly assign resources for implementation.

Although the MadHouse and TaskMasters initiatives had raised the innovation capability of the organization and by doing so had supported the strategy of the business, a number of key issues had to be addressed. Structuring the programmes effectively was going to be important. Convincing staff that they had a key role to play in the development of the company was also still a challenge.

LEARNING FROM THE RESULTS

With hindsight, Catherine Whelan sees that a clear understanding of the meaning of innovation is essential within an organization. This led her to develop the 'Innovation Quadrant' (Figure 3.5), as a categorization of the types of ideas that lead to successful innovations. Initially the Quadrant provided a communication tool, which was used to explain to all employees that innovation has a broad scope and is not simply ideas for new service products. It also allowed more emphasis to be placed on encouraging all employees to contribute to innovation and not just those selected to attend the MadHouse or work on new service products. Now, with the experience of focusing on innovation, it is interesting to see what types of ideas were applied successfully. The figures on Figure 3.5 indicate the percentage of ideas successfully implemented over the past two years and it can clearly be seen that new customer-focused opportunities (new service products) represent only 10 per cent of the implemented ideas. In contrast, improving processes through the elimination of non-value adding steps has had a major impact on many areas of the AXA business. Similarly, many improvements to existing service products have been made.

Overall, AXA Ireland has come a long way since the role of Innovation Manager was created. The company discovered the importance of communicating the role of innovation, creating well understood and effective filtering mechanisms, and knowing the types of ideas that are most likely to generate business returns. Furthermore, John O'Neill and Catherine Whelan have continued driving AXA's 'innovation journey' for over seven years. Specific initiatives have been launched every 12–18 months to encourage, for example, more customer-focused innovation. In some organizations such a number of innovation-related programmes might have led to 'initiative overload'. However, AXA Ireland has managed to keep the momentum going and capture

▶▶

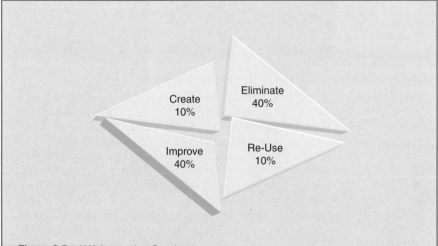

Figure 3.5   AXA Innovation Quadrant

the interest and full support of its staff. Their product range has clearly been transformed and as the AXA Ireland website says, 'you told us not all customers are the same and you would like to see an insurance package tailored to your specific need'. It then lists eight main car insurance packages, from packages for young drivers, female drivers and students, to specific packages for executive cars to classic cars.

AXA's 'innovation journey' has taken them a long way over the past eight years. The interesting thing is that even after eight years the results keep coming – illustrating the real value of a culture of innovation.

4 DEVELOPING AN INNOVATION STRATEGY

> Innovation is the capability by which we get the future we want as opposed to the future we receive by default.
>
> John Kao, 2008

INTRODUCTION

Innovation strategy is part of overall business strategy. It determines when and where innovation is required to meet the aims of the organization and lays out in broad terms what is to be done about it. It is a key element of the Pentathlon, shaping and influencing all the other elements, as is shown by Figure 4.1.

The first step in developing an innovation strategy is to identify where innovation is most needed. This is perhaps the most difficult task because the need for innovation often arises from long-term trends that may develop slowly or outside the immediate scope of the business. As a result the need may be difficult to recognize and painful to confront. The second step is to determine which dimension of innovation is needed to address the issue: for example, new products, new business processes, or a new approach to the market? The third step is to understand the degree of change required. Finally, managers must work out how best to defend the innovation from competition.

As Figure 4.1 indicates, innovation strategy influences all the other elements of the Pentathlon. It guides idea generation through setting goals for internal work, approval of research programmes and sponsorship of partnerships with others to explore new opportunities (Chapter 5). It guides project selection and prioritization (Chapter 6) through the criteria used in selecting projects; and perhaps directly by earmarking funds for strategically important work. Innovation strategy also guides training and recruitment (Chapter 8) and provides the framework for major investments in implementation (Chapter 7). An important thread running through all these considerations is 'Can we do all this by ourselves?' If, as is likely, the answer is 'no' the innovation strategy must indicate where and how outside help is to be sought. The topic of *Open Innovation* and how to apply it is a key part of innovation strategy.

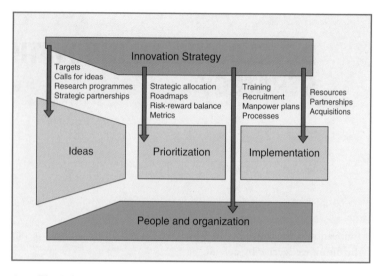

Figure 4.1   The influence of innovation strategy on other elements of the Pentathlon

In this chapter we cover the following topics:

- Strategic analysis
- Open Innovation
- Linking strategy to stakeholder needs
- Changing technology; technology maturity and dominant design
- Changing customer needs; disruptive technologies and strategies
- The effect of Competitors; appropriating the benefits of innovation in the long term
- Timing of innovation
- Tools for assembling and communicating the strategy: roadmapping and scenarios
- A main case study of Domino Printing Sciences

The need for innovation comes from a mismatch between the aims of an organization and what it can actually expect to achieve by continuing with its present policies. The logic of strategic analysis is illustrated in Figure 4.2. It involves making a prediction of the future, bearing in mind the effects of the key drivers of innovation mentioned in Chapter 1 – Technology, Customers, Competitors and the wider Environment – and asking whether the result is acceptable. If it is not, then the extent and manner of the mismatch points to what kind of innovation is required. For many organizations the main strategic impetus comes from the needs of customers and the demands of investors for growth and profitability, but the ambitions of the leaders of the company often play a vital role, as the fortunes of Microsoft under Bill Gates,[1] the Virgin group under Richard Branson, and (unfortunately) Enron under Ken Lay and Jeff Skilling attest. This vital component is shown as *Strategic intent* in Figure 4.2.

The analysis of long-term trends is a particularly important part of developing an innovation strategy because they may not be easy to spot and, if detected, are too often ignored. Many of the most serious threats (and opportunities) arise slowly and it is an important role of innovation strategy to look far enough ahead to see them coming and take action. For this reason we give considerable attention in this chapter to how long-term trends, particularly in technology, customer behaviour and competition, can demand innovative responses. Mini Cases 4.1 and 4.2 relate how two companies, Allianz in insurance and Zara in clothes retailing, reacted to long-term trends of commoditization and increasing competition in their industries. At the time of writing we can see Philips preparing to forsake the increasingly turbulent and competitive world of consumer electronics and Microsoft searching for new businesses to replace its threatened Windows product.

Analysis of the strategic situation may also highlight new, previously unacknowledged, opportunities. So there are likely to be several 'calls to action' and managers must decide which to tackle and how. In one activity, incremental improvements may be sufficient while another part of the business may face a serious problem requiring radical new solutions. Innovation strategy must identify these different themes and make it clear where the emphasis is to be placed.

Just as the effects of current policies must be considered against the background of changes in Technology, Customer Needs and Competition (as well as

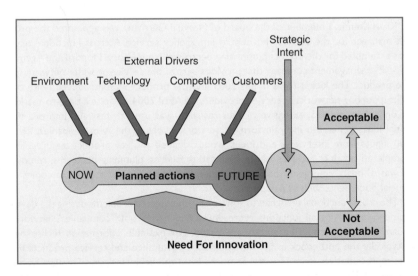

Figure 4.2   The need for innovation arising from the gap between acceptable and unacceptable projections for the future

more general aspects of the environment), so the same considerations must be applied to the innovation strategy itself. This forms the structure of the first part of this chapter, following on from an analysis of strategy from the stakeholder's point of view.

Mini Case 4.1

Allianz-Versicherungs-AG – Innovation Networking[2]

Increasingly companies need to bring in a fresh, outside perspective into the way they define their innovation strategy. Too often organizations view their field too narrowly and this prevents them from generating breakthrough ideas. Creativity is often the result of a market being viewed from different standpoints and this approach has been very successful at Allianz-Versicherungs-AG.

Allianz is the largest insurance provider in Germany. Dr Karl-Walter Gutberlet, an Allianz board member with responsibility for private customers, also serves on the board of Mondial Assistance Deutschland GmbH. This company is a business-to-business service provider focused on consumers' service needs related to travel, car transportation and living. Gutberlet's idea was to add this service philosophy to the insurance viewpoint. The result is an innovative new product that has taken the German market by storm and won an innovation prize from *Capital* magazine.

The new product was officially called 'Allianz Haus- und Wohnungsschutzbrief' (House and home emergency cover) but is better understood as the equivalent of a car breakdown service – a 'household emergency service'. Normal house insurance may cover the costs of solving a problem (for example, a blocked water pipe) but the consumer is still left with the hassle of finding someone to do the repair. Taking the analogy of the breakdown services available for cars, the new product covers the costs and also provides a hotline at Mondial, which organizes a quick repair by a qualified tradesman and the payment; and this is for approximately 5 euro per month.

Klaus Stemig, a member of the board of Mondial Germany, was appointed the project manager for the 24-hour household emergency service. A cross-functional team was assembled for the project comprising personnel from Allianz, Mondial and Agemis, a facility management company that provides part of the service provider network for the product. The kick-off was in July 2003 and the product was introduced (with the full supporting networks of service providers) in April 2004. Despite a time-to-market of only eight months, extensive market research was used to test and improve the initial ideas generated in brainstorming sessions involving the two companies. Over 400 inputs from interviews and focus groups defined the key product features. The completed product includes cover for heating failures, plumbing problems, removal of wasps' nests, emergency babysitting, emergency pet care and storage of copies of crucial documents such as passports.

The cross-functional team had to solve many unexpected problems during the development, but having all functions represented and having both companies' networks meant that these could be quickly addressed. 'For example, information technology is typically the bottleneck in the development of insurance and service products but our representatives from IT were on board from the beginning', says Stemig. Overall, 'we are proud that we not only developed a new concept but that we developed it

▶▶

on-time, matching a very challenging schedule. For example, it wasn't easy to create a new network of tradesmen set up to respond 24 hours a day across all of Germany but we did it'.

The product sold more than double the first year's goal of 25,000 policies and has established a reputation for Allianz as an innovative player in a conservative market. Spotting strategic opportunities is often about bringing in a different perspective and it is management's role to ensure that an organization's paradigms are challenged. Allianz is continuing to try and do this and is now rolling out further new products, such as 'Accident 60 Active' for senior citizens who need not only health insurance but also help in finding and organizing the health services they require.

INNOVATION STRATEGY AND STAKEHOLDER SATISFACTION

Organizations must aim to deliver increasing satisfaction to their stakeholders, and particularly the most important of these: the customer. So strategy must start with an analysis of the important benefits that an organization offers to its stakeholders and asking how their value is to be maintained and enhanced into the future.

Kano's Feature Analysis

A helpful and influential framework for thinking about the strategy for stakeholder satisfaction comes from the work of Noriaki Kano. He originally presented this analysis as a Quality Management tool linking product features to customer satisfaction,[3] but it has far more general application. Kano classified the features of a product into three categories according to the effect they have on customer satisfaction.[4]

1. *Basic* features. These are attributes without which a product or service would simply be unacceptable. Cars must start readily, window-glass must not distort the view, detergents should not irritate the skin. All of these features are expected nowadays (though it was not always so) and failure to provide them would cause great dissatisfaction. However, providing extra performance beyond the basic requirement gives no extra satisfaction to the customer. A car that fails to start only once in 10 years has no competitive advantage over one that fails once in nine years.

2. *Performance* features. These are features that provide a real benefit to the customer, and every improvement to them leads to greater satisfaction. Typical examples would be low price, fuel economy in a car, battery life in a portable phone, and reliable and increasing dividends for shareholders. For many products reliability or ease of use will also be performance features. Performance features are particularly important because they are the long-term focus of competition in any market. Companies gain competitive advantage

and profitability – perhaps over many years – by moving up the curve faster than their competitors. Every step is the basis for the next advance.

3. *Excitement* features, or *Delighters*. A customer is unlikely to demand these features because they are not part of the way the product is normally viewed, but when offered them he or she may be surprised and pleased. Such features often respond to *hidden needs* (see Chapter 5). They give an extra, unexpected value and may be attractive out of all proportion to the objective benefits they give. When it was first introduced, the remote control on a television was a classic example of a Delighter. We doubt it was invented in response to complaints about the chore of getting out of the seat to change channels, but once it was available it made a big impact. An unexpected new initiative such as an acquisition or expansion into a new market may have the same effect on investors in a company. Some delighter features are easily copied and so give only short-term advantage to the innovator, but some introduce a new dimension to customer satisfaction and hence to competition; they may then become new performance features.

Figure 4.3 illustrates Kano's classification of features in schematic form. The horizontal axis is the degree of implementation of a feature and the vertical is the customer satisfaction conveyed by it. The three categories of feature follow different curves reflecting their different effects on customer perception. A successful product needs to have an appropriate combination of basic, performance and delighter attributes. Customer or stakeholder satisfaction comes

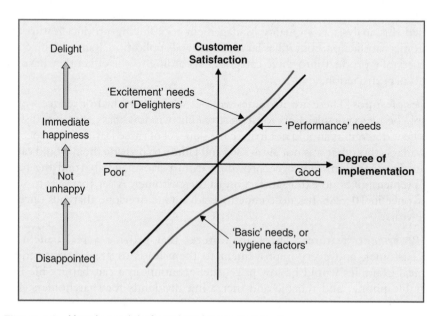

Figure 4.3   Kano's model of product (or service) features

Source: Based on Kano *et al.*, 1984, 1996.

from the basic and performance features, while their loyalty depends on delivering consistently superior performance, possibly accompanied by some excitement features.[5]

The features of a company's product may be allocated to the Kano categories by a simple questionnaire in which customers are asked how they would feel about a significant increase or decrease in their level of implementation (or possibly their presence or absence). A deeper understanding may be reached by Repertory Grid or Conjoint analysis, as described in Chapter 5. The answers are interpreted using the matrix shown in Figure 4.4. Thus if a respondent is unconcerned if the feature is reduced (or absent) but pleased if it is improved/present, then the feature is clearly a delighter. If he or she is uninterested in an improvement, but would be unhappy with a reduction, then it is a basic feature.

Features that fall in the central box (shaded grey) cause no particular response either way. It may be possible to reduce or even remove them.

A key strategic question for any organization is how it can enhance the value it delivers to stakeholders as time goes on. Hence strategic analysis should include a review of where key features will be on the Kano diagram in a few years time. This raises two vital questions. The first is whether the organization can continue to enhance the Performance features of the products and services it offers to stakeholders at the rate they require (or, at least, as fast as competitors do). The second, and more subtle, issue is whether stakeholders,

		'How do you feel about having less of this feature?'		
		Good	Don't care	Bad
'How do you feel about having more of this feature?'	Good		Delighter	Performance feature
	Don't care	Delighter when absent	Indifferent (Possibly an overprovided feature)	Basic
	Bad	Reduction is performance feature		

Figure 4.4   Matrix for allocating product features to their Kano categories

Source: Based on Kano *et al.*, 1984, 1996.

particularly customers, will continue to demand the same balance of features in future. We consider these two challenges in some detail in the following two sections.

Mini Case 4.2

Zara – a Revolution in Fashion[6]

The Spanish fashion retailer Zara has made a great success by overturning the established practices of the mass fashion business. Low margins at home and cheap labour overseas have driven European retailers increasingly to obtain supplies from the Far East, shipping them, in the main, by sea. But this makes the supply chain long and slow. Zara, which is the major part of the Inditex group, has reversed the trend. The majority of its goods are made in its own factories in northern Spain and Portugal from where it ships them by truck or air to more than 1500 stores around the world. The brand is very profitable – its return on sales has been as high as 15 per cent, five times the typical level in the sector. It is also growing strongly: from its foundation in 1975 it now has a turnover of more than 13 billion euros. Growth in sales, profits and outlets has quadrupled since 2000. It was described by Daniel Pielle of Louis Vuitton as 'possibly the most innovative and devastating retailer in the world'.

The key to Zara's success is the speed with which it can now get new designs to market, thanks to local manufacture and a very sophisticated logistics. 'The vertical integration of our production system allows us to place a garment in any store around the world in two to three weeks, provided the fabric is in stock', says Maria J. Garcia, a spokeswoman for Zara. The norm in the sector is five to ten *months*. No sooner has a new look made the headlines than it is on the hangers in Zara – weeks or months ahead of anyone else, and at a premium price. Moreover, the company's speed of response means it can follow the ups and downs of demand very closely. Twice-weekly deliveries mean that Zara shops are seldom short of popular lines and yet need to hold very little stock. So when demand turns down they can immediately switch to a new design. The company typically introduces 10,000 new lines a year.

In contrast, the much longer lead times elsewhere in the sector mean that competitors have to place orders months in advance. Forecasting that far ahead is almost bound to be wrong in such a fast-changing market and the result is a huge cost in obsolete stock that must be discounted or scrapped; a cost that Zara avoids.

Zara's business model ensures loyalty and premium prices by always offering its customers the most up to date designs. It has been noted that a Spanish woman will visit a typical clothing store 3 times a year, but 17 for Zara. The cost of making the clothes in its highly automated European factories is certainly higher than it would be to buy them from offshore suppliers (wages are typically $1650 a month compared with $206 in Guangdon province, China)[7] but the higher margins and savings in inventory costs and discounts more than compensate for this and give the company a unique positioning in its market. The Inditex group now claims to be one of the largest fashion retailers in the world and Zara is rapidly closing in on Gap as the largest clothing retailer in the world.

TECHNOLOGY: THE CAPABILITY CEILING

The Technology 'S' Curve

The first strategic challenge illustrated by Kano's analysis is the capability ceiling. This arises when an organization can no longer move its products and services up the performance curve on the Kano diagram at the rate demanded by customers. If key capabilities are approaching the limits of what they can do, the organization may become vulnerable to competitors with a better approach. Such limits frequently demand an innovative response so it is a vital part of innovation strategy to identify and confront the problem while there is still time to do something about it.

All technologies have a natural upper bound on their performance beyond which it simply cannot be pushed. The same applies to any kind of competence or capability, not just those that are overtly science-based, and we will use the terms technology and competence more or less interchangeably in what follows.

Foster[8] points out that, viewed over a sufficient length of time, the progress of any technology is likely to follow a recognizable path as illustrated in Figure 4.5. On the vertical axis we plot the performance of a key characteristic. It might be a physical attribute of a product, such as speed, price or comfort; the scope of a service (for example, the number of customers a salesperson can serve in a day); or any other parameter that is of value to the customer. On the horizontal axis is the cumulative investment made in developing that aspect of the technology. The curve tends to be 'S'-shaped. In the early stages, when the technology is in its infancy (the *emerging* stage), the performance is modest and the rate of progress is relatively slow; but each advance provides the basis for further improvement and so progress accelerates and the slope of improvement becomes steeper.

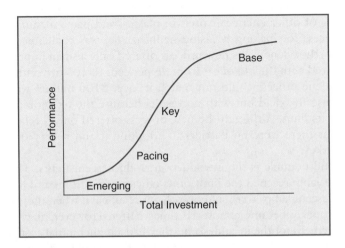

Figure 4.5 The Technology (or competence) 'S'-curve

Source: Based on Foster, 1986.

This improving trend may go on for a very long time, but eventually it comes to an end when some natural limit is approached. As a technology approaches this ceiling, progress becomes slower, investment becomes less and less productive, and the organization becomes vulnerable to attack. The various stages of development have been labelled *emerging, pacing, key* and *base*[9] to indicate their competitive significance.

History is full of examples where this drama has been played out. Foster quotes the example of commercial sailing ships.[10] They showed steady improvement from Roman times through the middle ages and into the nineteenth century, but the flowering of the great clipper ships like the *Cutty Sark* in the second half of the century signalled the top of their S-curve. Further attempts at improving their speed were unsuccessful, and indeed counter-productive: the only possibility was to add more sail, which led to instability in windy weather and a number of well-publicized disasters when the overdeveloped monsters capsized. Sail could improve no more, and gave place to steam.

A similar thing has happened in many modern instances: propeller-aircraft reached an absolute speed limit and jets took over for faster travel; waxed cylinders gave way to vinyl discs, and so to CDs as each reached its limit of audio fidelity; detergents replaced soap for washing clothes; trains replaced canals and so on.

An organization that relies on a capability that is approaching the top of its S-curve is vulnerable. It is therefore imperative to understand key capabilities well enough to be clear where their limits lie and what the alternatives might be. A maturing technology is always potentially at risk but the threat is *real* only if the limit to the capability is truly unavoidable and there is a genuine market demand for further improvement. It is *real* and *urgent* if an alternative technology is at hand that does not have disadvantages that outweigh its benefits.

The question of possible disadvantages of a competing technology is illustrated by two contrasting examples. The first (Figure 4.6)[11] concerns the chemical phthalic anhydride, which is an important feedstock for the manufacture of a number of other chemicals used in plastics and paint manufacture. The original process for making it, using naphthalene, was challenged by a new one, using orthoxylene. This new process offered only a small improvement in yield compared with the old one – from 95 per cent to 105 per cent. However, the naphthalene process could not match it; over $100 million was spent on efforts to raise the yield but with no results because the technology had simply reached its limit. Although the new process offered only a relatively small improvement there were no barriers to adopting it and it very quickly took over the market.

The second example is the introduction of fluorescent lights. The ordinary incandescent lamp reached the limit of its efficiency as a source of light around 1940. Fluorescent lamps were significantly more efficient when they were introduced and quickly became almost 10 times better. However, they were *not* a direct replacement for the incandescent: they had a higher initial cost, a different quality of the light and perhaps most important they would not, for a long time, fit into the existing light sockets. As a result, the two types coexisted for many

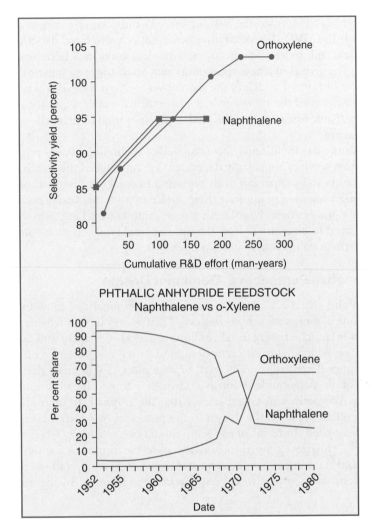

Figure 4.6   Replacement of naphthalene by orthoxylene as the feedstock for making phthalic anhydride

Source: Based on Foster, 1986.

years until recent pressure for energy conservation gave fluorescent lights a decisive advantage – just in time, perhaps, to be overtaken by LEDs!

Of course, technologies are not vulnerable to replacement *only* if they are reaching the top of their S-curve. Sometimes a better alternative appears while there is still plenty of scope for improvement in the incumbent technology. The two may then jostle for leadership for some time until one becomes dominant. For example, the first video discs were launched by Philips in the 1970s as an alternative to video tape.[12] They failed to make much progress and were eclipsed;

but the technology formed the basis of the CD and then re-emerged as a video format with the DVD. Petrol engines never entirely displaced diesel power for automobiles, and, indeed, diesel has now made a comeback because of its fuel economy. The arrival of a new technology may itself trigger a burst of improvement in the old one that delays the switchover.[13] Often the old will respond by adopting features of the new, as when conventional cameras quickly acquired a host of electronic features as established companies tried to delay the advance of digital imaging.

The S-curve has traditionally been applied to technology-based products but we stress that services are equally dependent on capabilities that reach a limit of capability and can be superseded. By replacing manual tracking methods by barcoding FedEx was able to improve their service in ways that had previously been impossible – for example, by offering online shipment tracking. Service companies, too, need to be aware of how the fundamental limits on their competences may make them vulnerable to new competition.

An Alternative Perspective: Dominant Design

Abernathy and Utterback[14] describe the evolution summarized above in a slightly different but illuminating way, as follows. They point out that when a new type of product is launched there usually follows a period of ferment and experimentation during which many different designs are tried out, often by many different companies. Eventually a preferred, or *dominant*, design arises that becomes an actual or *de facto* standard and is eventually adopted by all serious players. Thereafter Abernathy and Utterback say that the emphasis of innovation at the product level moves from the design to the processes by which it is made, marketed and supplied. In terms of the Kano model one would say when the dominant design emerges competition on the core Performance features is much curtailed and the competitive focus must move elsewhere: typically to cost, quality and brand value; but also to new Excitement features. In the automotive

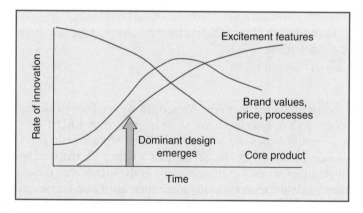

Figure 4.7   The effect of Dominant Design on product and process innovation

industry for example, the dominant design – petrol engine, four wheels, mono-coque construction – emerged in the 1930s – but competition on subsidiary features ranging from power assisted steering and automatic gears to parking sensors and entertainment systems has continued alongside brand and price differentiation. This change of focus is illustrated schematically in Figure 4.7. Such an evolution has been observed in many products from typewriters to automobiles and from aircraft to portable phones.

The emergence of a dominant design is good news for customers but may be a testing time for the incumbent players. Serious innovation is no longer possible at the whole-product level and so the added value goes elsewhere. They must now compete on their non-product business capabilities (or *complementary assets*, see below) such as marketing, production or brand, or by retaining dominance in key modules of the product.

Once a dominant design has emerged, it benefits from the accumulated efficiencies of scale and experience among the suppliers, and among the companies that provide components to them. As the automotive and PC industries demonstrate, design standardization allows manufacturers to use many common components, often specially designed for the purpose, with all the advantages of volume supply and specialization that go with it. New suppliers can now enter the component market because the interfaces are defined and stable. The whole supply chain rides down a learning curve, incrementally improving efficiencies and trimming costs. All this helps to maintain the advantages of the dominant design though the specialization that drives the improvement may also store up trouble for later (see later sections 'Disruptive technology' and 'The Success trap'; and Mini Case 4.5 on the automotive market).

A dominant design may emerge simply because it is the best way available at the time to perform the function. Axes, needles, woodscrews and forklift trucks are all examples of designs that are dominant simply because nobody can (as yet) improve on them. Another way for a dominant design to arise is by way of a formal standardization agreement at the national or international level. We all drive on the same side of the road (at least within each country); all postal systems use stamps; rails are now the same distance apart on virtually all European public railways. Such agreements are particularly useful when interfacing between interested parties is important. For example, the way mobile telephone systems work has been laid down by international agreement, rather than emerging in the marketplace, because it is more important that the way of operating should be agreed than that it should be optimum in any other sense. Once the choice has been made, innovation in the standard necessarily stops and competitive attention moves elsewhere.

In between these two extremes come a variety of situations where a leading design is held in place by *threshold* effects or *network* effects.

A threshold effect operates when a dominant design is held in place simply by the high cost of making a change. An excellent example is the 'Qwerty' keyboard (Mini Case 2.5). This design is inherently inefficient but it is so well established that attempts to replace it with a better one have always failed[15,16] because anyone who wants to change over has to unlearn a painfully acquired skill and learn a new one. The cost of making the change simply outweighs the benefits. The UK would long ago have changed to driving on the right like the rest of the world were it not for the cost – not to mention the dangers – of the transition.

Another, more powerful, way in which a dominant design becomes locked in place is through so-called *network effects* or *network externalities*. These occur when the value of a design becomes greater the more people adopt it. Telephones, email and the Internet are modern examples of this. The more popular they are the more valuable they become. The network effect may be direct, when the value is directly related to the number of customers; or it may be indirect, when the value is generated by related products and services. Thus the VHS video standard and the CD format became unassailable not because of the hardware but because of the huge amount of software products that are available to use on it. The same effects dominated in the emergence of DVD and its Blu-ray successor (see Mini Case 4.3).

Mini Case 4.3

Home Recording from Betamax to Blu-ray

The tussle for supremacy in the home recording market illustrates the power of network effects in a mass-market product.[17] The video tape recorder was pioneered for professional purposes by RCA and Ampex in the USA, with the latter eventually emerging as the dominant player. Many companies, including Philips, Sony, JVC and Matsushita took an interest in the technology from the 1950s but competition quickened in 1971 when Sony brought out the U-Matic, a cassette model that was suitable for semi-professional users such as schools, though not yet for home use. Sony, Matsushita and JVC agreed to cross-license their patents in 1970 and the race was on to open up the domestic market.

Sony launched the Betamax, the first video recorder designed for the home market, in 1975. JVC followed with the VHS a year later. Both designs used ideas from the U-Matic and neither had a fundamental advantage of cost or technology. Nevertheless, they used incompatible cassettes and recording formats. Sony had the advantage of being first-to-market but many customers felt their one-hour recording length was too short. VHS offered two hours from the start and a number of major companies, including Matsushita, decided to wait for it. In fact Sony launched a two-hour machine only five months after the launch of VHS and thereafter the two formats matched each other with innovations, neither drawing ahead for more than a few months at a time.

The market for VCRs grew dramatically, from approximately 20,000 units a year in 1975 to approximately 20 million in 1983 and 40 million in 1987. Sony's sales also grew until 1984 but their initial 100 per cent market share dropped to 61 per cent when VHS arrived in 1976 and was down to 50 per cent in 1978, 30 per cent in 1981/2 and below 10 per cent by 1985.[18]

Sony did not lose their initial advantage because of significant price or product disadvantages; their problem was that JVC, a much smaller and perhaps less arrogant company, gave much greater emphasis to signing up partners and distributors. They consequently gained a small but significant market lead early on, which was amplified

▶▶

into a greater dominance by network effects. These became particularly strong in the early 1980s when the market for pre-recorded videotapes took off. The higher market share of the VHS system made it the more attractive format for suppliers of the software. The better range of pre-recorded films in turn made VHS more popular with buyers of machines and so an upward spiral developed that turned JVC's 60/40 lead in terms of installed base (total machines sold) into a monopoly within a few years.

Another player in this market was Philips. They introduced their own video recorder, the 1700, in 1975/6 but did not market it aggressively. The technically superior 2000 system followed in the late 1970s but it was too late to stem the rise of VHS. But they learned the lesson of the importance of the network effects driven by software and when they launched the CD in 1979, it was in partnership with Sony. The companies immediately licensed the format widely and on favourable terms, creating a standard that was never threatened.

The VHS/Betamax battle was nearly repeated in January 1995 when Philips/Sony and Toshiba (in partnership with Warner Brothers) both announced competing videodisc recorders. This time the power of the software providers and potential licensees operated directly: they combined to push for a single standard and within the year both parties had agreed to adopt a common format, the DVD.

An onlooker would expect that the industry would have learned to avoid such struggles but the lure of the 'winner takes all' scenario that develops with strong network effects proved too strong. In 2002 a consortium of nine of the largest consumer electronics companies combined to announce a high-definition recording standard called Blu-ray. But Toshiba and NEC announced their intention to pursue an alternative, HD-DVD. Sony was the first-to-market in 2003 but with a very expensive product. NEC and Toshiba shipped HD-DVD drives on their computers in 2006, but the important battle was to win over the content suppliers. This time games consoles played a major role and Sony's presence in this market was an advantage; the PlayStation 3 launched in 2006 included a Blu-ray recorder. So was their position in Hollywood, after acquiring MGM and Columbia. HD-DVD was out of the game by the end of 2007.

We wait with interest to see how a standard for 3D display and recording will develop.

Where they occur, network and threshold effects both serve to make an established dominant design very difficult to shift. Together they can make an almost insuperable barrier, as people who tried to persuade the world to adopt an artificial new language, Esperanto, have found. Not only is the effort in learning a new language very large but it is also useful only when many other people have already done so. Microsoft's Windows operating system is another example where the threshold effect of familiarity is supported by the many independent application programs that have been written to run with it.

Evolution of Strategy as Technology Matures

As a company's core technology evolves through the stages shown in Figure 4.5, so the strategic focus of the company (or its business unit handling the technology) changes with it (Table 4.1).

To start with, the R&D department concentrates mainly on mastering the technology, while the market stance of the company as a whole emphasizes its technical competence and ability to supply the new product. Later on, as the technology moves up the S-curve, technical attention turns towards pushing forward the performance of the product and exploring the new applications that the extra capabilities open up. At this stage the company typically seeks to gain a strong market share and the marketing message concentrates on the functional advantages of the product. Then, as the technology reaches its later stages, attention inevitably moves away from the core performance (which has gone about as far as it can) to emphasize other aspects such as price, quality, reliability and service. The company now positions itself as a competent and reliable supplier, not only of the product itself but also perhaps of a range of supporting products and services. In a sense the competition is no longer between products so much as between whole companies, or brands.

All this, of course, applies only as long as the core technology is not superseded by another. If this happens when the incumbent technology is still in the Pacing stage the company will generally be able to absorb it without too much disruption, but if it arrives when everyone has adapted to working with a Base technology there may be some painful readjustments to be made to rekindle the entrepreneurial culture appropriate to rapidly improving capabilities.

Table 4.1 How Commercial and Technical Focus Evolves as Technology Matures

Technology Phase	Typical R&D Focus	Typical Company Focus
Emerging	• Technical understanding • Patents and IPR	• Find early adopters. • Gain practical experience • Publicise capability
Pacing	• Demonstrate capability • Establish standards • Explore variations • Understand limits	• Respond to early market feedback • Flexibility • Readiness to learn
Key	• Performance improvement • Customer focused features • Technical mastery • Design for manufacture	• Product performance improvement • Market share • Exploit new niches and applications
Base	• Reliability • Cost • Design and Ergonomics • Scan for new technologies	• Reliable and respected supplier • Brand image • Quality • Value • Complementary product / services • Business process improvement

CUSTOMER SATISFACTION: FEATURE FATIGUE

The second strategic issue that is illustrated by the Kano diagram (Figure 4.3) is that the position of features on the diagram tends to change in a regular and predictable way with time: the diagram rotates so that delighters eventually lose their impact and become performance features and performance features themselves become basic. This trend leads to important strategic challenges.

Consider the typical lifecycle of a new performance feature such as a TV remote control or a camera in a cell phone. When it is first offered, it causes admiring comment, and generates well-deserved sales advantage for the originator. But in the course of time, it is copied by competitors and loses its special impact. Its mere existence is then no longer a surprise and the scramble starts to make improved and refined versions. It may now become a performance feature, the focus of competitive improvement. Often the improvement continues until the performance of the best products completely meets the needs of even the most demanding of users. The products in the market will now be spread out along the Performance line and customers can choose what level they are willing to pay for. Eventually the market becomes so used to the feature that it is no longer a competitive element and drops below the axis as a Basic need. Table 4.2 gives some other everyday examples of these movements.

When a performance feature starts to run out of steam as a competitive advantage, it heralds a structural change in the basis of competition. Companies often find it very difficult to adapt to this change because the old focus of competition may be, quite literally, built into the fabric of the organization. It may be its core competence; and may very well be where management has habitually looked to protect and enhance margins. As a result companies often fail to notice that the game is changing and may continue to develop the familiar features of its products well beyond the point of interest to its customers. Customers themselves may not be helpful, either. When asked about the relative importance of various features, they will continue to rate basic features highly. Are comfortable seats important in a car? Of course they are. But that is not the same as saying that further padding will make a customer choose one car rather than another.

Table 4.2   Examples of the Evolution of Product Features on the Kano Diagram

Delighters that became Basic features	Performance features that became Basic
• Self-starters and heaters in cars • TV remote controls • Seat-back TV on long-haul flights • Lounges for business class travelers • 'Cash-back' at supermarket tills	• Price of ball-point pens • Accuracy of clocks and watches • Size of portable phones • Resolution of desktop printers • Service interval of (most) cars • Fidelity of audio systems

Continuing to develop basic features as if they were still performance features can be disastrous on three counts. First, the extra but useless performance can add unnecessary cost or complexity to the product; second, the chance to pursue features that will be of real interest to the customer is foregone; and third, the company may become vulnerable to an alternative, so-called *disruptive*, technology. An example of a company that recognized and profited from a disruptive opportunity is Formule 1 hotels, our Mini Case 4.4.

Mini Case 4.4

Formule 1 Hotels – a New Strategy for Customer Satisfaction[19]

In the early 1980s the board of Accor, a French hotel chain, challenged its managers to come up with a new concept for low-cost hotels. They asked them to reconsider what customers really valued from a night's stay and to see whether it was possible to find a better overall value proposition than the one generally on offer. The analysis showed that a number of features that were traditionally provided by even the lowest cost hotels were of comparatively little value to customers making an overnight stop. These included lounges, eating facilities, availability of a receptionist and spacious rooms. Such features were important for people staying in two or three-star accommodation, for whom a hotel stay was in part a cultural experience. However, most users of low-cost hotels simply wanted a good night's sleep. The other features were being oversupplied.

By moving to small rooms with only basic facilities, cutting out lounges and restaurants, and having receptionists available only at peak times, the company was able to reduce construction and operating costs for the new hotel chain significantly. But rather than merely reducing the price they also used the money to raise the standards of the features most important for overnight customers – comfort, cleanliness and quietness in the rooms – well above that usually available in the sector. The result was a new value proposition giving a much higher level of customer satisfaction. The 'Formule 1' hotel chain, launched in 1985, quickly became the market leader in the sector. Within ten years its market share exceeded that of its five nearest rivals combined.

Disruptive Innovation

The concept of *disruptive innovation*, or *disruptive technology* as it was originally called, was first identified by Clayton Christensen[20,21] at Harvard. He pointed out that companies often fall prey to a new technology or a new business model whose performance is actually inferior to that of the incumbent companies but which has other advantages. This can happen if a performance attribute that has previously been the focus of competition is starting to surpass the needs of a significant part of the market. (In other words the feature is dropping from the performance category towards basic.) Then a new approach can alter the basis of competition in a dramatic way.

Disruptive technologies which change the basis of competition are distinguished from *Sustaining* technologies which continue the current focus.

Sustaining technologies may undergo major transitions as one technology runs out of steam and is replaced by another, but essentially they represent 'business as usual'. So they tend to be well managed by competent companies. Disruptive technologies, however, change the competitive focus of the business and are much more difficult for established companies to adapt to. Mini Case 4.5 discusses the role of electric power as a disruptive technology in the automotive business.

Christensen's initial research was conducted on computer disc drives, a fast-moving market sector in which product life cycles are shorter than most. But further investigations have shown that the principles apply in other sectors from retail to earth-moving equipment. His ideas are based on the following observations:

- Companies succeed by serving their customers in markets that they understand well. They seek to improve the performance of their products to stay ahead of competition and protect their margins.
- The pace of technology development often exceeds the demands from the bulk of the market. This may be because the technology is developing particularly fast, driven by the requirements of the most demanding users; or because the need for the feature is becoming saturated.
- Disruptive technologies initially offer products that have poorer performance on the accepted features but other advantages such as price or size. They are first used either among the least-demanding users in the lower tier of the market or in new markets currently too small, or offering too low margins, to attract established companies.
- In the course of time a disruptive technology may improve enough to offer performance that is acceptable to most of the customers in the established market – even if never fully matching that of the existing approach. It can then compete fully with the established technology and its other features can catastrophically change the basis of competition.

Figure 4.8 illustrates the concept of disruptive technology, showing the performance curve of a sustaining technology related to user needs on a particular 'Feature A'. The speed at which it develops is driven by the competition between the established companies and may be faster than the rate at which customers' needs develop. Over time the technology enables product performance to increase from level $L3$ to $L1$. However, the needs of both 'high-end' and 'low-end' users (indicated by the shaded area on the diagram) increase more slowly. Nevertheless, companies that develop products with improved performance will often be successful and their market shares increase.

Disruptive technology is very different. Such a technology offers worse performance in respect of Feature A, so its first application may be in other applications, where its other attributes (such as lower price) are an advantage. It may not be attractive in the established market until it improves to level L2 when it starts to become attractive to low-end customers. At this point, the technology

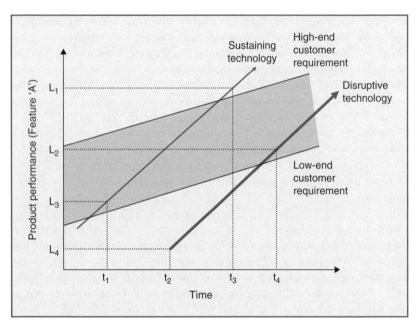

Figure 4.8 The development of sustaining and disruptive technologies

Source: Based on Christensen, 1995, 1997.

will start to disrupt the established market and customers may switch in significant numbers. Typically, established companies will tend to relinquish the lower end of the market and migrate upwards where margins are better, not recognizing the existential threat until too late.

An example given by Christensen is mechanical diggers. The early versions were based on motors linked to the digger buckets by drums and cabling and the key product features in the main market – open cast mining – were the reach of the arm and the capacity of the bucket. Over the years, the established manufacturers improved the technology to the extent that the reach and capacity were more than sufficient for the mining industry. In the 1940s, the British company JCB introduced hydraulic technology into the design. Both the reach and the bucket capacity achieved with this new technology were worse than that of the established products. But the mechanical arm using hydraulics was lighter and could be mounted on the back of farm tractors used for pipe-laying and small building projects – a new market. The success achieved by JCB and other entrants opened up the new market and over time hydraulic technology was developed to the level that met the needs of most of the mining market, too. Of the 34 companies operating in 1945, only 4 were able to successfully adopt hydraulic technology and survive to 1965. Over the same period, over twenty new companies entered the market.[22] The 30 manufacturers of mechanical excavators that did not make the transition from one technology to another were caught in the classic Disruptive technology trap. The new design was not suitable for their existing market and the markets it did suit were far from their own – and anyway too small to be attractive. So they had no way of using hydraulic technology, until it was too late.

Responses to a Disruptive Threat

The future of a company that faces a threat from a disruptive technology sounds bleak. It seems as if they must either pour investment into something that cannot be used in the current business or stand back while it develops elsewhere into an overwhelming threat. This is too alarmist. Of course a disruptive technology *may* precisely replace the functions of the old, bringing advantages but no disadvantages (as in the case of phthalic anhydride synthesis in Figure 4.6). More usually the incumbent technology will have some desirable features that the disrupting one does not. The newcomer will not necessarily sweep all before it; more likely the two will coexist,[23] sharing the market according to the different baskets of capability. And even if one does 'win', the victory may take a very long time. In fact a study by Charitou and Markides of a group of companies facing disruptive innovations found a variety of responses[24]:

Find a way to use it at once.   This is the 'classic' response to a disruptive technology and is the most appropriate if the disruptive technology really holds promise of eventually replacing the incumbent technology without any disadvantages. (Christensen's example of computer disc drives falls neatly into this category). By definition the disruptive technology is not suitable for the existing markets so the company must find a way to operate in a new market where it is. Typically this is done by setting up a new division. Hewlett-Packard took just this approach with its inkjet printer activity. When it first emerged, inkjet could not rival the quality of laser printing, but it had other attributes such as low cost, low noise and low power consumption. Rather than trying to get existing customers to buy the inferior technology HP set up a separate division tasked with exploiting inkjet in whatever applications it could find, operating whatever business model allowed it to make money. The strategy paid off handsomely when the quality of inkjet printing eventually rose to be good enough to displace laser from much of the desktop market. But if the improvement had not happened HP would still have had a profitable, if modest, business. IBM did a similar thing with the PC. Such an approach is easiest for large and diversified companies. Philips was able to use and develop LED lamps in its consumer electronics arm long before it emerged as a disruptive technology in its lighting business.

Mini Case 4.5

Electric Power in the Automotive Industry

The petrol-based internal combustion engine has been the overwhelmingly preferred power supply for personal transport since it won a brief struggle for dominance with electric, diesel and steam power in the first decade of the twentieth century.

▶▶

A Dominant Design emerged in the 1920s: a 4–6 cylinder petrol engine, hydraulic brakes, 3–5 gears and a steel body shell. The diesel engine retained a niche position in buses and trucks; and electric power hung on in a handful of specialist applications. Now, a century later, the industry is going through another period of creative turmoil as the industry tries to decide how to deal with the pressure for a less polluting means of transport.

There are many contenders for the new Dominant Design. They range from traditional designs powered by plant-derived ethanol at one extreme through high-efficiency diesel engines, petrol-electric hybrids, plug-in hybrids, hydrogen power and fuel cells to fully battery-powered cars at the other. The battle is peculiarly intense because as one moves along the list less and less of the established architecture remains. A hybrid, a fully battery-powered vehicle is architecturally very similar to a normal vehicle, with a central power unit supported by gears, clutch and transmission. But a fully electric car may consist only of a battery, four electric motors and a computer (together with steering and brakes and a cabin for the occupants). The power train – engine, clutch, gearbox, transmission – has gone, and with it 75 per cent of the manufacturing cost and the value of much of the design, manufacturing and support infrastructure on which the established companies have so long relied for their competitive position. This is a full-scale architectural revolution. It is not surprising that although Daimler-Benz, Toyota and Ford are active in diesels and hybrids the running in the fully electric race was first made by Tesla and other start-ups.

Electric vehicles are an example of a disruptive technology. For years the technology existed in a few niche applications but did not have the performance to compete in the mainstream. Now market requirements have changed to make low pollution and running costs very attractive, at least to some sectors. As their performance and range improve, electric vehicles will surely take a significant market share, even though they may never match petrol vehicles on the traditional criteria. But it is a competence-destroying innovation: the incumbent companies must embrace electric traction but the more successful it is the more it erodes their added value and destroys their core competences.

Focus on the existing business. If the disruptive technology does not precisely replace the incumbent one, an aggressive response may be successful, emphasizing and enhancing the features of the existing technology that are not shared by the new one. Examples of this are all around us: cinema responded to television with ever more impressive visual and sound experiences and is now more successful than ever; bookshops have responded to the Internet by offering easy chairs and coffee shops. And our clothes are *not* all made of artificial fibres. Disruptive technologies do not always win all the business.

Wait and see. Innovations do not always live up to their promise so a 'wait and see' strategy may work, combined perhaps with partnerships or investments designed to keep options open. The new technology may fail completely, or at least it may not develop far enough to be a threat. And in any case a late entrant may be able to buy in the new capability when it is sufficiently matured and use it to good effect.[25,26] We discuss this approach further in the next section.

Attack back – disrupt the disruption.   A final strategy is for incumbents not only to emphasize and enhance their intrinsic advantages against the new entrant, but also to add further ones, changing the basis of competition yet again. The Swiss watch industry is a classic example. Its success had been based on a long tradition of craftsmanship in making clockwork timepieces that were more accurate and reliable than any others. This advantage was wiped away by the arrival of extremely accurate electronic watches based on quartz crystals that were also very much cheaper. Faced with this dramatic change, the Swiss neither continued as they were nor attempted to follow the new competition on price and features. Instead, they re-disrupted the market by turning to a new way to compete – on style. The Swatch became a byword for novel visual design, a fashion accessory rather than a timepiece. To retain their valuable brand name Swiss Watch re-engineered the design of the watch, reducing the number of assembled components by 40 per cent so that it could still be made cost-effectively in Switzerland.

COMPETITION

Value Innovation: Blue Ocean Strategies

In our discussion so far we have implicitly assumed that innovation strategy will address opportunities and threats within an existing industry or market. W. Chan Kim and Renée Mauborgne of INSEAD point out that competing in the same game is not always the best policy. Sometimes the best innovation strategy is to outflank the competition by offering a different mix of benefits and so defining a new market space. Mini Case 4.6 on Caterpillar gives an example of this, as does Mini Case 4.2 on Zara. Such a *Value Innovation*[27] or *Blue Ocean*[28] strategy is especially attractive when players are competing head to head with similar offerings – as happens when feature fatigue has set in and no new delighters are available, or when the defining competence has met a competence ceiling that cannot be breached.

The scope for a Blue Ocean strategy may be detected by Value Gap analysis.[29,30] Figure 4.9 shows an example for a group of airline companies. This analysis compares the perceived performance offered by the companies in the market, and gives insight into the state of competition and possible opportunities for repositioning. Three of the curves in Figure 4.9 represent traditional airlines, whose value curves are all strikingly similar, indicating an uncomfortably tight state of competition. It immediately poses the strategic question of whether it is possible to find an alternative value offering that will be more attractive to some existing customers and may open the market to new ones. This, of course, was the opportunity recognized by South West Airlines in the USA and followed by Easyjet, Ryanair and others in Europe. Many of the customer service features,

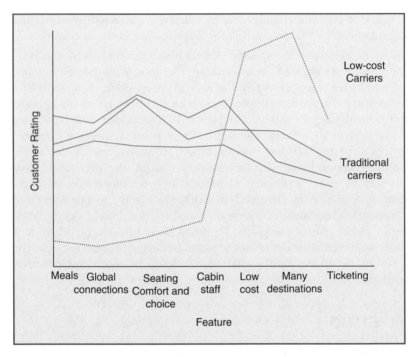

Figure 4.9 Feature analysis for airline companies showing the value gap exploited low-cost carriers.

Source: Adapted from Schoenberg 2003 and Kim and Mauborgne 2005.

such as gourmet meals, large seats and air miles that had for so long been the competitive focus for the traditional carriers, were seriously overprovided, especially on shorter flights. A radically different value proposition was possible, emphasizing convenience, multiple destinations and much lower cost.

Blue Ocean strategies have much in common with disruptive technologies in that they create a new basis for competition. The difference is that a disruptive technology offers a new technical capability and the particular interest is in how it may migrate from one market to another, completely dislodging existing players. A Blue Ocean, however, usually requires no new capabilities. The innovation comes from recognizing unmet, or over-met, needs and creating a new market, outflanking rather than demolishing other players.

Designing a Blue Ocean Strategy

In searching for a Blue Ocean strategy one needs to understand which of the existing features are oversupplied and so might be reduced or eliminated. Often a Kano analysis based on interviews and questionnaires will show the opportunities but in a well-established market more subtle tools may be needed to cut through the preconceptions of customers and managers. Repertory Grid and Conjoint analysis are examples, which we discuss fully in Chapter 5. The other side of the task is to create the new customer value by enhancing existing features or adding new ones. Kim and Mauborgne[31] give a number of possible strategies for finding these opportunities, which we summarize briefly below:

- Look across at other segments of the market and combine the most attractive features of both, eliminating the rest. 'Curves' is a US company that operates fitness facilities targeted at busy women who would normally be users of home exercise videos. Their low-cost women-only fitness clubs have relatively basic facilities but offer a large choice of locations so they are very convenient to get to and provide the supportive atmosphere of health club at low cost.
- Look across to other industries that provide the same type of function in a different way. Low-cost airlines aim to provide the speed of air transport with the cost, simplicity and multiple destinations of a bus.
- Target a different part of the buyer chain. Thanks to the Internet, many services that used to be provided through an intermediary can now be sold direct to the end-user; and in Europe there is a growing trend to supply customized boxes of produce directly from farms to the consumer.
- Offer a different mix of emotional and functional needs. QB Net (Mini Case 8.3) is making a great success from providing very quick and functional haircutting, eliminating the costly and time-consuming service of the traditional approach. On the other hand, health clubs have thrived by building a social atmosphere around the strict functionality of the gymnasium.
- Reach out to the other products and services that are used with the product. Dyson has built a successful business from bag-less vacuum cleaners, eliminating a tiresome related product. Allianz (Mini Case 4.1) found a new market space by offering a complete service for dealing with household emergencies when the established paradigm was merely to provide the money to pay for them.

Blue Ocean strategy is a relatively new concept in innovation management. It gives helpful insights into an important but neglected area of innovation and shows again how innovation so often comes from examining unnoticed and unchallenged assumptions about the business.

Mini Case 4.6

Caterpillar – Products AND Retail AND Services[32]

The Caterpillar company has a worldwide reputation for its range of innovative, robust range of earth-moving equipment. An example is its skid-steer loaders, which target the North American market. The development of these products included a focus on ease of operation and serviceability.

The loaders are designed for ease of operation for not only experienced but also inexperienced users. This was important because Caterpillar has also recently launched

▶▶

their own Rental Stores, and so inexperienced operators are increasingly using the equipment. Usability is supported by several features like ergonomics in the operator's compartment, excellent visibility; two instrument panels that always give the operator an overview of the loader's performance, and joystick controls.

The design of the loaders also focused on serviceability. For example, a sight gauge on the radiator enables quick checks to be made to the coolant level. Similarly, the cooling system has been simplified, improving the access to the engine required for daily checking and maintenance. Gearboxes are sealed-for-life units, the engine oil-change periods have been extended, and the testing of the hydraulic system has been simplified by the use of external pressure ports. Finally, service personnel can read the 'hour-meter', a device that measures the amount of time the product has been used, without having to enter the operator's compartment.[33]

Caterpillar has highlighted the advantages of these product improvements in their advertising. This means that customers are made aware of the benefits of a product designed for seviceability, even though they might not have previously considered it. Caterpillar has a long tradition of focusing on serviceability and even talk of 'negative downtime' for some products – their largest earth-moving equipment includes extensive remote monitoring capability, which monitors performance and arranges for preventive maintenance before a problem even occurs.

Protecting the Value

In launching a new product or service companies need consider right from the start how to defend their position against competition.

Intellectual property – patents and trade marks – is the most obvious and widely used way to create a barrier against competition (see Chapter 5) though in fact solid intellectual property that really blocks out competition is quite rare. For example EMI, who invented the body-scanner (and shared a Nobel prize for the idea), found that their intellectual property was not strong enough to protect them for long against GE, Siemens and others who had far stronger knowledge of the medical equipment market and access to it.[34]

Agreements with participants can also give at least a temporary monopoly position. For example, the barber shop QB Net (Mini Case 8.3), obtained deals to give them exclusive rights to place their innovative hairdressing outlets in airport concourses, blocking out the competition – at least for a while. Many specialist shops do the same in railway stations and other semi-public places. Signing up exclusive deals with key distributors can also work.

Disruptive technologies and Value Innovations may be protected from competitive response for a time simply because they alter the whole business model so that competitors take time to recognize the threat and may then find it difficult to adapt their ways of working. British Airways and KLM both started low-cost companies to compete with Ryanair and Easyjet but ended up selling out to them when the internal contradictions in running such contrary business models proved too great to handle.

Such strategies give at best temporary protection. In the long run (and earlier if the innovation can be copied or the patents 'worked round') a company's ability to profit from an innovation generally depends on its strength in the many other business capabilities that are necessary for success. Teece[35] calls these factors *complementary assets.* They may be generic assets, such as marketing, distribution, manufacturing expertise or brand image which could be applied to a range of projects, or they may be specifically adapted to the product in hand (a dedicated servicing activity or a capital-intensive factory, for example). If the innovator lacks the required complementary assets for the long run then it is vital to use the period of protection to build them up. For example, companies may push for a dominant market share that can be defended by the cost benefits of large scale operations.

As mentioned in a previous section, network externalities can be a powerful factor in holding a dominant design in place, and companies can seek the same effect for their own products by encouraging others to develop complementary products to use with it. The better such supporting offerings are, the more secure the main product becomes. This is a strategy used by games console manufacturers who seek to sign up the most creative game inventors to support their product. Philips and Sony used it with the CD standard and Microsoft with Windows. Support of film companies was a major factor in the battles for dominance of the market for video player markets, and more recently for high-definition DVD (Mini Case 4.5).

Products with network effects show a characteristic adoption curve: slow at first but reaching a rapid 'take-off' point when enough people have adopted it so that the network effects kick in. If two or more standards are competing in a market where network effects are prevalent, the network effect may be enhanced by the competition so that a 'tipping point' is reached[36] when one first emerges as the acknowledged leader and then grows rapidly at the expense of the others.

OPEN INNOVATION

As technology and business processes become more sophisticated, companies are driven to concentrate on their core competences and to outsource an increasing range of activities.[37] In the words of Frank Corrubba, chief technology officer of Philips: 'In this wonderful world of short lifecycles, eroding margins, dynamic economies and competitors coming out of the woodwork ... no one company can have all the core competencies necessary to introduce new products in a timely way'.[38] William Joy of Sun Microsystems says simply 'Not all the smart people work for Sun'.[39]

The term Open Innovation was popularized by Henry Chesbrough in his 2006 book of the same name[40] but the concept is as old as the hills. The term simply means that organizations can, and usually should, look outside their own doors both for innovative ideas and for ways of exploiting them. Many managers, when exhorted to do more Open Innovation reply, 'We've been doing that for years – working with design houses, consultancies and universities'. But Chesbrough points out that there are increasingly strong forces pushing companies to work in this way. The argument is this: The scientifically based industries that emerged in the aftermath of the war were generally vertically integrated in terms of technology for the very good reason that they had acquired a near-monopoly of knowledge in their field. Nobody knew more about computing than IBM or communications than Bell Telephone. The huge and successful research labs of AT&T, IBM and Philips produced a stream of new technologies and products which the companies developed and sold entirely by themselves. Anything they could not use immediately could be kept 'on the shelf' for later use. Nowadays, however, there are no monopolies of knowledge. Universities are much more open to industrial collaboration than they used to be and all of them try to teach useful and relevant subjects. The rise of the Venture Capital industry has made financing for start-ups much easier. Add to this the international spread of industrialization and the result is a huge proliferation of small firms, as well as other entities, developing new ideas and technologies all over the world. Any company that thinks it owns all the knowledge or all the talent is going to be wrong. As a senior research manager from Merck said 'Every senior scientist here running a project should think of herself or himself as being in charge of all the research in that field. Not just the 30 people in our lab, but the 3000, say, in the world in that field'.[41]

Many companies are reducing their in-house research teams and spending more on tapping into outside expertise and ideas. Proctor and Gamble have publicized their target that 50 per cent of their new products will originate outside the firm. Intel set up 'lablets' in or near universities to tap into their expertise. Many companies now have sections on their web sites inviting new ideas.

The move to open innovation means that the innovation funnel that forms the core of the Pentathlon is increasingly porous, with ideas coming in from the outside at all phases. Moreover, it is also porous in the other direction. The greater mobility of people between companies and the ready availability of capital means that if ideas are not used internally the people working on them are quite likely to decamp and set up a new venture elsewhere. In fact many larger companies have established Corporate Venture groups to sell or license technologies that they cannot use, or to spin out companies to exploit them.[42,43] Sometimes these companies are re-absorbed into the parent when they have pioneered a new application which turns out to be more relevant than had been thought. Chesbrough points out that the Open Innovation paradigm is particularly good at correcting 'false negatives' when an idea is judged to be unworkable but only because it does not fit into the markets or business model the company is used to. An exploitation route outside the company may then be the best way to generate value.

For most companies, however, Open Innovation means working with other organizations to find and develop new ideas for the existing business. The possibilities for collaboration range from simple subcontract, through joint development projects and licensing, to joint ventures, equity participation and acquisition.[44] This may involve acquiring ideas at the very early stage and developing them in-house; or taking them partly or fully developed. An increasing range of organizations exist[45] to help in these enterprises – ranging from patent brokers to contract design houses. For example, at the time of writing, the EU's Enterprise Europe network operates 240 offices in 33 countries with the sole function of linking providers of technology with potential users – free of charge; and see Mini Case 10.7 for how Philips successfully uses intermediaries to search for new ideas.

Managers must note, however, that Open Innovation forces companies to acquire new and difficult management skills.[46] For example, Corporate Venturing is not dissimilar to running a Venture Capital company, demanding a willingness to accept many failures for the sake of a few major successes, a philosophy that fits ill with the tight disciplines of large companies. And the collaborations between companies that are a central feature of open innovation are notoriously difficult to manage at the operational level; the particular issues being[47] how to handle intellectual property and how to accommodate the differences of expectation and culture between the parties. We cover this subject in more detail in Chapter 7. It is true to say that although the concept of Open Innovation is well established no paradigm has yet emerged for how best to manage the process itself. Nevertheless, many companies employ Open Innovation to great effect. Mini Case 4.7 on Microsoft and the Main Case of Chapter 9, on Sidler Automotive, are examples.

Mini Case 4.7

Microsoft – Open Innovation for the X Box[48]

Microsoft started work on the X Box games console in early 1999. The project was a combination of top-down direction from Bill Gates and his team, and a bottom-up initiative from games enthusiasts in the company. Microsoft faced a strategic threat that the TV would acquire processing and communications capabilities and eventually displace the PC and with it Microsoft's flagship, the 'Windows' operating system. Gates later said that in the strategic picture Microsoft needed twin pillars, with 'a PC in the den and an X Box in the living room'.[49]

But Microsoft had little competence in the design of many of the key elements that go to make up a games console, such as the audio and graphics chips that deliver the realistic pictures and sound on which the game depended. Nor did they have much experience in designing and manufacturing electronics hardware. Finally, although Microsoft already had a games division, they could expect to supply only a fraction (albeit a profitable one) of the games for the console. So, for a successful entry into this established and competitive market, Microsoft would have to assemble a coalition of suppliers, whose work would make or break the project. In such a fast-changing market, the chosen partners would have to be able to drive performance up and price down very aggressively. Sony had already shown the way: they forced the cost of their PlayStation down from $450 to $80 over 5 years by combining components

▶▶

and simplifying the design as technology progressed. And when the PlayStation 2 was launched, its graphics were 600 times better than those of its predecessor. Microsoft's job would not be easy.

Microsoft had one technical card to play: a suite of software called Direct X that made it easy to write games and other software for PCs. PCs come in a wide range of configurations with different processor speeds, memory sizes and peripherals. Direct X took care of the interfaces between the software and whatever hardware there was, and 'allowed game developers to make use of all the add-on gear that computers had gained without worrying about the particular mix[50].' Games developers would not have to learn a new set of programming techniques for each new generation of machine – as was the case, for example, with the PlayStation.

Microsoft's team approached all the major suppliers of PCs one by one, proposing they join the project as partners and handle the hardware. None found the business attractive because traditionally games consoles are sold at a loss and all the money is made on the games. So Microsoft now had to take full responsibility for the hardware; but they chose to subcontract the complete manufacturing task to an established contract manufacturer, Flextronics of Singapore who proposed to build two new factories to make the X Box, one in Mexico and one in Hungary.

The support of games designers inside and outside Microsoft was crucial for the success of the project. Even the choice of Nvidia as the maker of the vital graphics chip was heavily influenced by their preferences.

The launch date for the X Box was originally set for late in 2000 but it became clear that the performance that could be achieved at that time would not provide the impact that Microsoft, as a newcomer to the market, required. So it was decided to delay the project by a year to allow the use of Nvidia's next generation graphics chips and larger storage capacity.

Microsoft provided only the business and design concept, the finance, the styling, and the core operating software (not Windows, as it turned out). All the key components and the manufacturing were subcontracted. Microsoft would sell the hardware at a significant loss and generate income from its own games, and from a $7 license fee that it collects on games from third parties. The business plan forecasted a loss of $900 million, even if all went well, a price the company was prepared to pay to open up a new business area.

The X Box was launched in November 2001, 18 months after Sony's PlayStation 2 and 6 months after Nintendo launched their GameCube. By mid-2004, they had sold 14 million units, somewhat more than Nintendo's 13 million but well behind the 80 million sales of PlayStation 2.

The next round generation of games consoles looked like being a two-horse race between the X Box 2 and the PlayStation 3. But then Nintendo hit back with the Wii.

Strategic Issues

There can be great advantages in incorporating the cutting-edge capabilities of other organizations into one's service or product offering – indeed there may be little choice. But the loss of control that this implies may be a problem in the longer run. IBM's decision to outsource most of the components of its PC was hailed at the time as an object lesson in what was then called distributed innovation, and it certainly enabled them to move quickly into a market they had previously neglected. But in the long run it meant that they lost control of the design and they are now no longer a dominant player. Clearly it is important to have a robust strategy for collaboration and outsourcing.[51] Chesbrough, writing with David Teece of the University of California at Berkeley makes a distinction between *autonomous* innovations that affect only part of the product and *systemic* innovations that affect several parts of the design simultaneously.[52] Autonomous innovations can usually be safely and efficiently outsourced – the lamps on a car or transport to and from a hotel are examples. Systemic innovations, which on the other hand tend to relate to the architecture of the product and require coordination among several suppliers. These need to be directed by a single player, who in effect has control of the product itself. Supplier management for a supermarket and the power train of a car are examples of this. In general this implies that autonomous innovations may be outsourced but systemic ones should be kept in-house if possible. There are caveats however:

1. A company may not wish to relinquish control of an autonomous innovation if it is a particularly important competitive feature and the company has a special competence in it.
2. Control of systemic innovations is valuable only as long as the underlying design has a chance of emerging as a dominant design. Unlike IBM, Apple Computers retained control of the architecture of their product but lost out nevertheless because the PC architecture became the standard.
3. The value of controlling systemic features declines when these are no longer a source of performance improvement. An extreme case of this is mobile telephones, whose basic architecture is set by the internationally agreed system standard.

LINKING THE COMPONENTS OF STRATEGY

Roadmapping

In an effective strategic plan the components must be linked together in a coherent way that commands the understanding and engagement of all those involved. And it must clearly drive the actions that will make it happen. An effective way of achieving these aims is to construct a *roadmap*. This is a graphical representation of strategy that lays out and links the key aims of the organization, the means it will use to deliver them, and the new resources needed to make it all possible, in a single document. The roadmap format can be used as a way of presenting a strategy arrived at by other means, or as a vehicle for developing it. The map is typically structured in a series of layers representing the elements of the business issue being addressed, with links showing the dependencies between them. The horizontal axis is timing (too often missed out in so-called strategies!).

There are two main types of roadmaps. The first, which is often also the first step in a roadmapping process, is the Strategic Landscape, developed by Rob Phaal and colleagues at Cambridge.[53] This is used to explore the strategic situation facing an organization and identify the key issues that need further analysis. The map is simply a large sheet of paper divided horizontally into several layers which together represent all the significant aspects of the business that will remain important over the period being examined. These may be product lines, technologies, customer segments, competitors, core competences and so on. The horizontal axis is time. The team then considers each layer in term and populates it with the developments, possibilities and challenges that they expect at various times. They then look for links and influences between the layers and so identify key issues where innovative change may be called for. These issues are then taken away by smaller groups for closer analysis, as described below.

Some serious preparation is needed to make the process work well. In particular the layers of the map must be carefully chosen, to ensure that they represent all the continuingly important strands of the business. It is also helpful if a number of key players prepare a brief and structured presentation on the key issues facing the organization in the various layers in the short, medium and long term. These notes can be added onto the roadmap for reference.

Once a particular topic has been selected, a similar structure may be used to build a Roadmap to analyse and communicate a strategic proposal. The roadmap structure generally has far fewer layers than a Strategic Landscape and the emphasis will be on developing a coherent and structured approach to the issue, linking the main strategic goals to the activities necessary to make them happen. The upper level typically shows specific business aims such as a planned entry into a new market sector. Below this might be the physical or service products the company would need to achieve these aims; and below that the capabilities, resources or technologies it would have to develop to deliver them. Thus *know-how* (capabilities) is linked to *know-what* (products and services), *know-why* (aims) and *know-when* (timing). A simple and generic example is shown in Figure 4.10.

Describing their use in Rockwell Communications, McMillan[54] comments, 'Roadmaps are formal mechanisms for collecting data and sharing information in an open, partnering environment. Thus, roadmaps become knowledge-capture and communication tools for the company.' A roadmap is in many ways like a Gantt chart but at a rather high level of abstraction, the emphasis being on the logical structure and interdependencies rather than on completeness of detail.

The first consistent use of roadmapping in business was by Motorola and Corning in the 1980s.[55] The technique was adopted by a number of electronics companies in the 1990s, notably Philips[56], BP[57], Lucent and Hewlett-Packard, and this led to its use by communities of companies collaborating to plan the evolution of technologies for complete industry sectors. The roadmap for the semiconductor industry is perhaps the best known of these.[58] It has certainly been influential in guiding the progress of this industry. Subsequently roadmapping has been applied to even broader topics at the national level, such as the UK

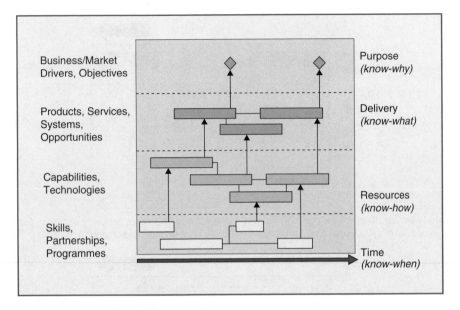

Figure 4.10 Generic roadmap structure

Source: Courtesy of R. Phaal.

Foresight activities for transport and other sectors,[59] and even in international politics.

The basic structure of the map can be varied in many ways to reflect the task in hand but it will usually retain the layered structure with links showing inter-dependencies. Roadmaps can be used for a variety of purposes, some of which are illustrated by the examples shown in Figure 4.11.

Building a Roadmap

The act of building the map is itself a learning process so it usually takes several iterations and much review before the plan settles down into a stable and accepted form. It is wise to do a rough draft quickly and refine and improve it as under-standing grows rather than to try and perfect each part separately before putting it all together. Much of the understanding comes from seeing the whole picture. Moreover, building the map takes a lot of effort and it is motivational to have an output early on so that participants can see the sense of what they are doing. Roadmaps gain much of their value from the process of review and critique.

In our experience representatives of all relevant technical and commercial departments must be involved because the purpose is to stimulate under-standing and debate about how the parts of the strategy work together; and ultimately to generate commitment to the plan. And it must have the active participation of the management team responsible for the aspect of the busi-ness under review. After all, the subject is nothing less than the future of their business.

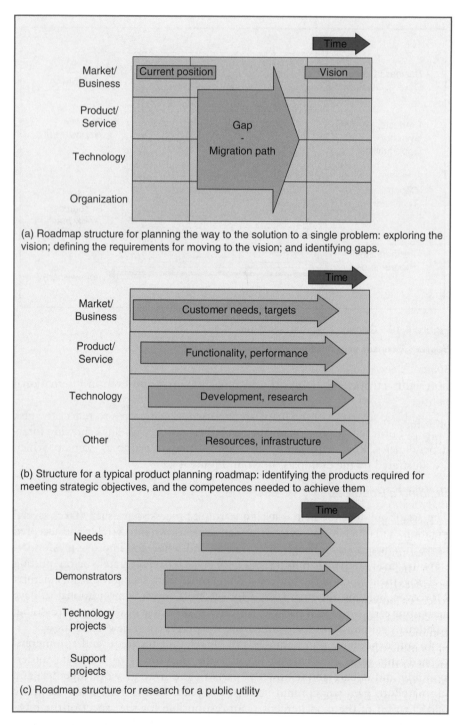

(a) Roadmap structure for planning the way to the solution to a single problem: exploring the vision; defining the requirements for moving to the vision; and identifying gaps.

(b) Structure for a typical product planning roadmap: identifying the products required for meeting strategic objectives, and the competences needed to achieve them

(c) Roadmap structure for research for a public utility

Figure 4.11(a-c)   A variety of roadmap formats

Source: Courtesy of R. Phaal.

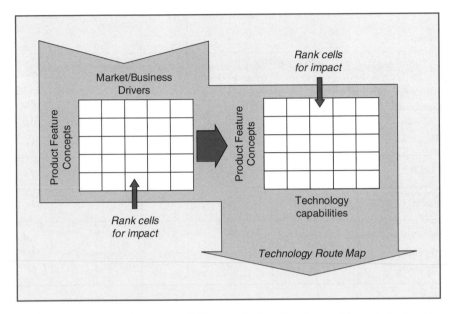

Figure 4.12   Cascaded matrices linking market and business drivers to technology requirements, via product features

Source: Courtesy of R. Phaal.

Although it is easy to imagine how useful a roadmap can be, getting started on it may not be so simple. Researchers at Cambridge University[60] have devised a quick way to generate a coherent 'first-cut' roadmap, which is particularly suitable for planning product or service strategy. The process consists of four stages, the first three of which are concerned with identifying the key market drivers, product features and technologies. A pair of *cross-impact matrices* is used as an analytical tool (Figure 4.12).

In the first stage, a prioritized set of market and business drivers is chosen. These are listed and given a weighting out of 10 according to the team's view of their importance.

In the second stage, participants consider the features or benefits of the product that drive competitive advantage. The first cross-impact matrix is used to check how well they support the key market and business drivers, using a process analogous to Quality Function Deployment (see Chapter 7 for a more complete description). Each feature is given a score according to the strength of its influence on each driver and these scores are multiplied by the weighting factor of the driver to give an overall score. This score shows how well that feature contributes to satisfying the set of drivers. This is a useful check that the right features have been chosen, and that all the drivers are addressed, but it is highly approximate so the precise rankings should not be taken too seriously. Any surprises should be carefully reviewed, though. This process is illustrated in Figure 4.13.

Driver Weight	4	10	2	6	6	10	8	4	
	Market Driver 1	Market Driver 2	Market Driver 3	Market Driver 4	Market Driver 5	Business Driver 1	Business Driver 2	Business Driver 3	Score
Feature 1	✓✓✓	✓		✓✓		✓✓✓	✓		72
Feature 2	✓	✓✓✓						✓✓	42
Feature 3			✓		✓✓✓	✓	✓		38
Feature 4	✓	✓		✓	✓	✓		✓✓	44
Feature 5	✓	✓✓✓		✓✓		✓✓✓	✓✓✓	✓	104
Feature 6	✓✓			✓✓✓		✓	✓✓	✓	56

Figure 4.13 Cross-impact matrix relating market drivers to product features in the first stage of the Quick-start process for product roadmapping

In the third stage, a similar analysis is done linking the product features (which now have weights derived from the first process) to the competences or technologies that the company has available. This shows what the critical competences are and how they contribute to the performance of the products, and so to the needs of the company and the market.

In the fourth stage, the information derived in the first three is used to generate a first roadmap. This is not an automatic process. The basic structure of the map – the key market events and their timing, the number of product lines and the frequency of new products and so on – are matters for top management judgement bearing in mind all the circumstances of the company and the market.

A useful starting point for the mapping session is for the participants to estimate what level of performance is achievable for each of the agreed product features at various times in the future. Extrapolation of past improvement trends, as we described earlier, is a useful tool to use at this stage. The team must also be aware of any possible limits to progress (are we reaching the top of an S-curve?) and, of course, must make some assumptions about what level of resources they can employ. In practice, the performances proposed are unlikely to be entirely acceptable, so the debate begins, trade-offs are made, and the team eventually homes in on a set of performances features that are both adequate and achievable. During the debate, managers should ask explicitly whether each feature is a Satisfier, a Performance feature or a Delighter in Kano terms; and more important whether they will continue to have the same status during the life of the map. Very probably, some features whose performance has driven success in the past may, with time, become mere Satisfiers. So it is worth establishing a vision for each feature: 'how far should we go with this?' 'can we envisage a time when it will no longer give us competitive advantage?' 'what new Delighters can we introduce to replace it?'

Keeping a Roadmap Alive

Roadmaps are sometimes used as a way of analysing individual issues, but more often they are intended to have a continuing life as part of the organization's strategy debate. If this is so then one cannot overemphasize the need to review and update regularly. There are four principal reasons for this. First, the world changes, often rapidly. A roadmap is not a page from an atlas but a sketch-map of a changing battlefield so the assumptions behind it are constantly being made obsolete by the march of events. The roadmap must adapt to new facts. Second, our own understanding of the world changes as we learn, think and debate with colleagues. The roadmap must adapt to new insights. Third, the process of thinking about strategy is more important than the strategy itself. Dwight Eisenhower wisely said: 'I have always found that plans are useless, but *planning* is indispensable' (our italics). Reviewing the roadmap deepens understanding and reinforces commitment to what has been agreed and so prepares us to meet the next challenge. Finally, old colleagues move on and are replaced with new. The act of reviewing the strategic roadmap with newcomers is an excellent way to acquaint them with the strategic thinking.[61]

Scenario Planning

The strategic planning techniques discussed so far in this chapter assume a certain level of predictability about the future. This may, of course, be an illusion. Scenario planning is a group of techniques designed to help organizations confront a future that contains significant unavoidable uncertainties and so may be quite unlike the present. The guiding principle is that although the future is unpredictable, cause and effect will still apply and this limits the range of possibilities. For example, a future in which global warming is a reality is pretty sure to have rising sea levels; a reduction in private motoring in the USA will certainly depress the motel business. So assumptions about a few key variables lead not to unlimited possibilities but to a restricted number of likely future states, or scenarios. Each of these is, in Michael Porter's words, 'An internally consistent view of what the future might turn out to be – not a forecast, but one possible future outcome'. Developing these scenarios opens the mind to alternative possibilities but in a disciplined way, seeking to:

- Understand the range of futures that might plausibly occur.
- Find indicators that can be used to give early warning of which scenario is evolving.
- Prepare the way, if only mentally, for possible disruptive changes.

- Avoid strategies that could be disastrous.
- If possible, find some strategies that are valid for all likely scenarios.

Scenario planning first arose after the Second World War, given impetus by the success of Operations Research. Its use in business was pioneered by Shell who used scenarios to examine what would happen if there were to be a political change in the Middle East leading to a sudden rise in the price of oil. This work did not allow them to predict the Yom Kippur war of 1973 but it left the company to some extent prepared for the price shock and able to react to it faster and more effectively than their competitors.[62]

Many scenarios have been developed to examine the impact of major geopolitical and social changes but they can be used on a smaller scale to examine the consequences of, say, the collapse of a competitor, a major regulatory change or a significant shift of customer behaviour.

Each scenario is a description of how the world would be if the uncertainties under consideration turned out in a particular way.[63,64] The scenarios are made as complete as possible and are presented in a colourful and compelling way so as to stimulate interest. The quality depends very much on the skill and knowledge of those participating in its definition. The key steps are as follows:

1. Identify the issues of concern and the timescale of interest.
2. Analyse the internal and external forces at work and agree on any assumptions to be made.
3. Identify trends in key factors and extrapolate to the chosen time.
4. Identify a small number (usually two or three) of high-impact developments whose outcomes are uncertain.
5. Consider all possible combinations of the key events. Reject any combinations that are incompatible or that contradict other assumptions.
6. Analyse the remaining scenarios in depth. Publicize and propose preparatory actions.

Figure 4.14 is a highly abbreviated summary of scenario work done in the 1980s looking at design criteria for future automobiles in the USA. Fuel price and consumer values were thought to be the major uncertainties influencing the kind of vehicles customers would want in the next two decades, and the combinations of these led to the four scenarios illustrated. This work was influential[65] in combating the assumption in Detroit that the big auto companies should continue with their policy of producing cars with only stylistic differences, for similar markets (a scenario called 'Long live Detroit'). At the time of writing (2009) it appears that the market is heading towards the opposite scenario ('Green Highways') faster than Detroit can move.

Managers using the technique emphasize that to be useful, scenarios must be carefully publicized and widely discussed in the company. Effective presentation graphics and attention-grabbing names for the scenarios all help to engage the debate and fix the issues in peoples' minds.

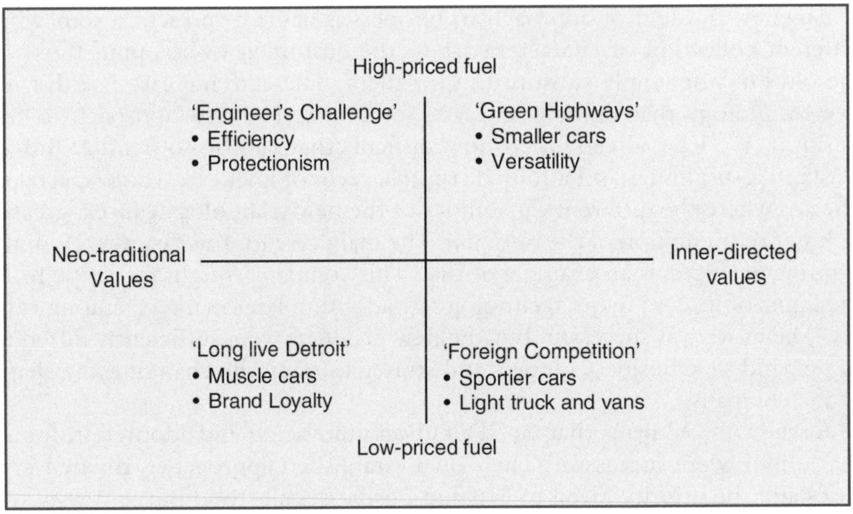

Figure 4.14   Scenarios for entry-level vehicle design Detroit 1980
Source: From Ringland 1998.

THE SUCCESS TRAP

A company that makes an innovative strategic change will itself be changed by the experience. As the new capability moves up its S-curve the competitive focus of the company typically moves away from dramatic service or product innovation towards improvements to business processes.[66] Financial, quality and manufacturing disciplines tighten; organization, capital investment and margins dominate management discussions. The disciplines of running a mature organization are very challenging and they become deeply embedded in the culture and thought patterns of the company. The trouble is that these habits can be quite wrong for handling something really novel. The most successful companies often find change most difficult because they have the most to change.

Indeed, in established companies the structure of the firm itself often comes to reflect the structure of the product it makes or the service it delivers and that may pose a huge barrier to radical change. Whole divisions of the organization may be formed to specialize in one module of the product. For example, Airbus makes the fuselage of its aircraft in France and the wing in Great Britain, a division of labour that has political as much as technical origins. Recently a radical new aircraft design was proposed, which is simply a flying wing with the passengers and cargo inside. Needless to say the proposal came from Boeing, not Airbus. It is almost impossible to imagine Airbus proposing, let alone developing, a concept that would destroy the very structure of the company. Any well-established company faced with a major change to the architecture of its product or service may face similar issues.[67]

Any new product or approach to business is liable to present a somewhat different collection of characteristics to the customer, overlapping those of the old but not simply substituting for them. The extreme case is a disruptive technology that, initially at least, forces a totally new approach to the business. We have already seen how difficult that can be to handle. But in between a sustaining and a fully disruptive technology lies a whole spectrum of cases where the different capabilities of the new technology cause a greater or lesser reorientation of the business. The main case for this chapter, Domino Printing Sciences, is an example of this. This company sought to escape from the limits of its core inkjet technology by adopting laser markers, among others. The move was successful but the new products were sufficiently different to demand new business models and strategies, radically changing the shape of the company.

A study[68] of 27 firms that faced a radical innovation and adopted it, found that only 7 were successful. Their own established approaches, divided loyalties and the priority given to existing businesses all stood in the way of the success they sought. Experience of spin-outs at Xerox[69] found that radical new activities kept within existing divisions seldom prospered because professional managers tried to force the new businesses to work within the patterns of the old. Hewlett-Packard had the same experiences with small disc drives.[70]

In summary 'An unhappy by-product of success in one generation of technology is a narrowing of focus and a vulnerability to competitors championing the next technological generation ... firms seem to fail by learning the lessons of survival in the short term too well'.[71]

SUMMARY

This chapter has covered the first element of the Pentathlon – innovation strategy. We have discussed the various factors, some subtle and some not so subtle, that demand innovative change. These have the common feature that they stem from the blocking of pre-existing routes to competitive advantage either through loss of scope for improvement or through satisfaction of market demand. This chapter has shown that

- An innovation strategy should identify and prioritize the needs for innovation, by examining the mismatch between the future as predicted and the future as desired.
- Innovation strategy must be an ongoing process not a single-point event.
- The need for innovative change often comes from slowly developing trends, which may be difficult to recognize and respond to. Among these are the Competence Ceiling, and Feature Fatigue (which opens the threat from disruptive technologies). Kano's analysis provides a useful structure for understanding these.

- Finding barriers such as intellectual property rights (IPR) to defend innovations from competition is very important, but strong complementary assets are required in the long run.
- As companies and competencies mature the focus of innovation moves from products and services to business processes.
- Organizations should choose the timing of innovations with care. Network and threshold effects can give advantages to earlier entrants.
- Roadmapping is a flexible way to formulate and communicate innovation strategy. Different formats are available for different strategic issues. Scenario planning can help in charting the more distant future.

MANAGEMENT RECOMMENDATIONS

- Understand the limits of your existing technologies or competences.
- Be clear whether these limits may put the organization at a competitive disadvantage.
- Be alert to the possibility that the market's demand for further improvements may be not as strong as it was. Avoid going further than required and find new sources of competitive advantage as the old run out.
- Consider early on how to defend your innovation from competition.
- Choose a competitive stance to each innovation: whether to shape the future, adapt to it, or reserve the right to play.
- Recognize how the management style and focus for success in established businesses are inimical to new ones. Set up separate activities for new businesses as far as possible.
- Plan well ahead, using tools such as roadmapping and scenarios that encourage participation from all concerned.

RECOMMENDED READING

1. Bower, J. L. and Christensen, C. M., 'Disruptive Technologies: Catching the Wave', *Harvard Business Review*, January–February (1995). [Summary of the theory of disruptive technology. Christensen has also written two books on the subject: *The Innovator's Dilemma* (1997) and *The Innovator's Solution* (2004).]
2. Teece, D. J., 'Profiting from Technological Innovation: Implications for Integration, Collaboration, Licencing and Public Policy', *Research Policy*, Vol. 15 (1986) pp. 285–305. [Seminal paper on the role of IPR and complementary assets in determining the distribution of advantage from innovations.]
3. Utterback, J. M., *Mastering the Dynamics of Innovation* (Boston, MA: Harvard Business School Press, 1996). [Covers the evolution of markets and technologies, and the concept of dominant design. Good case studies.]
4. Kim, W. Chan and Mauborgne, R., *Blue Ocean Strategy* (Boston, MA: Harvard Business School Press, 2005).

CASE STUDY
Domino Printing Sciences: Facing the Limits of Technology

Before reading this case, consider the following generic innovation management issues:

- How can companies recognize that their technology is facing a fundamental limit?
- Do such technological limits necessarily matter?
- What issues face a company adopting a new technology that fully replaces their current one?
- What issues face a company adopting a new technology that overcomes deficiencies of their current one but does not fully replace it?
- What problems may a single-technology company expect to face when it adopts new, overlapping products?

Domino was founded in 1978 as a spin-out from the technology consultancy Cambridge Consultants. Graeme Minto had led a project developing Continuous Inkjet (CIJ) technology for a client. Minto's client eventually lost interest but he believed the technology had promise so he licensed the know-how and set up on his own, working literally out of the garage of his home. The technology was not totally new: there had been academic work in the USA and Sweden in the 1960s; but only one company, Videojet in the USA, had yet applied it industrially.

Fortune favours the brave and by the early 1980s the company was prospering, helped by EU legislation requiring the date marking of perishable goods, an application for which CIJ was ideally suited. In 1985, Minto floated Domino very successfully on the UK stock market and set about handing over the reins to a new management team with experience in running large companies. He himself became chairman and after four years moved on to other things leaving a thriving company with a technology much in demand, albeit in specialist applications.

APPROACHING THE LIMITS OF TECHNOLOGY

It was in the early 1990s that Domino management started to be concerned about the restrictions that the technology itself would place on the growth of the company. As Howard Whitesmith, Domino's MD at the time commented:

> CIJ is a great printing technology. It's fully flexible, character by character; it can print at high speeds – up to 5 metres a second – and the drops fly up to a centimetre through the air. It's ideal for printing simple information onto products bouncing along a high-speed production line, like putting codes onto Coca Cola tins, for example. But it has serious limits: it's low resolution – well below what is acceptable on a printed page – and you can't make images more than about half an inch high. In fact as the characters get larger the printing speed goes down sharply [Figure 4.15]. By the end of the 1980s we'd made a lot of progress with better resolution and bigger images but it was becoming more and more difficult. The technical guys were quite clear that we were starting to push up against the laws of physics.
>
> The trouble is many of our customers already wanted to print larger characters, as well as images such as bar codes and logos but keeping the flexibility of non-contact printing. But

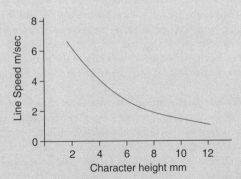

Figure 4.15 Relationship between maximum line speed and character height for continuous inkjet printing

we couldn't do it. And there were other things about CIJ that were less than ideal, such as the fact that we used solvent-based fluids. It's not as fundamental as the print size issue but here, too, we couldn't meet what our customers wanted.

The Domino board recognized that the fundamental limits on CIJ performance posed both a threat and an opportunity for the company. Without a new technology, Domino's rapid growth could soon come to an end. But there was obviously a demand for better performance if only it could be done. The big danger was that if a competitor moved in with something better Domino would not only miss out on a new business opportunity but could also lose many of its existing customers.

Meanwhile competition became more intense. As David Cope, Domino's operations director says 'In the 1980s we could still make regular improvements in product performance but in the 1990s there was less and less chance to keep a competitive edge in terms of the actual printing. These days the focus is on the quality and reliability of the product, and the back-up we give in service, distribution, and sales competence. And price, of course.'

THE SEARCH FOR NEW TECHNOLOGIES

During the 1990s, Domino staff looked for ways to print larger, higher-definition images onto moving products. 'It wasn't a big, concerted, project', says Steve Marriott, Domino's R&D manager at the time, 'We just all knew about the limitations of CIJ so we kept our eyes open for anything that might be better. We followed up magnetography, ion deposition and various kinds of contact printing such as mimeography. We even played with spraying a light-sensitive layer onto the surface and projecting an image onto it. But we didn't find anything that would replace and surpass CIJ'.

The nearest thing was 'binary' inkjet, a technology related to CIJ but using more than 100 jets for each inch of printing width instead of the single nozzle used in CIJ. This gave great printing speed and could be expanded to large printing widths. The equipment would be much more complex than Domino's existing products but there would be

▶▶

good applications in the commercial printing industry for addressing and personalizing magazines and envelopes, markets in which Domino already had some presence.

Another possibility was 'drop on demand', the technology used in desktop printers. This was a high-resolution technology and the print-heads could be stacked together to print large images. But it was slow, very sensitive to the distance from the print-head to the surface, and could print only onto paper or cardboard. Not a suitable technology for coding Coke tins.

A final possibility was laser marking. This works by rapidly scanning a small spot of laser energy over the product. It makes a mark by removing a layer (for example, of printed ink) and exposing the surface beneath; or by changing the colour of the surface itself. This technology would be fast, reliable and environmentally friendly but it wouldn't be suitable for all surfaces. One further drawback was that laser marking requires no ink, so Domino would forgo a very important source of revenue. Another was that nobody in the company knew much about lasers, either from a technical or from a marketing perspective.

The Domino board realized that there was no simple solution to their problem. No single technology would replace CIJ. 'I don't think we ever asked ourselves how many different technologies we might have to take on', says Whitesmith, 'we just took each one on its merits and made separate business cases'. Binary inkjet was easiest to decide because it was within the technical capabilities of the Domino R&D team, and there was a clear commercial demand for higher speed and higher resolution printing in the commercial printing market where the higher price would be acceptable. Developing binary technology proved more of a challenge than expected but Domino launched a product in 1997 which became successful and substantially replaced CIJ in the commercial printing sector.

Laser was clearly a case for acquisition. In 1994, Domino bought Directed Energy, a small laser company in California that had a unique small high-power laser tube already used in marking equipment. Domino's international distribution and knowledge of the marking market with Directed Energy's technical expertise allowed Domino to take the leading position in the expanding laser marking market.

Drop on demand proved more complex. Domino's technical team surveyed all the available examples in the early 1990s and found none that met their requirements. They adopted a 'watching brief' waiting for something suitable to be developed elsewhere. Eventually Xaar in UK and Spectra in USA, and others brought suitable print-heads to the market and Domino began to build them into products. They chose to act as integrators, selecting whatever type best suited each application.

THE DIFFICULTIES OF BECOMING A MULTI-TECHNOLOGY COMPANY

Within a few years Domino changed from being a single-technology company to one with a variety of technologies and products. The problem was that since none of the newcomers exactly replaced CIJ the company now had to handle four product lines with overlapping capabilities (Figure 4.16). 'To start with', says Whitesmith, 'we were very aware that the new technologies, especially laser, meant a big change and a big challenge to the company, especially to our distributors. So we set up separate divisions to drive the new products along, complete with their own sales forces. That

▶▶

didn't last long: it was too expensive and our customers were confused when they got calls from several Domino salespeople apparently in competition with each other. But most salesmen couldn't master the finer points of all the new products so they couldn't really sell them all properly.

We ended up with a hybrid arrangement where every salesman offered the complete range but they had local specialists in each technology to call on for support'.

Domino retained a divisional structure to give independence and focus to each product business. The CIJ-based coding and marking business continues to grow but the competitive focus is less on the product and more on price, quality, service and business processes. The newer technologies are still developing rapidly and their concentration is on new products and new applications.

	Cost (£)	Consumables	Reliability	Installation	Familiarity
CIJ	5,000–10,000	Yes	High	Difficult	High
Laser	12,000–20,000	Some	Very High	Easy	Low
Binary	20,000–30,000	Yes	Medium	Difficult	Medium
D.O.D.	5,000–12,000	Yes	Medium	Easy	Medium

Figure 4.16   Characteristics of Domino's new product range

Their management has to be correspondingly more exploratory and entrepreneurial. All the divisions still sell through the established sales channels but the newer technologies are also moving into new markets with new distribution. For example, lasers now sell into the semiconductor and clothing markets, entirely new ground for the company. Cope says this all makes for a more complex operation 'but that just reflects the real complexity of the markets and products'. By taking on new technologies to overcome the limits of its original one Domino has protected its existing customer base as it hoped. The new capabilities have driven them into new organizations and new markets that will change the very nature of the company.

GENERATING CREATIVE CUSTOMER-FOCUSED IDEAS

...chance favours only the prepared mind.

Louis Pasteur

INTRODUCTION

Companies that want to become better at innovation intuitively concentrate on generating more ideas through suggestions schemes and brainstorming. However, there is more to the second element of the Pentathlon than simply increasing the number of ideas generated by an organization. Innovation requires creativity, the application of knowledge, effective ways of recognizing customers' requirements and protection of the resulting ideas. Unfortunately, many of the commonly held views on creativity are incorrect. Too often creativity is simply perceived as 'completely new' ideas arising from 'eureka' moments. This overlooks the creativity required in solving known problems and the useful insights from the substantial research on individual and group creativity.

The potential contribution of customers and users in the search for innovative ideas should not be overlooked. Many researchers have recognized that customers are inept when it comes to articulating their needs. Therefore, it is necessary to move from traditional market research – which relies on direct questioning – to enhanced techniques, such as observation and indirect questioning. These can identify breakthrough ideas that either revitalize existing markets or create new ones.

In concentrating on ideas, creativity and knowledge this chapter aims to

- Explain how managers can enhance the levels of creativity in their organizations.
- Discuss the types of knowledge that are generated in organizations and how they can be harnessed to increase innovation performance.
- Give a detailed understanding of the best techniques for identifying customers' needs.
- Summarize the most effective ways to protect innovative ideas.

- Explain how the US company Texas Instruments manages creativity, knowledge and ideas.

CREATIVITY

Managers in both the service and manufacturing sectors 'need training if they are to be effective sponsors [of creativity and innovation]'[1] and should have an understanding of the following areas:

- The different types of business creativity.
- The factors which influence individual creativity.
- How group creativity can be managed.
- Key creativity techniques.

Types of Business Creativity

It is important to differentiate between business creativity and innovation. 'Business creativity is not only original thinking but also thinking that is appropriate and actionable'.[2] In other words, original thinking can lead to inventions but until these are commercialized, they do not become innovations.

There are three types of business creativity: *exploratory, normative* and *serendipitous creativity*. Exploratory creativity is closest to most people's understanding of creativity: the identification of new opportunities. It is 'unconventional thinking, which modifies or rejects previous ideas, clarifies vague or ill-defined problems in developing new views, or solutions'.[3]

In normative creativity, original thinking is used to solve known problems. Identifying problems which create real business opportunities is not easy. Problems are often articulated in a vague or indirect way. Therefore, an important task for managers is to identify and clarify the problems that their employees should focus on. Research has shown that a key part of innovation is solving the inevitable problems that arise in developing technological solutions to customers' needs.[4] Normative creativity is often required for process innovation, where customers are dissatisfied with service delivery, or a manufacturing facility that is not producing high enough quality. In the service sector the opportunities for normative creativity are enormous, as solving customer issues is a major catalyst for service innovation.

Serendipitous creativity acknowledges the role of accident and good fortune in, for example, discovering a new application for an existing idea. The most famous example is the 3M 'Post-It', where a glue that was being developed for permanent fixing failed but for which a very successful alternative use was found. Serendipitous creativity, by definition, cannot be managed easily, although looking for ideas from different sectors or bringing in experts from other fields can help because 'the best innovators aren't lone geniuses. They're people who can take an idea that is obvious in one context and apply it in not-so-obvious ways to a different context'.[5]

Knowing the three types of business creativity gives managers a greater ability to increase innovation. For example, asking employees for ideas for new products and services gives them an exploratory task, whereas specifying a customer problem that the product or service needs to solve gives employees a normative task (which is easier to respond to). Depending on the task involved, the most appropriate combination of individual and group creativity techniques can be selected.

Individual Creativity

Creativity can be the result of individual ideas, and in many organizations key individuals play an indispensable role. Individual creativity is a contentious subject in the academic literature. Some researchers take an *elitist* perspective and argue that most of the creativity in an organization originates from a few individuals. Others contend that creativity is a social process, and everyone has the potential to be creative under the right circumstances. We will discuss the factors that influence individual creativity and, then, how individuals' potential for creativity can best be unleashed in teams. The importance of linking individual to team creativity is well expressed in the following quote from a 2009 report from the Economist Intelligence Unit, 'Innovations may begin in the mind of a single individual, but if they are to generate valuable products or services they need to be developed by a community of thinkers'.[6]

From his extensive research, Mihaly Csikszentmihalyi a psychologist at the University of Chicago, stresses the importance of knowledge to make creativity possible. Both individuals and teams need experience, and access to relevant experts and information (*knowledge domains*) to be creative.[7] For example, in the complex field of pharmaceutical research, where hundreds of chemicals may be considered in the search for an effective medication, the volume of ideas being considered makes it necessary to have good data management – even highly talented individuals with good memories simply cannot remember all of the data that might be relevant. Similarly, with the growth of material being published, it is becoming increasingly difficult for scientists to have a grasp of more than their own specialized field. So, knowledge management is increasingly important to support creativity.

A myth has developed that individual creativity results from a flash of inspiration and the metaphor of the light bulb – invented by the American Thomas Edison – has become inseparable from creativity. However, one element of the metaphor is the instantaneous way a bulb lights and, for many, this stands for how creativity happens: without precedent, or planning. The view that creative ideas emerge spontaneously originates from the romantic era, where poems and other great works of art were credited by their authors to moments of inspiration (for example, Samuel Coleridge claimed that he wrote his famous poem Kublai Khan in one attempt), rather than through hard work over a period. Closer scrutiny of the many similar stories about spontaneous creativity shows them to be untrue (and earlier drafts of the poem were found in Coleridge's papers after his death). The quote at the beginning of this chapter from Louis Pasteur also indicates the role of knowledge and hard work in creativity, in contrast to pure serendipity.

Just as creative individuals are normally extremely knowledgeable and hard working, they might also be expected to exhibit definite personality traits. Much of the research looking for the typical traits of creative individuals is inconclusive and the search for *the profile* of a creative person is probably similar to alchemy. Csikszentmihalyi's work does show, however, that extremely creative individuals have 'complex personalities', by which he means that such people display contradictory traits. For example, they may switch quickly from being humble to being proud, introvert to extrovert, and traditional to being rebellious. This may make the job of managers harder but if this is the price to pay for more highly creative individuals, then it almost certainly is worthwhile. The work of Csikszentmihalyi and others shows that managers should nurture the creativity of their key individuals by

1. Giving them full access to the knowledge domain in which they are working. This means ensuring that company research scientists visit the leading conferences in their field and even allowing them to spend time at universities each year. In service, it would mean having key individuals visit leading service companies in other sectors, to gain a different perspective.
2. Motivating them to develop a passion for the subject on which they are concentrating.
3. Providing the time for them to immerse, even indulge themselves in the issues. Initially the process of creativity is divergent, when ideas, information and alternatives are being collected. Then the process becomes convergent, as some possibilities are rejected. Providing sufficient time is often a very difficult point because of the pressure for results in business. Managers need to be aware of the importance of avoiding extreme time pressure, as this is detrimental to creativity.[8]
4. Avoiding uncertainty. For example, the prolonged threat of a downsizing has a massive negative impact on personal creativity.[9]

Team Creativity and Culture

The level of creativity in an organization is not just dependent on individual creativity. Companies need to create a culture of creativity in which innovation project teams can excel. As this is intimately connected with the management of people (the fifth element of the Pentathlon) we will save our main discussion of this topic for Chapter 8 – Creating an Innovative Culture. The right culture for innovation is necessary; otherwise creativity levels will be low (see Mini Case 5.1 on PA Consulting). The vast majority of innovation projects involve teams. The lone inventor, striving to develop a successful product, is a rare phenomenon. (Although James Dyson, the inventor of the bag-less vacuum cleaner, worked in isolation on countless prototypes, before finding the right design.)

Research shows that nurturing team creativity is largely a question of avoiding barriers to creativity. Teresa Amabile of Harvard has conducted a number of studies and identified the key issues as

1. Matching the right group of individuals with the right challenge. Too often, the match of people to projects is poor, or the team is not diverse enough.
2. Giving teams the autonomy and the means to meet the challenge they are given but not the freedom to choose the challenge themselves.
3. Focusing discussions on defining the nature of problems; such discussions often lead to successful innovations.
4. Developing project strategy through discussions with the employees themselves, as this achieves 'buy-in'.
5. Making suitable resources available (including time and money). A certain amount of time pressure can be positive but team creativity plummets when unrealistic schedules set by management lead to mistrust and employee burnout.
6. Building teams with diversity, shared excitement in achieving the goals and a climate where the contribution of all employees is recognized.
7. Ensuring timely and appropriate supervisory encouragement. For example, if management takes too long to respond to team proposals, this has a negative impact on team motivation.
8. Guaranteeing support from the rest of the organization, particularly for innovation teams working under time pressure. Similarly, protecting teams from organizational politics is important.

Mini Case 5.1

PA Consulting Group – Tending the 'Garden' of Ideas[10]

'Creativity is a free spirit...it is an elusive subject to harness effectively into the delivery of business benefits'. With this philosophy, John Fisher, Technical Director of PA Consultancy Group's Technical Division manages nearly two hundred engineers, scientists and technicians in Cambridge, UK. The Division develops both product and process innovations for clients – organizations that often have encountered difficulties with product development projects. Fisher perceives his role as tending the 'garden' in which creativity can flourish. This requires leadership (including the communication of challenging goals); managing the politics to free the time for individuals to focus on the technical issues; providing excellent resources in terms of equipment, services and support; and providing access to information. The Division has been extremely successful in developing products and processes fast, even though this has often involved the solution of problems that others have failed to solve. As a result, the Division has been behind a number of hugely successful product innovations for well-known companies.

Researchers warn that very strong company cultures – *cults* – can decrease creativity.[11] Pressure for uniformity or elitism can block creativity, especially openness to others' ideas. At the team level, management must avoid *groupthink*, when a team develops an unrealistic view of the issues and disdains opposing views. Strong leadership can make groupthink more extreme.[12]

Team diversity helps creativity. Process innovation in manufacturing companies has largely been the responsibility of quality teams. Groups of manufacturing employees meet regularly to identify opportunities for improving the efficiency of processes. However, if the group consists only of manufacturing people, the ideas generated may be too narrow. For this reason, the JCB company which designs and manufactures earth-moving equipment (with manufacturing operations in the UK and Savannah Georgia) always includes representatives from other functional areas in their manufacturing quality meetings. For example, a sales representative is responsible for stimulating discussion on which of the process improvements being considered is likely to have a direct positive impact on customers.

Creativity Techniques for Innovation

Many creativity techniques can be used during innovation projects. The choice of which technique is most appropriate depends on the type of creativity needed (for example, normative or exploratory), and the number of individuals involved. J. Daniel Couger from the University of Colorado describes 22 creativity techniques, with recommendations as to whether they are best used with individuals or teams, and whether they can be used for exploratory or normative creativity.[13] The constant use of just *brainstorming* can lead employees to lose interest and so it is disappointing to learn that a major survey of executives still found that brainstorming was still the most popular technique for generating ideas.[14] So companies that are aware of the different techniques have two advantages: they can choose the most suitable techniques to match the issue at hand and provide variety.

Arthur Koestler wrote a classic book on creativity in the 1960s and his central premise provides a useful tool for innovators.[15] When we think, we do so using frames of reference – using particular ways of thinking (rules, habits, associative contexts and so on) that have been useful in the past. These are the mental equivalent of the physical reflexes and movements, which our bodies apply, unconsciously, to particular situations. Frames of reference and physical reflexes are highly efficient tools but can be difficult to shake off. According to Koestler, the creative act is bringing a new, previously un-associated, frame (F2 – Figure 5.1) to bear on a topic with an existing frame of reference (F1). Frames of reference are similar to the philosopher Thomas Kuhn's concept of paradigms: patterns and rules that define boundaries, and shared sets of assumptions. Creativity techniques bring a new frame of thinking and we will discuss five techniques that can be very helpful for innovation projects.

Brainstorming

The original and most widely known creativity technique is brainstorming, which was developed in the 1950s for use with groups. A group of people are

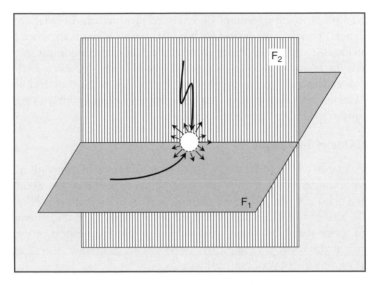

Figure 5.1   Creativity as the Intersection of Two Different Frames of Reference

asked to describe any ideas that come to mind as solutions to a problem (normative creativity), or as opportunities for new products, services of businesses (exploratory creativity). The ideas are written on a flip chart where everyone can read them and one idea leads to another. An experienced moderator typically records the ideas and reflects these back to the group to stimulate further discussion. The evaluation of each idea is suspended during the idea collection phase, so that potentially good ideas are not prematurely rejected (thus avoiding 'it will never work' judgements). An appropriate use of brainstorming would be, for example, to identify the reasons why certain customers are unhappy with a product whereas others are very satisfied.

Brainstorming is based on the assumption that people are naturally creative and that by deferring judgement on the quality of ideas until a sufficient quantity has been collected, means that some really good ones can be selected. One limitation of brainstorming is that certain people may dominate the discussion and so in the more effective variation *brainwriting,* ideas are written down by individuals before they are shared with the group.

Left-Right Brain Alternations

This technique ensures a 'whole-brain' approach to identifying an opportunity or solving a problem. Typical left-brain functions include speaking, writing, calculating, logic and deliberating, and so on. In contrast, our right brains control our abilities for intuition, spatial perception, art and visualization. A creativity task can be formulated to drive thoughts from both our left and right brains and two columns on a flip chart are used to summarize the contrasting ideas.

For example, the improvement of a service product can be analysed from a left (analytical) perspective, asking such questions as: What is the core product? How quickly is it delivered? What are the key performance indicators? In contrast, the right brain (emotional) approach would lead us to ask questions such as: How does the customer perceive our service? How do they feel about the service? The contrast between the insights gained from the left and right brain focused questions help to generate new ideas.

Five Ws, One H Technique

This is a versatile technique that can be used at all stages of innovation. It helps enhance our understanding of a problem or an opportunity by asking 5 'W' questions ('who', 'what', 'where', 'when', and 'why'?) and one 'H' ('how'?). Specific W and H questions are developed for the topic and the answers to the Ws tell us more about the issues. The answer to the H question provides ways to implement the ideas generated by the Ws. The technique is very useful for investigating reports of product problems.

A medical electronics company received a limited number of complaints that a widely sold blood pressure measuring device was not working properly. Investigation using the Five Ws One H technique helped understand the problem better. The 'where' and 'why' questions prompted an analysis of what was different about the hospitals that were filling complaints, compared with the majority of hospitals that had no problems. It emerged that the device worked well, except if the patient was shivering. The hospitals making complaints were found not to heat their recovery rooms (where patients are placed following operations), as a warm ambient temperature slightly slows the recovery from an anaesthetic. Most hospitals heat their recovery rooms to near normal room temperature. The H question was: how can the device be made to work when the patient is shivering? The answers to this led to improvements in the device and accurate blood pressure measurements in all conditions.

Mini Case 5.2

Nokia – Going to the Gemba[16]

One of the world's leading manufacturers of mobile telephones, Nokia, has recognized the importance of observation in understanding customer culture. The UK operation that is responsible for developing some of the company's products was aware that the Japanese market has different characteristics. Rather than employing a market research company, management decided that it was important for members of the new product development team to see the issues first-hand. Therefore, sales, marketing, R&D and managers were all paired up with Japanese colleagues. These pairs observed Japanese people using mobile phones in public places and gathered opinions, which meant that issues such as the delicacy of approaching people on the street had to be considered.

In Japanese quality management, the word *Gemba* means, 'where things actually occur; it is raw, untainted information'[17] and it is used to stress that managers must spend sufficient time on the production floor, if they are to learn how to improve production efficiency. Nokia's use of the term *Gemba* is analogous to the way anthropologists talk of *the field*.

Sending new product development employees into the Gemba to conduct the market research had the advantage of widening commitment but most of the employees were not experienced in market research. Therefore, Nokia produced a 'Training Guide' for the team: this consisted of an introduction to the objectives of the research; an explanation of the importance of the Gemba, guidelines for observation; guidelines for approaching and interviewing people; and obtaining volunteers for focus groups. Following the procedures in the Guide, Nokia employees collected photographs of the locations where they made their observations; the answers to a semi-structured questionnaire (a contextual interview) and short field notes following a set format.

The Nokia case demonstrates three important issues. First, the importance of having market research conducted by the NPD team and not just by a market research company. Second, the need to provide clear guidelines for the team involved, to ensure that observations are conducted systematically and consistently. Third, the reluctance of Japanese people to voice their opinions to strangers shows that cultural issues need to be addressed.

From the information that Nokia have published, it appears that the primary limitation of their research was that those involved had no previous experience of systematic observation. Although the Training Guide was prepared, it is difficult to learn systematic observation without practice. Inexperienced researchers can learn much more from working with skilled observers who are coding video tapes of consumer behaviour. An important part of any ethnographic research project can be the training of the team. Often the best way is to have the most experienced researchers make the first visits and use the data collected as an intricate part of training of the rest of the team.

Attribute Association

Attribute association can be used to solve a known problem with a product, process, or service (normative creativity), or identify new opportunities (exploratory creativity). The starting point is to create a list of the attributes of the product, service or process. This can be based on a company's internal views, or it can be based on market research exposing the customer's perception. For a vacuum cleaner, the list of attributes would include the ability to clean carpets, smooth surfaces, stairs, corners, and so on, plus other factors such as the manoeuvrability, design, and so on. Each of the product, service or process attributes is then reviewed using one or more of the approaches summarized in Table 5.1[18]: for example, can a useful attribute be multiplied?

The process of reviewing and modifying the attributes requires practice and there are no hard and fast rules for which of the approaches given in Table 5.1 is the most appropriate for a particular service or manufactured product. Complex products will most benefit from subtraction or task unification. Of course, the review of product attributes does not simply have to be conducted internally; observing users can give other insights (see Mini Case 5.2 on Nokia).

Table 5.1 Modifying Attributes

	Approach	Explanation	Service and Manufacturing Examples
1)	Modifying the nature of attributes	Also called *product morphology analysis*, this approach takes the main product attributes and sees how these can be modified.	• Home insurance normally covers the costs of repairs. The German Allianz Group has gone further and offers a home 'breakdown' service, with fast call-out of qualified tradesmen guaranteed for any household problem (see Mini Case 4.1). • Originally, domestic coffee machines had a simple glass pot to hold the freshly brewed coffee. However, companies such as Braun have changed this attribute to a vacuum flask, which keeps the coffee warm until needed.
2)	Subtraction or simplification of attributes	Removing certain attributes may simplify a product and make it more attractive to certain segments. This is an attempt to prevent what some writers have called *feature creep* – the tendency for development teams to always add more features to products.	• Some mobile telephone companies have successfully marketed a 'receive calls only' contract, which is popular with parents who want to be able to contact their children but do not want them making outgoing calls. • Not every subtraction attempt will be successful or positively perceived by customers. For example, the colourless Crystal Pepsi failed when it was introduced to the market in 1993.
3)	Multiplication of attributes	An existing product attribute is copied and offered, with a modification of the function of the repeated attribute, multiple times in the product. The multiplication leads to a specific benefit.	• A classic example is the Mach 3 razor from Gillette. The three blades all cut but the first two, which are set at different angles, drag across the skin to raise the beard for cutting by the second or third blade. • A service example is Europcar's multiple rental agreement. Busy executives can purchase rental agreements, for example, five days a month but these can be multiple rentals, such as one-day at five different airports.
4)	Division of attributes	This essentially looks at the product architecture and how physical or functional components are grouped together.	• In the automotive sector 'mechatronics' (the combination of software-driven electronics and mechanical components) is making a big impact. Companies such as DaimlerChrysler are moving previously mechanically controlled functions into software, to optimize vehicle performance. • DialA Flight, an Internet retailer of travel and tourism services, has carefully divided its service augmentation between its website and its call centre to give a personalized service (see Mini Case in Chapter 3).
5)	Unification of attributes	Assigning new functions to existing attributes. This can, for example, also lead to simplification.	• The US lawnmower manufacturer Toro has designed a cutting blade that circulates and cuts grass into much smaller pieces. Therefore, the pieces can be left on the lawn and the need for a grass-box has been removed. Effectively, a mixture of task unification and simplification.

Source: Goldenberg, J., Horowitz, R., Levav, A. and Mazursky, D., 'Finding Your Innovation Sweet Spot', *Harvard Business Review*, Vol. 81, No. 3 (March 2003), pp. 3–11; Altshuller, G., *And Suddenly the Inventor Appeared* (Worchester, MA: Technical Innovation Center Inc, 1996) and supplemented by examples collected by the authors.

TRIZ

No discussion about the use of innovation and creativity tools and techniques would be complete without stressing the value of TRIZ, a creative form of problem-solving developed by the Russian Genrich Altshuller.[19] The acronym TRIZ is based on the four Russian words for the Theory of Inventive Problem Solving. Altshuller, who worked in the Moscow patents office, based his ideas on his study of patents, and the work has since it started in the 1940s analysed over 2.8 million international patents.

Patents document how particular problems are solved and looking at large numbers of patents allows particular patterns to be identified. First, patents can be grouped by the generic problem they are solving – for example, an automotive patent might be specifically concerned with engine temperature control but at a generic level it is concerned with cooling. Altshuller grouped patterns by generic problems and found that, based on the underlying physical properties of materials, there are typically a limited number of ways to solve a particular problem. So the first advantage of a TRIZ database is that engineers involved with finding a specific problem can look up all the generic ways to approach the issue. In this way, rather than relying on brainstorming (which is dependent on the knowledge around the table), problem-solving based on a TRIZ database ensures that no possible solution is forgotten and provides example ways that problems have been solved (in example patents). In explaining TRIZ we often say that using the database provides ready access to the knowledge of previous generations of scientists and engineers.

The second advantage of TRIZ is that design trends can be identified and so opportunities for improvement can be spotted. For example, design tends to start with straight lines and forms and, over time, more complex lines and emerge. Comparing the type of products in a particular industry against these trends can bring useful ideas. The Mars group uses TRIZ regularly and a good example is the packaging of the ubiquitous Mars Bar. The wrapper used to have straight lines and was sealed like a parcel. Consequently, it was awkward to open. Nowadays, the ends of the wrapper have a serrated edge, which means that they can be torn open easily.

The third way that TRIZ helps is by providing insights into how *design trade-offs* can be managed. Say for example, a particular component needed to be strengthened to withstand wear but could not be heavier. TRIZ matrices allow designers to look at the ways in which this particular trade-off and many others have been solved previously. Once again, the theory of creative problem-solving provides access to a body of knowledge summarizing millions of inventions. Somewhere, sometime, the technical problems facing a product development team have been solved previously and so learning from this can be quicker and more effective that starting from scratch.

The Cold War led to TRIZ being largely unknown in the West until relatively recently. Now, it is being widely applied as a way of finding quicker solutions to product design problems. Slowly TRIZ is also being adopted into the service domain,[20] although currently there are no comprehensive databases of ideas available as there are for patents.

MANAGING KNOWLEDGE

Csikszentmihalyi's work showed that creativity is dependent on knowledge. Over the past 20 years much has been written on *knowledge management* – how an organization can stimulate and effectively utilize knowledge. From this vast field, we have selected two topics that we think are fundamental for those responsible for managing innovation. These are the nature of knowledge, and how knowledge can be captured and transferred.

Nature of Knowledge

Knowledge has two main forms: *explicit* and *tacit*.[21] Explicit knowledge (which is also known as *articulated*; or *declarative knowledge*) is formal and systematic, easily communicated and shared. It can be *codified* – summarized in a written or symbolic format that can be easily shared. Examples of explicit knowledge are instructions manuals, textbooks and service operations or manufacturing *standard operating practices* (SOPs). In contrast, tacit knowledge is hard to express, formalize or write-down. It is highly personal, often based on individuals' mental models (which they may not even be aware of themselves), and is usually taken for granted.

A common illustration of tacit knowledge is the master craftsman who can create a perfect artefact but cannot readily explain all of the steps taken, or the particular ways the materials are chosen, formed and worked. Master craftsmen have a high level of knowledge, most of which is not written down. Tacit knowledge is practical, context specific, and not easily shared as it is 'in the heads' of certain individuals. It can be very valuable to a company, as it is difficult to copy but, since it resides with individuals it is lost if they leave. Another example of tacit knowledge is the experienced cook who has a favourite dish that he or she can cook without weighing the ingredients or timing the stages of cooking. In order for the dish to be cooked by someone else, the recipe needs to be prepared, and the timings, weights and other details codified. Customers' tacit knowledge of how they use products can lead to breakthrough products (see Mini Case 5.3 on Miele).

The two types of knowledge reside in various locations within an organization. Databases, computer systems, publications and the Internet are repositories of explicit knowledge. Sometimes, however, what tends to be stored is information as opposed to knowledge. Information alone, without interpretation, recognition of its validity or experience is of limited use. Also, the sheer volume of data can sometimes limit its usefulness. In contrast, tacit knowledge resides with individuals, their expertise and heuristics ('rules of thumb'). Stimulating interaction between such individuals, including discussions on their 'routines for doing things' is a way for managers to stimulate tacit knowledge.

Mini Case 5.3

Miele – Listen and Watch Teams[22]

The mother was observed carefully 'hoovering' her child's mattress three times. When asked why, she said, 'Because then I know it's clean'.

Seizing an opportunity is what a German household products manufacturer has done in recognizing the influence on their markets of the growing number of people with allergies. The Miele company has introduced a vacuum cleaner that indicates when the floor being cleaned is dust-free. A hygiene sensor at the nozzle has a 'traffic light' indicator, which turns from red, through amber, to green as cleaning progresses. This sensor is a breakthrough feature for the increasing number of people who have allergies: because it allows the user to know when a room really is clean, or that an allergic child's mattress is free of dust and house mites have been eliminated. Interestingly, the feature was not developed in response to an explicit customer request. Rather, it was the subtle recognition that people with allergies spent more time cleaning; often vacuuming several times just to be certain a child's room was dust-free.

The market research behind this product was conducted in close cooperation with the *Deutscher Allergie- und Asthmabund* (German Allergy and Asthma Foundation – DAAB), an association for people with allergies. Through an innovative approach to its market research, Miele not only recognized the need for a hygiene sensor but also identified an important new opportunity: products specifically designed for people with allergies. People with allergies also have to be careful with their washing. Consequently, Miele has introduced a new washing machine, which has a special programme for washing pillows and a rinsing process to remove detergent residues. In addition, a tumble drier has been designed to minimize static electricity, as it exacerbates allergies.

Both these products were based on market research and ideas generated from working closely with the DAAB and customer groups. As Olaf Dietrich, Marketing and New Product Development Manager Vacuum Cleaners says: 'We are in regular contact with users and have a "listen and watch" philosophy at Miele. By this we mean that we realize that it is essential for not only marketing but also engineers to actually see the issues first-hand. Only if you are present do you really understand the issues'. The links established with the DAAB and other similar organizations also mean that Miele has established a lead over its competitors and is making its innovations harder to copy.

Core to Miele's approach is regular and intensive customer contact and the application of marketing and technical knowledge. 'For us, market research is all about understanding the customer's real problems. Once we have identified these, we use cross-functional teams to determine suitable solutions', says Mr Dietrich.

To manage tacit knowledge to support innovation, four recommendations can be given:

1. R&D and other managers involved in new product development need to ensure that the learning from innovation projects is identified. Lists of lessons learnt can help but promoting informal interactions between teams and departments can spread the knowledge more effectively.

2. Certain key solutions, approaches and the like will need to be documented in a way that the organization does not lose vital information if individuals leave.
3. Customers' tacit knowledge needs to be recognized and captured.
4. When certain individuals have tacit knowledge that is vital, companies need to ensure that it is shared with colleagues.

Capturing Tacit Knowledge

A leading researcher in the field of tacit knowledge has been Ikujiro Nonaka of Hitotsubishi University in Tokyo.[23] He recognized the importance of making tacit knowledge accessible, particularly in R&D settings, and identified transfer mechanisms such as *socialization* and *externalization*.[24] Tacit to tacit knowledge transfer is called socialization. The most commonly quoted example is the apprentice who over several years learns from the master through observation, discussion, and trial and error under the master's supervision. Once the apprentice has learned, their knowledge is also largely tacit. In an organization, managers can promote socialization by creating a work environment in which less experienced employees observe and learn from their most experienced colleagues. For example, some R&D departments have new project managers 'shadow' senior colleagues.

An example of converting tacit knowledge to explicit knowledge is music. Troubadours, the travelling medieval musicians, learnt both their music and texts through apprenticeships, travelling for years with older musicians. However, the sponsorship of Pope Gregory led to the development of an effective written notation. This enabled the spread of songs and music including the chants, which are consequently called Gregorian. Further developments such as the metronome allowed accurate capture of how fast the composer intended a piece of music to be played. Externalization is the name given to the process of converting tacit to explicit knowledge and this may require the development of new symbols and methods of codification, as was the case with music. Individuals with tacit knowledge may be reluctant to support the process of externalization because of the time required for this task. Evotec OAI, a German-owned provider of chemical services to the pharmaceutical sector, found that arranging informal weekly tutorials where their top scientists explained how they had solved specific problems, allowed experience to be externalized and passed on to newer colleagues. (This is also much easier than asking the most experienced scientists to document their knowledge in writing.) Metaphors, analogies and models are often effective means by which insider knowledge can be made understandable for outsiders. Our own research shows that engineers' knowledge can be stimulated by having them base their discussions of problems around metaphors and stories.[25]

Another key concept of knowledge management is *Communities of Practice* (CoPs). These are groups of people who share a common context to their work, use common practices, share identities and can provide the social context for transfer of knowledge across organizational boundaries. For example, engineers form a community with a common background, similar experiences and ideas that can make the communication between engineers in different organizations more effective than between engineers and marketing people within one organization. CoPs are important as they can be viewed as the means by which companies can profit from their employees' exchange of knowledge with broader communities. For example, the ideas for a 'Graphical User Interface' passed through the community of engineers from the Xerox Corporation to Microsoft, where they finally were implemented in the ubiquitous Microsoft 'Windows'. Hallmark Cards, the US greeting-card company,, has created what it calls 'customer communities of practice'.[26] Ideally, about 100–150 interested customers are linked via a website and encouraged to exchange ideas, comments, experiences and diaries. Hallmark's approach is a useful example of how Internet technology is being used to stimulate customer ideas. Similarly, Beiersdorf the German company which developed Nivea skin care products, uses its website to collect ideas directly from consumers and the idea of using virtual communities to improve NPD is gaining popularity.[27]

Capturing tacit knowledge from key employees is important, as is tapping customers' tacit knowledge on products and services. This latter point will be discussed later in this chapter, as we describe how to develop deep customer insights. Once knowledge has been captured, it needs to be transferred appropriately, to support innovation.

Promoting Knowledge Transfer

Both internal and external tacit knowledge can be helpful in innovation. The knowledge that certain individuals, or groups of individuals, hold can be important in solving problems, be it technical or commercial. Customers have tacit product knowledge that needs to be tapped using sophisticated market research techniques. Although it is intuitively easy to understand what tacit knowledge is, it is more difficult for managers to take advantage of tacit knowledge that is internal to a company, or external.

An anecdotal study of product design consultants IDEO in California showed that it brokered knowledge through four steps.[28] First, by bringing together people with knowledge of different markets, countries, products and technologies, the chance of unique ideas emerging is higher. Second, ideas need to be kept alive and providing easy access to information is important but simple Internet databases are not sufficient. Collections of tangibles, prototypes, toys and multitudes of other items are kept prominently in the company's offices, to remind people of ideas and stimulate further ones. Third, IDEO focus on creating new uses for old ideas. Fourth and finally, constant testing using prototypes will show what works and what can be commercialized.

The best-known theoretical contribution to the knowledge management debate is organizational learning. This is 'the capability, which enables an organization to acquire and process new information on a continuous basis to elevate knowledge and improve decision making'.[29] Peter Senge[30], an expert on organizational learning, identifies five key elements of learning organizations. They

1. Promote and value the *personal mastery* (expertise) of individual employees. Recognition of individuals helps generate a high level of commitment to the organization and its learning.
2. Develop *mental models*, which illustrate the way in which an organization and its processes work. Drawing and discussing key processes helps discover new ways of thinking.
3. Promote *team learning*, so that teams continuously adapt successful practices from other teams, both internal and external to the organization.
4. Have a *shared vision*, which is the collective form of personal mastery. This stimulates the organization's learning, which is only possible if it deeply matters to employees.
5. Utilize *systems thinking*, the ability to understand the cause and effect relationships inherent in organizational processes. It is the cornerstone of organizational learning and interlinks the other four elements.

As more becomes known about tacit knowledge and its generation and transfer, it is likely that managers will be provided with more concrete tools and approaches.

IDEAS AND INNOVATION

Innovations often fail. One study found that 34 per cent of new product developments do not fully reach their business objectives,[31] another study found the figure to be 90 per cent.[32] These studies clearly show that new products must be differentiated from existing ones. So product innovation is challenging and so is process innovation.[33] Companies that are successful at selling and implementing process innovations (for example, production line equipment) have been found to interact more intensively with their buyers.[34] Service products without original features (either in the service product or augmentation) have high instances of market failure. So, in product, service and process innovation it is essential to obtain effective customer input through market research.

Identifying Customer Needs – Traditional Approaches

Traditional market research uses *surveys*, *focus groups* and direct questions to obtain customers' inputs. However, customers and users may not be able to recognize or articulate their needs, as their ability to comment on the products and services is limited by their prior experience. Requirements that customers find difficult to articulate are termed *hidden needs* (or *emerging needs* or *latent needs*). Increasingly companies have found that traditional approaches lead to disappointment, as the output of such market research leads to incremental improvements rather than the breakthroughs that management hopes for.[35] The importance of new approaches to understanding customers has also been found in the service sector.[36]

In surveys, current knowledge of products, markets and customers is used to frame the questions to be asked and a suitable sample is determined. In selecting a sample, companies strive to identify a representative group of customers whose answers will be indicative of the whole market. It should be noted that in some markets the customers and users may be different persons and, in addition, the purchase decision may not be made by a single person but rather by what is called the *decision-making unit* (DMU) – this can consist of several people. In business-to-business markets particularly, the DMU can be complex as the individuals involved can have different expectations and requirements. Survey methodology is well known and will not be discussed here. Suffice to say that the design of a good questionnaire is not easy and, to be effective, questionnaires need to be *piloted*. For an overview of the crucial aspects of designing and using questionnaires, refer the classic texts on the subject by Oppenheim[37] and Dillman[38].

Focus groups are small groups of customers or users who have sufficient experiences in common to discuss a specific topic, related to products or services.[39] Normally, they are invited to meet at a neutral location, the discussion topic is introduced and visual examples of the subject matter are often on display. The discussion is stimulated with a broad question posed by the moderator, who also ensures that all participants contribute equally, and that all topics are discussed. Focus groups mix survey and interview techniques with, often, observers being hidden behind a two-way mirror. Video recordings may also be used. Once the data have been collected, the analysis of surveys or focus groups leads to a list of product attributes required by customers. Traditional methods are useful but they need to be combined with techniques to identify hidden needs.

Hidden Needs Analysis

The recognition of the limitations of surveys and focus groups has led to a range of enhanced techniques, which we will collectively term *hidden needs analysis* and Figure 5.2 shows how these techniques can be used in combination. The first point to note is that an organization consciously decides that it wants to identify radical product attributes and not just incremental ones. This decision means that, in addition to the traditional survey and focus group research, techniques such as *repertory grid analysis, empathic design* and *lead users* can be used in combination.

Ideas should be tested early on and in a practical way. Once potential product attributes have been identified, simple prototypes can be tested with customers and users. Such approaches allow intense interactions with customers; *experimentation, rapid prototyping* and attribute association all allow ideas to be further enhanced by obtaining customer reactions. This, in turn, leads to better product definition and then these product attributes can be prioritized using *conjoint analysis*. As shown by Figure 5.2, hidden needs analysis should lead to more

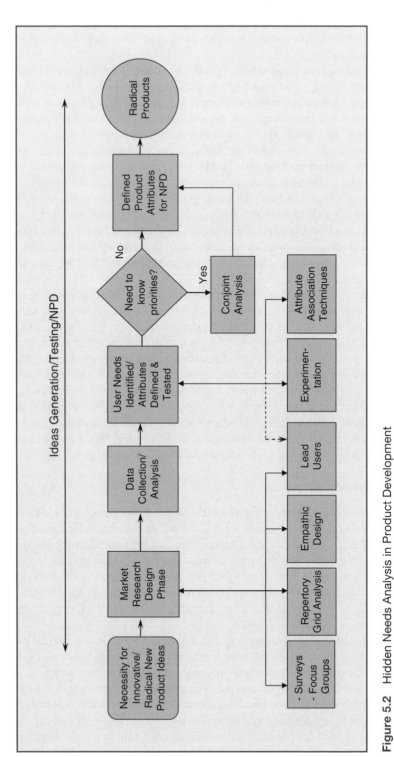

Figure 5.2 Hidden Needs Analysis in Product Development

radical products but there are no guarantees. There are an increasing number of published examples where companies have based successful product innovations on addressing hidden needs that they have identified (but this is an area where there is an urgent need for researchers to investigate how often such approaches lead to breakthrough products).

Surprisingly, the adoption of enhanced market research techniques has been slow. A survey of 70 Finnish companies producing business-to-business products showed the usage to be very low: 58 per cent of respondents do not use any technique and 27 per cent use only one technique.[40] The reasons these companies do not use innovative approaches to market research were management did not have the resources and perceived the data difficult to collect and analyse. Specialized consulting companies, such as IDEO in California, and PDD and WhatIf! in London, are the vanguard. We will look at each of the enhanced techniques in detail starting with repertory grid technique, so as to understand their potential for discovering hidden needs.

Repertory Grid Technique

Repertory Grid Technique is a powerful market research tool for identifying customer needs. The technique was developed for use in psychology. It enables interviewees to articulate their perceptions on products and services and taps their tacit knowledge. The technique is a structured form of interviewing which leads to a matrix of quantitative data – the *repertory grid*. Surprisingly, even though the potential of the technique has long been recognized, it is seldom used. This is partly due to the skills that an interviewer needs to conduct interviews.

To understand how the technique works, consider how an information technology (IT) service provider might use it. Such providers install and maintain computer networks for companies, including such tasks as upgrading personal computers and training employees in the operation of software. An IT service provider could use repertory grid analysis to gain creative ideas for improving its service offerings (consisting of both the service product and the service augmentation). Interviewees would be members of client companies who have experience of the services that they had outsourced (for example, purchasing managers). The interviewee would be asked to name six outsourced services with which they are familiar – these we will call service products A, B, C, D, E and F. The services are what are termed the *elements* of the test and each is written on a separate (postcard-sized) card, as shown in Figure 5.3(A). A wide range of services can be selected and Table 5.2 shows that the interviewee has selected a range, including facility management and financial auditing. The IT service provider's own service is also on the list, as is one direct competitor (Service E).

Note that the cards have been pre-numbered in a random sequence (5, 1, 4, 3, 2 and 6), to enable the selection of random sets of cards. From the figure it can be seen that the name of the first service ('A') has been written on the card numbered '5', whereas Service B is written on the card numbered '1'. After

Table 5.2 The Augmented Service Offerings
Chosen by the Interviewee

Service Products
Service A – Facility management (security and cleaning)
Service B – IT Services (IT Service Provider)
Service C – Data warehousing
Service D – Financial auditing
Service E – Competitor's IT Services
Service F – Employee training seminars

the cards have been annotated with services, the interviewee is presented with a set of three cards (termed a *triad*). Figure 5.3(B) shows the triad consists of Cards 1, 2 and 3, corresponding to Services B, E and D respectively. The interviewee is asked: 'Why is using two of these services similar and different from the third?' A typical response – a service attribute – could be that two of the service providers are 'easy to work with, good communications', whereas working with the third 'is difficult'. The way in which the interviewee differentiates between the elements in the triad reveals how they perceive the different services. Each of the three services is then rated against this first attribute. As shown in Figure 5.3(C), this is normally on a 5-point scale on which Service B has been highly rated on 'easy to work with' (a '1'), whereas Service D was given a minimum rating ('5').

Further triads are used to identify further attributes. The interviewee is not allowed to repeat attributes and so each new triad elicits at least one new attribute. As each attribute is determined, the interviewee is asked to explain what they mean by, for example, fast response and they will give details such as timings and the actions they expect. All this is recorded, as it gives insight into the customer's needs. Following each construct, the interviewee is required to rate all the services against it using the same 1–5 rating scale. These ratings form the repertory grid, as shown in Figure 5.4.

In Figure 5.4, the six elements of the test – Services B to F – are shown across the top of the grid. Down the side are the attributes identified during the interview. The stars around the ratings indicate which cards were in the triad that elicited particular attributes. For example, the first attribute was elicited using a triad consisting of Cards 1, 2 and 3 (indicated by the ratings with stars: *1*, *4*, *5*). It can be seen that the Service B is rated as '1' ('easy to work with, good communications') but Service D is difficult to work with and received a rating of '5'. Looking at the ratings, it can be seen that on the attribute 'fast response' Service C is rated mid-scale ('3') but rated as poor ('5') on the attribute 'absolutely reliable service (guarantee)'. The ratings tell us not only about how an interviewee perceives services; they also give us information on the importance of particular attributes. For example, the ratings on the attribute 'clearly defined service product' are not as widely spread (they only range from 1 to 3) as those for 'good value for money' (where the ratings range

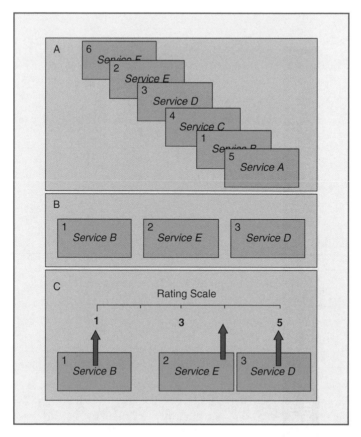

Figure 5.3 Example of a Repertory Grid Interview
A) The Elements of the Test – Services – Written on Cards; B) The First Triad
presented to the Interviewee; C) The Rating of the Services in the First Triad

from 1 to 5). This shows that this latter attribute differentiates more strongly between the elements. Hidden needs tend to be indicated by low ratings for all elements.

The grid can also be used to derive a *cognitive map* of an interviewee's perceptions of products and services. Deriving and interpreting this map is beyond the scope of this discussion but it can give further insights for product and service designers. Further details can be found in the book *Essential Skills for Management Research*.[41]

Repertory grid technique can also be used to generate ideas for manufactured products. The Hewlett-Packard Medical Products Group first used repertory grid interviewing over ten years ago and it helped the company identify the emerging importance of product attributes such as 'easy to set up' and 'easy-to-clean' in the medical equipment market.[42] A focus was placed on these factors in all subsequent developments. Mini Case 5.4 on Equant gives an example from the service sector.

ATTRIBUTES	CARD 1 Service B	CARD 2 Service E	CARD 3 Service D	CARD 4 Service C	CARD 5 Service A	CARD 6 Service F	POLES
Easy to work with, good communications	*1*	*4*	*5*	5	1	1	Difficult
Fast response to problems	1	4	5	*3*	*4*	*4*	Slow
Professional employees	*2*	5	*3*	4	*1*	1	Little knowledge
Clearly defined service product	3	*2*	1	*3*	1	*1*	Poorly defined ...
Service is good value for money	*3*	*3*	5	1	*5*	5	Expensive
Absolutely reliable service (guarantee)	5	4	*4*	*5*	5	*5*	Difficult

Figure 5.4 A Repertory Grid on Outsourced Services

Mini Case 5.4

Equant – Repertory Grids in Practice

One company that has used the repertory grid technique extensively is Equant, the world's largest data network provider – offering network design, integration, maintenance and support services in over 180 countries. The company always placed a high emphasis on being 'customer-focused' and regularly reviewed the results of customer satisfaction surveys, comparing their performance to competitors'. Although such surveys provided useful 'benchmarks', Equant recognized that they did not measure performance against the criteria, which were most important to customers.

In late 1990s, the company offered excellent network performance and global service availability. Consequently, it received better ratings than its competitors in surveys and this could have led to complacency. However, a project was launched to investigate whether there were aspects of service quality that were important to customers but were not covered by the surveys. Liam Mifsud, Business Support Manager at Equant, designed and conducted repertory grid interviews, in which the elements of the grid were a range of the customer's current service providers. Interviewees (IT Directors and Managers) were asked to name nine suppliers that their companies did business with, and these elements were presented in triads. The constructs elicited typically included a wide range of service quality criteria (far wider than those covered by the customer satisfaction surveys).

The results showed that customers' perceptions of service quality were not solely based on technical measures (such as coverage or network performance). Equant were able to identify ten new criteria on which their performance was being judged. For example, customers emphasized intangible elements of service quality, such as the responsiveness and flexibility of account management teams, and the quality and competence of the support staff they came into contact with. 'This provided us with a valuable means of understanding the changing needs of customers', says Mifsud.

Empathic Design

Dorothy Leonard-Barton from Harvard Business School has promoted empathic design and defines it as 'the creation of product or service concepts based on a deep (empathic) understanding of unarticulated user needs'.[43] The terms *ethnographic* or *anthropological* market research are also sometimes used, indicating that the data collection and analysis methods are largely drawn from these disciplines. The foundation of the technique is *systematic observation* but it also includes *discrete observation, contextual interviews* and what we will term *empathy building*. Empathic thinking should lead organizations to design products and services for people in developing countries and not just the affluent Western consumer (see Mini Case 5.5 on SEWA).

Systematic Observation

This technique assesses the use of products directly, rather than relying on customers' reported perceptions (as, for example, are derived in surveys).[46]

Mini Case 5.5

SEWA Banks – the Availability of Finance[44,45]

It is a shocking statistic but more people in India have to live on less than $1 a day than the entire population of the US. The cash-poor segment of the market is ignored by institutions in many countries but the emergence of India as a powerhouse for low-cost innovation is changing views. The 'bottom of the pyramid' or 'base of the pyramid' market as it is called is now attracting significant interest from companies. However, to successfully develop products that meet the needs of such customers will require companies to develop a deep understanding of the people in developing markets. Innovations in products and services are starting to be offered that until recently would have been thought unimaginable. In products, the Tata Nano car is poised to be a low-price breakthrough but, in some ways, it is in the heady world of finance that even more dramatic changes have taken place.

Microfinance – small loans for very poor people – has been very successful through the Grameen Bank in Bangladesh and SEWA in India. The SEWA Bank is a by-product of the Self-Employed Women's Association (SEWA), and it specializes in loans specifically for women, as women have been found to utilize loans more effectively than men and save some of their earnings. The Bank has a membership of over 10 million women in 7 Indian states. Enabling poor people to save and borrow has allowed many small businesses to flourish and the Bank now offers a wide range of services.

Microfinance is poised to develop further. As low-cost ATM technology becomes widely available (through Internet kiosks known in India as *sanchalaks*), insurance and other financial services previously unavailable to the poor will also enter the market. And as the *sanchalaks* and other IT solutions proliferate (for example, Vortex Engineering, an Indian technology company, has designed an ATM that does not need air conditioning and comes at a quarter of the normal cost of a terminal), access to healthcare and other services is likely to improve for the poor.

Systematic observation is time-consuming, the analysis is complex and difficult to learn, and significant preparation is needed.[47] It is for this reason that market research companies are increasingly hiring ethnographers, whose training enables them to observe and interpret effectively (that is accurately, unambiguously and in an unbiased way).

The key to effective observation is the preparation of a good *coding scheme*. Such a scheme is based on the research question: what is the observer looking to understand? Usually, in product innovation studies, observation aims to understand how customers use products in their day-to-day environment and to identify the unarticulated problems they face with these products. For example, a manufacturer might watch housewives operating washing machines in their own homes and this would yield a large amount of data on where (in the house), how (the process), and when (time of the day) washing machines are used. In the service sector, observations can be used to determine the typical stages of consumption of a service. The coding scheme gives the observer points to watch for and should prevent them missing key actions. This is particularly important, as the clues to unarticulated needs may be non-verbal.

Table 5.3 gives a generic coding scheme for observation and has seven categories of data: from the observed triggers for product usage up to the unarticulated needs. The table gives the main types of events to look for and the additional columns can be annotated with the timings of when these are observed and additional notes. It can be seen that the seven categories of data force the observer to not only look at how the product fits into the user's overall environment but also to look for signals that indicate unarticulated needs. For example, identifying the triggers for use can give insights. For a vacuum cleaner, the trigger for

Table 5.3   Generic Coding Scheme for Observational Studies

	Data categories	Events to look for	Observed?	Timings	Notes
1)	Triggers for acquiring the product or service	• Why, when and how?			
2)	Triggers for product usage	• Who, what, where, when, why, how?			
3)	The environment	• Physical layout/objects • Actors • Activities/events • Time sequence			
4)	Interactions with user's environment	• Physical interactions • Social interactions			
5)	Product usage	• Wasted time • Doing things right • Doing things wrong • Misuse • Confusion • Dangerous situations (for example, physical or data)			
6)	Intangible aspects and unarticulated needs	• Emotions • Frustration and wasted time • Fears and anxiety • Linguistic signals • Extralinguistic signals • Non-verbal signals (for example, body language) • Spatial signals			
7)	User customization	• User modifications of the product • User modifications of the (normal) process			

Source: Compiled by the authors from Leonard-Barton and a variety of other sources.

use could be the weekly clean of rooms, or something spilled. The latter trigger for use brings different requirements such as speed, which may influence product design. (The Black & Decker Company created the well-known hand-held 'Dustbuster' vacuum cleaners to address this need.)

As indicated by Table 5.3, frustration with services or products can indicate that a current design does not meet the user's needs, or it may indicate a poor user interface. A good observer will look for signs of frustration such as subtle *extralinguistic* signals (for example, the speed and emphasis in speech), *non-verbal* signs such as body language, and *spatial signals* (for example, the proximity of a user to others or objects). Another clue to unarticulated needs can be that users have modified the equipment to better meet their needs. Users may also modify their working pattern to get around the limitations of current products or services. Due to the multidimensional nature of good observation, often the best solution is to make video recordings, which can be viewed offline by a number of people all looking for the different clues. The disadvantage of video recording is that it may influence the user's actions.

Mini Case 5.6

Clarks – These Boots Are (Really) Made for Walking[48]

Clarks Shoes has been renowned for the quality and comfort of its products for over 175 years. The company was aware that the market for leisure footwear was significant and growing fast, and decided to enter what was for them a new market – walking boots. As this was a market about which they had no detailed knowledge of customer needs, they worked closely with PDD, a London-based market research consultancy. Product Manager Chris Towns said, 'I needed to understand the buying habits, end use and expectations of our new consumer. Understanding the motivations of walkers can only be guessed at from within the confines of your own office'.

PDD specialize in ethnographic studies and they conducted contextual interviews with walkers in UK national parks, home interviews with people who were members of walking and rambling clubs, and observed customers buying walking boots. The insights obtained from this market research allowed Clarks to clearly identify their target segments and, for each of these, to understand customer priorities. For example, 'comfort', 'fit' and 'safety' were quickly identified from interviews as important product attributes. However, the contextual interviews in the national parks allowed the design team to understand the real meaning of each of these terms and develop product characteristics to meet them. Much of the development involved experimentation with prototypes and this was conducted directly with walkers. Similarly, systematic observation of customers in shops found that they always feel the tongue of walking boots before they tried them on. Therefore, it appeared that the tongue was a feature of a boot that customers closely associated with comfort. This insight led the Clarks team to produce a particularly well-padded tongue in their final product. The Clarks range of 'Active' walking boots has been well received by both hobby and professional walkers and ramblers and is selling well.

The massive amount of data collected in systematic observation must be analysed and summarized in a form that is useful to management. New technology is helping here and the market research consultants PDD in London produce databases of key video clips, categorized by customer segment, for their clients. This database can be made available on a company's intranet to any department involved in product development. This helps to spread the understanding of the customer's world throughout the innovation project team (see Mini Case 5.6 on Clarks Shoes).

Another approach to analysing observations is to identify typical scenarios of how products are used, with associated problems and issues. Descriptive statistics on the number of times particular events occur, for example, can also be a useful way of summarizing data. Simple drawings and storyboards can also be used to summarize triggers for use and problems encountered. Storyboards are useful communication tools with both users and internally, to help the whole of the NPD team understand users' needs.

Discrete Observation

This approach, in which users are observed without their knowledge or permission, is only viable for consumer products and services that are used in public. For example, Nokia in Japan have had employees observe how users operate their products in public. Similarly, car manufacturers have built miniature cameras into cars at shows to observe how potential customers react to their new products. Using discrete observation raises ethical issues and the type of usage that can be discretely observed might not be typical. As discrete observation often deliberately eavesdrops on users' conversations, it has been colloquially dubbed capturing 'the murmur of the customer'.[49] It should be kept in mind that people normally quickly become aware that they are being observed and often react negatively. Obtaining permission in advance is safer.

Contextual Interviews

Contextual interviews are conducted in the user's environment but observation and a number of semi-structured questions are used, to understand the situation in which products are used. Questions collect background information, and then stimulate users to describe their actions. Typical questions are: 'Can you please describe what you are doing?' and 'When is that necessary?' Essentially, this produces verbal data on product usage that might not be generated in pure observation. Having people describe their actions can also unearth their tacit knowledge. Once again, video recording is commonly used. Contextual interviews are particularly useful for gaining insights into how the customer feels during the service delivery process and gaining ideas for improvement.

The London consultancy WhatIf! has made contextual interviewing easy for the manufacturers of consumer products, by negotiating access to all of the residents in one (long) street in Birmingham. All of the houses in 'The Street' can be visited with minimal notice and product managers have been able to both observe their products in use and ask questions. Intel has a number of projects which make use of contextual interviewing and employ a team of ethnographers, sociologists and behavioural scientists based in Oregon,[50] responsible for identifying the social backgrounds to product usage.

Empathy Building

Most authors concentrate on the data collection and analysis aspects of empathic design. However, the other side is the need to ensure that product designers develop not only an understanding of customers and users but also fully empathize with them. As yet, there is no formal methodology for this but a number of examples from industry demonstrate the approach. When the Ford Motor Company developed their Focus model, one target segment was elderly people. In order to get the engineers to understand the difficulties that older people have in getting into and out of cars, designers wore padded suits that reduced their ease of movement and simulated the restricted movement of later life. Similarly, a mobile telephone design team also working on a product for elderly people had its engineers wear thick gloves and glasses smeared with Vaseline for a week, to help them understand how difficult it can be for pensioners to operate today's products. No doubt in coming years the way in which companies attempt to generate true empathy will develop further. It is a case of finding ways in which the designers can 'step into the customer's shoes'.

Lead Users

Another approach to uncovering hidden needs was developed by Eric von Hippel at MIT. *Lead users* are groups of customers or users that face more challenging requirements than most of the current marketplace (see Mini Case 5.7 on Lego). Their needs can be ahead of the market, by months or by years but they become mainstream over time. As the market vanguard, lead users face urgent, challenging needs and can benefit significantly from solutions to these. One word of caution is necessary – the theory on disruptive technology discussed in Chapter 4 shows the drawbacks of solely concentrating on existing customers needs. Organizations need to be cautious because extreme needs might not be interesting for mainstream customers. However, if applied correctly, lead-user technique looks at the needs of demanding users, collects ideas from users of similar products and services in other markets, and checks the mainstream market for the relevance of the ideas generated.[51]

In contrast to traditional market research, where the sample is chosen to be representative, lead users face particular issues and are not representative of normal users. The selection of a lead-user group normally follows four steps. First, a screening process is used with existing users to identify which of them have more demanding needs. Figure 5.5 illustrates the process in which the starting point is screening normal users. From these, the *extreme users* are at the top of what can be perceived as a pyramid of users. They are extreme in terms of the demands

---

Mini Case 5.7

Lego – Mindstorming Better Product Ideas[52]

Since its introduction in 1998, the Lego Mindstorms robot kit has been a huge success, selling upwards of 40,000 units a year. The kit includes a large robot brick that can be used in combination with a range of motors, lights, bricks and sensors to build highly intelligent devices – for example, a robot that can manipulate and solve Rubik's Cube. Writing the control programs for such devices is a complex and challenging task, which is conducted on a laptop. The market for Mindstorms has developed into two distinct segments: parents buying the $200 kit for teenagers hooked on engineering; and adult enthusiasts ('geeks') who love programming in their spare time. Geeks love to exhibit their creations at the annual Lego 'Brickfest' conference.

When Lego decided to improve the Mindstorms product, they turned their attention to the geeks and chose to involve some of them in the new product development from a very early stage. After signing a non-disclosure agreement, four geeks were invited to exchange their ideas about the existing product in a secure chat room, hosted by Seren Lund, the director of Mindstorms. Over the next year, the four lead users were in regular contact with Lego, giving a wealth of ideas about how to make significant improvements to Mindstorms. Involving the four enthusiasts at such an early stage led Lego to develop a very different product, based on their suggestions. The new product, which was introduced in August 2006 looks very different and is not backwards compatible. The new robot brick has more computing power, uses an improved programming language, and comes with a vastly improved array of motors, sensors and (new style) bricks. Interestingly, although the four dedicated enthusiasts were fundamental to the project and had a very strong influence over the final design, they were not paid by Lego – the prototype kits they were given, the peer recognition they received, and the opportunity to influence the new product were enough motivation for them.

In the original Mindstorms development, Lego had learned the difficulties in managing a project including electronics and software (both of which are a mile away from plastic bricks). Therefore, making radical improvements to the Mindstorms software was outsourced. The shock came when within weeks of the product being introduced, a Stanford graduate had reverse-engineered the robot brick and posted all his findings about its control and software on the Internet. Lego considered legal action but decided that this would be counter to the spirit of Mindstorms. Now the software licence that comes with every kit includes a clause allowing hacking. Consequently, the worldwide community of Mindstorms enthusiasts has grown fast and Lego's philosophy of deeply involving customers in NPD is here to stay.

---

that they place on products or services and also, normally, in their expertise in dealing with the particular challenges they face. For example, extreme users may have the ability to modify standard products or processes in order to cope with the particular challenges of their working environment.[53] Once the extreme users have been identified, the important next step is to identify analogous fields where similar but even more extreme challenges are faced than the ones in the current market.

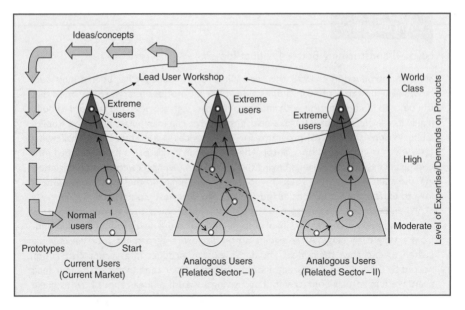

Figure 5.5 Selecting a Lead User Group

Source: Adapted from von Hippel, E., Thomke, S. and Sonnack, M., 'Creating Breakthroughs at 3M', *Harvard Business Review*, Vol. 77, No. 5 (September–October 1999), pp. 47–57.

To understand the process, consider the example of 3M, where lead users helped develop improved medical drapes. Drapes are adhesive films applied to the skin to minimize infections during surgery. The key attributes of the product were discussed with normal users – these were adhesion to skin and infection prevention. The discussions also identified that an increased risk of infection was a worrying trend in many hospitals. Next, extreme users were identified as surgeons who had to deal with higher risk of infection than in normal hospitals. Here both military field surgeons and surgeons working in developing countries with lower hygiene levels were consulted. Discussions with these extreme users identified two related sectors. The problem of infection is also an issue for veterinary surgeons, who have to operate on animals in non-hygienic environments and have problem fixing drapes on fur and hair. Finally, an unusual second set of *analogous users* was identified – Hollywood make-up artists, who have to attach masks to skin.

Extreme users from the current market and those from related sectors form the full lead-user group. For each of the lead users identified, techniques such as observation and contextual interviewing should be used to understand their working environment and issues. One of the advantages of working with analogous users from related sectors is that they normally do not mind sharing their experience, as competitive issues are not involved, and so it is normal to organize a workshop with the lead-user group. This is used to not only tap their individual expertise but also to learn from the discussions that result from bringing together users from what can be very different sectors and backgrounds (referring back to Figure 5.1, this can be seen as the bringing together of different frames of reference). The discussions are moderated and produce ideas for products that address the challenging needs lead users face. The development of these ideas into prototypes can also be conducted in close cooperation – called *co-development* – with the lead users, before the products themselves are tested with normal users. Hilti, a European manufacturer of industrial mounting equipment has found that the combination of a workshop and co-development was particularly effective and less expensive than their normal market research.

Experimentation

Users are often unable to describe the sort of product solutions they require, as they do not have sufficient technical knowledge. A creative exchange of ideas between the user (their needs) and the designer (potential solutions) is needed.[54] This needs to be an iterative process, as potential solutions need to be tested and modified to be effective. Therefore, it is useful to produce both *physical* and *virtual prototypes* that can be tried out and discussed by users and customers. It is also sometimes called *co-development*, as noted earlier, and takes advantage of the much-improved technologies for the production of prototypes. Whether it is stereo-lithography development of physical models, computer simulations of car crash scenarios, or virtual reality mock-ups of products, which allow users to interact with them, there are many possibilities to make prototypes. Co-development is also being adopted by the service sector, as customer inputs are critical to good service product design. Allowing customers and users to try and test products at an early stage means that it is still possible to make changes to the final product or service design (for ideas on how this can be implemented, see the section on *Agile Project Management* in Chapter 7).

Virtual Communities

The worldwide web has enabled groups of people with common interests to exchange their ideas easily and such virtual communities are being tapped by companies looking for ideas and even help with product development. *Online communities* have been defined as a group of customers that have a high level of interest and knowledge about a particular group of products.[55] At its simplest, the use of online communities involves online surveys that customers can voluntarily complete and which can give insights into their needs (obviously such questionnaires have limitations such as their validity). However, a range of interactions are now being used, from interactive question-and-answer games (which are designed to gain understanding of how products are perceived and used), to *user design software*, where customers can participate in the design process. *Open source software* is a prime example of where users and customers are intimately involved in product development but other examples are emerging. Facebook was able to have its website translated into different languages by allowing users to do the work and video game companies have also had their customers help in major development projects.[56] The term *crowdsourcing* is the popular term now being applied to the use by companies of virtual communities. One of the main advantages to web approaches are that they can tap the collective intelligence of users[57] and so it is an emerging type of market research that is likely to be an important complement to the other methods we have described.

Identifying Priorities – Conjoint Analysis

Essentially all of the techniques discussed up until now identify product or service attributes. Once these are clear, the priorities from the perspective of the customer can be determined using conjoint analysis, as indicated on Figure 5.2. Conjoint analysis (or *stated preference technique* or *trade-off analysis*) is one of the more widely applied scientific approaches to market research. Provided the product attributes have been appropriately elicited from customers, conjoint analysis is a very useful method for understanding the *utility* of each of them. Conjoint analysis can be used in the service sector to understand the trade-offs that a customer is willing to make between elements of the service product and service augmentation.

There are three main stages in conjoint analysis:

1. Identifying characteristics of each of the product attributes and hypothetical product descriptions;
2. Interviewing a suitable sample of customers;
3. Calculating the customer's perceived value of each attribute (the utility).

To understand this, we will consider the example of the development of a new laptop computer.

Various methods will have been used to identify product attributes and hidden needs. Let us assume that six attributes were identified in market research with business users: (1) Display size (2) Hard disk capacity (3) Processing speed (4) Physical size and weight (5) Connectivity (ease of integration with other devices) and (6) Price. An important question during product development is: on which of these attributes does the customer place most value? Only with this information can development priorities be effectively set. For example, how much effort should be invested in developing a large screen compared with attempting to reduce the overall weight?

The first stage involves the identification of levels for each of the attributes and the typical range of values of existing products. For example, the weight of a laptop is typically around 3 kg. Once the attribute measures and their ranges have been determined, the next stage is to prepare descriptions of a hypothetical set of products, as shown in Table 5.4. Naturally, attributes change over time and in a fast-moving market such as laptops, the price and performance will need to be checked regularly. There are many possible combinations of attributes and so many hypothetical products can be developed, although only three (Product A, Product B ... Product n) are shown in the table. The number of hypothetical products that need to be considered depends on the number of attributes and their possible levels. For example, with six attributes, each with at least three

Table 5.4   Attribute Levels

	Product attribute	Product A	Product B	... Product n
1)	Display size	14 inch	15.4 inch	17 inch
2)	Hard disk capacity	400 Gbyte	320 Gbyte	250 Gbyte
3)	Processing speed	2 × 2.26 GHz	2 × 2 GHz	2 × 2.4 GHz
4)	Physical size and weight	3.5 kg	2.5 kg	2.1 kg
5)	Connectivity	WLAN, network and internal modem cards. 3 USB.	WLAN, network card, infra red connections. 2 USB.	WLAN, 4 USB, multiple interfaces.
6)	Price	1349	849	1799

levels (as shown in Table 5.4), results in $3^6 = 729$ theoretical combinations (but far fewer will be used in data collection).

The next stage is to interview customers and to present them with alternative products. In the so-called *pairwise* version of conjoint analysis, the customer would be presented with simplified descriptions of Products A and B and would be asked: 'Which do you prefer?' Each product has advantages and disadvantages; although Product A has a bigger hard drive, it is more expensive than B and has a smaller display. Therefore, the customer makes trade-offs between the values of the attributes in choosing their preference. Next, the customer is presented with another two products and asked the same question. The process of presenting the products and collecting answers is made easier by conjoint analysis software packages (such as the widely used ACA developed by Sawtooth Software), where this is automated and many researchers now administer conjoint analysis via the Internet. The sample of customers to be interviewed needs to be representative of the target market.

The interviews collect a significant amount of data on how customers view attributes and make trade-offs. Conjoint analysis software takes this data and uses mathematical principles to determine the value or utility a customer places on each attribute. Figure 5.6 shows the typical output of conjoint analysis, for the attributes speed and hard disk capacity. A graph of the utility versus the attribute level is shown and the slope of this graph indicates the importance of the attribute. For example, the faster speed appears to be important to customers to a degree, as the 2 × 2 speed has a lower utility than 2 × 2.26 GHz but 2 × 2.4 GHz speed is not perceived as significantly better. But the hard disk capacities of 250 and 320 Gbytes are not perceived as anything like the 400 Gbyte.

Utility graphs can be derived for all attributes and they give an understanding of how customers make their trade-off decisions, which in turn allows product development decisions to be made more effectively. In addition, analysis of the results pertaining to price can allow pricing decisions for new products to be

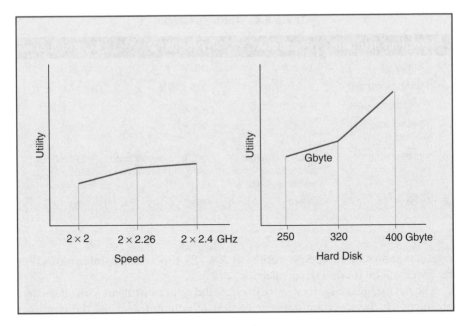

Figure 5.6 Conjoint Analysis Utility Graphs for a Laptop Computer

made. For readers who want to know more about conjoint analysis, it is recommended to consult the textbooks of Caroll et al.[58] and Gustafsson et al.[59]. Referring back to Figure 5.2, conjoint analysis is shown as the last step in using market research for improved product development. It should be stressed that although conjoint analysis is a very effective method, it is critically dependent on the identification of product attributes that are pertinent to customers (including hidden needs). Conjoint analysis is nowadays also being applied via the worldwide web.

Choosing the Correct Approach to Market Research

To help choose the most appropriate approaches for a specific piece of market research, Table 5.5 gives the advantages and limitations of the seven techniques discussed in this chapter. To achieve effective results and uncover hidden needs, a combination of techniques is almost always needed.

For example, one of Robert Bosch's business units which designs and manufactures production line equipment used observation of operators working in their customers' factories and repertory grid interviews, thus gaining insights into product requirements. A survey was then used to collect data from a representative sample of users and the results are now being incorporated into a new product design. Real customer insights are often the result of using a blend of the techniques.

Table 5.5 Different Approaches to Identifying Customer Problems and Requirements

	Approach	Overview	Applications/Advantages	Limitations
1)	Survey Research	• Use of direct questions to determine customers' views on what they think are their requirements. • Open-ended questions allow respondents some freedom to give creative ideas.	• Widely used method of collecting customer inputs. • Can be applied as a postal survey, telephone or direct interviews.	• Questionnaires are often thought to be easy to design. In fact, it is the opposite and many surveys are poorly designed and consequently produce equivocal results. • Response rates are often low, which raises the question of whether the results are representative of the market. • Respondents may find it difficult to articulate their answers to open questions.
2)	Focus Groups	• Small groups of selected users or non-users, paid to discuss product needs. • Discussions are stimulated by an initial question and by having example products in the room. • A moderator guides discussions. • Market researchers often observe the discussions through a two-way mirror.	• Help to define customer problems and give background information, rather than identifying solutions. • In vitro discussion of products (that is users are taken outside their normal environment).	• The somewhat artificial nature of the situation can limit the effectiveness. • Particular individuals can dominate the discussions. Therefore good moderation is required. • Some companies try to save costs by using inexperienced moderators; this wastes the potential of focus groups discussion.
3)	Repertory Grid Technique	• Users or customers undergo a structured interview. • Interviewees are stimulated to identify product attributes by being asked to compare triads of different products and/or services.	• Repertory grid technique is powerful at enabling users and customers to articulate their issues. • The technique taps tacit knowledge of hidden needs	• The technique is not well known. • Interviewees need to have experience with 5–6 different products and services to make the technique work. • Interviewer needs specific training in the technique, although it is easy to apply. • Time-consuming interviews.

Continued

Table 5.5 Continued

	Approach	Overview	Applications/Advantages	Limitations
4)	Empathic Design	• A range of approaches of which the main ones are systematic observation, contextual interviews and putting product designers 'in the shoes of users'.	• Becoming more popular. • Gives an in-depth understanding of customers' and users' product use models. • Contextual interviews are in vivo and the environment gives valuable information.	• Systematic observation is not easy and using specialists may be the best approach (otherwise base studies on a suitable coding scheme developed from Table 5.3). • Vast amounts of qualitative data may be generated, which requires effective analysis strategies.
5)	Lead Users	• Identification of users that have extreme needs in your current market. Further identification of analogous users in related sectors. • It is usual to run a workshop with extreme and analogous users, to develop product concepts.	• Workshop brings together very different users and stimulates creative discussions. • Can be combined with experimentation, to test the concepts identified in the workshop.	• Difficulties in identifying lead users. • Workshops are time-consuming and lead users may need to be motivated to give their time. • Workshop is outside the normal working environment (although it can be combined with a visit to a lead-user environment).
6)	Experimentation	• Customers are presented with early prototypes of products (or services) and base their suggestions on these. • Seeing and using a tangible product often enables customers and users to articulate their views better.	• Observing in a realistic scenario how customers react to tangible product ideas. • Can be an extension of the lead-user approach.	• May require expensive virtual prototyping equipment. • Superficially, services cannot easily be prototyped. However, leaders such as HSBC Bank prototype their services and collect reactions.
7)	Conjoint Analysis	• Identifies the trade-offs customers make in deciding between different products. • Customers are presented with descriptions of products or service products and must choose their preferences.	• Identification of the product attributes that customers perceive as their key priorities. • Development of pricing models.	• If the wrong attributes are fed into the analysis, then the prioritization will not be useful (it will encourage a continuing focus on incremental products). • The somewhat artificial nature of the decisions can limit the accuracy of the findings. • Relatively complex method that usually needs expert support.

Source: Compiled by the authors.

PROTECTING IDEAS

In order to gain the maximum advantage from their innovations, companies need to protect and exploit their knowledge. The most obvious mechanism for protecting innovations is patents: a 'legal right granted to exclusive commercial use of an invention, normally for a limited period of time'.[60] Most countries in the world have laws that protect intellectual property – ideas, designs, works of art, literature or music – and allow their originators to establish and defend their ownership of them. The field of *intellectual property rights* (IPR) is complex, constantly changing and varies to some extent from country to country. IPR is a matter of civil, not criminal law and companies must police their own IPR and take action at their own expense to protect it. In this section we will concentrate on the aspects of importance to managers, but we stress the importance of taking legal advice before making serious commitments.

There are many kinds of IPR but only the four main kinds need concern us: *copyright*, *design right*, *trademarks* and *patents*.

Copyright

Copyright protects writing, music, computer programs, electronic circuit layouts, web pages, photographs, works of art and so on from unauthorized copying for commercial use. It protects the overt content or appearance of the work but not its meaning (if any). So a particular drawing of an invention would be covered by copyright but not the invention itself, and another drawing of the same thing, not obviously copied from the first would not be protected. Limited copying for personal use or study is allowed: typically one chapter of a book, one article from a journal, a short excerpt from a piece of music. In the UK, copyright for musical and artistic works lasts for 70 years. For published editions the term is 25 years. There is discussion as to whether copyright will be used to protect fashion designs (see Mini Case 5.8 on Versace).

Copyright is created automatically when the work is complete and requires no registration or payment. Generally, the copyright for anything done by an employee in the course of his or her job would belong to the company, but there may be ambiguity about work done by contractors or freelance workers. Always clarify who owns the IPR in innovation projects; it can be embarrassing to find that a subcontractor owns the copyright to the manual produced for you, the artwork for your sales campaign, or the computer program that runs your new product.

One defence against an allegation of copyright infringement is that the work was separately created and appears the same merely because there was little choice in how the function could be performed. This may be plausible in software and so some programmers deliberately include sections of code that have no real function as a way of proving if their program has been copied.

Mini Case 5.8

Versace – Fashion Copyright or Right to Copy?[61]

The spring collections of leading designers such as Versace are eagerly awaited by not only the pundits of the fashion world but also by the many copycat retailers that produce similar designs at lower cost. Versace designs that are priced at upwards of $5000 are regularly copied by companies such as A.B.S and Eci, which sell dresses at around $400. Then there are the many counterfeiters that simply try and make copies that are not easily identified as such, and are sold at a fraction of the price of the original. Counterfeiting is illegal in most countries but protecting the basic cut and design of a dress from the 'knockoff' industry is more difficult. The European Union offers three year copyright-like protection for 'original fashion designs' and the US is considering similar legislation. However, in a $100 billion industry where inspiration often comes from the past, or from different cultures, or from the competition, the effectiveness of legislation is probably going to be limited.

Design Right

Design means the appearance of all or part of a product, especially its shape, colour, texture or ornamentation (or a combination of them). Design protection can prevent another company copying the product directly, or marketing an apparently identical one, even if they can show that they designed it themselves. It is a useful way to protect an original piece of design, and the brand recognition that may go with it, such as the Coca Cola bottle shape. In services, aspects of the servicescape can be used to strengthen the brand, such as McDonald's double arches.

In many countries an *unregistered design right* exists that protects against copying but not against separate creation. More powerful is the *registered design right,* which gives a monopoly right to the design for up to 25 years, and can apply internationally. The design has to be registered through a Patent Office and it is granted only to designs that are novel and would be viewed as 'fresh' by an 'informed user'. Expert advice is essential. There is a one-year period of grace after public disclosure so it is possible to test market a design before registering it.

Trademarks

A trademark is defined as 'any sign capable of being represented graphically, which is capable of distinguishing goods or services of one undertaking from those of other undertakings'.[62] It can be a name, a symbol, a special font or script, a colour, or – more often – a combination of them. There are many familiar examples. A registered trademark can be obtained through the Patent Office and typically costs up to €100. Protection is granted separately for different categories of product so that the same mark may be used by quite different companies provided their activities do not overlap. Separate protection is needed in each country but there are arrangements to extend cover to many territories for quite modest fees. Failure to trademark in different countries can cause problems. For example, the international clothing company La Chemise Lacosta has a right facing crocodile. Crocodile International, a Singapore-based clothing manufacturer, registered its own left-facing crocodile motif across Asia in the 1960s. Now with Lacosta trying to dominate the high-end Asian market, the two companies have become locked in a number of legal actions.[63]

A trademark may not be purely descriptive (like 'bread' or 'washing powder'), or too similar to another one already in use for the same category of product. So it is important to check the availability of the proposed name of a new product or service if you may want to trademark it later.

There are two reasons for seeking protection for a trademark in a particular country. One is to be able to prevent other companies using it and so 'passing off' their products as yours. The other is to establish your own right to use it; because, unlike other types of intellectual property, trademarks are, by and large, granted to the first applicant in each country (the USA and Canada are notable exceptions). So if you do not register early you may lose the chance to do so later.

Patents

Patents are the most powerful and influential way to establish ownership of an innovation because they protect the idea itself. A patent grants the legal right to exclusive use of an invention in exchange for a fee and a full disclosure of it, including a clear description of how it can be embodied. Protection typically lasts for about 20 years, depending on the country, but often with renewal fees to be paid at intervals, which get steeper as time goes on.

Patents are granted separately in each country where protection is required (though a single patent covers the European Community), so such protection can be expensive. The initial costs for writing a patent and processing it as far successful grant is typically several thousand pounds per country (and may take several years) followed by renewal fees of a further five or ten thousand over the first 10 or 12 years. The decision to patent is not one to be taken lightly.

What Can Be Patented?

To be patentable, an idea must pass four tests. It must be *novel*; it must involve an *inventive step*; it must have a *practical application*; and it must not be in an *excluded category* (which includes, among other things scientific theories, mathematical methods, and – with some restrictions – methods of doing business). The most demanding test from the management point of view is the first, which requires that the invention has never been publicly revealed before the filing date of the patent. (Patenting services is consequently difficult). A patent application for a means of raising sunken ships by filling them full of small airbags was refused because the idea had been shown (using table tennis balls) in a Disney cartoon in the 1940s. The Patent Office will search existing patents but this does not guarantee that the idea has not been published in some other way. Of course it also means that the inventor must keep the invention secret until a patent is filed.

Infringement of Patents

If a company manufactures or offers for sale a product incorporating a patented idea they are said to infringe the patent. The owner, or licensee, of the patent can force them to stop and may be able to extract substantial damages, particularly if the infringer was aware of the problem. This is the primary power that a patent gives. However, infringement is a quite separate matter from patentability. For example, suppose long ago 'Company X' invented the first chair with a back and was granted a patent on it. If 'Company Y' already had a patent on a stool (an essential constituent of a chair) then Company X would infringe this if they actually sell any of their chairs. They will need to seek a licence from Company Y before they can market their product. But their own patent could still be valid, and Company Y (or any other) would have to seek a licence from them to market a chair.

A company that wants to use a patented idea has a number of options. One is to seek a licence to use it. Another is to challenge the validity of the patent, particularly if it can find a prior disclosure of the idea. The third, which is often possible, is to work round the patent by finding a way to perform the same function but outside the legal scope of the patent. The full disclosure required in the patent document often helps competitors 'design-around' the patent and copies proliferate.[64] A survey of 600 European companies showed that 60 per cent had suffered from copies of their products but only 20 per cent went to trial.[65]

The Business Use of Patents

Patents have four main uses in a company. The first, as noted above, is to enforce a monopoly by taking legal action to prevent others using the idea. This can create a competition-free and possibly very lucrative market. The second is to licence the patent to others in return for a fee, or royalties, or both. The third is as a bargaining counter in relations between companies: large companies often agree to swap rights to each other's patent portfolio, each one using its own IPR to gain access to that of the other. Finally, small companies use their patents as objective proof of their technical depth and inventiveness so as to enhance their value on sale or flotation.

One of the drawbacks of the patent system is that it is less useful for small companies than for large. A survey with results from European SMEs found that patents are used less than they might be, although many respondent companies had suffered financially when copies of their products and services were made, often by larger companies.[66] The perceived limitations were that patent protection took a lot of effort to acquire and, in practice, gave only limited protection because legal action was expensive and seldom successful. Because of this, both SMEs and larger companies often adopt other strategies to protect their knowledge. One is simply to keep the knowledge secret, an effective strategy for process innovations or others that are not visible to people buying the product. As discussed in the sections on the scope of innovation, the matching of product innovation with process innovation is often a good way to protect knowledge because innovative process technology 'can block or stymie would-be imitator's push into the market'.[67] It is also normally hard to apply patent protection to services and often the best approach is to concentrate on developing a unique augmentation. Other measures are discussed in Mini Case 5.9 on Micro Scooters and also in Sidler, the main case study in Chapter 9.

Mini Case 5.9

Micro Scooters – Success, Even When Patents Don't Help[68]

Its popularity may have waned but the urban scooter was a smash hit that continues to be popular with teenagers. What used to be considered as simply a child's toy has become a high-tech product, aimed at a range of age groups. The story behind this phenomenally successful product is an interesting one, which shows the need for innovative marketing, fast product development and the limitations of international patent protection. Surprisingly, the product idea itself almost failed to get to market.

Wim Obouter is the Swiss inventor of the original Micro City-Scooter. He studied international marketing in the US and had worked in both financial services and the manufacturing sector in Switzerland. However, it was his love of sports – windsurfing and cycling – that helped him to identify a niche in the transport market. Over ten years ago, Wim recognized that, when he wanted to go out for a drink or a meal in the evening, it was often too far to walk but not far enough to warrant getting his bicycle out of the cellar, or to drive. Later he was to coin the phrase *micro-distances* for these sorts of journeys. As he often travelled micro-distances, he set about designing a solution to the problem. He considered a skateboard but decided on a scooter, as it would be easier to ride. So he handmade himself a simple scooter that turned out to be 2–3 times faster than walking and which could be folded together, so that it would be easy to take into a bar. This prototype worked well and turned heads in Zürich. 'When I was on it, people always used to stop and stare at me. So much so that I started to think that it wasn't very "cool" to be seen riding a scooter! So I stopped riding it during daylight hours'. Soon the prototype fell into disuse and the whole idea might have died, had not Wim still believed that there was a need for such a product.

Over the next few years, the idea did not die entirely and Wim even wrote a marketing plan. In this he described a market need for not only an updated children's toy but also for a lifestyle product, which addressed the micro-distance issue. However, friends and colleagues were sceptical. They told him that he had a 'respectable job in a Swiss bank so why on earth was he playing around with ideas for children's toys?' So the prototype was literally shelved – it was left unused in Wim's garage.

That was until the summer of 1996 when, by chance, the prototype was spotted by neighbours' children, who asked if they could try it out. They were hooked immediately. From then on, throughout the summer, up to twenty kids per day took turns to use the scooter – 'they just kept coming to borrow it and my wife kept saying there

▸▸

really is something in this idea'. Finally, Wim had proof that the city-scooter had great potential for the kids market, although he still felt convinced that the potential was far greater. The success with the local neighbourhood finally convinced him and his wife to take the idea further. At the time, the launch of the Smart car with its advertising slogans of 'Reduce to Max' and 'The Future of Mobility' inspired Wim to make a video of his prototype and approach the car manufacturer. The Smart organization was impressed and considered integrating a scooter within the boot of the car as an ideal combination – a city car with the city-scooter for the last lap of the journey. Later, however, this decision was reversed at the time that the Smart project – a cooperation between Swatch and Daimler – experienced problems. Therefore, Wim was forced to look for an alternative route to market.

When Smart backed out, Wim turned to Far East manufacturers looking for a source of funding. He found a partner company with enough faith in the project to fund the tooling and other set-up costs and who helped find a Japanese retail partner willing to try the product – with an opening order of 20,000 scooters. These sold immediately and the market grew quickly to sales of 75,000 units per week – almost an instant success.

City Bug UK Ltd handled the UK marketing. One of the partners, Seth Bishop, says they quickly realized that 'the product was great but it would attract competitors quickly. And without many international patents it would need a strong brand to maintain a market leadership position'. This was difficult because City Bug did not have the 'marketing spend' of a big company. Therefore, they adopted what some marketing professionals now refer to as 'stealth marketing' – finding novel ways to reach their target segments, without resorting to conventional advertising. The marketing plan concentrated on establishing the profile of Micro as a premium product. 'We wanted it to achieve cult status quickly, to make it stand apart from the copies'. Therefore, the marketing team concentrated on getting fashion journalists interested so that they would write articles in magazines such as *The Face* and selecting distribution channels such as design shops as opposed to retail chains. From the start, the Micro product was promoted as a top design.

The Micro product is manufactured in China and Wim knew that, by the time production of the Micro had ramped up, the word would have spread and a host of Asian copies would be inevitable. However, he knew that high labour content of his product would make it uneconomical to produce in Switzerland. Also, he saw a need to increase production volumes fast and his experience in the manufacturing sector told him that the length of time required to gain approval and build new facilities in Switzerland would be disadvantageous. The downside of Asian manufacturing is the speed and frequency with which copies emerge and, as he later discovered, it is impossible to use patents as a protection mechanism.

With hindsight, Wim sees two issues with patents: the time required before cover is achieved and the investment needed to enforce them. Typically it takes up to two years to be granted a patent. During this time, a host of copies will be on the market, many from countries where patent rights are difficult, or even impossible to enforce. 'The difference between innovation in my markets and, for example, the pharmaceutical sector is time-scales. Product life cycles are typically six months for me and so the market moves much faster that the bureaucracy of patents. And so I need to compete through constant product innovation, not through law suits'.

▶▶

> With over 15 million units of the Micro brand sold since 1999, the product is an outstanding success. For the future Wim intends to innovate in both the product design (for example, sophisticated suspension mechanisms and ABS brakes are planned) and the brand. Finally the product has achieved the 'cool' image and broad market appeal that Wim intended.

The key points for managers are as follows:

1. When launching a product with new features, check carefully whether some could be patented. This must be done, and a patent filed, before the product is shown to any third party (unless covered by a confidentiality agreement);
2. Check new product features to make sure they do not infringe other patents. This requires a professional search of patent databases;
3. Leave enough time to act on the results of these investigations before the product launch;
4. Encourage staff to patent ideas that may be valuable but choose the countries to file in with care because of the considerable cost;
5. When subcontracting any work that may result in registerable IPR, ensure that the contract defines who will own it;
6. When licensing a patent or when starting a joint venture that may lead to patents, establish who is responsible for filing costs and maintenance fees; for choosing countries to file in; for detecting and taking action following infringements; and for defence of the patent if attacked. And establish what the rights of all parties are if the patent is successfully challenged or worked round.

SUMMARY

This chapter covered the second element of the Pentathlon – managing ideas. It explained how creativity is often misunderstood and managers need to look for effective ways to stimulate constant creativity through the exchange of information and knowledge. One of the key areas of knowledge is capturing the elusive voice of the customer. Here, traditional market research has serious limitations and, therefore, companies need to understand and adopt appropriate enhanced approaches. Overall, this chapter explained

- The nature of individual and team creativity with ideas on how to stimulate creativity levels.
- Some of the most useful techniques to invigorate the process of generating ideas for new products and new services.
- The main types of knowledge and how they can be best utilized and, as necessary, protected.

- The most appropriate ways to conduct market research into customers' and users' needs, so that radical innovations can be developed.
- If the strategic goals of the organization focus on achieving product and technology breakthroughs, then creative links need to be made between the strategy and the generation of ideas. This is the subject of the main case study for this chapter, which looks at Texas Instruments.

MANAGEMENT RECOMMENDATIONS

- Foster an understanding of the different types of creativity in your organization and use this to stimulate a constant flow of ideas.
- Encourage staff to recognize the importance of actively collecting ideas from outside sources.
- Take active steps to establish and maintain a 'culture of innovation' that supports idea generation.
- Promote the exchange of knowledge within and between innovation project teams. Recognize and protect knowledge that is vital to the organization.
- Employ an appropriate combination of market research techniques to identify your customers' hidden needs.
- Identify suitable ways to protect innovative ideas from competitors.

RECOMMENDED READING

1. Squires, S. and Byrne, B. (eds) *Creating Breakthrough Ideas: The Collaboration of Anthropologists and Designers in the Product Development Industry* (Bergin and Garvey: Westport, CT, USA, 2002). [Interesting perspectives on how product design studies can be improved through ethnographic methods.]
2. Couger, J. D. *Creative Problem Solving and Opportunity Finding* (Danvers, MA: Boyd and Fraser, 1995). [Comprehensive coverage of many creativity techniques and their applications. Unfortunately, gives little information on empirical research into creativity.]

CASE STUDY
Texas Instruments – Defining Innovation[69]

Before reading this case, consider the following generic innovation management issues:

- How does the chosen innovation strategy impact the management of ideas?
- If end-users do not understand the technology, how can they generate useful inputs for product designers?
- How can managers match market trends to technological advances?
- How can customers be encouraged to give ideas that are not simply based on improving current functionality?   ▶▶

Texas Instruments Incorporated (TI) is based in Dallas. It is a world leader in semiconductors, producing a wide range digital signal processing (DSP) and analogue devices and has over 29,500 employees worldwide. In 2007, revenues of $13.8billion were earned, of which a massive $2.15billion (16 per cent) was invested in R&D – a clear demonstration of TI's commitment to technology and new products. Its products provide the processing capability for a multitude of consumer devices such as mobile telephones, digital stereo, car navigation systems, interactive toys and digital cameras. Developing technology that will satisfy the demands of manufacturers such as Nokia and NEC, technology experts themselves, constantly tests TI's ability to anticipate requirements. However, the company has a tradition of going beyond existing customer needs.

For example, TI is famous for developing the first integrated circuit (chip) in 1958. Back then, inventor Jack Kilby knowingly broke 'the customer is always right' rule. He was specifically asked by a customer to develop some discrete circuits but he thought of how, by packing these onto a single piece of silicon, a more efficient overall device could be manufactured. As a result of his foresight, the applications of electronics have multiplied and, today, millions of chips are produced every day. A brilliant idea, for which Kilby won the 2000 Nobel Prize for physics, and the sort of feat that is difficult to repeat. Today, just as in 1958, it is important to exceed customer needs. But how can radical ideas be generated?

With the increased complexity of electronics, TI has recognized that technical intuition alone is seldom sufficient. Trying to extrapolate customer needs in the isolation of the laboratory was found to be too risky. 'For a while, we had a bunch of engineers who used to figure out what the customer wanted and throw it over the wall to the sales guys, who would figure out how to sell it...but not now', says Bob McKune with TI's Wireless Marketing team. Over the past ten years, TI has developed a variety of approaches to support the process of anticipating customers' needs and predicting technology trajectories. These are based around a new function and its interface to people in the business units, both in marketing and technology management.

STRATEGIC MARKETING

One of TI's most effective means for stimulating innovative ideas has been the Strategic Marketing function, which is staffed by technical, business and market experts. They collect and develop ideas for new markets and evaluate potential projects very much in the way venture capitalists work. The group was founded in 1998 and has been responsible for developing some major new businesses, such as the OMAP™ family of applications processors for mobile telephones. Ideas are honed by comparing data from the market, technology and financial scenarios. Every idea has to undergo top-management scrutiny and, if approved, seed funding is available, resources are quickly identified and high-level priorities are set. To keep the development of new business focused, a simple 'top-three priorities' rule is often applied. And to speed progress even further, the strategic marketing people most closely associated with the development of an idea transfer to the 'start-up' business unit. 'Being in one of the strategic marketing teams is about as close as you can get to external start-up mentality...inside of a big company', is how one of the original members of the OMAP team described it.

▶▶

One of the ways Strategic Marketing and the business units go further than many of TI's competitors is in studying end-users and not just direct customers. It is recognized that end-users determine what will be needed in the future and although these end-users understand little if any of the technology going into a mobile phone, for example, identifying trends in requirements is vital. Therefore, Strategic Marketing closely follows markets and conducts significant consumer research. Doug Rasor, VP of Strategic Marketing, says that understanding end-user trends helped TI recognize very early how 'the combination of convenience and increased functionality would transform gadgets from "luxury" or "techie" items to "must-haves" for today's busy consumer'. Similarly, tracking the consumer gave an early prediction of the need for every mobile phone to support high-quality photographic capability. Such insights into the world of the consumer have had a major impact on how TI products are designed, often pushing R&D to deliver what could be called 'over the horizon performance'.

MARKETING AND LEAD CUSTOMERS

Just as Strategic Marketing focuses on new markets, marketing in the business units is tasked with developing ideas for radical new products. McKune says, 'TI has shifted to become not only technology-oriented but also customer- and end-user oriented'. In the process, new approaches have been adopted to help customers articulate the future and a strong focus on end-users comes from close cooperation with Strategic Marketing. Lead-user technique has also been used extensively and the view of McKune is that choosing the right people for lead-user groups is the critical part of the process. 'Literally, you have to look years ahead and a lot of our customers can only look out about 12 months. Others can only look out six months to the next introduction'. Therefore, 'industry thoroughbreds', as McKune calls them, are carefully chosen and experts are also brought in from related sectors. This stimulates broader discussions around technology and emerging customer issues, which in turn identifies real opportunities. Leading these discussions is a role shared by McKune and the Chief Technologist.

Chief Technologist

The Chief Technologist for the OMAP platform, Michael Yonker, works in an office directly opposite to McKune's. Their respective doors are always open and they constantly trade jokes, accusing each other of either an inability to properly interpret the market, the technology, or both. Behind the jest, however, both Yonker and McKune are very serious about their goal of matching future technology to hidden needs. Yonker describes his role as 'the technical guy, who also understands the business side and who has a prominent role with our customers. In a sense I have to bridge the gap, acting as an evangelist to both R&D [convincing them about the importance of interpreting and leading the market] and marketing [convincing them of the potential of new technology]'.

'A lot of technology managers are pure R, or pure D but I put a premium on internal and external communication', says Yonker. Product technology roadmaps are used extensively as an internal planning and communication tool. By using roadmaps to show the links between the market and technology, Yonker aims to avoid 'technology

▶▶

being developed that is not effectively applied. That's what we call "nerd products" – nobody wants to buy them and we don't want to develop them'. This in turn has led to the 'customer is always right' rule being broken regularly. Usually customers have a tendency to demand ever more functionality. However, McKune and Yonker have found that appropriate communication can identify product simplification opportunities. Removing product features can be a tough negotiation with customers but when all five key criteria – cost; size, weight and volume; power consumption; performance; and time-to-market – are discussed in unison, as opposed to features alone, TI have found that interesting alternatives emerge more easily than might be expected. 'Through introducing this broader view and discussing all five criteria with customers, the whole technical thing has taken on a different light', says Yonker.

INNOVATION: DEFINE NOT REFINE

In common with their competitors, each year TI is introducing new chips that are half the size, one-quarter of the price of previous ones, and have half the power require-ment (and therefore require fewer battery changes). In terms of performance, how-ever, the work of Strategic Marketing, lead-user discussions and end-user studies are providing TI with ideas for exceeding expectations. For example, the OMAP™ team is now working on a 'superchip', which will offer manufacturers the capability of design-ing all of the features they want to include in a mobile telephone from voice-only to multimedia. This is one product but the result of what Yonker and McKune see as the clear innovation philosophy of their business unit; 'our goal is to define new customer needs, not just refine existing ones'.

SELECTING AND MANAGING AN INNOVATION PORTFOLIO

As living and moving beings we are forced to act ... [even when] our existing knowledge does not provide a sufficient basis for a calculated mathematical expectation.

John Maynard Keynes

Our knowledge of the way things work, in Society or in Nature, comes trailing clouds of vagueness. Vast ills have followed the belief in certainty.

Kenneth Arrow (Nobel Laureate in Economics)

INTRODUCTION

Any organization is likely to have a number of innovation projects running at any one time. Allocating resources between them to achieve optimum returns is always difficult, the more so when some have high levels of uncertainty. Managers face three challenges: the first is deciding which projects are intrinsically worth doing in themselves (the *valuation problem*); the second is choosing a group, or *portfolio* of them that best meets the overall needs of the organization (the *balance problem*); and the third is to retain the understanding and commitment of the people involved, especially those whose projects are rejected. Choosing and managing a portfolio is a dynamic activity because innovation projects change as they proceed and, as a result, some may have to be pushed forward, some delayed and some stopped altogether. Setting and managing the changing priorities among innovation projects is the third element of the Innovation Pentathlon.

A key difficulty in selecting the right innovation projects is that much of the information on which the decision should be based may be unknown, or at least uncertain, at the outset. A great deal of preparatory work may be needed to resolve the uncertainties, and indeed some risks may remain until very near the end of some projects. So project selection is often not a single decision made at the start of the project, but rather an interim decision followed by

Table 6.1   Some Acronyms Used in Project
Selection and Portfolio Management

Acronym	Meaning
DCF	Discounted Cash Flow
DTA	Decision Tree Analysis
ECV	Expected Commercial value
IRR	Internal Rate of Return
NPV	Net Present Value
TBE	Time to Break Even
BSM	Black, Scholls, Merton

an investigation and a review – perhaps several times over – before a 'point of no return' is reached when a full commitment is made. Often companies use separate teams, or even departments, for exploring new concepts and for the more focused and disciplined activity of implementation (see Mini Case 6.7 on Richardson's knives).

Management action plays a vital role in steering a portfolio of innovation projects to success. As each project progresses and the uncertainties unravel, managers will face not only unanticipated obstacles but also unexpected opportunities. There will be upsides to exploit as well as downsides to manage. The first step in successful portfolio management is to embrace the inevitable uncertainty, and aim to turn it to advantage. This requires a flexible and open attitude backed up with some strong management disciplines, and a few simple tools. This chapter covers

- The principles of portfolio management.
- Financial valuation methods.
- Accounting for uncertainty in project valuation.
- Non-financial ways to value projects.
- Selecting and balancing a portfolio of projects.
- Management processes.
- A Main Case on Britannia Building Society.

Management, and especially financial management, is notorious for its use of obscure acronyms. Portfolio management has more than its fair share of these and we give a glossary in Table 6.1.

PRINCIPLES OF PORTFOLIO MANAGEMENT

The Need for a Process

Portfolio management is not just about making the right decisions about which projects to start. It is also about reviewing those decisions regularly, changing them when necessary and helping staff and colleagues to understand and accept the changes. The ideas element of the Pentathlon diagram is drawn as a funnel to emphasize the fact that there should always be more ideas available than are finally used. The more novel ones may require some work before it is possible to make a decision, and inevitably this work will sometimes turn out to be wasted. Many companies find it difficult to accept this; but any organization that is not prepared to invest adequately in the early process of investigation and risk removal either will produce only trivial innovations or, worse, will have to cancel many projects later on when far more money has been invested. 'Fail soon to succeed quicker' is a good motto, used by the product design consultancy, Ideo. Stopping projects is often painful because people have invested much energy, enthusiasm and even their personal credibility in them, so it is very helpful to have a clear and objective process for making these difficult selection decisions.[1] The process should aim to ensure that all the key issues are understood and debated. It should encourage clarity, and where possible quantification, but at the same time allow scope for the exercise of management judgement.

An inadequate portfolio management process leads to slow decisions, a tendency to choose only low-impact 'me-too' projects and a failure to stop projects that have lost their way. The typical results of these are summarized in Table 6.2.

Portfolio management is a complex and multifaceted task. Management judgement is required but appropriate tools also help. In selecting the tools to use it is vital to remember that their role is to help managers come quickly to decisions that are not only good but can also be justified and communicated. Mini Case 6.1 describes how the World Bank redesigned its selection process to achieve these aims.

Table 6.2 Business Impact of Poor Project Selection Processes

Management Issue	Resulting Problems
Slow decision-making	• Projects that start late will be late to complete • Late to market means lost profit • Rush to make up for lost time causes excess cost and temptation to cut corners • Frustrated staff
Unadventurous, low-impact projects	• Poor profitability • Lost opportunities to gain market share • Poor morale
Too many projects	• Resources stretched so that some or all projects run late • Lack of management attention • Bottlenecks
Poor projects not killed early	• Unnecessary waste of money and time • Lack of resources for good projects

| Mini Case 6.1 |

The World Bank – the Vision for Selecting Programmes[2]

Most people expect innovation to be particularly difficult in large, bureaucratic organizations. The World Bank, with its headquarters in Washington DC, might be seen as such an organization and not a hub of innovation. However, appearances can be deceptive as during the past four years the World Bank has built a reputation for being creative and innovative. How?

Much of the credit must go to the insights provided by the team at the corporate strategy unit that has radically changed the way projects are chosen for World Bank funding. The aim of the Bank is to alleviate poverty and traditionally only large, relatively conservative programmes were funded. Large amounts of money were involved so everybody wanted to make the best use of the cash available and avoid funding anything with a high risk. The decision process was normally complicated, conducted at the highest levels in the organization, and was slow.

Now the Bank has completely changed the way it selects the best proposals from the myriad it receives. The vision was to base the selection process on the way venture capitalists make funding decisions in stages and spread their risks over a range of projects rather than 'just going for the big one'. Initial funding is now available for the first stages of a programme and subsequent financing is dependent on defined results being achieved in a set timeframe. Now the World Bank is experimenting more, and is running pilot programmes to test radical ideas. The range of projects being considered and the selection process have also become highly transparent. Decisions are made by a panel of judges drawn from industry and a variety of non-profit organizations, such as Oxfam and World Vision and centres on a 'Development Marketplace'. This is done at a day-long meeting in which proposals are presented and selected in the style of an industrial show, with booths set up for each proposal, presentations and the like. Not only does this make the selection process transparent to all employees and applicants but the resulting exchange of ideas spurs everyone involved towards the production of better proposals, year on year.

Finally, managers must remember that different tools are appropriate at different stages in the life of an innovation project. In the early, investigative stages judgements may be mostly intuitive, and only later, as the facts clarify, will full financial analysis be helpful (see Figure 6.13).

Elements of a Good Portfolio

The overall purpose of portfolio management is to ensure that the organization's collection of innovation projects delivers the best value over time. The key issues that must be considered are[3]

Valuation Criteria

- Each individual project should represent good value to the organization.

- The collection of projects must make efficient use of the resources available. Where projects compete for scarce resources it must be clear how the allocation between them is to be made.

Portfolio Balance Criteria

- High-risk projects may have to be balanced by low-risk ones to ensure that the overall exposure to risk is acceptable. The organization may also want to maintain a balance of projects over time and possibly across the areas of the business.
- The innovation portfolio must fit and respond to the company's strategic needs. Perfectly good projects may have to be delayed or aborted in favour of others in more strategically important parts of the business.

Management Criteria

- The management process should be as open as possible.
- The information on which decisions are made should be collected with care, to minimize avoidable bias.
- When ongoing projects are cancelled, the process must ensure that staff motivation is retained.

We will examine each of these requirements in more detail later in this chapter.

VALUING INDIVIDUAL PROJECTS

Types of Project

In discussing valuation methods it is convenient to distinguish three generic types of project. The simplest is a *single-stage* project that is expected to run through from start to finish without interruption, as shown in Figure 6.1a. Small or low-risk projects are generally treated in this way. The second is a *multistage* project, which is conducted in phases with a progress review after each one when a decision is made whether or not to continue. This is obviously appropriate for high-risk projects and especially those where preliminary investigations are needed to establish what can (or should) be done. Projects with high levels of technical novelty, such as drug development, would be examples. It may be possible to give figures for the probability of cancellation at each phase, as shown schematically in Figure 6.1b, and these figures can be useful in valuing the project, as we show later. These are not probabilities in the normal sense but rather estimates of the confidence that managers have that the decision will go one way or the other. The third type of project is one where the reviews after each phase may lead to alternative courses of action, rather than a simple go or stop decision so that the project plan could branch into a network of possibilities (Figure 6.1c). Such *network* projects require more sophisticated valuation methods.

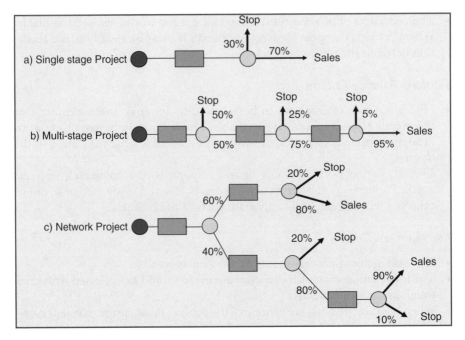

Figure 6.1   Single-stage, Multistage and Network projects

Note: The boxes are activities, the circles decision points. The percentages represent confidence estimates of which way the decision will go.

Financial Valuation Methods

The most obvious way of valuing a project is by financial analysis. Indeed this is the most common, and often the only, method used.[4] It is often necessary to supplement it by other techniques, especially in the early stages of projects when the financial data are often unreliable. But appropriate financial assessment is obviously important at any stage and should, of course, dominate the argument as the project nears fruition. The analysis can be done with varying degrees of sophistication, and somewhat different methods are appropriate for simple and for complex projects.

Single-Stage Projects

The most straightforward and the most commonly used way of determining the value (V) of a project is simply to estimate the financial benefits (B) accruing from it and subtract the costs (C) to give a net value.

$$V = B - C \tag{1}$$

Many levels of sophistication are possible in estimating the components of this simple equation, but before we discuss them further it is worth remembering that extra sophistication does not necessarily make for better decision-making. If the basic data are flawed or uncertain, elaborate computation will not make it any better. Indeed it may obscure the logic or, worse still, may lend a spurious authority to a fundamentally unsound deduction. Remember the adage: garbage in, garbage out.

That said, some enhancements are certainly useful. The first is to take account of the time-related value of money. Income today is worth more than income next year because money in hand today could be invested to earn one year's worth of interest. For the same reason early expenditure is more costly than later. The first modification of Equation 6.1 is therefore to take account of this effect by using *Discounted Cash Flow* (DCF). In this approach, every element of income or expenditure is discounted by a factor that takes account of when it occurs.[5] An income or cost in one year's time is multiplied by a discount factor $1/(1 + s)$, where s is the yearly cost of money: so if money costs 5 per cent a year, the discount is $1/(1.05)$, or 0.95. Income made in two years' time is multiplied by a discount factor of $1/(1.05)^2$, or 0.91, and so on.

When discount factors are included for both income and costs, the value of the project is called the *Net Present Value*, or NPV:

$$NPV = C_1 + C_2/(1 + s) + C_3/(1 + s)^2 + C_4/(1 + s)^3 + ... \qquad (2)$$

Here C_1, C_2, C_3, and so on are the cash flows (costs or incomes) into the project in the first, second, third time periods and so on.

The discount rate, s, should be the average cost of capital to the organization and so should include the cost of equity and of debt in the proportions found in the balance sheet.[6] Some financial managers choose a higher discount rate on the income stream as a way of taking account of a high level of risk in the project. This practice is subject to three criticisms: First, the particular figure used tends to be a 'gut feel' that can seldom be justified.[7,8] Second, it makes the assumption that uncertainty is always a negative factor, which is wrong. Uncertainty means that a project faces a range of possible outcomes, not just a single one; and this range may well include results that are better than hoped as well as worse. Third, risk is not merely an aspect of value. It is an entirely different thing, requiring specific management. Burying risk in a financial discount hides it from scrutiny and so undermines the management process.

Net present value is very widely used[9] and is worth the comparatively small amount of effort involved in the calculation, especially if the timescales of the project are long or money costs are high.

Sensitivity Analysis

The next enhancement is to estimate how robust the value of the project is. The simplest approach is to re-run the financial calculations several times with different assumptions about the major component parts. This basic and valuable step is surprisingly often omitted, even in these days of easy spreadsheet analysis. Yet the information may be critical in deciding whether to go ahead with a project

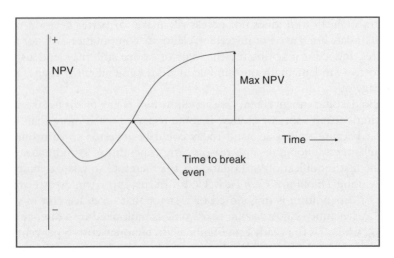

Figure 6.2   Development of the NPV of a typical project with time

if it turns out to be very sensitive to some factor that cannot be relied on. It is also very useful as the project progresses because it highlights which elements the project manager must control to ensure financial success. We will discuss this further in Chapter 7 on implementation.

Another approach to robustness is to calculate how quickly the project delivers its results. A convenient measure for this is the 'payback time', or *Time to Break Even* (TBE). The financial returns from most projects will follow a curve like that shown in Figure 6.2, starting with a period of loss when expenditure is made but income has not yet begun, moving to the 'break-even point' when the income balances the expenditure; and then on to overall profit. Other things being equal, a project with a short TBE is more secure than one that takes longer, simply because there is less time for unexpected things to happen. A more subtle approach is to calculate the *Internal Rate of Return* or IRR, which is the value of the discount factor, s, in Equation 6.2 that would reduce the NPV of the project to zero.[10] Clearly, the higher the IRR is, the more financially robust the project: an IRR of 25 per cent would mean that the interest rate would have to be greater than 25 per cent before it would be a better option to keep money in the bank than to invest it in the project. Companies often reject projects that do not meet a threshold value for TBE or IRR.[11]

Single Projects with a Risk of Cancellation

Innovative projects often face the possibility of cancellation before it reaches the end. How does one include this in the valuation? Suppose our confidence in a successful outcome is a percentage, p. There are two possible outcomes: a loss equal to the costs ($-C$) if the project is stopped; and a profit equal to the difference of income and cost ($I-C$) if not. The classical approach is to add the two possible outcomes multiplied by their probabilities. This gives the mean or, in statistical terms the expected outcome or *Expectation*:

$$\text{Expectation} = p(I - C) + (1 - p)(-C) = I.p - C \qquad (3)$$

The result, as one might expect, is simply to reduce the income by the factor p. Notice that the effect on profit can be quite severe: a healthy 50 per cent profit margin is reduced to zero if p is 50 per cent.

But what actually is this Expectation? It is merely the average outcome to be expected from running a large number of such projects. (Just how large a number is discussed later). For an individual project however, the result will be *either* a profit of $I-C$ *or* a loss of $-C$. It will never actually be $Ip-C$; so for a single project the mean value is literally meaningless. One is reminded of the British trade union leader in the 1960s who said, 'Don't talk to me about 8 per cent unemployment. If it's you, it's 100 per cent'. He might have added '... or 0'. Certainly, faced with 8 per cent unemployment few people ask themselves how they can manage on 92 per cent of their salary. The average figure has meaning for governments but not for individuals.

Risky or uncertain projects fundamentally face a range of possible outcomes. It is a mistake (though a very common one) to seek to accommodate the risk in the valuation just by altering the estimate to another single figure estimate. We show below, however, that it is perfectly possible to compare projects and to construct an optimal portfolio without resorting to this fiction.

Estimating Probabilities in Projects

The objective assessment and management of risk is a relatively recent develop-ment in the history of human thought, let alone of business management.[12] For example, the modern concept of probability was not formulated until the mid-seventeenth century by Pascal and Fermat, who built on the earlier work of Galileo, Huyghens and others.[13,14] The fact that such illustrious names were involved should remind us that this is not an easy topic to think clearly about. Even today we are easily misled, as the number of people who believe in winning systems and 'runs of luck' at roulette makes clear.

What do we really mean when we say 'I give this project a 30 per cent chance of success'? Thirty per cent of what? And what use is the number? Let us start with the question of how to estimate the probability of an event.

In most games of chance the probability of an event can be worked out just from the logic of the situation: the chance of drawing a king from a well-shuffled pack of cards has to be 4/52 because there are four kings in a total of 52 cards. In the business world, of course, such logical simplicity is rare. Thought alone will not tell us the probability that the dimensions of a part made in a factory will fall in a particular range, or the proportion of a population who need shoes of a particular size. These must be measured. Yet it is impossible to examine every person's foot or every part made in a factory; instead one must look at a finite number of cases and deduce the underlying proportions of sizes from them.

Sampling Theory is the study of how the characteristics of a population can be calculated from measurements of a restricted sample of cases. Three considerations are important here:

- The samples must be representative of the population. There is no point in looking at a sample of Japanese people and hoping to deduce the foot sizes of Norwegians.
- The situation must be stable. If new machinery is introduced into a factory it is likely to change the process and new samples must be taken.
- The accuracy of the estimate depends on the number of samples taken. Roughly (because the details depend on the statistics of the underlying process), the uncertainty in the estimate improves only with the square root of the number of samples.[15] This means that accurate estimation requires a surprisingly large number of samples: about 100 are needed to give 10 per cent accuracy, and opinion pollsters have to interview over 1000 people to get an accuracy of a few per cent.

In estimating the probability that a particular project will be successful, one relies on comparisons with similar ones in the past. But most people are familiar with very few projects, and fewer still that are genuinely comparable to the one in hand. So these are not probability estimates at all but expressions of personal confidence based on a combination of experience and judgement. There is nothing wrong with this: it's all we have. But managers of innovation projects must recognize that these confidence assessments are very, very approximate. They can be improved by pooling the views of several people, as we discuss at the end of this chapter, but they remain expressions of confidence, not calculations of probability in the strict sense.

Multistage and Network Projects

In a multistage project, managers can take action to deal with problems as they arise, if necessary abandoning the project if its prospects become unattractive. They can also recognize good fortune and capitalize on it. Management action during the course of a project can radically improve its value and this must be taken into account in the calculations. Failing to include this 'undervalues everything'.[16] The following simplified calculation shows how important management intervention can be.

Decision Tree Analysis

Consider a project, which we will call Project Alpha, which proceeds in four stages with decision points between. Each stage has a different cost and at the start of the project, managers estimate their confidence of each being a success, in the sense that progress will be good enough for the project to continue. These are shown in the form of a *Decision Tree*, in Figure 6.3. If the project comes to fruition the expected income, appropriately discounted, is €75m.

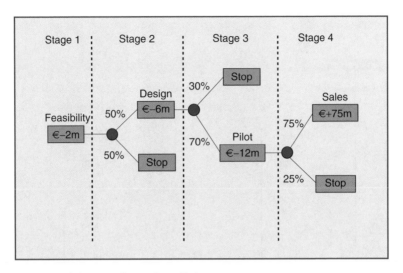

Figure 6.3   Decision tree for project Alpha

Note: The boxes show activities and their (discounted) cash flow.

The total discounted cost of the project is €20m and the overall confidence in success is $0.5 \times 0.7 \times 0.75$ or about 26 per cent. If the project goes ahead with no intervention the Expected revenue is 26 per cent of €75m, or €19.5m. With costs of €20m, the NPV is projected to be a loss of €0.5m, so the project looks thoroughly unattractive financially.

The picture changes dramatically if we take into account the option for management to stop the project after each stage if the prospects look poor. The cost of the first stage must be included in full but there is only a 50 per cent chance that the cost of the second will actually be incurred. The third-stage cost will occur only if both the first and second phases are successful, confidence in which is 35 per cent (0.5×0.7). The correct calculation for the likely costs is therefore

$$€(2 + 0.5 \times 6 + (0.5 \times 0.7) \times 12)m = €9.2m \qquad (4)$$

Thus the project as a whole really has a projected NPV of €(19.5 − 9.2)m = €10.3m. This straightforward calculation emphasizes how misleading over-simplistic financial projections can be. Good management decisions add value (arguably €10.8m in the above example!). Neglecting the possibilities for choice and action during a project can lead to serious undervaluation and the likely rejection of potentially excellent opportunities.[17]

The estimated value for a multistage project derived in this way is known[18] as the *Expected Commercial Value* (ECV) and the process of analysis itself is called[19] *Decision Tree Analysis* (DTA). Clearly, it is more realistic than a simple DCF calculation for such projects, though one must always remember that the figures used are estimates, not facts.

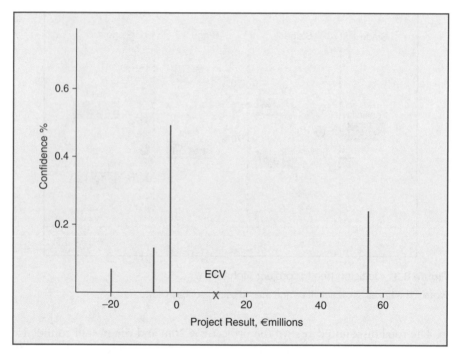

Figure 6.4   The actual possible outcomes of project Alpha

   The ECV calculation yields a single figure for the value of the project, taking into account the confidence levels ascribed to the outcomes at the various stages. It is very convenient to have a single value but of course it actually represents the average outcome of a large number of such projects. If one undertook project Alpha alone it would actually have just one of four outcomes: a profit of €55m if it went to completion; or a loss of €2m, €8m or €20m if it stopped at an intermediate stage. This is illustrated in Figure 6.4. The ECV is not itself a possible outcome at all.

Monte Carlo Simulation

The range of possibilities for a project can be explored more completely using a *Monte Carlo* simulation.[20] This used to be considered a rather esoteric technique but it can now be done very easily using a spreadsheet and a simple application package.[21] The idea is to run a large number of calculations using a random number generator to represent the confidence levels in the decision tree. For example, the confidence in success of the first phase of project Alpha is 50 per cent, so the simulation first generates a random number between 0 and 100 and if this is less than 50, the phase is deemed to have failed so the simulation records a project loss of €2m and stops. Otherwise it stores the €2m cost and generates another random number to decide whether the next phase is successful. If this number is less than 30, the second phase has failed so a project loss of

€8m is recorded. Otherwise the accumulated cost would increase by €6m and the simulation would move to the next phase, and so on until completion. The simulation is then repeated. Each run will generally have a different outcome, but repeating the process a very large number of times and accumulating the results generates a full view of all the possible outcomes and how relatively often they occur.

A simple calculation such as we have just done does not strictly require the Monte Carlo treatment. But it is very useful if we wish to make the model more realistic, for example, by replacing the single values for the costs of each phase by a range of possibilities. For example, instead of putting €6m for the cost of phase two of Project Alpha the model would allow, more realistically, a distribution of cost between perhaps €4m and €7m. Figure 6.5 shows the result of a Monte Carlo simulation of a project similar to Project Alpha, where ranges of costs and of income have been allowed in place of the single-point estimates.

The Monte Carlo simulation is a helpful and surprisingly easy technique to use. It has the healthy effect of showing the full range of possibilities that management may actually face on the particular project. Of these outcomes the 'average' may itself actually be very unlikely – as it is, for example, in the project shown in Figure 6.5.

Comparing the Values of Risky Projects

The additional information provided by this more complete analysis is helpful in managing the project but the complexity of diagrams such as Figure 6.5 does seem daunting when it comes to making priority decisions between projects.

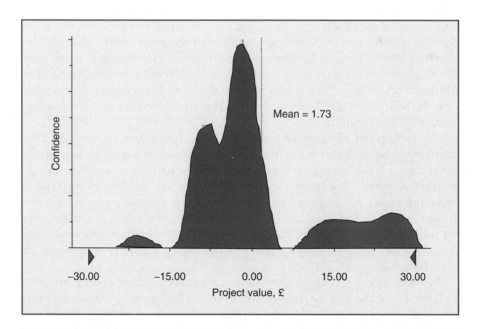

Figure 6.5   Result of Monte Carlo simulation for a project similar to project Alpha

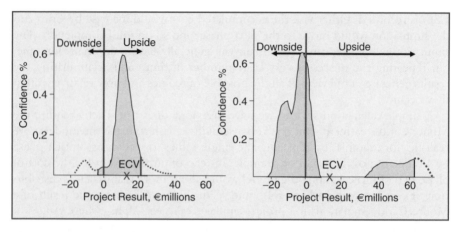

Figure 6.6 Two value distributions truncated to remove extremes, showing their different Upside and Downside measures in relation to a benchmark

However, comparisons can be made quite simply by treating each project as a wager in which the possible loss is balanced against the possible gain.[22] The most attractive project is the one with the best balance. One must first recognize that the detail of the probability diagrams has no predictive value for individual projects for the reasons already explored, so the analysis should aim merely to establish upper and lower limits of the value – the best and worst outcomes that are reasonably likely to happen. This will usually involve rejecting the tails of the distribution as shown in the two different cases illustrated in Figure 6.6. This may be done by rejecting the upper and lower tails representing, say, 5 per cent of the outcomes; or by making a judgement about the manageability of the extremes. A performance benchmark is then chosen (for example, break-even or a target return on investment) and projects considered as potential wagers in which the possibility of loss represented by the worst likely outcome compared with the benchmark (the Value at Risk, or Downside) is set against the possible positive result (Upside).

The appropriate measure of Downside is the lower edge of the truncated distribution because this is the amount that the project stands to lose in the worst case; it is the budget managers must commit for the project. The Upside measure requires a bit more thought. Managers are usually uncomfortable using the upper edge of the distribution which is the maximum return the project is ever likely to make. A more conservative measure is to use the area (or integral) under the curve to the right of the threshold, which represents the *probability-weighted* Upside. This was the measure chosen by Embraer in Mini Case 6.2.

The ratio of the Upside to Downside is a measure of how good a prospect each project is, and a rational portfolio can be selected simply by choosing projects in the order of Upside/Downside until the available risk budget is used up. Note that in this approach the concept of Risk as a separate variable disappears entirely. Risk is seen merely as a way of thinking about the range of outcomes that each project faces. There is no question of 'balancing' risk and return.

Mini Case 6.2

Embraer Aerospace – Using Decision Trees[23]

Embraer, the Brazilian aerospace company wanted to determine the most effective way to introduce radio tagging (RFID) technology into part of its operations. It was unclear whether it would be better to proceed via one or two-pilot implementations to minimize the risk, or to go for a single implementation with no preliminaries.

A group of managers first constructed the three decision trees working as a team. They then made their own individual estimates of confidence levels and of cost and income data. Recognizing that their estimates could only be approximate they agreed to set the confidence values on the tree by allocating 12 tokens between the tree branches representing their relative confidence in each of the outcomes. They estimated costs or incomes (suitably discounted) for each stage as upper and lower limits with either a triangular or flat distribution between them. Finally, the estimates were pooled and discussed as a team to come to agreed values. This process took a few hours. The Monte Carlo analysis was then done offline and the resulting value distributions presented to the team the next day for discussion and review. In this case it was agreed to truncate the distributions by simply removing the 5 per cent tails at either end. One of the decision trees and the associated Monte Carlo results are shown in Figure 6.7.

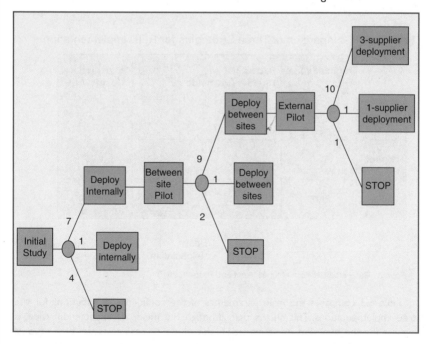

Figure 6.7   Decision tree and Monte Carlo simulation for RFID project for Embraer

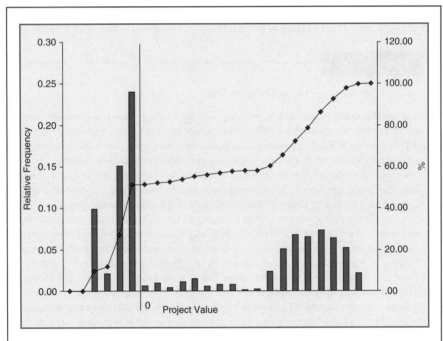

Figure 6.7   Continued

Table 6.3   Comparison of Three Strategies for RFID Implementation

	Highest value (HLV) $	Expected Upside/ Downside	Mean $	Expected Upside/ LLV
No pilot	475	3.1	135	1.0
1 pilot	765	3.2	160	1.25
2 pilots	697	5.3	190	1.0

Best "expectation"   Most secure "bet"

Source: Case adapted from Mitchell, Hunt and Probert, 2010.

Table 6.3 compares the main parameters of the confidence distributions for the tree implementations. This shows that although the mean, or expectation value, is highest for the two-pilot implementation, the one-pilot case gives the best ratio of Upside to LLV, which, as argued above, is a more secure basis for choice. This is the implementation that the company chose to follow.

Valuing Large and Small Portfolios of Projects

We have already emphasized that the ECV or mean outcome is a misleading concept when applied to an individual project. Nevertheless, it can be used for sufficiently large portfolio. This is because the uncertainties in the individual projects tend to cancel out, and so as more projects are added the value of the whole portfolio becomes relatively closer to the sum of the means of the individual projects. Unfortunately, the uncertainty reduces rather slowly as the size of the portfolio increases. Roughly (because the details depend on the statistics) it takes 10 projects to reduce the relative spread to 1/3 of what it was for one project, and 100 to reduce it to 1/10 – and that is assuming there is no correlation between the factors causing success or failure in the projects, a rather bold assumption if they are happening in the same organization. Any such correlation slows down the reduction of the spread.

Anyone who uses the mean as the measure of the value of a risky project is implicitly assuming that it forms part of a very large portfolio. This may be right, but very often it is not.

Real Options

Many authors[24] have noted that projects in the physical world have much in common with financial instruments called *Options*. An option on a stock is a contract that allows, but does not compel, the holder to buy that stock at a fixed price at some point in the future. If the price of the stock goes up, the holder of an option can make money by exercising the option and then selling the stock at the (higher) prevailing price. However, if the stock goes down, the option holder does not have to make a purchase and loses only the cost of purchasing the option itself, which is usually much less than the value of the stock. Many innovation projects have the same logic in that they give management an option, but not the obligation, to take an innovation forward after each stage. This analogy suggests that the extensive theory developed for valuing financial options might be applied to valuing the flexibility that managers have in managing projects. This is known as the *Real Options* approach to valuation.[25] Its application to innovation projects, and especially to new product introduction, is an area of active research at the moment.[26]

The theory of option valuation for financial stocks was worked out fully in the 1970s by Fischer Black, Myron Scholls and Robert Merton (BSM). The full treatment involves an elegant partial differential equation, the Black-Scholls equation, which allows analysis of a large range of varied cases.[27] The analysis has been extremely influential in the financial community but attempts to apply it to innovation projects have not been particularly convincing and we consider that the idea is flawed because the financial and project domains are seldom closely comparable.[28] The first discrepancy is that in the BSM treatment the value of the stock follows a 'random walk' path, with its possible range spreading upwards and downwards as time goes on. This means that the possibility of gain from holding an option increases over time, so the value of a long-dated option is greater than a short-dated one. This is a good model for the stock market where securities can be traded at any time but innovation projects generally have no realizable value until they are complete. Moreover, the value of the options that they provide is more likely to decline with time because of competitive pressures, expiry of patents or market lifecycle. If it were not so managers would be observed diligently slowing down their innovation projects! The second discrepancy is that the BSM analysis relies on being able to identify a *hedge position*. In essence a hedge is a mirror image of the stock: an asset whose value tracks it in reverse, going down if the stock goes up, and up if it goes down.[29] In the world of innovation projects, however, much of the risk will be within the project itself (so-called *specific*, or *private*, risk) and cannot usually be hedged. How could one arrange to profit from an idea that simply proved to be unworkable? Real options may be useful in evaluating 'real' projects where the risks are mostly in market conditions but not for the majority of innovation projects where most of the risks are internal.

Non-financial Methods

In an ideal world financial calculations would be all you need in selecting projects in a portfolio. Unfortunately, the financial information available in the early stages of a project may well be incomplete or unreliable – or more likely, both. There are two reasons for this: the first is that the completion date may be some way in the future so there may be genuine uncertainty about what can be achieved and what the customer's reaction will be. The second is that developing a detailed business plan with reliable financial information requires a lot of effort that companies may feel is not justified when the project is still in the concept stage. So even if realistic financial projections could be made, the truth is that they seldom are. This fact is well attested by research: in a wide-ranging study, Robert Cooper and co-workers[30] found that of all the possible ways of selecting projects, practicing managers had the least faith in purely financial projections.

The limitations of financial projections have led companies to look for more broadly based approaches to portfolio management in which financial data may be included but as only one of several factors. The approach is analogous to the *Balanced Scorecard* approach to measuring company performance.[31] The argument is that where financial figures are considered unreliable one can improve the project selection process by including other criteria that are known to be well-correlated with the success in new products.[32,33] The simplest set of such generic factors for a new product might include market size and growth rate; level of competition; how well the project fits with company strategy and so on. But companies will often use factors that are more industry-specific.

The criteria may simply be used as a checklist to guide the review process and ensure that all relevant factors are being considered. Alternatively managers may allocate a score against each factor and so arrive at an overall score for each project to give a clearer sense of priorities. An example of such a process used by

Table 6.4   Project Scoring System Used by Dupont[34]

	Score		
	15	**10**	**5**
1. Strategy Alignment	Fits Strategy	Supports	Neutral
2. Value	Significant differentiation	Moderate	Slight
3. Competitive Advantage	Strong	Moderate	Slight
4. Market Attractiveness	Highly profitable	Moderately profitable	Low Profitability
5. Fit to Existing Supply Chain	Fits current channels	Some change, not significant	Significant change
6. Time to Break Even	< 4 years	4 – 6 years	> 6 years
7. NPV	> $20 m	$4 - $20m	< $5 m

DuPont is shown in Table 6.4. Managers allocate a score against each of seven factors, using the statements in the boxes as guidance, and the results are added to give an overall figure.

Designing and Using a Scoring System

Checklists and scoring systems usually have to be customized for the job in hand. For example, the system used by Domino Lasers a company with a restricted product range and a turnover of $30 million at the time (see Table 6.5) is quite different from that used by Dupont, a diverse company with a turnover closer to $30 billion. Indeed, different criteria may apply for different types of projects. Managers at a large engineering company once told us they had rejected scoring methods because they 'rejected all the innovative projects'. The problem turned out to be that they were selecting research proposals using a checklist designed for small product improvements. Its first three items, Technical Risk, Commercial Risk and Financial Risk, though quite appropriate for minor enhancements, were enough to kill off any really novel idea.

Designing a checklist or scoring system is a useful learning experience for the management team and there is plenty of help in the literature[35] so the time spent is not wasted. The following issues are the most important:

- Avoid too many factors. There must be enough separate points to give structure to the debate and to ensure that nothing important is overlooked, but too many can inhibit good discussion. Six factors are probably about right, ten the maximum.
- Avoid factors that express the same issue in different ways, such as 'sales' and 'market share'. This leads to overemphasis of one factor.

- Ideally, the factors chosen should be of roughly equal importance, if only because the team will probably spend roughly equal times on scoring each of them. Of course it is possible to allocate a weighting to each factor and then multiply the scores by these weightings. But beware of spending more time discussing the weightings than the projects!
- The scales used for the factors should as far as possible represent equivalent value to the organization. For example, in Table 6.5 the scales for Increased Sales and Cost Reduction were chosen so that a particular score on either would yield approximately the same profit level, taking into account the financial structure of the business.
- Demand facts and numbers rather than 'gut-feel' responses wherever possible.

An important part of constructing a project scoring system is to give adequate guidance on how to interpret the scales. It is arguable that DuPont does not go far enough in this respect; for example, people with the same opinion of the competitive advantage of a project may have different views about whether this should be given the rating 'strong', 'moderate' or 'slight'. This unnecessary ambiguity can be reduced by using a more complete set of *anchoring statements* to help ensure that all participants use the scales in a comparable way. (An alternative is for certain people to be responsible for scoring one parameter for all projects – see the main case for this chapter: Britannia Building Society. This at least ensures consistency.) A set of anchoring statements, used by Domino Lasers, is shown in Table 6.5.

There are different opinions about whether scoring should be done individually or as a group and whether a group should aim to reach a consensus on each factor. The advantages of sharing information in an open way are obvious but it has often been noted that the discussions and conclusions can be driven to a false consensus driven by one dominant or senior member.[36] We discuss these issues in more depth in the final section of this chapter.

The value of scoring systems often lies as much in the discipline of collecting and discussing information on all aspects of the project as in the final scoring. Helpful as they are, these are rough-and-ready methods designed to aid decision-making in highly uncertain situations. If one project should score a few points more than another, recognize that the precision of the tool is not enough to differentiate them. Find another consideration – the quality of the project manager or the morale of the team perhaps – to separate them.

Scoring systems are very widely used in project selection but our experience is that people often have a vague feeling of dissatisfaction with them. Probably this is simply because scoring is used most often in the early stages of projects when information is clearly patchy and nobody feels really comfortable in making decisions. However, it is the best – indeed virtually the only – technique that is suitable for such situations.

Table 6.5 Project Scoring Matrix Used by Domino Lasers with Anchoring Statements (see also Mini Case 6.3)

Rating	0	4	7	10	Total
Key Items					
'HARD' Increased Sales (or lost sales saved) in first 3 years after launch	None	$2 million (e.g., 100 machines at 20K)	$4 million (e.g., 200 machines at 20K)	$6 million (e.g., 300 machines at 20K)	
Cost reduction savings over 3 years	None	$0.5 million	$1 million	$1.5 million	
Price premium/gross margin in target market	Worse than in our main business	Margins similar to our main business. Little or no price premium	Improved margin. Price premium equivalent to $1m over 3 years	Significantly better margin. Price premium equivalent to $1.5m over 3 years	
Channel cost or efficiency benefits	More difficult to sell or service than existing products. Significant training needed	Selling and servicing much the same as existing products	Easier to sell or service than existing products. Efficiencies worth $1m over 3 years	Significant benefits to the channels. Efficiencies worth $1.5m over 3 years	
'SOFT' Customer impact	Offers no unique customer benefits or features	Some unique benefits. Enhances corporate image	Clear unique benefits. Something to talk about. A 'door opener'	Eye-catching benefits. A talking point at shows, gives an entry to competitor laser accounts	
Technology offers a platform for growth	Dead end/ one of a kind	Can be used in other products or for business expansion	Potential for use throughout the business or for business expansion	Opens up entirely new markets	
Comments					Total %

Mini Case 6.3

Domino Lasers – Portfolio Scoring[37]

Simon Bradley, the Managing Director of Domino lasers a manufacturer of laser systems based in the USA and Germany, became concerned that the company was concentrating too much on small, low-impact projects, possibly to the exclusion of larger but riskier enterprises. The company had between 10 and 15 projects in hand, some quite mature but others in the early formative stages. Bradley wanted to include the management of the newly acquired German subsidiary in the review of the project portfolio to ensure there would be support from all parts of the company for any changes that had to be made. But it would not be easy, as it was clear that managers in the two parts of the company had different tolerances of risk. The two teams also tended to emphasize different aspects of the market, the Americans being more used to seeking high-volume opportunities while the Germans tended to pursue applications with lower volume but higher margins. Doing a portfolio analysis together could help to align the views of the two management teams but there would have to be a clear structure to guide the discussion.

Bradley spent some time in preparing a structured risk-reward analysis. It had to be useable for early-stage projects, where detailed financial information was not available, as well as for more mature ones. Carefully anchored scales were clearly needed to help align the approaches of the two teams. The scales used are shown in Tables 6.5 and 6.6.

A trial run for the scoring system quickly revealed a problem. While all the participants were familiar with some of the projects, almost nobody really understood them all. The review could not go ahead without more shared information. Accordingly, three of the participants undertook to collect data on all the projects and circulate it for comment and review so that at the next meeting everyone would start from an agreed set of facts.

The teams met by video link to discuss the projects and assign scores for risk and reward to each one. Richard Blackburn, manager of the US factory commented:

> We started out trying to reach a consensus on each factor but we quickly decided that if there really was a range of opinion about something then we ought not to lose sight of that. So we discussed the facts of each project and then scored them individually. Then we discussed the scores. Sometimes people changed their minds when they understood where the others were coming from, but not always. At the end we recorded the range of each score as well as the mean. People felt much more comfortable not trying to force a consensus.

Bradley comments: 'The most useful thing about the scoring system was that it forced us to think about all the aspects of the projects – not just the cost and technical feasibility, which had tended to dominate our thoughts before. For example, we had a couple of research projects where the biggest risks were actually to do with the market acceptance. So we decided to put effort into the market research first and hold off on the technical work for the moment'.

Choosing a Valuation Method

Every evaluation method has its strengths and weaknesses, and the choice of which to use depends on the level of uncertainty and the amount of choice open to managers as the project progresses. An NPV calculation is appropriate for a single-phase, relatively low-risk project. However, if there are many decision points, ECV or a Monte Carlo simulation are more useful. Greater uncertainty demands an Internal Rate of Return calculation at least, or a switch from financial methods to a scoring system. It is often appropriate to use several methods to provide extra certainty, as Agilent found (Mini Case 6.4).

The choices are illustrated in Figure 6.8.

Mini Case 6.4

Agilent – Riding the Market Waves[38]

Agilent Technologies provides testing technology for communications, life sciences, chemical analysis and semiconductors. Within the semiconductor test business (which became independent as Verigy in 2006) the Systems on the Chip Business Unit (SOC BU) has four manufacturing and R&D sites employing over 650 employees who develop and manufacture a range of highly sophisticated 'chip testing solutions'. These products cost between $600K and $4M. Agilent's customers include 'testhouses' (high-volume integrated circuit testers) and many of the major electronics manufacturers worldwide.

Financial management is given much emphasis at Agilent and the financial controller of the SOC BU, Werner Widmann has deliberately spread his team across the four sites. This ensures the close cooperation necessary with all aspects of the business, from hardware and software R&D, to marketing, to manufacturing and supply chain management.

Key success factors in the chip tester business are time-to-market; meeting the customers' demanding technical specifications; and achieving fast, low-cost chip testing. The business is highly volatile – within a year the quarterly sales figures can fluctuate by as much as 150 per cent. With such uncertainty, it is difficult to maintain R&D spending during downturns in the market; so part of Widmann's responsibility is to ensure that the SOC BU makes significant return on investments during the market upturns and does not suffer from cash flow problems during the downturns.

To deal with the challenges Widmann's team has adopted a much wider role than many financial controllers.'For example, my team led a Portfolio Management Taskforce to develop tools and processes to support top management in the SOC BU Business Board', he says. Gauging the technical risks of a project, and forecasting product sales are notoriously difficult so the team developed a set of tools to be used in parallel. These are based on portfolio assessment questions, market uncertainty analysis and project scoring matrices. Communications throughout the worldwide management team have been significantly improved through the adoption of this standard set of portfolio management tools. And, to promote learning, managers' previous estimations of sales and risks are compared with actual figures and fed back to them. 'The new SOC BU Portfolio Framework has greatly helped in the way it presents the data and makes the trade-offs visible. The Management Team now has the information it requires to make fact-based decisions on which projects to back and which to kill, or postpone. We are now starting to get much better at understanding market attractiveness and risk' says Widmann.

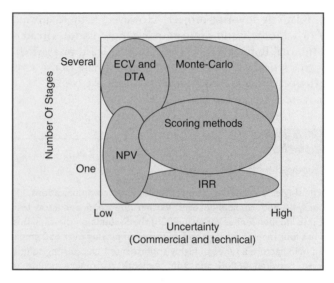

Figure 6.8   Appropriate valuation methods for different types of project

CHOOSING AND MANAGING A PORTFOLIO

Ranking Projects for Selection

Assigning a potential value to each project, by financial calculation or scoring, is the first step in managing a portfolio. The projects can now be ranked in terms of Upside/Downside ratio or by return on investment. Money is the most usual criterion of course, but other things may be important. Progress may be limited by the availability of specialist staff such as good project managers; or it may simply be a departmental budget that cannot easily be changed. Portfolio selection then amounts to getting the best return from this bottleneck resource. Return on investment may be replaced by some other ratio such as 'Return on R&D spend' or 'Return on marketing spend'. If a scoring system has been used, rather than financial assessment, the expenditure may already be factored into the score, giving an overall figure of merit directly.

Actually, of course, each project in the portfolio will use a variety of resources, human and material. Mathematical optimization techniques are available to calculate how to select the group of projects that will produce the best financial return subject to the constraints on several different resources. However, such techniques seem rather seldom used in practice,[39] probably because the mathematics hides the process. Managers cannot readily review or justify the results, nor can they adjust or amend them to take account of other factors. And how do you explain to a team that their project has been terminated because an optimization programme said so? Better to use simpler methods that help to clarify the logic, without removing the scope for management judgement and interpretation.

Managers will often start the project selection process by discarding all proposals that do not offer a certain return on investment, or that fail to achieve a required score, or have too long a payback period. The remainder may now be ranked in terms of financial returns or score and, if no other considerations were involved, one would simply select from the top as many projects as funds or facilities allow. However, in practice the overall balance and strategic fit of the portfolio must also be considered and we consider these techniques in the next section.

Balance

The first aim of portfolio management is to assemble a collection of projects that all represent potentially good value to the company and good use of its resources. We must next consider whether the portfolio represents a good balance of activities in other respects, in particular, *strategic alignment, time and resources*, and the *risk/reward* profile.

Strategic Alignment

The first aspect of portfolio balance to consider is strategic alignment. For example, if a company has a long-term aim to move into a new technology or to enter a new market, a proportion of its innovation investment must be in projects directed towards that end. This priority may override most others and so must be injected into the portfolio management process by some 'top-down' approach that gives special emphasis to projects that express the strategic thrust of the organization, at the expense of others.

There seem to be only three generic ways in which strategic aims can feed into portfolio management. The first is by directly earmarking money for a group of projects, perhaps identified by a roadmapping process (see Chapter 4), that constitute a plan to achieve the required strategy. The resources for these strategic projects must be 'ring-fenced'. Certain types of projects may receive priority treatment as a matter of course: safety issues or compliance with legal regulations would be examples.

The second approach is for management to declare that, as a matter of policy, a certain amount or proportion of funding will be allocated to particular types of project. This approach is known as *strategic buckets*. It may mean allocating funds to particular market sectors or product types (Figure 6.9) or to certain classes of project. The AXA insurance company,[40] which provides our main case study in Chapter 3, aimed that 10 per cent of its innovation projects should be entirely novel, 10 per cent should be based on the reuse of existing ideas in new applications, 40 per cent should be incremental improvements and 40 per cent should eliminate unnecessary activities.

The third approach is simply to include strategic priorities as factors in the project scoring system. This gently guides the selection process in a particular direction rather than imposing an overt policy.

Time and Resources

The projects in the portfolio must also be balanced with respect to completion times. A spread of delivery dates will usually be desirable because there

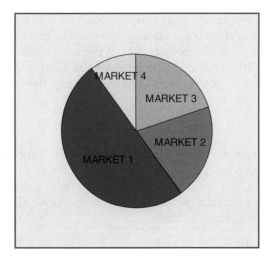

Figure 6.9   Strategic alignment of project budgets according to markets served

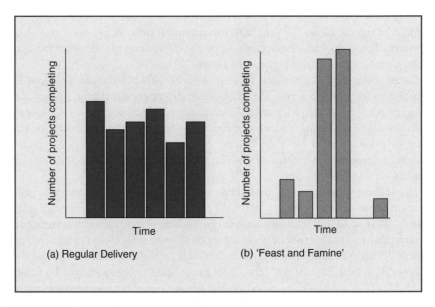

Figure 6.10   Time balance in a project Portfolio

will be a limit to how much change an organization can manage at one time. A steady flow of new products is generally more motivating for the sales force and easier to handle throughout the supply chain than a glut followed by famine (Figure 6.10). On the other hand, there may be good reasons to launch some innovations together to maximize their impact. For example, several new products may be required together for a trade show or an exhibition. Whatever the reason, the timing of the projects in the portfolio must be considered and managed.

Risk and Reward

Another important element of portfolio balance is risk. Organizations may be willing to take on some high-risk, high-reward projects but only if they have a sufficient number of low-risk projects going on at the same time to provide security. Conversely many companies worry that they are 'risk-averse'. By this they do not mean that they take too few gambles, but that they do not undertake enough of the long-term, difficult and innovative projects that have potential for generating really high returns. The *risk-reward* or *risk-impact* diagram is a convenient way to display the balance of risks among the projects and so aid decision-making (see Figure 6.11). Projects are displayed on a grid where one dimension is a measure of the estimated value of the project – for example, its NPV or the rating from a scoring system – while the other is a measure of the uncertainty or risk of the project. The diagram gives a display of the state of the portfolio but not a diagnosis of how healthy it is. That is left to the judgement of the management team.

There are several good reasons for separating perceptions of risk from perceptions of value in this way:

- Risk and reward are different things and require different kinds of management action. The potential reward from a project is often determined mostly by external forces and so is relatively constant, while risk, particularly technical risk, can often be dramatically affected by some investigative work or experiment.
- Risk and reward often become entwined in our minds in unhelpful ways. We have already observed that managers often down-rate their estimates of the potential of projects as a way of accounting for the risks. Risk does not necessarily make a project less valuable; it may merely mean that work is needed to clarify the situation.
- When there is doubt about feasibility, it is all too easy not to ask basic, and perhaps easily answered, questions about value (and vice versa). We have heard managers argue: 'There's no point in worrying about the market when we don't know whether the thing will work'. As a result much time and money is wasted in proving the feasibility of some product that in fact had no market potential. Separating risk and reward explicitly poses questions and prompts action on both.

Figure 6.11 is a typical risk-reward diagram. It shows the balance of the portfolio between the four quadrants, which are often named as *Bread and Butter* (low risk but low rewards); *Pearls* (low risk and high rewards); *Oysters* (high risk

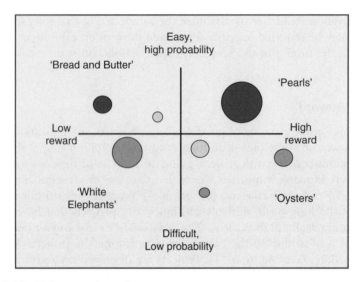

Figure 6.11   Risk-reward matrix

but potentially high reward); and *White Elephants* (high risk, low returns – and proverbially difficult to kill!). In this figure, the area of the circles represents the investment in the current phase of each project and so the diagram shows the distribution of effort over the whole portfolio. The shading can be used to show how near the projects are to launch, or for any other distinction – for example, to show which market sector or part of the business they relate to. Fruit of the Loom (Mini Case 6.5) used it to show how their innovation projects related to the critical stages of their manufacturing process.

The fact that projects may be found in any part of the risk-reward diagram emphasizes the point we made in the section on Real Options: that the world of projects is very different from the world of financial stocks. In the financial world the operation of the market ensures that low-risk stocks generate a low reward and high reward goes only with high risk. Innovation projects are generally quite different because the assets that they represent are not traded openly. No market mechanism operates against Pearls or White Elephants.

A risk-reward diagram carries a lot of useful information in a simple and accessible way but managers must use their own judgement to decide whether the portfolio best meets the needs of the organization. Such diagrams are most useful for early-stage projects. Scoring systems will usually be used to position them on the axes and the balance between risk and reward is determined intuitively. In the later stages, when enough financial information is available to draw value-confidence plots, the more formal and logical methods described above can be used.

Scoring the Risk Dimension

Risk is very difficult to estimate but a carefully designed scoring system can take some of the subjectivity out of the process. The principles are exactly the

Mini Case 6.5

Fruit of the Loom – a Portfolio of Process Innovations[41]

Fruit of the Loom is an international clothing manufacturer employing over 23,000 people and based in Bowling Green, Kentucky. The business is strongly vertically integrated, spanning the complete product process from spinning the yarn and weaving and dyeing the fabric, to creating and packaging the final garment. Consequently the company is very diverse, operating from over 50 sites around the world.

Process innovation – ranging from improvements in existing processes to the application of radically new manufacturing technology – is very important to the continuing success of the company and the target for regular significant financial investment. Management were concerned that, without some central coordination, innovation efforts might be concentrated in too few parts of the business. Moreover, the best practices being developed in some parts of the business were not necessarily being shared with all the sites that could benefit. In 1998, Dr Michael Mallon, VP Manufacturing and Sourcing, set out to understand the portfolio of process innovation projects better, aiming to get better value for money and to ensure that all parts of the business were receiving appropriate attention: 'Previously, each process innovation investment had been assessed individually purely on a financial basis. There also wasn't much interaction between the different functional areas involved. We wanted to improve this process.' Mallon looked at how product portfolios were managed and started to apply these ideas to Fruit of the Loom's process innovation – probably the first company to apply this level of sophistication to process innovation projects.

A survey across all sites showed that more than 100 process innovation projects were being conducted. A portfolio bubble diagram was prepared showing the expected return on each project in one dimension and the degree of innovation in the other

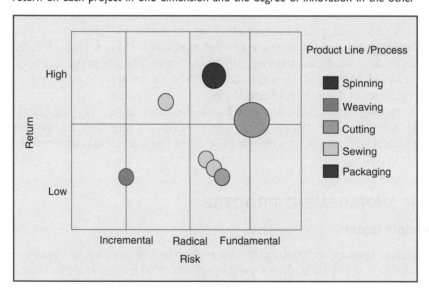

Figure 6.12   Risk-reward matrix used by Fruit of the Loom

▶▶

(Figure 6.12 – simplified to show only a few projects). Financial returns were estimated using 'Expected Manufacturing Benefit' (EMB) – a calculation based on the ideas of ECV. The size of the circles on the diagram represents the level of investment. Some projects at different sites were found to be very similar; a clear waste of precious resources. So the first task was to eliminate duplication while ensuring that the experience gained from the selected projects was made fully available across the company. Once this was done, attention moved to prioritizing the remaining projects. Colour coding was added to the bubble diagram to show the stage of the manufacturing process (spinning, sewing, weaving, packaging and cutting) involved. The resulting diagram allowed managers to see the complete balance of their innovation programme on a single sheet. 'This forced all functional areas to sit down and discuss the portfolio in detail. Not only do we consider each individual project but we monitor whether we were innovating sufficiently at each of the process stages, such as spinning and packaging.' As the diagram indicates, the more radical innovation efforts were concentrated on the clothing stages, and packaging, a promising area for cost reduction, was being neglected.

It is now several years since Fruit of the Loom introduced process innovation bubble diagrams. However, as Mallon says, 'my colleagues still find them a highly relevant tool that creates the interaction necessary to make better investment decisions. Combined with our improved approaches to assessing technical risks, EMB, and even whether the appropriate human resources are available has helped us become much more effective at managing our manufacturing technology. Senior managers have welcomed this more formal process, as they see that it has delivered significantly superior projects than was previously the case.'

same as discussed earlier for appraising project value. In Table 6.6 we give an example of such a score-sheet used by Domino Lasers (Mini Case 6.3). This risk matrix splits each dimension into only six elements. The risk dimension is called 'Likelihood of Success' to emphasize that the scores are not supposed to be probabilities in the strict numerical sense.

Somewhat similar scales have been published elsewhere.[42] Having a checklist of factors can ensure that no major aspects of risk are forgotten; and anchoring statements help people turn information about uncertainty into a shared assessment of risk.

THE MANAGEMENT PROCESS

People Issues

Managers responsible for the portfolio process face two related 'people issues'.

The first is the difficulty of getting reliable information on which to base selection decisions. This is an unavoidable problem, especially early on, simply because decisions have to be based on predictions about the future, not just on facts about the present. But it is compounded by the fact that the people who

Table 6.6 Scoring Sheet Used by Domino Lasers for Assessing Project Risk (see Mini Case 6.3)

Rating	0	4	7	10	Total
Key Items					
'TECHNICAL' Size of technical (in at least 1 parameter)	New concept or order of magnitude change	Step change short of order of magnitude or significant novelty of method	Less than 50% change. No major novelty	Incremental improvement	
Technical uncertainty	Many major technical uncertainties or very high complexity	Several significant technical uncertainties or high complexity	Technical solution defined but uncertainties remain	A defined and straight-forward technical risk	
Demonstrated feasibility	Have not yet been able to demonstrate feasibility	Limited demonstration achieved. Or outline plan for cost reduction	Almost demonstrated. Full demonstration planned. Or detailed plan for cost reduction	Full technical feasibility clearly demonstrated	
Knowledge of market for this product	Pure guesswork	Rough estimate available but no specific study yet done	Specific study done but more work needed. (e.g. market known within a factor of 2)	Market size well defined. No further work needed (e.g. +/-20%)	
'COMMERCIAL' Market readiness	Extensive market development required. No apparent demand	Need or benefit must be highlighted to customers	Clear relationship between product and customer need; or substitutes a competitor product	Meets a clearly expressed customer need; or substitutes one of our products	
Channel capability	No relevant expertise or experience in our channels	Some relevant experience or expertise	Considerable relevant resources available	Leverages our existing skills and resources well	
Comments					Total %

know most about a project are those working on it, and they have a vested interest. Project selection can degenerate into a contest of advocacy skills between passionately committed, and not necessarily objective, project leaders. The only way out of this is to make the collection of the information that is used in the selection process as open and objective as possible, and to allocate enough effort to reviewing it. Larger companies can make good use of experts from other departments. A good example is the process used by SmithKline Beecham (now Glaxo SmithKline) and described in Mini Case 6.6, in which they took pains to separate the valuation of projects from the final portfolio selection.

Since all predictions contain an element of judgement, it is clearly best not to rely on the view of a single person but to seek and combine the views of several people – provided they all have the requisite competence. The improvement that can come from numbers can be negated if a powerful or charismatic figure dominates the proceedings so if the views are pooled in an open meeting it must be carefully managed. The Delphi process[44] avoids this problem by having each participant put forward his or her opinion anonymously. The group discusses them without seeking to identify who said what. A further round ensues, and continues until consensus is reached. Originally this was done by letter or email. A modification that we have found works well is for participants to make initial

---

Mini Case 6.6

Selection and Portfolio Management at SmithKline Beecham[43]

SmithKline Beecham, now GlaxoSmithKline, is a large pharmaceutical company. The merger that created the company five years before left them with a large R&D portfolio of more than half a billion dollars in 1994 which needed reorientation in the face of new pressures. Management were unhappy that their selection process appeared to have become politicized as strong-willed project leaders competed for resources for projects that only they fully understood. The process was seen as neither efficient nor objective. As one manager said 'Figures can't lie, but liars can figure'. The problem was to install a process that was much more open and objective and that could gain the support of all concerned. Their improved approach had three phases.

The first was to ask teams to make not one but four proposals: a base-line proposal, to continue the project as planned; a 'buy-up' proposal in which they could ask for larger resources for an enhanced project scope or speed; a 'buy-down' proposal for smaller scope; and a 'minimal' that would close the project but retain the maximum benefits. This had the effect of moving teams away from 'all or nothing' advocacy towards a more business-centred approach. These new proposals were discussed with senior managers and with the group who would later form the selection panel. In a number of cases the teams themselves, or the subsequent discussions, produced new approaches that were better than the single track to which the team had become committed. The selection panel now understood all the projects well and were clear that the best routes to success had been chosen.

In the second phase, a common set of information was compiled about each project with the help of consultants and colleagues inside and outside the project. Valuations

▶▶

were produced using decision trees and resulting in an upper and a lower valuation for each project rather than a single-point valuation. These valuations were reviewed and debated by the selection panel until everyone was content. Only then was the portfolio selected, and this was done by an independent internal consultancy group who then presented it to the selection panel for review. The selection panel could now concentrate on the portfolio debate, without getting drawn back into valuation issues.

The process is reported to be very successful. The careful and open valuation process was accepted as fair. Many projects were changed to the Buy up or Buy down proposal and the new portfolio projected a 3-fold improvement in return on assets. As a result, management agreed to increase overall R&D expenditure by 50 per cent.

estimates alone which are then discussed anonymously in a structured meeting where the aim is to understand the facts and reasoning. Then participants re-do their estimates and the average is taken, though also noting any serious outlying views. Particular care is needed in eliciting views of project risks and we discuss this further in Chapter 7.

The second people issue arises because innovation necessarily involves waste. A few years of effort that leads nowhere may be no problem for a company, but it will be a lot for the individuals concerned, especially as they often get to feel passionately about their work. This means that the selection process must be as open and objective as possible so that the inevitable disappointment when a project is cancelled does not turn into general disillusionment. It must also give credit to people who do good work on unsuccessful projects, otherwise the pool of innovators will surely dry up. Research laboratories do this by allowing their scientists to publish papers so that they can build a reputation for the quality of their work. At the very least project teams should be able to present and defend their innovation ideas directly to senior management so that they know they have received a fair hearing and that their work is understood and valued by their seniors. Many companies – Richardson Sheffield (Mini Case 6.7) is one, Philips is another – hold well-publicized exhibitions in which new ideas are promoted and top managers discuss and debate the proposals with the innovation teams before making decisions. Innovation is risky, but the risk must be borne by the company, not individuals.

Mini Case 6.7

Richardson's Knives[45]

Richardson Sheffield now part of the House of Fraser manufactures kitchen knives and scissors. Until fairly recently the company's success was primarily based on one main product range: the 'Laser' knife. With its fine serrated edge profile, this product had a 25-year 'stay sharp' guarantee. The Laser with its patents provided the company with a technological advantage that enabled it to grow dramatically throughout the 1980s.

▶▶

In recent years new entrants to the market, weakening intellectual property rights, and the growing importance of 'fashion' in all kitchen products had started to weaken the company's position.

MAJOR PROBLEMS

One of the key issues facing Richardson was that the company had adopted a strategy of giving every major retailer exactly what they wanted, no matter how difficult the variations were. As a result, David Williams, group technical director for McPherson's, who owned the company at the time, explains: 'We had ended up with an increasing number of customer-specific variations – and enormous business complexity, and all within a block of business that actually had not grown at all. We realized we had to stop clinging to old technology and an old definition of what constituted "customer service"'.

The main R&D department had increasingly become overloaded, and one-off special designs were pushing out core product development. Even when an early filtering system was set up, it was far too bureaucratic. The NPD process itself suffered from many typical problems; in particular there was no 'front-end' coordination and control, and no real R&D focus. 'Instead of focusing on major projects, we used to start and develop many projects, and then cherry pick the best ideas for final design', explains Williams. 'Many ideas almost got to market before being dropped, because only right at the end did we get any marketing input'. Also, decision-making was very slow and poor. 'All major project decisions were taken by the Group's senior executives at regular business review meetings', notes Williams. 'R&D was only one item on the agenda at these reviews – and usually the last one. Consequently decisions were often rushed, with executives dismissing ideas and re-directing projects without proper consideration'. Also, the reasons why some projects were chosen in preference to others were not transparent to most of the organization, as only those present at the business review meeting were informed.

Another key problem was a poor understanding of the market and consumers. As with many companies that grow through technological dominance, and with products that effectively sell themselves, Richardson Sheffield had lost contact with its customers. As its technological lead diminished, the company found it increasingly difficult to develop new products that met consumers' expectations.

THE INNOVATION PROCESS

The changes to managing innovation at Richardson Sheffield were summarized in the company's Three-Stage Model: this consists of a front-end process, the NPD process, and tooling to production process. The pre-development 'front-end' is based around a process framework developed by Williams. 'Essentially the first key ingredient was to establish that there was only one process...and all projects should follow this route, and be subjected to the same filter screens – no more product extensions, or projects being completed by the back door route', he says. To enforce this, marketing has become the originator of all new product projects, and works jointly with R&D to develop product ideas that can be presented to retailers as a combination of technology, consumer and customer-driven concepts, rather than simply asking what retailers want.

▶▶

A key part of this approach is the offline development of new technology. 'We have found in the past that it is very difficult to get new technologies to work, and impossible to say when the technology will be ready. So we have formalized the approach whereby I keep the technical developments on one side, only pushing them forward when they are ready', explains Williams. 'Once I have proved the material technology, and if I can sell the benefits to the marketing people – and through concepts to the customer – then the technology is taken up and developed into a full project brief. This way customers are not left waiting for promised new technology, and from the market's point of view the development cycle from them seeing a technology to the finished product is very short'.

For all projects that are to be progressed, the company now appoints a new product manager – from within marketing – who is made responsible for that project, and who works directly with the R&D team once they are given the brief. The coordinated work up-front ensures that only those projects which are likely to have a high market impact come into R&D for development. 'R&D no longer gets bombarded with hundreds of half-baked and badly thought through ideas', notes Williams. To enforce this, full authority for specific projects has been delegated to the marketing product managers and the development teams. Projects no longer have to be continually assessed by senior executives.

'Development projects are now very much in the hands of the marketing product managers. Therefore projects are much less likely to be "political solutions" – a design which tries to harmonize all the division's requirements and customer demands into one product, which often led to products that did not really meet anyone's requirements', says Williams. He adds: 'The senior executive review now only looks at future product strategy rather than specific projects, and this was again something that we dramatically needed to achieve'.

Selecting the Tools

We have already observed that the financial tools used in evaluating individual projects must be chosen to fit the complexity and risk involved, and that scoring systems may change as projects mature. In the same way, the tools and methods used for evaluating portfolios need to evolve as the projects progress, from the broad and subjective methods in the early stages towards 'hard', financial analysis later on. For example, if we imagine a project that starts in a research laboratory and makes its way eventually to a commercial product the choice of portfolio management tools may evolve as indicated in Figure 6.13.

In the very early stages the only important thing is to identify some possibilities that excite enough interest to motivate the team. Later on, scoring methods and risk-reward assessments help, but in the final stages most companies would expect fully costed business plans.

The team that does this review must be in a position to take the necessary actions so it will generally be at a divisional or corporate level in order to have the scope and power to do the job. There is, however, some debate about whether portfolio reviews should generally be conducted together with those for individual projects, or separately. Cooper[46] advocates that project reviews should be

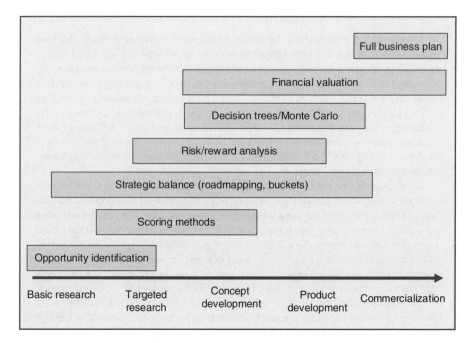

Figure 6.13 Appropriated selection tools at various stages of the innovation process

conducted at times required by the work programme and not constrained to an artificial timetable. Hence portfolio reviews should be separate. However, good communication between the processes is essential; one would not wish to give a project the go-ahead at its project review only to have it axed by the portfolio process the next day.

SUMMARY

Selecting and managing the portfolio of innovation projects are difficult but vital parts of managing innovation. Failure to make good and timely decisions is bad for efficiency in the short term, and for profit, or even survival, in the long term. In this chapter we have reviewed a variety of techniques to help managers select the innovation projects to pursue:

- Financial methods of varying degrees of sophistication take centre stage, but they must be backed up by more subjective methods that allow strategic and other factors to be included in the analysis.
- Particular care is necessary in valuing risky projects. It is a mistake to use single estimates of value such as the mean. The range of possible outcomes must always be considered.
- Scoring systems are particularly helpful in the early stages of projects when financial information may not be reliable.

- The portfolio of projects selected must not only represent the best possible use of resources, but must also be balanced in terms of risk, timing and strategic impact.
- No one set of tools suits all situations; the choice depends on the information available, the type and complexity of the projects involved and how close they are to commercialization.

RECOMMENDED READING

1. Bernstein, P. L., *Against the Gods: The Remarkable Story of Risk* (New York: John Wiley, 1998). [An excellent and readable account of the history and ideas of risk and risk management.]

2. Boer, F. P., 'Financial Management of R&D', *Research-Technology Management*, Vol. 44, No. 4 (July 2002), pp. 23–34. [Good survey of the available methods for valuing innovation projects.]

3. Sharpe, P. and Keelin, T., 'How SmithKline Beecham Makes Better Resource Allocation Decisions', *Harvard Business Review* (March–April 1998) pp. 3–10. [Best practice for a disciplined and inclusive management process.]

4. Cooper, R. G., Edgett, S. J. and Kleinschmidt, E. J., *Portfolio Management for New Projects* (Cambridge, MA: Perseus Books, 2nd Edition, 2001). [A complete and authoritative review of portfolio management practices.]

MANAGEMENT RECOMMENDATIONS

- Choose project valuation tools that are appropriate for the types of project: using subjective measures such as scoring when uncertainty is high, but emphasizing financial measures more as commercialization approaches.
- Keep valuation tools simple and transparent so that the decision process remains open to review, and leaves scope for management judgement.
- Treat numerical measures of risk with caution; they are always very approximate.
- Avoid point forecasts; try and understand the range of possibilities open to each project.
- Ensure that the portfolio is balanced in terms of time and strategy.
- Give close attention to the management process, ensuring that the valuation process is objective and that unsuccessful innovators are rewarded for their efforts.

CASE STUDY
Britannia Building Society – Building and Evolving a Portfolio Management Process[47]

Before reading this case study, consider the following generic innovation management issues:

- What are the difficulties a company faces when it tries to create an innovative culture where one did not exist before?
- Can innovation be imported into an organization from outside or must it grow from within?

▶▶

- How does innovation management differ in service and manufacturing enterprises?
- What criteria are appropriate for evaluating projects in the service sector?

The Britannia is a building society (the British equivalent of a Mutual Fund), founded in 1856 in Staffordshire in the north of England. It provides mortgages, loans, related insurances, savings and investment products. The Society's traditional values of reliability, accessibility and personal service served it well for many years and innovation was not high on the agenda.

THE 'SKUNK WORKS'

The arrival of the Internet in the 1990s caused a shift in Britannia's attitude to innovation, and in 2000 a special task force, the 'E-Business Unit', was set up to explore the opportunities and threats it posed, and to promote higher levels of innovation in general. Within this team a subgroup, called 'The Incubator', was given the task of generating new product possibilities and pushing them forward. The team operated as a 'skunk works', in a separate location, away from the day-to-day running of the business. The E-Business Unit was headed by Tim Franklin, who reported directly to the then Group Chief Executive, Graham Stow.

Mark Chizlett, the programme coordinator, approved of this organization: 'Skunk works teams are focussed, fast and open to innovation. In a very disciplined, data-rational, company like ours we needed a team with some independence and the ability to experiment with running new products; and with a real sense that it is OK to fail.' The Incubator team worked closely with the Board, initially in a three-month intensive strategy review, and later by regular meetings every three months to review projects and manage the portfolio.

From the start the team used a process with four gates to ensure that good ideas were selected and that the balance of projects was appropriate:

Gate 1: Presentation of ideas and decision on which to take forward;
Gate 2: Review of solutions and decision whether to do a controlled pilot, 'launch and learn';
Gate 3: Decision whether to proceed to a scale implementation;
Gate 4: Review of experience and decision to 'plant out' or sell off.

Review meetings started with a presentation of the existing portfolio and ended with a review of how it stood after the decisions just made. Projects that had reached a milestone were assessed and rated against a 'balanced scorecard' of criteria before being approved to move on. The criteria were different at each gate, being initially rather subjective but getting steadily more rational as the projects matured. Detailed financial analysis was not used, at least in the early phases. It was a learning experience for everyone. Chizlett says the Board were not always in their comfort zone: 'They were used to carefully-documented proposals full of data that had already been reviewed by other committees. But, with appropriate stakeholder management by Tim, they came to find the different approach refreshing and thought-provoking. And it worked: we completed six quite major new projects in the first two years'.

▸▸

Britannia was well aware of the deficiencies of running innovation teams outside the mainstream business. Chizlett commented: 'A skunk works is insulated from the day-to-day business and that means it can lose touch with the business case'. So a team of directors oversaw the activities of the Incubator, ensuring that it focused on business results and that it had support for the new initiatives. A policy of short-term secondments to the Incubator meant that their new ideas had ready-made champions throughout the business.

One of the objectives the board gave the Incubator was to be torch-bearers for a new culture for the Society. Chizlett thinks that was probably a mistake: 'It was just too much of a cross to bear for the individuals in the team: to set up a new process and new products and change the Society's culture as well. Culture must be generated from within, not by a guerrilla group sniping from outside'.

INNOVATION MOVES INTO THE MAIN STREAM

By early 2003, it was time to devolve the E-Business team. As Mark Chizlett put it 'We realised the Internet is no longer something new; it's something that needs to be put back in the business. Anyway, by this time most of the team were implementing the new products and running the Internet as a channel'

But Chizlett was worried about who would now be the 'conscience for innovation': who would search actively for new opportunities? Making NPD part of the value chain rather than a separate function promised to give a clearer route to implementation; and it was felt that the new product ideas would benefit from the insights of people further upstream, who were in regular contact with customers. An NPD mission statement expressed the need very clearly: 'If we don't respond quickly to new products from the competition our members (customers) and prospective members will take their business to those that do, limiting our ability to meet targets and strategic ambitions'.

Britannia would be a fast-follower in innovation, a stance driven by both their brand values and resources.

The arrival of a new Group Chief Executive, Neville Richardson, in 2003 provided a trigger for a more concerted move to change the culture of the society and to embed NPD activities more directly in the fabric of the organization. The 'Living the Values' culture-change programme was headed and driven by Richardson. All staff attended a briefing and a roadshow followed by intensive training sessions, company publications and reinforced by new personal objectives. The new culture generated several new sources of ideas: all mangers now have continuous improvement goals in their objectives; the suggestions scheme was revitalized; and a route was created from the customer care department to NPD to feed in opportunities raised by customers.

The position of New Product Development as an integral part of the company was formalized in a new management process, launched in 2003. The NPD manager has the job of collecting propositions and ideas from throughout the company and selecting the most promising ones. A committee with representatives from Marketing, Treasury, IT, Administration, Finance and the Sales channels helps with the selection. The managing board, chaired by Tim Franklin, now the Managing Director of the Member Business and a main board Director, reviews the chosen ideas using a balanced scorecard of nine elements, illustrated in Figure 6.14. Individual members of the board themselves

▶▶

provide the scores for the projects, ensuring a high level of consistency from project to project.

ELEMENT	WEIGHT	MANAGER RESPONSIBLE FOR SCORING
Benefits	4	Marketing *and* Finance
Customer need	3	Customer Excellence
Strategic fit	3	Marketing
Business risk	4	Product Management
Systems and processes	3	Information Services
Operational complexity	3	Operations *and* Sales
Delivery cost	4	Finance
Dependencies	3	Information Services
Priority	3	Managing Director

Figure 6.14   Britannia's project scoring system

'I don't say that what we've done would be right for everyone but it's right for us, here, now', says Chizlett, now promoted to manage the Savings and Investments division, 'There will still be conflicts, compromises, choices. We'll start some things and have to stop and try again. But the conditions for success are all well in train.'

7 IMPLEMENTING INNOVATIONS

There is nothing more difficult to take in hand, more perilous to conduct nor more uncertain in its success, than to take the lead in the introduction of a new order of things.

Nicolo Machiavelli

INTRODUCTION

Turning an idea for an innovation into reality is bound to be something of a unique experience that must be treated as a *project*: a finite activity with its own objectives and resources, and above all its own leadership.

Successful implementation of an innovation starts with good *Project Management*, nowadays properly regarded as a professional discipline in its own right. No project of any size has much of a chance without a well-trained project manager with the power to get things done and the support of higher management. He or she will need good people skills because the more innovative the project is the more impact it is likely to have on people not directly involved in the project itself and this often generates resistance. Managing the reactions of the various stakeholders who are affected is a particularly important job for the manager of an innovation project.

New Product Development (NPD) is the most frequent type of innovation project for most companies, and most of best practices in innovation management have their origins in the development of new hardware or software products. But innovation projects of all types share the basic problem of NPD: managing complex projects that demand learning and experimentation on the route to a novel result. This chapter is about this management problem.

Implementation is shown at the end of the innovation funnel in the Pentathlon framework but this does not mean that it is a separate activity that follows on after ideas have been collected and a selection decision made. The Ideas and Selection phases may involve investigations, trials and pilot studies which may be thought of as early parts of the implementation process. Certainly they require similar management techniques. In such projects what is learned at each stage

227

may change the aims and direction of the whole enterprise so the overall project plan is open to modification as learning develops (see Mini Case 7.1 on Organon, for example).

Mini Case 7.1

Organon – NPD, Demand and the Supply Chain[1]

Organon is the human health-care division of AkzoNobel, a Dutch multinational. It creates, produces and markets prescription drugs mainly for reproductive medicine, psychiatry and anaesthesia. Although the majority of its product development is concentrated in the Netherlands, the company has 10 manufacturing sites and over 12,000 employees around the globe, required to provide fast and efficient service to its geographical markets. Organon has learned to plan for demand uncertainty during NPD, to integrate the needs of its manufacturing plants into its product planning process and to design the supply chain alongside the product development.

The main risks related to the uncertain demand for pharmaceuticals are overcapacity and lost sales. It is expensive to set up pharmaceutical production facilities and, on the one hand, overcapacity must be avoided. On the other hand, a product being unavailable reduces sales and brings a loss in market share that can seldom be recovered. Consequently, Organon product launch plans include different sales scenarios: best, expected and worst cases. Based on these sales scenarios, a number of supply-chain design options (including the suppliers to be used worldwide, the manufacturing sites to be used and its inventory strategies, and the delivery logistics selected) are prepared. Each supply-chain design option is quantitatively evaluated on five criteria: finance, risk, available resources, flexibility to scale production up and down and (interestingly) a measure of confidence in the assumptions.

Erik Hoppenbrouwer, Supply Chain Director, says,

> Early in the NPD process we have added demand and supply scenario planning. We review it regularly and have increased our overall success with product innovations. It is important not only to have an excellent product but also to match it with the best supply chain design. It is not easy as you are dealing often with high uncertainties. Since we have started assessing our confidence in the forecasted figures, we have increased the quality of our decisions. As a result, we can avoid over-capacity whilst minimizing lost sales.

The evocative term *the design factory* has been used to describe a department, such as an R&D group, that is devoted to innovation projects.[2] A design factory needs a process of innovation that can be used repeatedly and with some confidence, as Pizza Hut have found (see Mini Case 7.2). Such a process allows the organization to capture the lessons from previous experiences and using them to guide what is done next time. This learning process is exemplified by the experience of the New Zealand Department of Conservation described in Mini Case 7.3.

Implementing innovative projects is inevitably a team matter and it is important that people from all parts of the organization that will be affected by the project contribute to it from the start as a *cross-functional team*. Team structure and management are crucial and the reader is referred to Chapter 8 for a full discussion of these and related issues.

This chapter will describe the following:

- The basic techniques of project management.
- Risk management.
- Linking customer needs to product design.
- Managing stakeholders.
- Managing the people and processes in an innovation department.

Mini Case 7.2

Pizza Hut – New Product Development

To the uninitiated, the development of a new pizza might be seen as a trivial selection of a new set of toppings. However, in the fast-food business where product consistency and fast 'roll-out' are essential, it is not that simple. Pizza Hut has a seven-stage NPD process called the FRPP – the 'Field Ready Product Process'. This process ensures that a robust product is developed, by defining the steps that are necessary to develop the recipe, select suppliers for the ingredients, test the 'manufacturability' of the product in a typical Pizza Hut restaurant, and ensure positive consumer reactions to the new product. Everything is done to ensure that no time is wasted between a product concept being selected and it being available at the majority of the chain's restaurants. Part of the FRPP ensures that the employees in the restaurants are adequately trained on the product before it is released. Increasingly, competition in the fast-food industry is based on special meals that are only available for limited periods and matched to major events, such as sport championships, or film releases. In such cases, Pizza Hut has found that a reliable but flexible NPD process is essential, even if the resulting product is 'only' a pizza.

PROJECT MANAGEMENT TECHNIQUES[3]

The following is only a brief introduction to this important subject. Our message to managers is that if you do nothing else to improve your company's implementation of innovations at least recognize the importance of project management and make sure that your project managers receive good, formal training for their task.

Projects are classically considered to have four phases: the *concept* phase in which the aims and deliverables of the project are worked out; the *design* phase in which detailed design work is done; the *planning* phase when the implementation is planned in detail; and the *implementation* phase in which the job is actually done. In straightforward, low-risk projects, such as building a road or a house, the parties expect to deal quickly with the issues in the concept phase and so it may scarcely consider it to be within the project at all. In innovation

other hand, the concept phase is not a curtain-raiser to the main part of the whole. It may last a long time and be divided into [stages] such as research, pre-development and concept validation; indeed [a] project may very well stop before it is over. The concept phase embraces the Ideas and Selection parts of the Pentathlon. In the product development literature the concept phase is often called the 'fuzzy front end'. The irreverent name is appropriate because the 'front end' is difficult to define and needs focused attention that it often does not receive. Consequently it is often ill-done and takes too long.

Ideally the concept phase ends with most of the technical and commercial uncertainties removed so that the project can proceed with little risk of failure. There is no doubt that this is the most efficient approach, but it is not always possible to eliminate all the risks early on, so a real possibility of change, and even of outright failure, may remain until near the end of the project. The management process must recognize this unpalatable fact and accommodate it.

Five elements are fundamental to the successful management of any type of innovation project:

- Clear and precise aims, including clear understanding and management of trade-offs.
- A breakdown of the work into elements small enough to be planned and managed.
- A scheduling plan that ensures that the tasks are undertaken in the right order and at the right times.
- A resource plan to ensure that people and facilities will be available to do the tasks as required.
- Active management of stakeholders (the subject of a later section).

We will consider each of these elements in more detail in the following sections.

Setting Project Aims and Tradeoffs

No project can succeed unless its aims are clear from the start. This is obvious, and yet ill-defined objectives – such as ambiguous product specifications – are probably responsible for more project failures than any other factor. This does not mean that every aspect of the project must, or can, be specified right at the start. But every innovation project should at least have a clear *project charter*: a one-page brief that sets out the purpose and key objectives of the project – the elements that are essential to success. As the project progresses, the aims will harden into a firm specification (and the sooner the better), but in the early stages the project charter is an essential guide.

Most of the outcomes of any project or product are essentially committed by decisions made early on, so this is the time when management involvement pays most dividends (Figure 7.1). Sadly, top management attention is too often concentrated in the later stages when the activity and expenditure is highest.

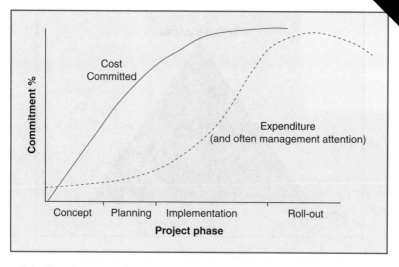

Figure 7.1 Development of committed cost, actual expenditure and management attention in a typical project

Source: After Roussel, P. A., Saad, K. N. and Erickson, T. J., *Third Generation R&D* (Boston, MA: Harvard Business School Press, 1991), p. 85.

Every project is essentially defined by the task itself (the specification); the time allowed; and the cost of doing the work. If something happens to any of these three factors it can generally be recovered only by changing one of the others. This is illustrated in the *project management triangle* in Figure 7.2. For example, if part of the project runs significantly late, the time can generally be recovered only by adding extra resources and so increasing the cost, or altering the deliverables. Similarly, a change to the project specification will impact either time or cost. There is no escaping this. The project charter should therefore state clearly what the trade-off strategy will be and not leave it to the project team to work out in the heat of the moment when problems arise (as they certainly will). The effect of a cost overrun is usually easy to work out but it may be more difficult to calculate the impact that a late launch or a reduced specification will have on the commercial benefits. 'Program managers who know to a penny what an additional engineer will cost and what profits will be lost if the company misses manufacturing cost targets, seldom can quantify the losses associated with a six-month slippage in the development process'.[4] However, the truth is always useful and often surprising.

Studies[5,6] have shown that the time taken to bring a new product or service to market often has the greatest impact on profitability. Several factors contribute to this; for example, a late launch reduces not only the total lifetime sales but also the opportunities for premium pricing as a leading product in the market. The reduced sales volume also affects costs, through less-efficient use of fixed costs and the loss of 'learning-curve' efficiencies that come from accumulated operating experience. Don Reinertsen[7] reported the figures shown in Table 7.1 for how the profitability of a laser printer project by Hewlett-Packard would be affected by various issues in the development process.

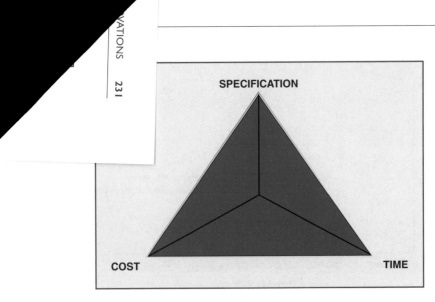

Figure 7.2 The Project Management Triangle

Table 7.1 Project Tradeoffs

Issue	Reduction in project profit (%)
Product introduced 6 months late	31
Quality problems reduce selling price by 10%	15
Compatibility problems reduce sales volume by 10%	4
10% product cost excess	4
30% development project budget overrun	2

Source: From Reinertsen, D. G., 'Whodunnit? The Search for New Product Killers', *Electronic Business* (July 1983), pp. 62–66.

These sensitivities are often quoted to emphasize the importance of time in new product development. However, they must be treated with care because they apply to a particular case: the product lifetime was five years; the market was growing at 20 per cent a year; and prices were expected to fall by 12 per cent a year. A different set of assumptions leads to quite different conclusions. For example, we calculate that a project to reduce the cost of a product by 30 per cent, in a basically static market with static pricing, would have the sensitivities shown in Table 7.2. In this case, the profitability of the project would be much more sensitive to product quality and cost than to the time taken. In medical projects, product performance and safety rightly outweigh time to market. The design of oil and gas platforms is another example. Managers must know the actual sensitivities of each particular project because they may seriously affect

Table 7.2   Project Trade-offs on Different Assumptions

Issue	Reduction in project profit (%)
Product introduced 6 months late	10
Quality problems reduce selling price by 10%	66
Compatibility problems reduce sales volume by 10%	10
10% product cost excess	23
30% development project budget overrun	2

Note: The calculation assumes a 50 per cent gross margin and a five-year product lifetime.

how the project is run. For example, in the case shown in Table 7.1 it may pay to spend more money on the development process, or to choose a cheaper design if it will speed-up delivery.

Mini Case 7.3

The New Zealand Department of Conservation's Pest Eradication Programme – Restoring the Dawn Chorus[8]

Many islands in the South Pacific have been invaded by rats introduced from overseas, and these pests often wipe out indigenous species entirely. As part of its biodiversity programme, the NZ Department of Conservation (DoC) looked at the possibility of eliminating rodents entirely from some of the islands. The scientific view was that this was simply not possible, but DoC staff were not convinced: As one staff member said: 'What we were looking at, at the time, was rats invading islands and species going extinct as a consequence ... The accepted wisdom was that the best you can do is to go out there and grab what you can and rescue them and take them somewhere else ... You wouldn't have to be involved in too much work before you'd realize there's got to be a better way than that ... Pretty soon you're going to run out of places that you can stick these things'.

The mindshift towards trying eradication took place in the early 1980s. The development of new poisons led to experiments on small islands eliminating only a single type of rodent, and moved on later to larger and more complex islands and several species. As more difficult islands were attempted, new techniques were tested and applied. Aerial application of bait was first tried in 1989 and the technique was later developed using helicopters with specially developed underslung baskets. When global positioning systems (GPS) became available they were adopted to improve accuracy. By 1990, 13 species of rodents had been eradicated from 60 islands. This increased to 20 species by 2001. The biggest operation to date has been the elimination of the estimated 200,000 rats from the 11,000 hectare Campbell Island in 2001 at a cost of $2.6 million.

The vision and passion of DoC staff were the most important factors of the success of the pest-eradication programme. Although international experts had concluded that

▶▶

eradication was highly unlikely, key DoC staff refused to accept this. Their refusal to give up on the vision led to experimentation and success with small projects which in turn bred the confidence to take on more ambitious ones. But the right kind of senior management support was very important. For example, the Campbell Island project was jeopardized when a lorry full of rat poison crashed into the sea. Senior managers stepped in to deal with the consequences and protected the project manager from blame and interference so that he could continue to get on with the job. A common theme in the programme was the need to have a culture of trust, forgiveness and not punishing failures. Management accepted that project teams had to experiment to find the best solutions and that some experiments would fail. Care was necessary to manage expectations. The Campbell Island project manager talked about his strong conviction that the organization trusted him to manage the project and to work through issues without second-guessing or unhelpful interference.

A special team, the Island Eradication Advisory Group (IEAG), consisting of administrative experts and managers from previous eradication projects played an important role in giving expert advice to project teams and ensuring that lessons were carried forward from one project to the next. The IEAG also helped to protect the team from political interference.

Other countries are now copying the idea. As biologist Sir David Bellamy put it, 'New Zealand is the only country which has turned pest eradication into an export industry'.

Work Breakdown Structure

Successful execution of any project requires a detailed understanding of what has to be done. The starting point for this is the *work breakdown structure (WBS)* which lists all the *work packages* (or, more simply, *tasks*) and the relationship between them (Figure 7.3). All work packages should be self-contained entities,

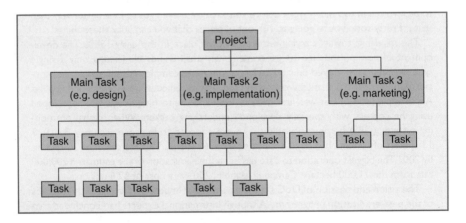

Figure 7.3   A Typical Work Breakdown Structure

to be done by identified people. The WBS is a simple tool and yet is often over-looked, especially in innovative projects where it may be said that the uncertain-ties makes such analysis useless. In fact the converse is true: the WBS is useful precisely for the help it gives in understanding those uncertainties and address-ing them. A review of the WBS is also a very effective communication tool at the beginning of a project as it shows everyone the full scope of what is to be done – not just the core design or manufacturing tasks – and highlights how each task depends on others. Organon, for example, found how important it was to include supply-chain issues in the planning (see Mini Case 7.1).

The WBS is also vital for monitoring progress. Completed work packages are the only unambiguous measure of what has been achieved.

The Project Schedule

Once the tasks have been identified using the WBS, it is time to consider the order in which they are to be done. The ordering is vitally important but it is not always straightforward to work out. Some tasks may be done at almost any time during the project while others cannot be started until earlier ones are complete, which themselves have to wait for others to be done, and so on. Most projects will contain several such sequences of tasks but there will always be one chain that is longer than the rest. This is called the *critical path*.[9] It is very important because the sum of the times required to complete all the work packages on the critical path defines the minimum length of the project. Managers will look very closely at these tasks to see if any can be rescheduled or speeded up because that is the way to reduce the time the project will take. Once the work is in progress the tasks on the critical path should be moni-tored with particular care to ensure that whatever else happens, they, at least, will be on time.

Nowadays a wide range of software is available to simplify the task of plan-ning projects. The familiar bar chart, or Gantt chart,[10] is a very effective way to summarize the activities in a project for communication inside and outside the project team. In a Gantt chart all the project tasks are represented as bars whose length shows their duration. It shows at a glance what tasks are being done at any one time and which are to come; and by shading in the completed tasks the project manager can show clearly how the work is progressing.

The Resource Plan

The next stage in constructing a project plan is to ensure that the required resources can be made available and that they are used efficiently. Most projects will require a range of skills or resources, which may not be interchangeable, so the first thing is to analyse the requirements for different types of resource, especially people. The analysis will usually show peaks when some people or resources will be overloaded. This will obviously mean that their tasks may run late. If these are on the critical path the schedule for the whole project is jeopar-dized, so extra resource must be found or the plan modified in some other way to reduce the overload. Many iterations may be needed to produce the most effective resource plan.

Agile Project Management

The formal disciplines of project management were developed to control complex projects with a well-defined aim – including vast innovative enterprises such as the NASA Apollo project. But like all process disciplines project management can easily become a straitjacket, and a school of thought has arisen that emphasizes that there are circumstances when the formal techniques should be applied with a light touch. This idea, called *agile project management*[11] is especially relevant when the project proceeds by a series of exploratory steps rather than by defining a goal and going for it. This is obviously so in the early stages of innovative projects but the same also applies whenever rapid prototyping is possible. For example, in software engineering it is usually impractical to specify in advance every detail of how the interface with the user should work, but it is a simple matter to build prototypes, offer them to potential users and go through a series of refinements until the result is acceptable. Not surprisingly, agile project management was first applied to such software projects.[12] Effective simulation has long been possible for electronic circuit design, and in recent years the same capability has become available for mechanical designs including 3-D Computer Aided Design and Virtual reality presentations; and in some branches of chemistry it is possible to make and test hundreds of options simultaneously. The best way to proceed may be to quickly build a prototype, test and evaluate it and then build the learning into a new version. The project proceeds by a series of iterations rather than in a single run and may be thought of as a spiral, rather than a linear process. In these contexts, the project management moves from a top-down focus with careful documentation and long-term formal planning towards a more egalitarian approach. This centres on more individual autonomy, and close interaction between the development team and the customer, while keeping planning and documentation to a minimum. Teams working in this way operate 'on the edge of chaos' but the discipline of testing and appraising prototypes at frequent intervals forms the framework for monitoring and controlling progress. Project management disciplines are slimmed down and adapted to the rapid cycle of exploration but are not forsaken. For example, stage-gate reviews, as described later in this chapter, are still required to ensure that all parts of the project – not just the design element – are progressing and that the business case remains robust. The agile management concept is described in full by Jim Highsmith (ref 11) and others.

MANAGING PROJECT RISKS

Innovation projects often face high levels of uncertainty, so effective risk management techniques are very important. Risk considerations enter both in the initial selection of the project and in its subsequent management. These two aspects overlap because the resolution of the uncertainties as the project unfolds may cause reassessment of whether it is right to go on. The continuing process of choosing a group of projects and re-evaluating that choice – portfolio management – was covered in Chapter 6. Managing the risks within a particular project is an aspect of project implementation.

Early attention to risks pays dividends. Toyota[13] reported 30–40 per cent reductions in costs and lead times in R&D projects when they introduced careful risk management processes. Similar results were reported at Xerox.[14]

Collecting Risk Information

The first and crucial stage of risk management[15] is to form as complete a picture as possible of the risks facing the project. This is not at all an easy task.[16] The information is bound to be somewhat speculative, and moreover people are often unwilling to voice their concerns especially if the problem lies in someone else's area of work. It is particularly difficult to maintain a negative point of view in the face of opposition by a forceful or charismatic individual. And it is well documented that successful teams can easily become overconfident, a phenomenon known as 'groupthink'.[17] It is therefore helpful to use an independent person to collect and collate responses anonymously[18] and then present them to the team for open review, carefully facilitating the meeting to keep it objective.[19]

Checklists can be very helpful throughout this process in reminding people of problems encountered on previous projects that might be relevant to the current one. Table 7.3 gives examples of some of the topics in a checklist of marketing risks used successfully in Philips and Unilever's 'Risk Diagnosing Methodology'.[20]

Table 7.3   Example of a Risk Checklist (Marketing Factors)

Risk Element
Target market clearly defined and agreed
Market targets based on convincing research data
Direct feedback from key customers documented
Specification meets consumer standards
Fits consumer habits and/or conditions
Non-intended use by customers adequately anticipated
Communication about new product can be based on realistic product claims
Target consumers attitudes will remain stable during development period
Product will provide easy-in-use advantages compared with the competition
Niche marketing available if required

Source: From Kaiser, J. A., Halman, J. I. M. and Song, M., 'From Experience: Applying the Risk Diagnosing Methodology', *Journal of Product Innovation Management*, Vol. 19 (2002) pp. 213–232.

Appraising the Risks: The FMEA Process

Failure Mode and Effect Analysis (FMEA)[21] is a systematic technique for assessing the risk factors that have been identified and ranking them according to their importance. It is most widely used for exploring the failure modes of new products or processes but it applies equally well to projects. Every part of the product or aspect of the project is assessed in detail to determine all the ways in which it might fail. Each failure mode is then ascribed a score of 1–10 according to how likely it is to happen and a further score of 1–10 according to the severity of the impact it would have if it did. Safety issues are conventionally assigned the maximum score. A third score is often used to indicate the likelihood that the failure will not be detected (or, in the case of a project, that the problem will not be corrected in time).[22] The product of the scores is the *Risk Priority Score*, which gives an overall indication of the risk posed by that element. Table 7.4 shows an example of such an analysis, applied to the checkout process at a supermarket.

FMEA is essentially a team activity. It is often helpful to include people from outside the project who have relevant experience but the important next step of deciding how to deal with each risk is essentially a job for the project team itself. Any 'show-stoppers' that might cause the total failure of the project should be tackled first, of course.

Table 7.4   FMEA Analysis Applied to a Supermarket Checkout Process

Failure mode	Likeli-hood	Severity of impact	Failure to detect	Risk Priority Score	Action
No bar code on product	5	2	4	40	Review process. Consider reward for detection
Bar code reader fails	1	2	1	2	
Product wrongly recorded/priced in computer system	3	8	6	144	Special project required
Item not on computer	5	2	1	10	
Assistant enters same item twice	2	8	7	112	Investigate software prompt
Assistant fails to enter item	2	2	9	36	Training
Out of bags	4	8	1	32	Plenty of spares
Item dropped or broken	6	6	1	36	Review flooring

The problem of risk reduction is particularly difficult in service-related projects because important aspects of the customer interaction may not be testable except by trialling the complete service. Bank of America addressed this problem by creating a mock banking facility for initial testing and designating some outlets as further test-beds, as described in Mini Case 7.4.

Mini Case 7.4

Bank of America – Testing Service Innovation[23]

When a new Chief Executive joined Bank of America in 1999 he quickly recognized the need to raise the level of innovation in the bank's services and formed a new Innovation and Development Team (IDT), tasked with spearheading new services and delivery mechanisms. The IDT reviewed ideas for innovations but had the foresight to realize that testing new services and delivery mechanisms is just as important as making physical prototypes is for tangible products. Initial testing was made possible by setting up a mock branch created by the IDT at headquarters. However, experimentation to determine the reaction of real customers was the next step so, 20 of the Bank's branches in Atlanta were selected as test branches. These were equipped with new systems and the staff received training on the test services that would be offered in parallel to the normal range of services. Through 'live' testing, including the careful monitoring of customers' reactions, the Bank has been able to swiftly determine the viability of new services.

The staff members at the test branches were initially highly motivated to support the development of new services. However, problems arose soon afterwards. Staff members are normally paid on a commission basis and so they found that their incomes were dropping significantly because of the time that they had to spend being trained on the new services being tested. This was solved by putting the staff on a fixed salary but this caused friction with staff at other branches who felt they were under more pressure on commission. It also meant that the new services under test were not linked to tellers' commission, as were all the existing products at the Bank.

Bank of America's experiences demonstrate two main tenets of new service development. First, it shows the need to iron out design problems in a realistic setting off-line, before moving to interact with customers. Second, it shows that the motivation of employees can be a key consideration in the design of new service products.

LINKING CUSTOMER NEEDS TO PRODUCT DESIGN

Embedding the Features: Quality Function Deployment

When customers describe what they want from a product, or managers specify the requirements for a new process, it will usually be in terms of the overall utility or experience that they seek, not the way it is achieved. Thus a customer's perspective for a car might include 'reliable', 'luxurious' or 'fun to drive' but would be vague about what this means in terms of road-holding, acceleration or acoustics. In designing an innovation it is vital to ensure that the customer's needs drive the choices that are made in the design and that the elements all contribute effectively to satisfying them. An effective tool for this is *Quality Function Deployment* (QFD).

The first step in QFD is to understand the customer's needs and desires from their point of view. Techniques such as hidden needs analysis, empathic design, repertory grids, contextual interviews and lead-user consultation may be used, as described in Chapter 5. The needs elicited by these studies are summarized into simple statements in the language the customer might use. They are likely to be subjective, qualitative and non-technical. These needs, and the responses of the organization to them, are assembled into what is known as the *House of Quality*. In its most complete form the house can have as many as eight sections, or *rooms*, but we use only five here for the purposes of illustration (Figure 7.4). More complete treatments are to be found in the work of Don Clausing of MIT[24], and others[25].

The first section of the House of Quality contains the customer requirements. As an example we will take the final stages of a postal delivery service, for which the customer requirements might be

- Reliability.
- Daily delivery.
- Undamaged mail.
- Easy to divert mail when someone moves.
- Arrangements for handling parcels when nobody at home.
- Low cost.

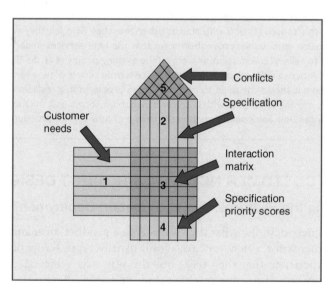

Figure 7.4   The House of Quality

These requirements are unlikely to be all equally important to the customer so it is convenient to allocate a weighting to them to express this. At this point the Kano analysis of features into basic, performance and excitement categories (see Chapter 4) is useful.[26]

The second section (specification) contains the main performance elements of the product or process in the language of the organization providing it. For a product, this would be the technical specification; for the postal service it might include factors that the organization would provide, such as

- Local distribution points.
- Local delivery staff.
- Local transport.
- Address-reading system.
- Sorting.
- Customer profile information.

The impact of each element of the product performance on the customer need is now assessed and noted where the two intersect in the Interaction matrix (section 3). It is usual to define three levels of impact, which we represent in Figure 7.5 with one, two or three stars. Scores out of 10 are also used; it is

		Local distribution depots	Staff quality + incentives	Local transport	Address reading system	Sorting process	Customer profile info.	Low cost
Reliable	7	*	*		*	***		
Daily Delivery	10	**		*	**			
Mail not damaged	9		***	**				
Mail can be diverted	5						***	
Low cost	6							***
Arrangements for absence	4	*	**				***	
		41	100	73	37	63	81	54

Figure 7.5 QFD analysis of local Postal Delivery Service

usual[27] to give 9 for a high impact, 3 for a medium and 1 for low in order to avoid the situation where a feature providing a very minor impact on several needs is rated more highly than one giving outstanding benefits to only one or two. These figures are multiplied by the weighting of the customer need (shown alongside each in Figure 7.5) and displayed in the interaction matrix (section 3). The results are added to give overall importance scores for the various features (section 4). The interaction matrix shows at once which features of the specification contribute most to satisfying the various customer needs. The most important must be given priority in the design phase and those with low impact are candidates for elimination. The matrix may also highlight where important customer needs are *not* being served by the product features.

The final part of the House of Quality is the roof, where any conflicts between features are noted (shown by crosses in Figure 7.6). For example, in the postal system case, it may not be possible to install address-reading equipment in local depots; and holding customer profile information may conflict with the need for low cost. These conflicts cannot be resolved within existing thinking and so indicate that one benefit must be traded off against another. More important, however, this part of the house points to where there are opportunities for innovation that might avoid the trade-off altogether.

Quality function deployment is a valuable tool for ensuring that the detailed features of the product or service really do align with the needs of the customer.

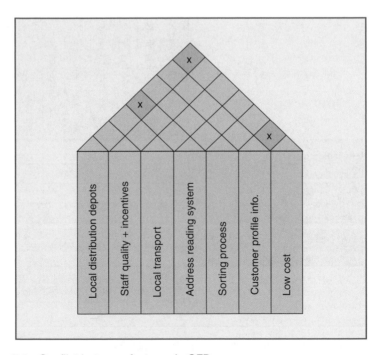

Figure 7.6   Conflict between features in QFD

Like all such tools it is an aid to thought not a substitute for it, so much of the value often comes from the discussion it stimulates. The simple and compact form of the presentation is a great advantage.

Mini Case 7.5

Boxer – Bacon Butties, Brazilian Beer and Branding Birmingham[28]

What is the real value of design? Is it just a way of making products look good? Or a way of bringing creativity into business? How valuable is design to most companies? The team at Boxer Design Consultants, based in Birmingham England and Chicago are faced with these questions on a day-to-day basis and see their challenge as balancing the creative and the rational aspects of business. Their business has 45 staff and a turnover of £5 million.

When most people think of design they tend to think of the aerodynamic lines of a sports car, or a visually stunning kitchen utensil from Alessi. However, design is more than pure aesthetics and Boxer has conducted a number of challenging projects ranging from rebranding of a Brazilian beer, to fast-food packaging, to working on the image of a city. The challenge with the beer was to help Brazil's best-selling beer position itself in the UK as a premium brand for the style-conscious segment and an innovative approach was needed. Boxer came up with the idea of a competition for budding artists to design wrapping for the beer bottles and packaging. Over two million bottle and pack wraps were printed with the winning designs and specially painted buses toured cities to visit clubs and promote the beer. The campaign was nominated as one of the best in the industry.

From Brazilian beer to Birmingham's brand: Boxer was tasked with creating a campaign that not only challenged outdated perceptions of England's second city, but also present Birmingham as a city re-born, bursting with energy and enriched by cultural diversity. Boxer strategically defined the City of Birmingham's brand identity and built the campaign upon the proposition, 'Many worlds, one great city'. The campaign was rolled out across a variety of media including advertising, print and online and given the extensive range of organizations and companies who would use the brand, Boxer also created brand guidelines.

In order to constantly come up with such creative ideas, part of Boxer's culture is the 'Soak-It-Up' Friday team gathering. The whole of the studio and client services teams chat over Brummie bacon butties (Birmingham bacon sandwiches), discussing examples of design practice the teams have collected over the previous week. The purpose is two fold: seeking ideas from the wider world and to stimulate debate around other people's designs to inform decisions in current projects.

Angelique Green, Chief Operating Officer for Boxer, not only has responsibility for managing the company but she also plays a major role in creative projects such as those with McDonalds in the US. 'My role is to guide and inspire the overall direction of the business, so the Soak-It-Up initiatives are very important. Clients look for inspirational creative solutions that lead to real business benefits. We therefore have to partner both at a practical level with our designers and on strategic level leading the business direction.' The key to producing leading-edge solutions for business is to understand challenges and balance the creative and the rational, so she is assisted by

▶▶

other directors such as Julian Glyn-Owen. With a design degree, international business experience and an MBA, Julian can focus on rational business benefits for clients whilst designers create breakthrough design. Julian's interests lie in developing the skills required to translate and transition client needs into breakthrough design. 'Often we see global brand owners carrying out leading-edge positioning and analysis. But what they don't do, for understandable cultural, organisational and professional reasons, is to make the leap from their valuable analysis to an emotional, meaningful experience for the consumer. Our clients need help in *translating* the literal into the *emotional* – this is what we do everyday in creating attractive, powerful, even magnetic context for the targeted consumer.'

Defining and Delivering Service Products

Everything that we have covered in this chapter applies equally to services as to manufacturing, but, as discussed in Chapter 3, defining and managing service innovation raises new issues (see Mini Case 7.6 on Cruise Liners) and requires some additional tools. 'Because services are intangible, variable, and delivered over time and space, people frequently resort to using words alone to specify them, resulting in oversimplification and incompleteness'.[29] In this section we will present two approaches that can be used to enhance the analysis and hence the management of service innovation projects: these are the *service concept* and *service blueprinting*. Both are simple approaches that, in combination, allow service products to be better understood and discussed more effectively (and as customers are intimately involved in the service experience, it is fundamentally important to make it easier for them to articulate their ideas on better or improved services).

The Service Concept

This is an approach that is useful in identifying strategic opportunities for innovation, something too often missed as most service innovations are only incremental.[30] Using the service concept consists of writing short descriptions of four elements: the value, form, nature of the experience, and the outcomes from a service.[31] Table 7.5 shows a number of questions that can be asked in generating ideas for innovative services, looking at each of the elements of the service concept. Often the best ideas come from looking for unmet needs; optimizing the form and function; improving the customer experience; and making the outcomes more tangible.

Preparing a single-sheet description of the service concept will generate ideas for innovation and it can be used in discussions with customers. It also dovetails with the service blueprint, which is a detailed diagram of the form and function of the service.

Mini Case 7.6

Cruise Liners – New Service Development[33]

The world cruise business is 8 million guests per year, and there are approximately 150 luxury cruise liners currently sailing the world's oceans. A typical guest invests $2500 for 7 nights and the clientele is conservative. Synthiea Kaldi is a former Guest Relations Manager with six years' experience in the industry, working for two of the most successful operators. One of these operators commissioned a new liner and Kaldi's experience on that project shows the critical importance of a cross-functional team being involved from the beginning if the service concept is to be successful. The problems encountered with the design of the new ship mean that the cruise operator involved is best left anonymous.

Kaldi says,

> What was good was that the whole service team came together to discuss the new liner as it was being built. Looking back, though, not enough time was spent to iron out problems, and discussing blueprints wasn't a very effective way to recognize the issues. We did see some things that had been forgotten such as safety deposit boxes. Fortunately these could still be installed. Other basics were also missing, such as locking cash drawers in the reception desk for the Front Desk Attendants. These were later added but they were never as secure as desired.

Customers also noticed the lack of drawer space leading to a regular complaint about the staterooms.

> One of the attributes of the new cruise concept was the "Food Court". This buffet restaurant was designed to give passengers fast and efficient service in pleasant surroundings. However, it was not as successful as hoped due to a number of factors. The limited number of drink stations slowed the overall service considerably. A serious issue was that the trolleys to bring the food efficiently from the galley, many decks below, did not fit in the lift.

Worse still, one of the vents into a main guest corridor captured the sewage type odour from the water processing plant many decks below. This led to guests perceiving the ship as not being as new or clean as it really was. 'Line of sight' issues in the show lounge were identified too late, although most were remedied before the ship went into service. Again, this was not spotted from the blueprints and it cost the company hundreds of thousands of dollars as each seat had to be individually elevated and tilted to give a good view of the stage. Once the ship was in service, it was realized that the signage for the toilets, while visible to wheelchair bound guests, was not visible to those who were standing. 'It quickly became apparent to the team that line of sight issues are nearly impossible to identify from blueprints and the ship designers should have found a better way to deal with this', states Kaldi.

Fortunately, she says, there were also some notable successes built on some good designs for the servicescape (see Chapter 3). The disco was intended to draw the younger, late-night crowd and its decoration, which was pure 1960s, was very effective at achieving this. 'And the ambience chosen for the alternative restaurant, which was only available upon reservation at an additional charge, worked so well that the guests actually felt they weren't paying enough for the experience! It really shows how getting the design right is crucial to the service concept.'

Table 7.5   The Service Concept

Element	Key Questions to Ask
The value of the service	• What the customer is willing to pay for? • What value does the customer gain? • What hidden and unsatisfied customer needs are there? • Does the customer have to invest too much time or resources to receive the value?
The form and function of the service	• What are the key steps in the delivery of the service? • What does the service blueprint look like? • What opportunities are there to streamline (remove stages that are not perceived as value-adding)? • What opportunities are there to add stages that add value?
The nature of the service experience	• What are the key steps in which the experience occurs? • What is perceived as negative about the experience with current services? • How are competitors' services perceived?
The service outcomes	• What tangible and intangible outcomes are there? • Are the outcomes clear and tangible? • What additional outcomes would be appreciated? • How can a superior customer benefit be provided?

Service Blueprinting

This tool was first developed over twenty years ago. A number of organizations in the US have used it very successfully but in many other countries it is not well known. A service blueprint is a flow diagram of the critical interactions between the customer and the service provider,[32] clarifying how the various functions of the organization contribute to the customer's experience at each stage. It is generically related to the QFD approach but with the emphasis on the time dimension, a factor that is not usually a concern for physical products. It starts with the actions the customer takes in deciding to purchase and consume a service. Sometimes blueprints for complex services will need to be broken into several stages.

Figure 7.7 shows a blueprint for the initial stage in a professional service – business consultancy. The analysis starts with the *customer actions* (second row from the top). It is important to understand these from the customer's perspective, for example, by conducting observation and contextual interviewing – see Chapter 5. The first customer action is typically to visit the website and therefore the website is the first physical evidence of the interaction – albeit indirect – with the company (shown in the top row of the diagram). It is important that the site is attractive, easy to use, informative and convincing, for example, using case studies and testimonials from previous customers. If the customer is persuaded then they will probably call the consulting company and their interactions first with the telephone switchboard and then with an expert consultant all should be designed to demonstrate the efficiency, competence and knowledge that the company offers. This should lead to an appointment where the customer visits the consultancy company for the first time.

The first direct contact is when the customer visits the company and encounters the main physical evidence of the company's competence (the *servicescape*,

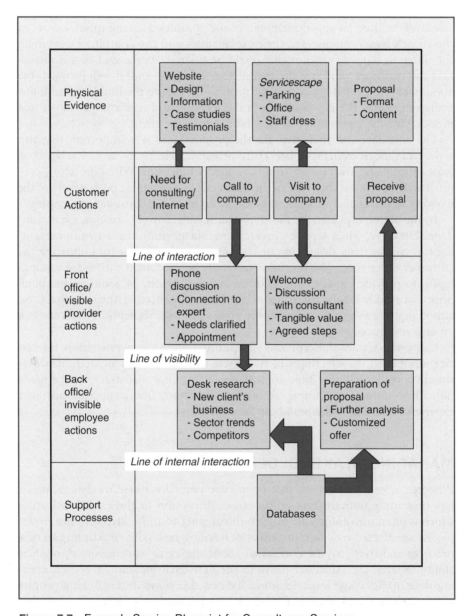

Figure 7.7 Example Service Blueprint for Consultancy Services

see Chapter 3). 'First impressions count' and so the consultancy company must make sure that their offices and staff all give the right impression. (Consider for example, how many companies have security staff running their reception areas and the often negative first impression that this makes.) After a welcome, the customer will probably have detailed discussions with a particular consultant, who should be well informed about the client's business and who will have accesses to data on competitors, and so on. The discussions should be run professionally and be an appropriate mix of the consultant asking questions about the client's issues, listening to their explanations and the consultant explaining the different types of services that could be offered. At the end of this discussion the customer will leave the consultancy company and, if well planned, the consultant will probably accompany them as they leave the building and informally summarize the key points from the meeting and confirm when a written proposal for the consultancy work will be sent to the client.

The customer will then wait for the proposal and it is important that this arrives on time or earlier (not later) than promised. The proposal will be based on back-office work, with input from the support functions. When the actual proposal arrives, it is another type of physical evidence (its style and content) of the working of the quality of work to be expected from the consultancy company.

In the above explanation, the steps will seem relatively obvious, even mundane. However, when service providers use blueprinting the act of documenting the various steps always, in our experience, leads to ideas for improving the customer experience. The blueprint can easily be combined with video ethnography, to provide visual examples of moments of truth. In addition, the blueprint can readily be discussed with customers, in collecting their feedback. So although it is a simple instrument, the power of service blueprinting should not be underestimated.

Using the service concept and blueprinting always generates ideas for service innovation. In selecting which of these should be implemented, managers should consider whether they are scalable (as business increases); can be made difficult to copy (for example, through staff training and a superior customer experience); and how the brand can be established.

MANAGING STAKEHOLDERS

Whether or not you believe that people are naturally averse to change, it is a fact that any significant innovation causes disruption to the established order which is often uncomfortable or even threatening to those involved. For example, those affected may face the effort of learning new skills or adapting to new practices and they may be concerned about the extra work involved, or their ability to learn the skills and thrive in the new environment. Moreover, existing skills may become less relevant as the new tide flows in threatening peoples worth, influence and status in the organization. These are genuine concerns that often lead to strong but entirely reasonable resistance to change. Such resistance can ruin a project just as surely as can the technical, commercial or staffing issues that project managers are trained to expect.

In understanding and overcoming resistance to change, the project team must first understand who is interested in the project and how much power they have to affect it. These Stakeholders may be directly involved in the project or may merely be affected by the ripples it causes in the company or the wider world. The Power-Interest matrix, illustrated in Figure 7.8, separates them into four groups according to the influence they have and the attention they should receive.

The least significant stakeholders are the *Bystanders*. They have little interest in the project and little influence over it, so they need no deliberate attention. The second group, the *Supporters*, are more or less keenly interested in the outcome but have little direct power over the project or policy. In a company launching a new product these might be the shop floor staff, service personnel and perhaps the majority of the sales force. Supporters are not powerful individually but they may carry influence because of their number. They have a right to be kept informed and may turn out to be important in influencing the more powerful stakeholders.

The *Key Players* are clearly the most important group. They have both a strong interest in the project and the power to affect it. This group will include the senior managers directly involved and often others, such as trade union representatives and key account salesmen, who represent important interests among the Supporters. Clearly, they must be kept closely involved and consulted on any major change of direction. The final group, the *Dark Lords* are those who have powerful influence on the organization but are not directly involved with this particular project. Examples may be senior managers in departments not directly involved in the project; non-executive directors; major investors or key

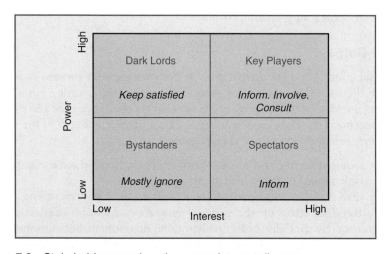

Figure 7.8   Stakeholder mapping: the power-interest diagram

Source: Adapted from Johnson and Scholes.

customers. Since they are powerful people, their public endorsement of the project may be very helpful although generally they do not interfere. However, if their interest is stirred they may suddenly move from a passive position to become Key Players, and hostile ones at that (see Mini Case 7.3). They must be kept informed and their needs satisfied. In particular, with an innovative project the project leader must take care to understand where the project may have knock-on effects that may impinge on the domain or interests of one of these 'big hitters'; and then to work to avert trouble.

The *change equation* which is described in detail in Chapter 8 is a helpful tool for understanding and addressing resistance to change among the various stakeholders.

MANAGING AN INNOVATION DEPARTMENT

Most companies rightly see innovation not as a 'one-off' event but as a continuing need, and so they look for management processes designed to help them manage a stream of projects, some of them simultaneously.[34] New product development (NPD) is an example of such a project stream and much of the most influential work in the field has been done in the context of managing the R&D function.[35,36] The Stagegate® process of Robert Cooper[37] of McMaster University has been particularly influential. We concentrate in this chapter on the formal processes for managing an innovation group; the 'softer' issues including questions of team structure are no less important, however. These are discussed in Chapter 8.

Managers should install a specific process for managing innovation projects for several reasons: as an aid to monitoring progress; to ensure that priorities are regularly reviewed (and, if necessary, changed); to improve communication; and as a vehicle for learning and improvement.

Phase Gates

The basic control and standardization in the management process is imposed through the use of milestones, or *gates*. Each gate is the occasion for a careful and formal review of the project, bringing together the experience and expertise of the organization. Phase review meetings are an important part of the innovation management process for several reasons:

1. They require a formal and objective review of progress, which serves to identify problems and plan the next steps.
2. They give managers an opportunity to update their understanding of each project and its effect on the wider organization. Most innovation projects are not merely specialist tasks involving one department but business developments, leading to new business activities and perhaps new markets. The gate reviews are a chance to review not just the immediate activities but the progress of resulting changes in the wider business.

3. They give an opportunity to review the environment of the project to check whether there have been any changes that might affect its viability.
4. Finally, they are formal decision points: if all is well, formal approval is given to go on to the next phase; if not, the project is stopped, or at least delayed until the deficiencies are corrected. For this reason the process is often called a *Phase Review* or *Stage Gate*.[38]

A phase-gate process must operate over all the stages of a project, from concept to delivery. How many phases there should be depends on the needs of the organization, the speed and complexity of the projects and to some extent the strength of the project management function. Weaker project organizations can be helped by a more formal process. Clearly, more gates allow closer scrutiny but at the expense of time spent in preparing for and attending the review meetings. When adopting phase gates for the first time, companies often opt for a large number (we have seen 12- or even 14-phase processes!). Experience points to simplicity, however, and a current consensus favours somewhere between four and eight phases. Standard process designs are available in the literature with suggestions for what should be expected by each phase.[39,40] These are useful but should be used only as a framework. The formal process and the checklists that back it up, must suit the organization and, crucially, must evolve to reflect and embody the learning carried over from project to project. Figure 7.9 illustrates a typical phase-gate process. The activities expected in each phase are summarized in the upper section, and the scope of the reviews at each gate are shown in summary below. Most innovative companies will have something of the sort.

The Stage-Gate process is well established and almost universally used, but managers must guard against a 'one size fits all' mentality. For very big or innovative projects a complete and formal process is essential but small or simple projects need less intervention. Most companies either have two versions or decide at the start of the project which parts of their standard process should be used on this occasion. But managers must beware of changing the process during the project. Many project failures can be tracked back to 'cutting corners' when the project is in trouble. Choose the process at the start and stick with it.

Management Process at the Gates

One key role of a phase-gate process is to prevent projects rolling steadily forward when they actually contain serious problems not addressed and perhaps not fully acknowledged. This common problem is, of course, a manifestation of the tendencies such as 'groupthink' that make risk appraisal so difficult.

A powerful way to avoid overconfidence is the *peer review*. This practice, originally known as a *design review* is widely used by electronic hardware designers among others. The design team invites a group of colleagues from outside the project to do an in-depth review with the aim of picking up any problems that the team may have missed, 'before', as one engineer put it, 'Mother Nature tells us herself'. The members of the reviewing team do not take over, or even share,

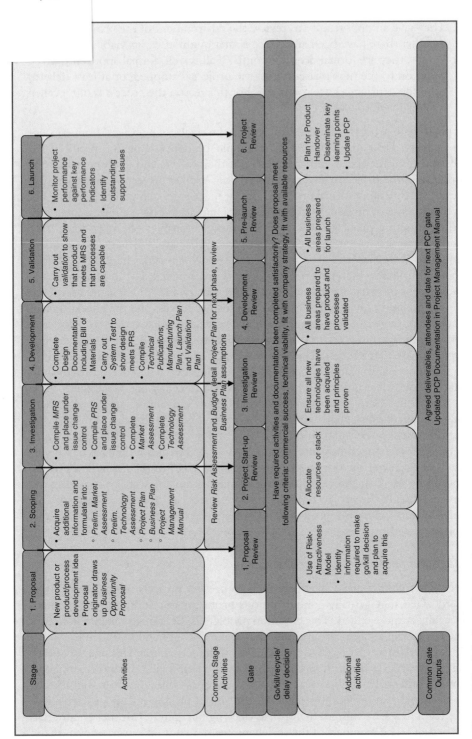

Figure 7.9 A 6-stage phase-gate process

responsibility for the work. Their job is only to offer advice for the responsible team to use as it sees fit. Design reviews should be built into the phase gates so they are expected as a matter of course at the critical points, and they should be instigated and run by the design team. The role of managers is to check that the reviews happen but otherwise to stand clear.

In addition to the results of peer reviews, other documents or evidence of progress may be required at phase gates. Test results, market survey reports, financial analyses, marketing plans and so on may be expected, and if not produced may stop the progress of the project. The formality of the occasion forces everyone to pause, take stock and to address difficult questions. Senior managers can probe for weaknesses and ask for proofs and demonstrations of key aspects of the project. In doing so they assure themselves that the project is on track; and in giving the formal go-ahead for the next phase they also assure the project team of their continuing support.

It used to be said that gate reviews should be strictly 'go/no-go' occasions: if any of the elements were not complete then everything should stop until they were. Modern practice is to allow for softer decisions so that the project may keep moving for a time if one of the gate conditions is not met, but under careful control.[41]

Post Project Reviews

Every innovation management process should include a *post-project reviews* (PPR) in which project team members discuss how the project was conducted and what could have been improved.[42] Ideally this knowledge is then built into the formal process to be available for future projects. Although the value of PPRs is well established, research shows that most companies do not use them and therefore miss a learning opportunity.[43] There are a number of key points to consider when organizing PPRs[44]:

- *Timing.* It is important that reviews are held relatively soon after the innovation project has been completed, otherwise the availability of the key players is likely to prove difficult and also their interest and memories of the project will be less reliable.
- *Scope, atmosphere and moderation.* The PPR meeting needs to be effective at uncovering issues and so may need to enter the 'zone of uncomfortable debate'. This normally requires a 'no-blame' atmosphere and a skilled *moderator*. The moderator should normally be from outside the project team and have prior experience of leading probing debate.
- *Learning from success and failures.* PPRs should be conducted for successful and for failed projects. Both may have valuable lessons.
- *Learning at different levels.* All aspects of the project should be reviewed. Technical problem-solving is an obvious area but more important lessons may be derived about the process used for running the project. And individuals may have personal lessons to learn.

- *Dissemination of the results.* The time and effort invested in running a review is wasted unless the key findings are efficiently disseminated and are available when they are relevant to other projects. The impact of key messages is often lost if they are simply documented in (yet another) report that is distributed to other project managers. To combat this, Hewlett-Packard has recorded short 'what I learnt from this project' video interviews with project managers and made these available on their intranet. Others have recognized that the results of post-project reviews should be discussed at the start of new projects, or should be a focus for mentoring schemes for project managers. Often it is convenient to include checklists for each gate to remind people of problems to avoid. But these must be brief; only the really important lessons should be included, otherwise the stage-gate documentation can balloon out of control.
- *Linking the learning to actions.* Recent research shows the benefit of appointing a *project knowledge broker,* whose role is to concentrate on the transfer of learning between project teams.[45] In particular, this broker is tasked with ensuring that new projects have specific actions linked to the learning from previous projects, in order to avoid repeating mistakes.

Recent research that we have completed indicates that some of the most important lessons learnt from innovation projects are closely related to tacit knowledge.[46] For example, experienced new product developers know that dealing with changes in product specifications; managing budgets for projects that are highly innovative; and solving technical problems are all highly complex. Dealing with these three issues appears to require a high degree of experience and is based on tacit knowledge. Therefore, senior managers must put suitable mentoring schemes in place that are focused on teaching new project mangers these essential skills.

A good innovation management process may be written down very readily but it needs steady effort and improvement [47,48] for it to become fully embedded in the organization. 'Every company that really improves the new product development process goes through evolutionary stages'.[49] Table 7.6 shows the kind of maturity process that may be expected.[50] A more detailed analysis of how the component parts of the process may mature is to be found in McGrath 1996.[51]

Evolution is desirable but decay is also possible. A surprising number of managers we have spoken to report difficulty with maintaining an effective Stage-Gate process in the long run. What seems to happen is that the process is put in place, often following a bad experience with projects running out of control, and is initially welcomed. However, over the course of time more and more checks and balances are added, responding to things learned at the review meetings. At the same time the effectiveness of the process means that there are fewer problems with projects so people start to question whether all the formality is actually worthwhile. Eventually the process falls into disuse. Then another crisis occurs and it is reinstated, usually in a simpler form.

Table 7.6   Maturity of a Product Development Process

STAGE	CHARACTERISTICS
1	No formal NPI process Resource conflicts across projects No documented procedure Successful outcomes due to heroics and individual skill Frequent time-cost overruns and rework
2	A process exists, but It is not respected and is used inconsistently It is often ignored by project teams It is over-bureaucratic and seen as a burden not an aid Still frequent overruns and rework
3	Process used and understood Clear roles and responsibilities Process moderately well understood by all It is not bureaucratic It supports consistent new product innovation
4	Continuous Process Improvement Metrics exist for performance of products and process Regular process reviews Learning stimulated at all stages of development and disseminated to other teams Process is culturally ingrained and understood across the business

Source: Adapted from Fraser, P., *Managing Product Development Collaborations* (Cambridge: University of Cambridge Institute for Manufacturing, 2003).

Managers can do two things to avoid this cycle. The first and most important is to resist creeping complication. The learning gained from the PPRs should be captured as checklist of things to remember, not as requirements for more formal reports. Better a set of reminders than a mass of detail that nobody respects. Second, milestone reviews must be treated as positive occasions. A certain adversarial element is inevitable because people have to show that work has been done, and done well. But the purpose of the review is to ensure the success of the project, not just to 'hold people's feet to the fire'. If project members regard reviews purely as trials to be survived then the process will eventually decay or be subverted. If they habitually go away feeling more secure that their project is on the right track then the process is alive and well.

Managing Simultaneous Projects

Any project organization other than the independent autonomous team is likely to require some members of staff to work on more than one project at a time. This may be inevitable but it raises problems. The most obvious is that individuals often become overloaded if they work for more than one boss, and so their projects will slip.

Another problem is the inefficiency that comes from changing from one job to another. Every change needs a period of readjustment to the new task. This may be no more than recalling the details of the new job, but it may involve meetings, visits, even relocation. All this is time wasted. Wheelwright and Clark report[52] that for engineering work the wastage is such that working on four jobs simultaneously halves effectiveness. Their results are shown in detail in Figure 7.10. Interestingly, the optimum is not necessarily to work on only one project. This is because a person working on a single job may have periods of waiting time if the flow of work is not perfectly scheduled, as is quite likely. Nevertheless, these figures give substance to the intuitive feeling that it is usually better to finish one task at a time rather than to try and keep lots of balls in the air.

A further inefficiency is more subtle and less well recognized. It is the time that is wasted in waiting and queuing due to variations in scheduling. This problem would not arise if all the projects were perfectly scheduled so that each individual or department receives a new task at the precise moment when they complete the previous one. But in reality this seldom happens, even if the project plan says it should because few tasks ever take exactly their allotted time. In a chain of tasks performed one after the other, these uncertainties quickly add up so that in the later part of the chain the actual times have a large random element even though the *average* workload may be as planned. The result is periods without work followed by a time of overload. Queues build up and tasks are delayed. This situation is familiar to anyone who has ever queued in a shop or at a motorway toll station. The problem is not a shortage of capacity to deal with customers, on average, but the irregularity with which the work arrives.

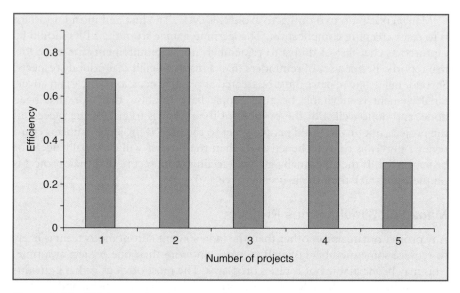

Figure 7.10 Efficiency of engineers working on several projects simultaneously

Source: After Wheelwright, S. C. and Clarke, K., *Revolutionizing Product Development: Quantum Leaps in Speed, Efficiency, and Quality* (New York: The Free Press, 1992).

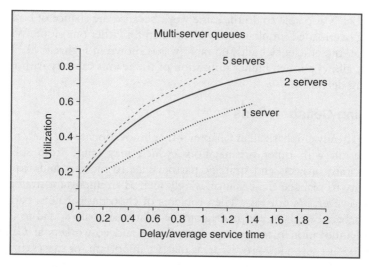

Figure 7.11   Improvement in utilisation by sharing peak load among a number of staff (servers)

Service companies seldom have an R&D department and so their problem is that employees responsible for innovation often have to do this in parallel to their normal activities, which tend to take precedence, adding a further random element. The result is that neither the normal work, nor the innovation, is done on time. Service managers need to ensure that sufficient capacity is available and reserved for innovation activities.

Randomness in scheduling can mean queues and delays even if the flow of work is quite low. Maybe the effect is not surprising; but what may come as a shock is just how strong the effect is. Figure 7.11 shows that a single person dealing with a stream of tasks arriving at random intervals causes a waiting time equal to the length of each task if he or she is busy on average 50 per cent of the time (if the tasks also have random lengths). To get the queuing time below 10 per cent, the worker must be prepared to be idle 80 per cent of the time! The delays reduce substantially if the task lengths are constant so that the only random element is in the scheduling.

There are four things managers can do to reduce scheduling inefficiencies in managing innovation projects:

1. As already discussed, avoid working on too many projects at once. Better to complete one job and move on than to juggle several, with the increased randomness that results.
2. Reduce the variability of the duration of jobs as far as possible by detailed planning and preparation and by learning and using the lessons of past projects.[53]
3. Arrange flexibility of capacity, for example, by arranging for temporary contract staff to be available when necessary to cover transient peaks.
4. Arrange to share work among members of the project team. Transient loads on any one person can be accommodated without extra staff if another team

member is also able to do the same work because the chance of both people being overloaded simultaneously is less than for either one alone. With more people, the efficiency builds up rapidly as is shown in Figure 7.11. The flexibility allows a much higher utilization of the team's capacity without introducing delays.

Managing Collaborations

We have already emphasized in Chapter 4 that innovation is very likely to require collaboration with other organizations, which may range from subcontract through joint projects and strategic partnerships to mergers and acquisitions. The ability to manage these is increasingly seen as an important strategic capability. However, it's not easy. The problems of choosing partners, partitioning the work between them and managing the relationship are added to the usual issues of innovation management. Pete Fraser and co-workers at Cambridge University[54] list seven key process areas that are important for success in collaboration projects, and at least five of them represent major additional tasks beyond those normally required in innovation projects. Organizations cannot expect

Table 7.7   Maturity Stages for the Key Processes of Collaboration in NPI

	Level 1	Level 2	Level 3	Level 4
Collaboration strategy	(Not) invented here	Occasional ad-hoc partnering	Some established partners	Regular review of joint competencies
Structured NPI process	No formal NPI Process	A process exists, but not well used or appreciated	Process used and understood	Continuous NPI process improvement
Task Partitioning	Interfaces not well defined	Modularity considered intuitively	Formal configuration planning	Conscious simultaneous design
Partner Selection	Cross fingers and hope. Little structured assessment	Based on word-of-mouth reputation	Good review of technical capabilities	Broad assessment of capabilities
Getting started	Work starts before agreements in place or IPR ownership clear	Contract, but without full buy-in. Problems with resourcing.	Agreement in place	All ground rules agreed. Clear role definition. Resources agreed
Partnership management	Misunderstandings. Changes come as an unpleasant surprise. Specs too loose or too constraining	Managed but not championed. Normal project management but no more	Collaboration champions on both sides	Frequent and open communication
Partnership development	'Them and us' attitude. New skills jealously protected	Little effort to improve but cost of changing partner considered too great	Growing trust and confidence	Mutual trust. Clear sense of 'Win-win'. Combined effort to develop joint capabilities

to become excellent at all of these at once and there is typically a steady maturing of competence with experience, as we noted above for in-house processes. Table 7.7 shows the seven processes with summary statements indicating typical stages of maturity.

Clear contractual relationships are important in managing collaborations but there are limits to what can be written into a contract to ensure success, especially when there is an element of discovery in the work. Alliances typically fail because operating managers do not make them work, not because contracts are poorly written.[55] For this reason, care is needed to ensure that there is a climate of trust and confidence between the partners, that communication is open and frequent, and that the arrangement is clearly understood to be a 'win-win' situation.[56] Wipro, one of the largest and most successful contract R&D always start projects with one or more extended workshops aimed at building relationships and understanding; and have communications between partners as a key topic at all stage reviews.

SUMMARY

The key points covered in this chapter were

- Managing the implementation of innovations requires all the normal techniques of effective project management augmented with some specialist processes to control the high levels of uncertainty often encountered.
- The most important of these are the adequate appraisal and treatment of risk and ensuring that the needs of the customer are fully reflected in the design.
- Innovation projects often have repercussions beyond the project itself. The project manager must take care to ensure and maintain the support of those affected, especially if they are in positions of power.
- A disciplined management process with clear review points not only helps control and monitoring of progress but also facilitates learning so that competence in innovation management can mature over time.
- Managing multiple projects simultaneously demands extra care, especially to avoid queuing.
- Increasingly, innovation projects involve collaboration with others and organizations need to develop competence in doing so effectively while not jeopardizing their strategic position.

MANAGEMENT RECOMMENDATIONS

- Ensure that strong project management processes are in place.
- Identify and manage all the important stakeholders affected by the project.
- Appraise and manage risk.
- Handle trade-offs when unexpected events occur.
- Install control processes such as the Phase Gate that allow clear management, and facilitate the transfer of learning from one project to another.
- Avoid queues and delays when managing a number of projects simultaneously.
- Develop a competence in managing collaborations with others.

RECOMMENDED READING

1. Wheelwright, S. C. and Clarke, K. B., *Revolutionizing Product Development* (New York: The Free Press, 1992). [Authoritative and readable introduction to the subject.]
2. Cooper, R. G., 'Third-Generation New Product Processes', *Journal of Product Innovation Management*, Vol. 11, No. 1 (January 1994), pp. 3–14. [Summary of the stage-gate process pioneered by Cooper and his co-workers.]
3. Cooper, R. G., 'From Experience. The Invisible Success Factors in Product Innovation', *Journal of Product Innovation Management*, Vol. 16 (1999), pp. 115–133. [Excellent and practical survey of do's and don'ts in managing innovation projects.]
4. Keizer, J. A., Halman, J. I. M. and Song, M., 'From Experience: Applying the Risk Diagnosing Methodology', *Journal of Product Innovation Management, Vol. 19 (2002), pp. 213–232. [Detailed description of a successful process for identifying and managing risks in innovation projects.]*

CASE STUDY
Wipro Technologies, India – Optimizing NPD[57]

Before reading this case, consider the following generic innovation management issues:

- *What are the potential problems that arise when new product development is conducted at multiple sites and across organizational boundaries? How can these issues be addressed in the NPD process?*
- *What are lessons that can be learnt from NPD projects?*
- *What should companies do to stimulate learning that is not just related to specific new product development projects?*

Wipro Technologies is a world leader in IT Services with revenues of over $5B and more than 97,000 employees around the world. It serves a wide range of sectors including manufacturing (18 per cent of revenues), banking and financial services (17 per cent), retail and transportation (16 per cent), and technology (13 per cent). Wipro is also the world's largest provider of R&D services and employs over 18,500 engineers in this domain. Founded over twenty five years ago, it has eight development centres, including major facilities in Bangalore, India. It provides offshore product engineering for a wide range of companies covering automotive electronics, medical devices, telecommunications, computing (hardware and software), consumer electronics, semiconductors, avionics, and industrial automation. The company has an approach that it calls 'Extended Engineering', whereby clients can outsource any part of the value chain, including complete product development, product 'sustenance', and support. The demand for cost-effective product development is high, as companies attempt to bring products to market faster but at the same time reduce costs.

OFFSHORE ENGINEERING

The downturn in the world economy has limited the amount of money that many companies can afford to invest in R&D and heightened the interest in offshore engineering. Advances in information technology have made it easier to co-ordinate outsourced

▶▶

activities and the number of companies using this approach has increased significantly. Sachin Mulay, General Manager – Strategic Marketing, says there are a number of factors driving companies towards offshore engineering. 'Initially, it was the cost advantage that caught people's attention. That is still important but there has been subsequent recognition that offshore engineering can improve speed to market and the quality of the finished product. Interestingly, companies are now starting to recognize that we can not only help them with product development but also give them access to leading edge ideas on R&D management'.

Where are the leading edge ideas being generated? 'We currently manage over 1000 R&D projects a year and so we want to learn as much as possible about these, so we can apply it in the future for our clients' says Mulay. In addition, the relatively new 'Wipro Council for Industrial Research' is creating a network of domain and technology experts from Wipro, who are working in collaboration with leading academic institutions and industry bodies to study market trends. The Council has been set up to address the needs of Wipro's customers, specifically to look at the innovative strategies that will help them facilitate their IT and business strategies and gain competitive advantage.

MAKING EXTENDED ENGINEERING WORK

It is well known that co-location makes NPD teamwork easier. However, as an offshore R&D service provider, Wipro always has to deal effectively with multiple sites, organizational boundaries, and a global delivery model. A. Vasudevan is the Vice President of VLSI & System Design and manages over 2100 engineers working on clients' projects. He has clear views on the challenges in new product development and says, 'We must excel at running multiple-site projects. To achieve this, we put a lot of emphasis on defining roles and responsibilities at the beginning of projects. We also have a "handshake" concept, where we put milestones into the schedule to deliberately check that both parties are 100 per cent satisfied with both the technical progress and quality of our communications.'

To apply the handshake concept effectively, Wipro engineers need to be technology experts and also highly skilled project managers. 'As part of our "Talent Transformation" programme, engineers receive intensive coaching in cross-cultural issues, project management techniques, optimizing communications, and negotiation. These skills are all essential for our work that covers multiple sites, different time zones, disparate organizations, and diverse cultures', says Vasudevan. Wipro also has a strong mentoring scheme whereby experienced project leaders support their more junior colleagues in learning these skills and ensure that tacit knowledge is transferred from one generation of engineers to the next.

TECHNICAL CHALLENGE

The projects that are given to Wipro by their clients are technically very challenging and the devil is in the detail. For example, an innovative start-up company recently came to Wipro for help in achieving their goal of producing PC-based gaming hardware with such exceptional performance that the gaming community would be really impressed. One of the limitations of previous games was that the pictures generated

▶▶

were not that realistic, for example impacts and the movement of debris were not real-istically represented (and did not follow the laws of physics). But game enthusiasts do not want realism, they want reality. So there was a need to produce the computational power (in hardware and software) that could ensure that the pictures generated were real and the movement of every object, be it a car involved in a collision or a bullet ricocheting off a wall, followed an exact, calculated path.

The goal was clear but achieving it was by no means simple. Normal game proces-sors at the time were accurately calculating the path of about 40 objects but that was insufficient to represent the movement of, for example, an avalanche in a skiing game. Calculating the exact way an avalanche will move requires a set of very complex phys-ics algorithms to be coded, massive use of memory in making the calculations, and fast hardware to support calculations that will accurately pinpoint the movement of over 40,000 objects. High-performance hardware with ASIC (Application Specific Integrated Circuit) technology needed to be developed hand-in-hand with the software.

The technical challenge that Wipro faced was matched by a management challenge of equal magnitude. The client, game developers, key suppliers, and some of the own-ers of the required IP (intellectual property) were spread across the globe, and time-to-market was crucial as the idea of using physics algorithms in gaming software had already been muted (and there were rumours that other gaming companies were working on it). In such a situation, the project management needed to be executed flawlessly so that the 'physics hardware and software' would be available on-time proj-ect. Rising to the challenge, the development team met all the milestones and passed all of the technical tests first-time. Most importantly, this enabled their client to be first-to-market with the capability to represent the laws of physics 100per cent accurately in pictures—pictures that show true-to-life explosions that cause dust and debris, characters with human movement, clothes that drape and tear the way you would expect, and dense smoke and fog that billow around an object.

Wipro's development expertise was initially seen by some clients to be purely tech-nical. That meant that clients' projects were managed using their own NPD processes. 'However, increasingly clients are recognizing our process expertise and are interested in us helping them speed-up their own processes. Wipro conducts so many projects each year that we have a greater opportunity to learn about the strengths and weak-nesses of the product development process than many of our clients, who work on a more limited number of projects', says Vasudevan. 'After every project we analyze what the technical and managerial lessons are, and in the VLSI Design space we have defined our design methodology called 'EagleVision'. Effective reuse and automation are the basic tenets of this design methodology.

SERVING THE SERVICE SECTOR

Although Wipro is very active in electronics and manufacturing, it also has a history of working in the service sector, particularly banks and financial services. These clients are served by a specific organization that has gained significant expertise in the different field of supporting new service development.

Prudential is a leading life and pensions supplier in the United Kingdom, with a cus-tomer base of around 7 million. The company had numerous call centres spread across diverse locations in UK, with each call centre dedicated to handle customer enquiries

▶▶

related to a single product line. This meant that customers had separate numbers for each of their products and the call centre consultant had to sometimes transfer them to a different department for each product. As a strategic IT partner Wipro rationalized Prudential's product categories and business processes, and provided an integrated view of transactions across products. The most important initiative was the integration of multiple front-end customer services applications into a single consolidated system. This will give Prudential's customer service agents a consolidated view of the customer allowing them to deal with a significantly larger number of transactions. Prudential will be able to deliver on the brand promise of 'one operation', reducing costs and delivering even better customer service.

THE INNOVATION COUNCIL AND THE FUTURE

One of the potential dangers of R&D consultancy work is that all of the innovation at Wipro could be solely in response to clients' specific requirements. Management recognized that innovation should not be solely project-driven and several years ago formed the 'Innovation Council', made up of senior managers from Wipro and some of their leading clients. 'We recognized that we consistently need to push forward our own expertise. From our knowledge of a wide range of technologies, we saw that we could identify opportunities', says Mulay. The Council brings understanding to the changing business and consumer landscape in key business domains, spots the latest industry trends in various technologies, looks out for innovation best practice and business solutions that can be practically applied. 'Such projects demonstrate our ability to offer leading edge technology to our customers. They see a roadmap of the components and technologies we are planning and know that it is not just a single product development project where we can serve them but really in the long-term' says Vasudevan.

Ideas for new technology are also gathered 'bottom-up'. 'It is our engineers and project managers who are immersed in the technical issues who often have the creative long-term ideas. The Council's job is to choose the best ones, based on our analysis of how the resulting technologies and components will, in turn, both increase the quality and speed of NPD for our customers' says Vasudevan, 'and, for example, we have recently developed some key technology for wireless networking'.

Although the R&D services arm of Wipro Technologies initially focused on client-driven product engineering, it has come a long way. It has also become a leader in spotting technological opportunities, optimizing processes, managing effective NPD, optimizing processes, and driving project-to-project learning. It is a hotbed of NPD learning that is likely to provide a lot of managerial lessons for the future.

CREATING AN INNOVATIVE CULTURE

Ordinary people cannot be innovative all of the time. However, if somebody gives them a target...

Akio Morita (Sony)

INTRODUCTION

The fifth and final element of the Pentathlon concerns people and organization. In many ways it is the foundation stone of innovation as without the right culture, companies can never be innovative. Finding effective ways to manage people, teams, organizations, and create a real *culture of innovation* is one of the most challenging aspects of innovation management.

Figure 8.1 illustrates how the people and organizational issues underpin all of the other elements of the Pentathlon. First, successful innovation strategy is dependent on leadership and achieving a culture of innovation. Second, creativity and ideas depend on the right atmosphere and rewards. For example, for open innovation to work, the employees of an organization must be willing to adopt the best ideas, even if these are from outside. Third, people issues impact the prioritization of projects. Project selection is contingent upon the availability of good team leaders and team members for the types of innovations planned. Finally, successful implementation builds on cross-functional relationships, charismatic innovation champions and project-to-project organizational learning. Employees' willingness to take risks very much depends on the existence of a 'no-blame' culture.

This chapter covers three levels of human resource management (HRM) – the organizational, team and individual levels and covers

- How organizational culture should promote innovation.
- The effective management of teams for innovation projects.
- Recruiting, motivating and rewarding individual employees to contribute to innovation.

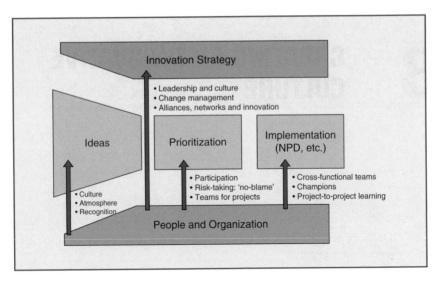

Figure 8.1   The Links of People and Organization to the Other Elements of the Pentathlon Framework

The majority of organizations have a personnel department or human resource management function. This function needs to play a proactive role in innovation management as people can be thought of as the 'building blocks' of an innovative organization. In the literature such an approach is referred to as *strategic* HRM (this is in contrast to a purely reactive role, in which a personnel department only concerns itself with administration, recruitment, pay and conditions). As Figure 8.1 shows, the influence of people and organization is fundamental to innovation and so a strategic approach to human resources is essential to support innovation.

ORGANIZATIONAL CULTURE AND INNOVATION

Organizations can have very different cultures and the characteristics of these cultures impact innovation. Culture has been defined as: 'the set of values, understandings and ways of thinking that is shared by the majority of members of a work organization, and that is taught to new employees as correct'.[1] Some companies, such as Sony and 3M, have proudly built a culture of innovation and gone out of their way to allow employees a level of freedom to support this. Corporate culture can have a positive impact on product innovation.[2] But culture alone does not guarantee performance – as the quote at the beginning of this chapter indicates, clear goals and targets are a necessary precursor for employees to be consistently innovative. A recent survey of over 1000 US HR managers showed that the majority of them perceived creating a culture of innovation to be highly important. To achieve this, making organizations customer-focused and

generating effective cross-functional teamwork were seen as the two most important elements.[3] The first step in creating an appropriate culture is to understand
how culture relates to innovation (see Mini Case 8.1 on UPS).

Mini Case 8.1

United Parcel Service – Culture and Innovation[4]

UPS is one of only sixteen *Fortune 100* companies from 1900 that have survived and
it attributes much of its success to its strong company culture. At UPS, culture is
perceived as 'myths, rituals, language, ideas, goals, and values'[5] that are shared by the
company's 350,000 employees. Some of the aspects of the culture are tangible. For
example, the *Policy Book* and *Code of Business Conduct* give specific advice on dealing
with customers and conflicts. Employees receive detailed feedback annually in their
Quality Performance Review, in which managers, peers and team members contribute to
the evaluation. Promotions are largely internal. Regular communications are key, and
most departments use the *Prework Communications Meeting* approach, where employees
informally update each other at the start of their shift.

Less tangible are the drivers of technical innovation at UPS. These can be traced
back to the founder Jim Casey, who was the first to modify the Model T Ford for parcel deliveries, the first to utilize conveyer belts for parcel sorting, and also led UPS to
be the first logistics company to experiment with air freight (in 1925). UPS is still clear
that being at the forefront of technology is important and has recently made significant
investments in the development of databases.

All of the company's routines, rituals, and control systems focused on being a provider of cost-effective package shipping (rather than premium-priced fast delivery). A
strong culture can, of course, have its disadvantages and UPS was relatively slow to
react when FedEx launched its next-day service. This shows that, just as formal organizational structures need to be reviewed regularly, so does culture. Corporate culture
should not be left in abeyance. The culture at UPS now focuses on offering customers a
choice of services (options on delivery and price), and optimizing the coordinated flow
of goods, data and funds, through advanced information technology.

Understanding and Assessing Culture

Although the widespread opinion is that it is difficult to manage culture, it is by
no means impossible.[6] Many of today's ideas on culture stem from the ground-
breaking work of Edgar Schein at the MIT Sloan School of Management.[7] He
was the first management researcher to identify the different levels of culture,
from the visible aspects (for example, the formal organization), to the values and
basic assumptions within an organization. Schein's work led to practical ideas on
how managers can perceive, interpret and work with culture.

A simple and effective tool for assessment is the *cultural web* from Gerry
Johnson of Lancaster University in the UK.[8] It was developed from empirical
studies of organizations and identifies six partially overlapping aspects of culture,

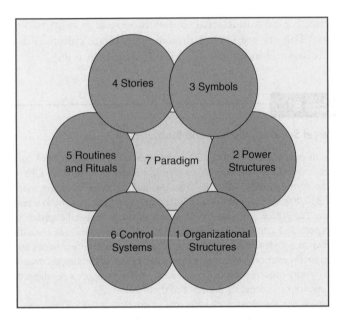

Figure 8.2   The Cultural Web

Source: Balogun, J., Hope Hailey, V. with Johnson, G. and Scholes, K., *Exploring Strategic Change*, (London: Prentice Hall, 1999), pp. 229–234.

as illustrated by Figure 8.2. The web identifies direct manifestations like the formal organization as well as the 'taken-for-granted', intangible characteristics. Six aspects of culture are identified and these are used to help recognize the so-called *central paradigm* of the organization, the key aspects of its culture. The diagram helps to make the different levels of culture cogent and acts as a management tool for 'diagnosing' culture and understanding how it can be positively influenced.

The key aspects of culture as captured by the web are

1. *Organizational structures.* The formal organization is the most obvious aspect of culture. Formal structures are normally based around what is important to an organization (or what was important to it in the past). It is also the aspect that most managers focus on, if they want to change culture. Such managers miss the opportunity to address the other aspects of culture – organizational changes need to be viewed within the wider context of the web.

2. *Power structures.* These are related to the formal structure of an organization but not easily recognizable from organization charts. The power in an organization might lie more with R&D than marketing, although the two departments and their managers are at equivalent levels in the formal organization. In a service organization the real power might lie in the back office. Power structures often reflect the central beliefs of the organization and, for example,

Hewlett-Packard was famous in the 1980s for being 'an engineering company'. The real power in an organization may reside with certain individuals and outside of the formal structure.

3. *Symbols.* Just as tribes have symbols that represent their culture, so it is with business organizations. These symbols include advertising and logos, the style of offices, company cars, titles and dress codes. The language, terminology and acronyms strongly reflect culture.

4. *Stories.* Every organization has stories that capture the essence of key events and share 'folklore'. Such stories are told to new recruits and visitors and act to reinforce behaviours.[9] FedEx tells a story of an employee who organized a helicopter to get an important package to a customer on time. Although the cost was exorbitantly high, the employee was not disciplined because management was impressed by the dedication to the customer that it demonstrated and recognized the potential of such a story. 3M have several stories about mavericks championing the development of what eventually become successful products, despite the initial opposition of management. Such stories are like myths that persist because they express some important aspect of the organization.

5. *Routines and rituals.* Routines are the ways employees in an organization learn to act towards each other and to process work. Such routines enable an organization to run smoothly. An absolutely fundamental routine for innovation is how an organization develops its understanding of customer needs (and Chapter 5 included many approaches that can be used to generate a more customer-focused culture). In addition to formal processes, organizations develop what become 'taken-for-granted' approaches to particular issues. This, for instance, could be an unwritten rule about how different departments interact during the innovation process. The routines underlying interaction can mean that formal processes are applied very differently from how they are described on paper. Routines can be difficult to change because they are often based on tacit knowledge and may strongly support the overall paradigm of the organization. Organizations have *rituals*, such as neophyte programmes, sales conferences, promotion criteria and appraisals, all of which indicate to employees what is valued in the organization.

6. *Control systems.* These include formal processes, measurement systems, and reward and recognition systems. All of these show what the organization values and help to set the focus of attention. The most important control systems for innovation are those used to generate ideas, select the best ones and implement them efficiently (this corresponds to the middle slice of the Pentathlon). Control systems, as shown in Figure 8.2, overlap with routines and rituals, and organizational structures.

7. *Paradigm.* Reflecting back to the definition of culture given above, the central paradigm is expressed as a statement summarizing the main points about how an organization 'thinks' and 'acts'. The paradigm is the distillation of the points from the six surrounding circles.

Applying the Cultural Web

Overall, there are three steps to using the web in an innovation context:

1. Determine the current cultural web – how well does the existing culture support innovation?
2. Identify a 'desired' cultural web that supports innovation more effectively.
3. Determine the changes necessary and how they can be achieved.

To determine the cultural web, it is normal for outsiders (consultants or researchers) to talk to a representative sample of employees, taking into account different functions and the hierarchy. Once the elements of the cultural web have been explained, simple open questions can be used to gather each individual's opinions on culture.[10] A workshop with employees is useful for extracting the central paradigm from the six indicators of culture. The web is effective at identifying aspects of culture that can hinder the further development of an organization. For example, Hay Management Consultants, the well-known international human resources consultancy, recognized from their cultural web that they were too narrowly focused on 'job evaluation' services (analysis of remuneration), whereas the market required a broader mix of consultancy services.[11]

To understand how to use the cultural web in an innovation management context, we will give an example.

Determining the Current Web

Figure 8.3 shows the cultural web derived for a multinational manufacturer of building materials, which we will refer to as 'BuildCo'.[12] Information was gathered in 36 one-to-one interviews and a workshop with employees from 5 departments. Employees were asked to identify aspects of the cultural web and discussions were used to define the paradigm. A strong degree of alignment was found between the individuals' views on the current culture:

1. *Organizational structures.* The formal organization had recently been changed to link it with a new Stage-Gate product development process and several employees said words to the effect that 'this has been interpreted by the Process Managers as [a licence to] "command and control"'. In addition, a strong functional orientation in the organization hindered the use of cross-functional teams for new product development. Certain individuals such as Process Managers and the Head of Business Development had a strong influence. Specifically, the Process Managers were seen as championing their processes rather than adding real value to actual projects.

2. *Power structures* were seen as rigid and centralized and this led to conflicts for the business units. One manager said, 'the parent company's over-riding philosophy of being a low-cost commodity...company is at odds with a business unit which seeks to add value through the application of technical and market knowledge'.

3. *Symbols.* Although it was relatively new, the Gate Review Board (responsible for assessing the progress of all new product development projects) had already achieved a symbolic status; it represented how BuildCo was extending its predisposition for tight controls into the area of innovation. Moreover, the Stage-Gate manual had quickly become identified as symbolic of an organization with what employees termed 'a reliance on paperwork and red tape'.

4. *Stories.* In order to improve their new product development, the company had recently implemented the recommendations of a large management consultancy firm (including the Stage-Gate NPD process). One of the common stories was about the modus operandi of the consultants and their influence on top management. Another commonly related story berated the way the Board wanted to make every decision. This was reflected in the power structure, which was concentrated at the centre; employees said the 'parent calls [the] shots'. Although BuildCo was profitable, operational problems were frequent and almost seen as inevitable in the way they were presented in common anecdotes. Finally, the story of an unsuccessful alliance reinforced the view that such ventures are risky and therefore undesirable.

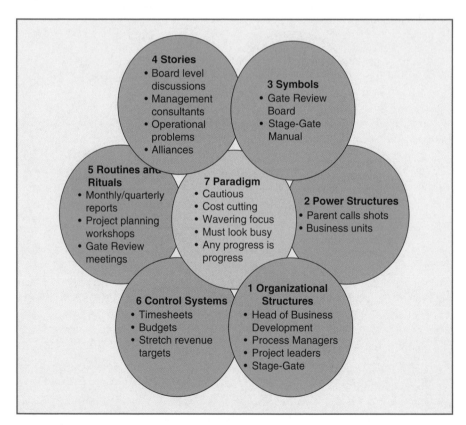

Figure 8.3 The Current Cultural Web for BuildCo

5. *Routines and rituals.* The most important routines and rituals were identified as the monthly and quarterly reporting, and project planning meetings.

6. *Control systems.* Matching the power and the organization, the building materials company had many control mechanisms, from timesheets that individual employees were required to submit, to budget reports at the department level, and challenging revenue targets for the business units. Overall, BuildCo was tightly controlled and hierarchical.

7. *Paradigm.* Having identified the different aspects of their culture, the workshop participants described the central paradigm under five headings: including 'cautious', 'cost cutting', and '... with a varying focus'. Such a paradigm was perceived as incongruous for a company with the aim of being more innovative.

Identifying a 'Desired' Web

The second stage of applying the cultural web to innovation management is to identify an appropriate culture of innovation for an organization. To achieve

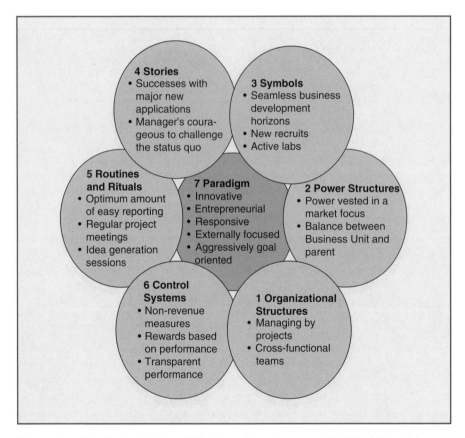

Figure 8.4   The Desired Cultural Web for a Manufacturer of Building Materials

this, BuildCo ran a second workshop. First, the participants (a range of employees) were asked to define a desirable and achievable new paradigm. Second, they were required to look at the six aspects of culture that would reflect this central paradigm. The overall result is shown in Figure 8.4. It can be seen that to achieve the central paradigm of an 'innovative, entrepreneurial, responsive and goal-orientated' company, many changes were deemed necessary.

To become more innovative, there was a perception that the formal and informal power structures at BuildCo must become decentralized. Participants had widely differing views on the most feasible organizational changes and discussions were lively. Market-focused projects and cross-functional teams were seen as the way to start. Connected to this, new symbols of innovation were needed, such as new recruits bringing a fresh wind, seamless business development (across the functions) and more dynamic laboratories (R&D). Stories that would communicate the paradigm would concern 'successful innovations', or 'managers having the courage to challenge the status quo'. It was clear that a new culture was needed, which would generate success stories. Similarly, new routines, rituals were perceived as necessary to stimulate more positive project meetings and generate more innovative ideas.

Effecting the Change

The final step in using the cultural web for innovation purposes is to gather ideas on how culture can be modified to the desired state. The main ideas that emerged within BuildCo were

- The CEO should communicate a clear innovation strategy, and give autonomy to the business units to develop new products and markets.
- Reporting should be streamlined and aligned to the goals of each business unit.
- Cross-functional teams would become an integral part of development projects and project managers who had the ability to drive these projects would be selected.
- The Process Managers should be moved directly into project management, where they could make a direct contribution.
- The results of the cultural web exercise shocked management but it galvanized them into making a range of changes to move towards the desired culture.

One aspect of using the cultural web for change – stories – is often perceived by managers to be open to manipulation. Here we stress that it is management's role to create the atmosphere and opportunities for top performance to be possible so that success stories arise, rather than 'making up' stories. Research shows it is unwise to make 'grand declarations about innovation' that are not matched by real results.[13] An innovative organization creates success and the stories should follow. Innovative organizations also recognize that culture needs to be managed (see Mini Case 8.2 on Texas Instruments).

Mini Case 8.2

Texas Instruments – Realigning R&D Culture

Some organizations are focused on being first-to-market and so the ability to invent is essential. This said, there can be a downside to inventiveness if it becomes the strongest component of R&D culture – it can lead to the proverbial reinvention of the wheel. In dealing with technical issues, solutions to similar problems are often known and so R&D engineers do not need to start from scratch. Unfortunately, the *not invented here* (NIH) syndrome, where researchers do not adopt or adapt existing ideas, instead insisting on developing their own original solutions, wastes resources. Research-intensive companies, including ABB, Aerospatiale, Audi, BASF, BMW, BT, Nestle, Nokia, Philips, Renault, Royal Dutch Shell, Siemens and 3M, have recognized NIH as a common problem.[14]

Texas Instruments (TI), the developer and manufacturer of integrated circuits, has taken steps to avoid NIH as part of their 'Vision 2005' initiative. This includes an annual 'NIHBWDIA prize' for the R&D employee who takes an idea from somewhere else and makes a significant contribution to product or process innovation.[15] The 'not invented here but we did it anyway prize' has been instrumental in making an important improvement to the culture of innovation at TI.

Studies of Innovation Culture

Research can give us ideas on how to make organizations more innovative but these ideas need to be adapted for particular contexts – there are no universal solutions. We should bear two things in mind. First, many papers base their discussion of innovation culture on anecdotal examples and so their recommendations are not likely to be reliable.[16] Second, many of the more reliable studies have been conducted in famous organizations that have particular characteristics, such as 3M, Hewlett-Packard, Toshiba and Texas Instruments. The ideas and recommendations from such studies must be adapted specifically to the organization whose innovation performance we are trying to improve. We will discuss three major studies.

Two US scholars of organizational behaviour, Mariann Jelinek (College of William and Mary, Virginia) and Claudia Schoonhoven (University of California), conducted a major longitudinal study of culture and innovation.[17] They spent eight years investigating five successful electronics firms in the US: Intel, Hewlett-Packard, National Semiconductor, Texas Instruments and Motorola. The main source of data was in-depth interviews with senior managers covering strategic planning, idea generation, project management and company organization (and reorganization). Their results show that routines and rituals underpin formal processes and, 'a strategy of innovation is contained not in "plans", but in the pattern of commitments, decisions, approaches and persistent behaviours that facilitate doing new things'.[18]

Jelinek and Schoonhoven show that sustained innovation is possible in a large organization but is dependent on several factors. First, the innovation strategy needs to be relevant and understood throughout the organization. It is important to create relatively small business units, as these will be more focused and communication will be easier. Frequent reorganizations help to keep a company closely aligned to its markets and to keep employees flexible and positively disposed towards change. A strong company culture can help during periods of market turmoil. But strong organizational cultures will foster innovation only if they are built on norms such as accepting failure, questioning decisions and conclusions. Strong cultures can suppress new ideas (by causing everyone to think in a certain, unquestioning way – *groupthink*) and companies can become slow to recognize opportunities. Jelinek and Schoonhoven found that managing organizational culture requires significant amounts of top managers' time.

In another study, Charles O'Reilly of Stanford and Michael Tushman of Harvard conducted 200 in-depth interviews with managers in Silicon Valley, to determine the aspects of culture that promote innovation. They structured their research around their belief that 'two component processes underlie all innovation: *creativity*...and *implementation*'.[19] Best practices identified included people challenging the status quo, reward and recognition for risk taking, and a positive management attitude towards the inevitable problems that arise. Furthermore, a tolerance of mistakes was identified as essential. The norms that promote efficient implementation are teams with the authority to make quick decisions, and open sharing of information between functions.

The third study is from two researchers at the Polaroid Corporation, Karen Zien and Sheldon Buckler.[20] They used in-depth video interviews, analysed by anthropologists, to examine the culture of 11 innovative companies in Asia, Europe and the US. The research elicited seven principles of culture: such companies were staunchly proud of their reputation for innovativeness; experimentation was encouraged; relationships between marketing and R&D were excellent; the companies had a deep understanding of the customer; the whole organization was engaged; both individuals' and the organization's capacity to innovate was tapped; and, finally, stories acted as a *leitmotif* for innovation.

Ideas for Creating a Culture of Innovation

There are many parallels between the three studies. Relating back to the cultural web, Table 8.1 summarizes how to apply such ideas to establish a culture of innovation:

1. *Organizational structures.* Four different best practices can be identified for organizational structures to promote innovation: market-orientation; frequent reorganizations; autonomous teams and 'innovation managers'. Aligning organizations to markets is a common and effective practice, provided it is matched with the delegation of authority to these units. In large organizations, the role of the CEO is that of an 'organizational architect' who needs to find the best way to match the organization to the constantly changing markets – frequent reorganizations are an important approach.[21] Autonomous teams can be the best

way of dealing with radical innovations, which cannot efficiently be developed within the existing organization and processes. One new approach that has not yet received much coverage in the management literature is the creation of specific positions for 'innovation managers'. Having this role creates a figurehead for innovation improvement programmes. For example, GlaxoSmithKline and Zurich financial services have innovation managers responsible for improving innovation processes throughout their organizations. Proctor and Gamble have a manager who is responsible for driving open innovation through external sourcing of ideas.[22]

2. *Power structures.* Both researchers[23] and practitioners have recognized the value of cross-functional awareness. ShinEtsu is a Japanese-owned manufacturer of polished silicon wafers and has customers such as Intel and Samsung. In their Malaysian operation, part of the culture is a very strong relationship between R&D and manufacturing. This is fostered through *routines* which lead to a balance of power. A 'freshman's program' for new R&D engineers requires them to learn how to operate manufacturing equipment and actively participate in kaizen teams, constructive criticism is actively encouraged and sometimes whole teams will transfer from R&D into manufacturing in a 'cradle to maturity' approach to responsibility (rather than the 'over the wall' de facto approach of many companies).[24]

3. *Symbols.* Three sorts of best practice can be identified. Communication, both internal and external needs to have an innovation focus and, for example, Hewlett-Packard recently adopted the 'HP Invent' slogan in all of their advertising. As an internal communication tool, the AXA Quadrant has been very successful and is a symbol of their new understanding of innovation (see main case at the end of Chapter 3). Displays of product and process innovations can and should inspire and at Unilever displays of new products at the entrance to manufacturing facilities make innovation highly visible. Ideo, the Californian innovation consultancy, have dozens of gadgets around the workplace to trigger ideas and experimentation (and even have 'librarians' responsible for collecting artefacts).[25] Outstanding individual contributions can be recognized through plaques and certificates that are visible in the workplace and act as symbols of innovation.

4. *Stories.* Talented managers can develop an ability to use stories effectively.[26] Zien and Buckler developed a typology of management styles related to organizational culture. They found that some managers do not narrate stories, focus entirely on figures and thus miss the opportunity to promote innovation. Others relate anecdotes from the 'good old days', which alienates and places innovation in the past. 'Innovative leaders' reshape old stories and inspire the future. The research indicates that managers can be 'transformational leaders' if they develop and constantly tell enlightening stories in staff meetings, interviews and outside speeches.

5. *Routines and rituals* can be used to support innovation. Two categories of best practice are promoting new ideas and tolerating mistakes. A leading innovator in

the US hospitality sector, Joie de Vivre, has an interesting routine.[27] The 'Fresh Eyes' programme takes advantage of the different perspectives that new employees bring to the business. In most service companies, new employees have a top-down performance evaluation after 30 days. The roles are reversed at Joie de Vivre and new employees are encouraged to challenge complacency by asking questions such as: 'why is it done this way?' and giving their evaluation of what they have seen. Motivating employees by giving them more interesting tasks is central to the philosophy of Hamilton Acorn, an award-winning UK manufacturer of professional quality paintbrushes. For example, production engineers are encouraged to design and build complex production equipment and not just focus on running the existing production lines.[28] Making the funding available for new ideas within organizations is a key step in encouraging people to recognize commercial opportunities. Tolerance of mistakes is part of the culture at Johnson and Johnson and enshrined in the founder's maxim that failure is an important 'product'. Other approaches that promote tolerance and creativity include: Dupont's use of the phrase 'it was a good try' to avoid negative criticism and; the symbolic burying in the woods of a prototype scanner that was a market failure (this allowed the engineers to vent their frustration) for Hewlett-Packard Medical.

6. *Control systems.* There must be mechanisms that enable employees to suggest ideas and obtain the resources to investigate them further. But processes for portfolio management and NPD are also essential. Metrics can be used to measure and promote innovation throughout an organization and Schafenacker, a supplier of automotive mirror systems, excels at this by 'cascading' management goals all the way to the level of the individual employee.[29] Later in this chapter we will discuss reward and recognition.

Human resource management best practices are particularly difficult to transfer because how they are viewed and accepted is subjective. Consultants recommended that EvotecOAI, a German-owned chemical research services company, adopt 3M's 'rule' that every researcher is free to spend 10–15 per cent of their time to work on their own projects. The CEO was sceptical that this would bring a return on what he saw to be a large investment of time for a small organization. Therefore, the idea was modified and top performers, voted by their peers, were allowed 10 per cent free time for a period of one year. This focused programme was very effective at spurring on researchers to achieve peer recognition. Additionally, the work of the top performers in the 10 per cent of their time dedicated to 'personal projects' turned into ideas that were very profitable for the company.[30]

In using Table 8.1, managers should choose the ideas which appear most relevant. A combination of changes will be necessary to move towards the desired culture. Best practices in human resource management and culture provide useful starting ideas; managers must find ways to adapt them to their own organization.[31] Changes to the culture should be integrated with the other actions to increase innovation and how this is best done is the subject of Chapter 9: Boosting Innovation Performance.

Table 8.1   Best Practices for Achieving a 'Culture of Innovation'

	Aspects of Culture/ Best Practices	Explanation and Company Examples
1)	**Organizational Structures** • Market-oriented structures • Frequent reorganizations • Teams • 'Innovation managers'	• Market-oriented organizations engender focus and urgency. Miele, a household products company, is organized by customer segments rather than technologies. • Large organizations can stay more adaptable through reorganizations (Motorola; Hewlett-Packard). • Creating autonomous teams for new ventures (for example, IBM, DuPont and the Xerox Corporation). • Formally appointing an innovation manager gives focus to performance improvements (GlaxoSmithKline; AXA; Bank of America). To tap outside resources more effectively, Proctor and Gamble recently created the post of 'Director of External Innovation'.
2)	**Power Structures** • Training • Cross-functional rotation	• ShinEtsu promote excellent R&D and manufacturing relationships through their 'freshman's program' and thus achieve a balance of power between these functions. 3M trained their top manager's to 'let go' and delegate authority more effectively. • Sony managers place particular emphasis on managing cross-functional boundaries.
3)	**Symbols** • Communication • Displays of innovation successes and other artefacts • Symbolic recognition and awards	• Company logos and slogans are a symbol and some companies update them regularly to ensure the typeface and style is modern. Hewlett-Packard recently added a focus on invention with the line 'HP Invent'; AXA have developed the 'Innovation Quadrant', which has become both an internal symbol of innovation (for example, as a screen-saver) and a tool for communicating the meaning of innovation. • The workplace and the reception area should celebrate innovation by displaying relevant product and process innovations: 'artefacts'. Unilever has interesting displays of not only their product innovations but also their process improvements (see main case study at the end of this chapter). Artefacts are used to encourage experimentation at Ideo. Axa have an 'innovation corridor' (outside the staff canteen). • Plaques, certificates and other recognition for innovative employees can become symbols. When Hewlett-Packard introduced a new reporting metrics for NPD* and every division manager trained in the approach received a Perspex desk block with a diagram of the metrics.
4)	**Stories**	• 3M 'mavericks'; Sony Corporation's Walkman. Managers can compare their style with Zien and Buckler's typology, in order to learn how to use stories more effectively.

Table 8.1   Continued

	Aspects of Culture/ Best Practices	Explanation and Company Examples
5)	**Routines and Rituals** • Promoting ideas for new products, new services and process improvements • Tolerating mistakes	• 'Fresh Eyes' Joie de Vivre; 'tinker time' at 3M; NIH at Texas Instruments (see mini case in this chapter). Giving a sufficient challenge to employees is essential (Hamilton Acorn). • Internal venture management: making finance available for funding entrepreneurial ideas and opportunities. • 'Failure is our most important product' Johnson and Johnson; DuPont 'good try' language; 'Bury the dead' party HP (now Philips).
6)	**Control Systems** • Processes • Metrics • Reward and recognition	• Ensure that there are simple mechanisms for staff to propose ideas and obtain resources to investigate them (AXA does this). • Most companies have introduced Stage-Gate or other formal NPD processes. Leading organizations have moved more to having a flexible process for the whole of innovation. Systems and processes to promote entrepreneurial thinking (for example, Richardsons: see main case in Chapter 2). • Company goals and metrics are 'cascaded to all levels' (Schefenacker is particularly good at this). Canon set notoriously tough NPD goals. • Rewards and recognition are linked to innovation closely, including employee performance appraisals (Fischer GmbH has an interesting approach described later in this chapter).

Note: *House, C. H. and Price, R. L., 'The Return Map: Tracking Product Teams', *Harvard Business Review*, Vol. 69, No. 1 (January–February 1991), pp. 92–101.

Source: Based on the literature, supplemented with further examples collected by the authors.

Efforts to stimulate innovation are often difficult and results may not be fast in coming, so senior managers need stamina if they are to be successful at leading innovation.[32] In the context of innovation, leadership includes communicating clearly how important innovation is to the organization; demonstrating this importance by investing top management time in supporting projects; selecting the right people and structures; establishing key aspects of the culture, such as the freedom to experiment; and constantly driving projects.

Most of the examples in the literature on innovation culture come from manufacturing as service sector research is rare. Bearing in mind the contrasting nature of service companies (Chapter 3), building a culture of innovation in services includes stimulating more ideas on the service augmentation, and making innovation processes more tangible but not bureaucratic.

Promoting Entrepreneurial Spirit

Many organizations hope to instil an entrepreneurial spirit amongst their employees. Successful entrepreneurs generate many business ideas, quickly screen-out ideas that do not look promising and drive the better ideas forward. They make quick assessments, which can be in stark contrast to decision-making in large organizations. Therefore, there are a number of points that organizations should strive to emulate.

Research[33] has shown that entrepreneurs focus on three areas in their assessment of potential businesses. First, the scope of the venture is important, as the resources (including finance) required can be vastly different, depending on the market to be served. (For example, the founder of FedEx needed a dedicated fleet of aircraft and over $90million investment before opening for business.) Second, entrepreneurs focus on identifying market factors that leverage demand and develop new products and services to solve problems faced (but not necessarily articulated) by customers[34] (see Mini Case 8.3 on QB House). Third, entrepreneurs raise the barriers to competitors, in order to survive.

Over 70 per cent of successful entrepreneurs 'replicated or modified an idea encountered through previous employment'.[35] It also is interesting to note that employees that are frustrated with the working atmosphere at established

---

Mini Case 8.3

QB House Japanese Barbershops – Entrepreneurial Thinking[38]

QB Net is the largest chain of barbers in Japan and the brainchild of entrepreneur Kuniyoshi Konishi, who was dissatisfied with the expensive and time-consuming traditional hairdressers in Japan. Konishi-san's hunch was that Japanese business people just did not want to lose an hour for a haircut and did not value the hot towels and other aspects of the traditional approach. A simple market survey showed that 30 per cent of respondents said they were interested in a fast, low-price alternative, and this led him to open his first QB Barbershop in Tokyo in 1996. Now he runs over 200 outlets in Japan, with revenues of over $14million and plans to expand throughout Asia.

The QB Net approach is systematic and high-tech. Each and every opportunity is used to reduce costs and achieve the target of a haircut in 10 minutes, for 1000 yen. Locations are chosen directly in business districts. Customers can tell the waiting time from green, yellow and red indicator lights mounted outside every shop. The stylish layout of salons has also been linked to speeding the process of haircutting and special chairs with sensors are used to determine the waiting time. A contribution to both lowering costs and accelerating the process is that customers must buy a ticket from a vending machine, thus eliminating the need for a cash register. Customers sit in a small cabin for their haircut (a 'QB Shell'). This has a seat, a sliding door, mirror and just those utensils needed by the hairdresser for fast and efficient hairdressing. For example, a vacuum 'airwash' tube mounted from the ceiling is used to clean the customer's neck and clothes of loose hair (and eliminate the need for a time-consuming hair wash). QB

▶▶

Shells have even been installed on railway platforms in Japan and at Singapore Airport in 2008.

The basis of Konishi-san's hugely successful business was recognizing a problem faced by a large number of people: lack of time. What is impressive is the way in which he systematically analysed the process flow in a barbershop and developed the optimal solution.

companies create most entrepreneurial ventures.[36] This means that established companies have to find ways to encourage *intrapreneurship* (entrepreneurship in existing organizations). Peter Drucker has said 'it takes special effort for the existing business to become entrepreneurial and innovative'. Mechanisms that can help are initiatives where employees can propose innovations and quickly receive special funding for such projects – this is normally referred to as *internal venture management*. Management needs to be willing to focus on recognizing opportunities. Once such opportunities are seen, clear and separate entrepreneurial organizations need to be created and these need to be staffed with people with the right personality.[37]

Counter-Culture of Innovation

All too easily a culture can emerge that stifles innovation. Uncertainty, strong hierarchical control, lack of recognition, and simply not making it clear to employees that innovation is the responsibility of everyone are common faults. Organizational change, with reduction in employee numbers – downsizing in the vernacular – is probably the most destructive. Research has shown that the uncertainty surrounding such reorganizations, which has been termed *anticipated downsizing,* is worse in lowering creativity levels than *actual downsizing.*[39] Negative impacts can persist for a long time after actual downsizing and these are the result of the depressed atmosphere in the workplace directly lowering creativity, and, second, those employees who are still creative keeping their ideas to themselves (for personal advantage). For managers the messages are clear: if downsizing is necessary, then the process needs to be completed as fast as possible and active steps need to be taken to prevent a negative atmosphere arising.

It should be recognized that companies that need cultural change often have the least time and money to go through the necessary steps: identifying the problems, selecting champions, building commitment to change, auditing progress, rewarding intended outcomes, and so on. Companies operating in highly volatile contexts, but with bureaucratic mentalities and structures, tend to tighten up even further (imposing more hierarchical control). That may lead to short-term success (for example, cost savings), but limits long-term adaptability even further. And such companies do not succeed at building a culture of innovation.[40] Research shows that in difficult times, organizations need to experiment with new ideas and create new structures.[41]

MANAGING INNOVATION TEAMS

How successfully an organization can implement its innovation projects depends significantly on how efficient it is at managing teams and developing the necessary leadership skills within the organization. The HR function should take a leadership role in this.

Team Structures

Most of the studies of project teams have focused on their use in new product development but the findings are also relevant to new services and process innovations. Innovation requires a mix of skills and viewpoints and so the importance of cross-functional teamwork has long been recognized in the manufacturing sector. In new service product development, the recognition of the value of cross-functional teamwork is emerging. It is the mix and even clash of different functional perspectives that can generate really good ideas and prevent implementation problems.

There are different types of project team structure, each with advantages and limitations. So it is important to consider what most appropriate structure for each innovation project is. This consideration should also take account of the culture of the organization; it is not realistic to try to move 'overnight' from a strong functional approach to a more autonomous approach. We will discuss five types of teams that are relevant for innovation projects, as shown by the work of researchers such as Michael Martin[42] (Dalhousie University, USA) and Steven Wheelwright and Kim Clark at Harvard[43]:

- Functional teams.
- Cross-Functional teams.
- Heavyweight (cross-functional) teams.
- Autonomous teams.
- Virtual teams.

One word of caution before these team structures are discussed. It is not just the formal structure chosen that influences the success of innovation teams. The informal links they have both within and outside the organization need to be supported.[44]

Functional Teams

It is rare but possible that members of only one function are needed for some innovation projects – *functional teams*. Figure 8.5 shows the organization of a typical business unit, with R&D, operations, marketing and finance. A functional team might be formed in any of the functional areas. Normally functional teams are used for simple innovation projects and perhaps the best example is the continuous improvement (*kaizen*) team working together to optimize a manufacturing process. In the service sector, groups of operations employees

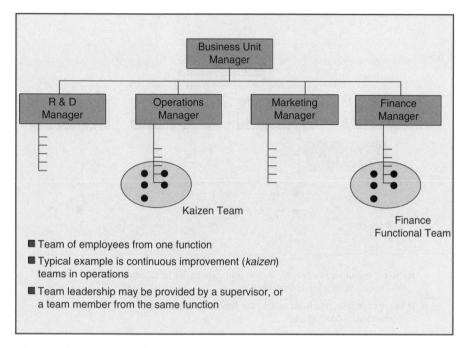

Figure 8.5   Functional Teams

may also work together on improving a process in a function: axa insurance have a 'Taskmasters' programme to encourage teams of employees from operations to identify where they can eliminate non-value adding steps in key processes.

A functional team has the advantage that its members all have similar goals and so little management time will be required to set-up the team. Often the team itself can nominate a team leader and so functional teams do not tie up precious project management talent. The limitations of functional teams are that the perspectives and range of skills included may be too narrow, or a suitable team leader may not be available. In this case, a moderator could be assigned from another function.

Cross-Functional Teams

It is not feasible to rely on inputs from only one functional area for the major-ity of innovation projects and so each functional area needs to assign people to the innovation project. As shown in Figure 8.6, the project manager is normally from one of the functional areas and reports to their normal manager (in the figure, the project manager is shown as having been assigned from R&D).

Cross-functional teams combine expertise from every function and so it is less likely that a key point will be forgotten. For example, team members from operations will start discussions about how a product or service product will be prepared and delivered. The disadvantages of cross-functional teams are that

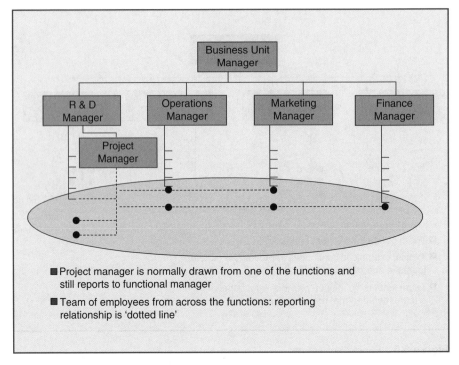

■ Project manager is normally drawn from one of the functions and still reports to functional manager

■ Team of employees from across the functions: reporting relationship is 'dotted line'

Figure 8.6 A Cross-Functional Team

they need management attention to make them work (conflicts of interest often arise between the functions represented), and the project manager does not have direct authority over the team members (normally it is a 'dotted line' reporting relationship). Sometimes they require management to delegate more responsibility (see Mini Case 8.4 on 3M). It can be hard to gain the full commitment of team members, who still report to their functional managers. Consequently,

---

Mini Case 8.4

3M – Myth, or Motivation and Mentality?

In the extensive management literature there is one company that stands out in terms of innovation culture; 3M has been regularly discussed and both its practices and products eulogized (including the ubiquitous 'Post-it'). So much has been said about 3M that there is almost a myth surrounding the way the company manages its people and its innovation. Looking at it objectively, there are three levels at which 3M has taken steps to stimulate more innovation: at the company, team and individual level.

In the early 1990s, 3M's performance was stagnant. Few enhancements were being made to the massive portfolio of 60,000 products and to combat this CEO 'Desi' DeSimone, introduced a set of measures of innovation performance at the company level.[45] These goals were: 30 per cent of revenues must be from products less than 4-years-old; and 10 per cent from products less than 1-year-old. To support this, the 'Challenge 95' programme provided extra funding, fast-track management decisions on innovative projects and encouragement to combine ideas across the company's wide range of businesses. These steps invigorated innovation in the company and many new products were launched. However, many of these innovations were only incremental products (such as variations on the Post-it theme) that had little market impact. To drive radical innovation, various steps were taken. First, the internal view of what constitutes a 'new product' was revised in order to swing the focus away from incremental projects. Second, it was perceived that customers may not recognize their needs or be able to articulate them and the lead-user approach (see Chapter 5) was adopted to generate more radical ideas.[46] Third, 3M management stressed that they were expecting innovation in all areas of the business, from the R&D laboratories, to marketing and sales, and after-care.

Although company measures are essential, it is at the team level that projects are conducted and projects in aggregate constitute company performance. Therefore, 'Action Teams' were introduced for NPD.[47] Management recognized the dichotomy that a tight organization could lead to process efficiency but a looser process would devolve authority and be more effective. 3M found that not only the Action Teams needed training but also top management needed coaching to 'back off' and really empower the team.

At the individual level, 3M have taken steps to promote and reward innovation. In hiring, 3M look for people that are creative, have broad interests, are self-motivated, energetic, have a strong work ethic and are resourceful. During the interview process, applicants' problem-solving ability is tested thoroughly in group exercises. A range of approaches promotes innovation through employees. The rule that development people can spend up to 15 per cent of their time on investigating their personal ideas is almost as famous as the Post-it. 'Genesis grants' are available to fund the first investigations of personal ideas. Taking promising ideas further is supported by the 'Pacing Plus' scheme, which motivates by what 3M term the 'Pinball Effect' (success gives you the chance to play again); and the Carlton Award is 3M's 'highest recognition, their "Nobel Prize"'.[48]

the project manager may not have access to the appropriate level of resources. Unfortunately, some companies assign their employees to several cross-functional projects in parallel and this exacerbates the problem.

Heavyweight Cross-Functional Teams

The main limitations of cross-functional teams relate to the conflicts of interest that may arise. If the project manager does not have a high degree of personal charisma or negotiation skills, the fact that they do not have formal authority over team members can be a problem. As the formal reporting of team members to the project leader is a 'dotted line', employees may give more weight to their functional allegiance than to the project.

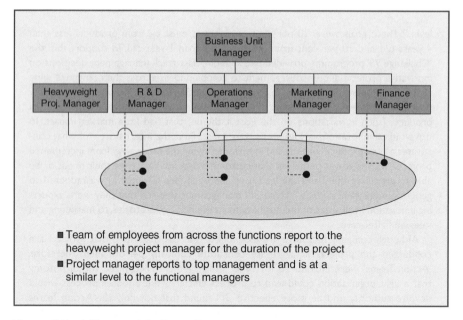

Figure 8.7   A Heavyweight Cross-Functional Team

Therefore, the formal organization is often modified to give a stronger reporting relationship. Figure 8.7 shows that a *heavyweight project manager* is designated to lead the team and, to give this manager the necessary authority, they are at the same hierarchical level as the functional managers.

The heavyweight cross-functional team has similar advantages to a normal cross-functional team. In addition, the project manager has direct authority and can drive a project. One disadvantage of heavyweight cross-functional teams is the scarcity of suitable project managers to lead them. Therefore, such teams are not a panacea. Also, an influential heavyweight team manager can tend to divert resources from cross-functional teams led by more junior project managers. Consequently, it is essential that the project selection is linked to the available resources. It is important to consider project leadership requirements as part of portfolio management.

Autonomous Teams

In the *autonomous* team shown in Figure 8.8, an entrepreneurial project manager (*new venture manager*) is selected and assigned a small team. Many of the 'rules' of start-up ventures apply to the design of an autonomous team. It is crucial to have people experienced in certain functions. A small number of participants is ideal and they need to define a simple but effective process for driving an idea to

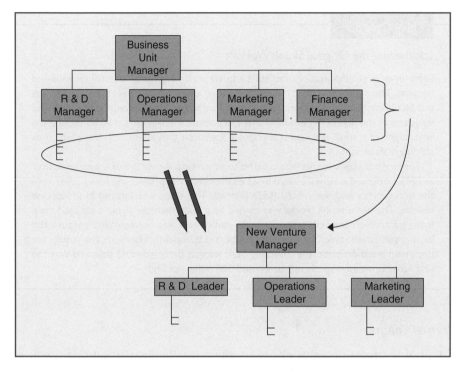

Figure 8.8   An Autonomous Team

market. A wide number of companies, including IBM and DuPont, have used autonomous teams and these are also called *skunk works* (see Mini Case 8.5 on Lockheed). Provisional studies[49] have shown the importance of the team being placed in a separate location and being led by a high-level manager, freed from bureaucracy.

Autonomous teams have the advantage that they can adopt different ways of working and do not have to fit within the parent's cost structure. There are several limitations. They require an entrepreneurial style of management and finding suitable candidates to lead them may be difficult. (BASF has recognized this and focuses its management development programmes to the provision of such managers.) The projects allocated to autonomous teams are normally challenging and inherently risky. Consequently, the first project may not be successful but in this case the idea of using such teams should not be rejected. An issue for the parent organization is that the autonomous team will quickly develop a sub-culture that may challenge many of the values of the parent. Other disadvantages can be the disruption to other projects, and the problems with reintegrating members of the autonomous team at the end of the project. Top management need to be prepared to deal with such issues.

Mini Case 8.5

Lockheed – the Original Skunk Works[50]

Sometimes large organizations can stifle innovation through their control systems and routines. The approaches that help make innovation more effective, for example, formal NPD processes, can sometimes be too constraining. More often, it is the overhead structure of the parent organization that can prevent innovation and so mimicking the advantages of a small start-up is a popular approach that is normally referred to as starting a *skunk works*.

   The original skunk works was created to accelerate the design of a new jet fighter in 1943. Lockheed assigned a team of 23 engineers to the project and freed them from the bureaucracy and the official R&D process. The team was located in a separate building. The name skunk works was coined by a team member (from a cartoon strip featuring an illicit brewery with the same name) and was not so-called because the 'new organization stinks' (as many people have subsequently assumed). The results for Lockheed were dramatic; the 'Shooting Star' jet was designed in 43 days and was the first American-designed aircraft to exceed 500 miles per hour.

Virtual Teams

In all of the types of teams discussed, there may be links to outside suppliers (although these have been omitted from the diagrams). In many industries suppliers make major contributions to innovation projects. Sourcing expertise for innovation from outside (open innovation) is increasingly important and when resources from a number of different organizations are brought together, a *virtual team* is formed.

Figure 8.9 shows a virtual team where the different competencies needed are sourced from a variety of organizations but the project management is provided by the organization that launches the project. Increasingly, virtual teams, drawn from a mixture of organizations, run innovation projects. Essentially virtual teams are very fast for the development of innovations that are not dependent on an organization's other products, processes and services.[51] The advantages of such teams are that they can bring together expertise, which is not available in a single organization, and can be fast and entrepreneurial in nature. On the downside, they are not co-located, communications can be difficult, and the cost of the external resources can be very high (although cheaper in the long term than developing internal expertise). An example of a virtual team that achieved excellent results is the Wingspan Internet bank development team. This pulled together experts from a number of information technology companies and launched an online bank within 90 days.[52] The basis of this success included a clear definition of the responsibilities of each of the suppliers, an 'immersion day' to launch the project, in which all contributors met and focused on defining the interfaces between their work and others. Regular videoconferences were

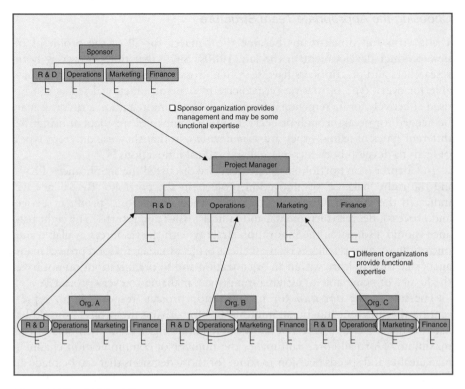

Figure 8.9   A Virtual Team

also held to keep the whole of the virtual team informed of progress and to identify problems.

Making Project Teams Work

The portfolio of innovation projects needs to be matched to a suitable set of
project teams. When empowered teams are working effectively they can reduce
the information overload on top management and improve the quality of decisions as these are made at a lower but more appropriate level in the organization.
Ensuring that innovation project teams work effectively involves

- Selecting the most appropriate team structure.
- Assigning team members.
- Creating a team and managing cross-functional relationships.
- Using project champions.
- Co- and virtual location.
- Project leaders and champions.
- Dealing with project failure.

Choosing the Appropriate Team Structure

Using cross-functional teams became the panacea for all of the problems of new product development in the late 1980s. Since that time, however, both researchers and practitioners have seen that cross-functional teams are not suitable for every type of innovation project. In general, functional teams can be used effectively for incremental innovation, whereas more radical structures may be needed for breakthrough projects. Leading companies are adept at using the different types of teams – they are *ambidextrous*, in that they use different types of team to develop both incremental and radical innovations.[53]

In Chapter 6 on portfolio management, we discussed the significance of having the right 'balance' of innovation projects in the portfolio. By balance we indicated the mix of innovation projects by their dimensions (product, service and process); degree (incremental and radical); risks; and returns. The right balance should also match the innovation strategy with the resources available and one of the scarcest resources is an excellent project manager. Good project managers take time to learn within an organization and so organizations do not have the luxury of being able to assign a top project manager to every project.[54]

The size of the *core team* for an innovation project (responsible for representing the different functional interests and for driving the project) should be kept manageable, and research shows that about eight team members is the maximum.[55] A small core team makes the number of communication channels manageable and speeds decision-making, for those decisions that can be made at the team level (obviously some decisions require management involvement).

Table 8.2 summarizes the advantages and limitations of the five types of project teams and can be used as a tool for deciding which type of team is most appropriate for a particular project.

Selecting Team Members

Selection of the team members is nearly always a compromise. Whilst it is not difficult to ensure that all the relevant functions (or skills sets) are represented in the core team, it is not possible to have the best people from each function. Top people are always in demand so, in practice, the project team will consist of people with different performance levels. In choosing the team members, both functional expertise and team working ability are key and the latter consists of a person's commitment to team goals, being able to get along with others (particularly when under pressure), and their ability to listen and make constructive criticism.[56] Higher risk, radical innovations require the highest level of teamwork.

In choosing a team, it is essential to consider personality traits, as these have an influence on team working. It is not simply a case of gathering the cleverest people. Various tests have been developed, such as Myers-Briggs[57] or that developed by R. Meredith Belbin's work at Henley Management College in the UK. Essentially all such tests look at how the traits of the individuals in a team match with the range of skills needed in an ideal team. There is no generally

Table 8.2 Choosing the Right Type of Team

	Functional Teams	Cross-Functional Teams	Heavyweight Cross-Functional Teams	Autonomous Teams	Virtual Teams
Advantages	• Simple to organize. Do not monopolize management time. • Ideal for 'tactical' improvements to the day-to-day processes within a function.	• Bring together knowledge and responsibilities of all functions. • Work well for projects where something similar has already been successfully completed. • Require relatively low management commitment.	• Due to an experienced manager taking responsibility for the heavyweight team, it has more influence. • Can use existing processes and resources.	• Autonomous teams are freed of the bureaucracy and overheads of the parent organization. • Separate location reinforces the independence of the team. • The team spirit will quickly encourage entrepreneurship.	• Brings together levels of expertise not available in a single organization. • Can be much faster moving than projects resourced internally. • Such teams are entrepreneurial in nature.
Limitations	• Team may miss opportunities, as they have a narrow perspective. • Team learning is not applicable to cross-functional projects.	• Project manager has little formal power and so may not be able to control cross-functional differences. • In competition for resources are likely to lose out to heavyweight teams.	• Require a very experienced manager to lead the project. • May require significant amounts of management time. • May not work well for new ventures, as they are too closely tied to the parent organization.	• Radical approaches will test the capacity of the parent organization to accept change. • Entrepreneurial management talent is hard to find.	• Are not co-located. • Need good communication and a simple, effective innovation process. • Sourcing outside expertise can be very expensive. • Intellectual property rights (IPR) need to be carefully managed.
Recommended Application(s)	• Kaizen projects in all functions. • Developing a process orientation within the functions.	• Incremental innovation projects. • More complex kaizen projects, where a cross-functional view may add a better understanding.	• Radical innovation projects (not recommended for low complexity projects). • Heavyweight teams offer a good training ground for managers with top potential.	• New ventures: new products in new markets. • Dealing with disruptive technology.	• Development of new technology, where the internal competence does not exist. • Essential for effective open innovation.

acknowledged 'best' test and so, in the absence of good empirical data, we have selected the Belbin test to describe in detail, as it is easy to apply to innovation teams and provides a categorization.[58] Belbin defined *team role* as a 'tendency to behave, contribute and interrelate with others in a particular way'. He identified eight team roles, which are summarized in Table 8.3. For example, the *coordinator* tends to focus on ensuring that the objectives are clear, responsibilities are allocated, and on summarizing team conclusions. Each of the eight roles, with their particular characteristics, brings particular strengths to a team.[59] The *implementer* pushes for action, whereas the *team worker* is supportive. Typically, individuals have a tendency to a particular team role, with one or two subsidiary traits. The best teams have a mix of roles.

Belbin's work helps both in choosing and forming teams. A simple question-naire allows individuals' roles to be determined and a balanced team can then be chosen. Often the ideal team members are not available, and in this case, the Belbin methodology can form the basis of a team 'kick-off' workshop. In this workshop, a moderator explains the method, uses the questionnaire and then creates an open atmosphere in which the team members discuss their individual characteristics and how, together, the team can best function. For example, if there are no obvious implementers in the team, how this deficit can be addressed?

Table 8.3   Team Roles

Role Designations	Characteristics	Typical Focus
Coordinator	Positive-minded, self-confident and impartial individual. Often of average intellect.	Clarifies objectives, helps allocate responsibilities, articulates team conclusions and seeks consensus.
Shaper	Often an over-achiever who is impatient, provocative, emotional and outgoing.	Articulates the findings in group discussions, presses for agreement and decision-making in their own way.
Plant	Intellectual and knowledgeable. Individualistic and unorthodox.	Makes proposals, generates new ideas.
Monitor/evaluator	Sanguine, cool-headed and clever.	Analyses problems and issues, evaluates others' contributions.
Implementer	Tough, pragmatic, conscientious.	Wants to turn talk into action and effective implementation.
Team worker	Team-oriented, gregarious, may be indecisive.	Gives personal support to others.
Resource investigator	Inquisitive, innovative and communicative.	Brings in new ideas, negotiates with outsiders.
Completer-finisher	Attention to detail, conscientious perfectionist.	Emphasizes the importance of meeting schedules and achieving goals.

Source: Adapted from Belbin.

It should be stressed that the moderator must set an appropriate atmosphere in the workshop, as some individuals may otherwise object to being 'tested' and having the results openly discussed. If it is applied sensitively, Belbin is a valuable tool for launching and managing teams.

Creating a Team and Managing Relationships

One of the most important aspects of project team management is establishing effective relationships from the beginning. This depends on individual interactions and cross-functional issues.

Early research by Bruce Tuckman from the Ohio State University showed that newly created teams typically progress through a number of phases.[60] This is often presented as the *teamwork wheel*, as shown in Figure 8.10. Initially, in the *forming* phase, members tend to be guarded, polite and the team works together cautiously. Next, as the first tasks are tackled, conflicts or personality clashes may occur, or even fundamental disagreements because of different functional backgrounds – this is the *storming* phase. Some of the clashes can be healthy and bring better ideas or identify problems. The team will then move into a phase of *norming*, where it addresses the conflicts and develops rules or ways of effectively working together. Lastly, teams should move to and remain in the *performing*

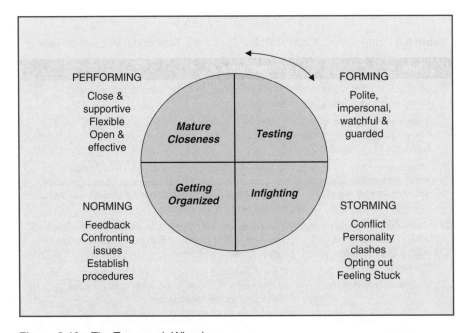

Figure 8.10   The Teamwork Wheel

Note: Tuckman himself did not draw a diagram of how teams develop. However, based on his work, various 'teamwork wheels' have been drawn over the years based. The version we show originates from Cranfield School of Management.

Source: Based on Tuckman.

quadrant. Sometimes, new conflicts can move the team back into storming but good team management should move the group quickly back to performing.

The teamwork wheel can be used to support teams in their own development. It is useful at kick-off meetings and can be used to create team understanding throughout a project. In the forming phase teams can develop their own 'ground rules'. Developing such rules early on can minimize the negative aspects of storming and accelerate the transition to performing. Table 8.4 shows a number of suggested rules. (This is based on our extensive work with NPD teams.)

Functional and Other Interfaces

One of the most talked about aspects of teamwork, particularly in NPD, is the relationship between R&D and marketing. Many researchers have investigated the 'wall' that often exists between these two functions. It appears to be a perennial issue. In a major study of nearly three hundred projects at 50 companies, frequent conflicts were identified and various relationships were found,[61] ranging from *severe dissatisfaction*, to *mild dissatisfaction*, and *harmony*. What is particularly interesting is that each of these categories was found to have advantages and disadvantages. In the former, distrust leads marketing and R&D to mutual disrespect and poor consolidation of market and technical ideas. Such friction can often result from personality conflicts and the fact

Table 8.4 Suggested 'Ground Rules' for Cross-Functional Innovation Teams

	Rule	Comments
1)	Respect all team members' opinions and expertise.	This should help to avoid cross-functional friction.
2)	Customer-focus and quality should not be **compromised**, without a team decision.	Stops internal views or technology push dominating.
3)	Deliver your work on-time or warn the team in advance, if you expect problems.	Underlines the importance of everyone delivering on time, in order for the whole project not to experience delays. Also encourages individuals to ask the team for support before it is too late.
4)	Communicate efficiently and always consider how your work can impact others in the team.	Communication is too often poor and the interfaces between different work packages or functions are not sufficiently considered.
5)	Question, question, question ...	Helps teams 'keep an open mind' and be more innovative in their approaches.
6)	Assess risk but expect the unexpected.	Should allow some problems to be anticipated, the unexpected should be dealt with quickly as some resources are 'reserved' for unseen problems.
7)	Make it a winning team!	All individuals should focus on making the project team something special and achieving extraordinary results.

that employees 'never see any signs from management that collaboration is desired'.[62] Management needs to lead by example in demonstrating the value of both functions and, particularly, the value of collaboration. Mild dissatisfaction can be the result of too few meetings between the functions and even R&D and marketing being 'too good friends'. This can stifle healthy professional disagreements (that often can lead to excellent ideas). Finally, full harmony, where both functions are equal partners can be positive for incremental projects but the 'give and take' attitude may lack the fire that sometimes is necessary to make innovation breakthroughs.

Although the R&D to marketing interface is the most commonly discussed issue, it is not the only one that managers should consider. An emerging issue is the interface between R&D and the financial controlling function.[63] Complex R&D projects, particularly technology development, require good risk assessment. However, the adequate assessment of risk requires both technical and financial aspects to be considered and this requires excellent working relationships between finance experts and R&D leaders. The interface between these two functions has a significant influence on the effectiveness of portfolio management and is increasingly an area where organizations need to concentrate.

Cross-functional boundaries have been widely recognized as problematic. In addition, the different opinions and 'language' used by management and engineering means that these groups often do not communicate effectively.[64] Organizing effective cross-functional communication is a key management task.[65]

Co- and Virtual-Locations

Co-location is an important mechanism for innovation projects. If all team members can be brought together, then both communications and team spirit improve dramatically. Open plan offices where furniture is on wheels make the bringing together of project teams much easier. Email is no substitute for bringing people within speaking distance. Where co-location is not possible, extra effort must be made to coordinate and integrate the efforts of the various members of the team. Modern video-conferencing technology certainly makes the management of virtual teams easier (although it is still not a direct replacement; face-to-face contact is just as important as ever).

Different physical locations and locations in different time zones make communication more difficult but they can bring some advantages. For example, 21Torr is a German marketing and Internet consultancy company that has used separate location to its advantage. Customers in California have found it useful to choose 21Torr as a service provider, which because of the time difference can implement site modifications 'overnight'.

Project Leaders and Champions

The role of the innovation project manager cannot be overstated. In more simple, incremental projects the leader must act as a communicator, a climate-setter, planner and interface. However, for radical innovations the team leader must act as a real *champion,* pushing the cause when the project requires more support or encounters resistance.[66] Research has shown that wider skills and the ability to identify and adopt unconventional approaches are essential for radical projects.[67]

As good project leaders are rare, organizations need to take active steps to ensure that they assign their best managers to the more complex projects. Development of skilled champions takes time and direct coaching of junior colleagues by experienced managers helps, but individual personality plays a role. Not everyone has the passion and energy that is required to be an effective champion. To avoid such key employees as champions being lost, special rewards and recognitions may be necessary.

Launching Innovation Projects

Several times we have mentioned the value of kick-off meetings for innovation teams. Although these have not been strongly researched, a number of highly successful projects have used them and our personal experience is that they are highly valuable. Bringing the whole team together (even if it will subsequently work virtually) is very useful. In addition to teambuilding, the meeting can establish ground rules, define the work breakdown structure (see Chapter 7), consider the issues at the boundaries of the work packages, and consider the implications of the characteristics of the individuals in the team.

Dealing with Failure – Project Termination

Although success is the aim of every team, this can be elusive. Studies have shown that many products fail and many process innovations are also unsuccessful.

Empirical evidence confirms that few organizations are efficient at determining when projects should be terminated and often such projects continue unabated. Too many organizations do not have clear termination criteria and so do not act at an appropriate time.[68] This results in wasted resources and, too often, significant demotivation.[69] Members of teams responsible for projects that are not successful, particularly those where the failure was perceived in advance to be inevitable, are particularly likely to feel demotivated. Personal careers can be damaged by association with a failure unless there is a culture that accepts that not all projects can be a success. Certainly, there must be sanctions for incompetence, but good individual performance should always be recognized even in unsuccessful projects.

Terminations should be carried out as early as possible and the team members need to be re-assigned very quickly, in order to prevent demotivation. There is much that can be learnt from projects that are not successful and researchers have found evidence that companies that were good at this were able to 'build on this failure' to be successful on subsequent projects.[70]

MANAGING PEOPLE FOR INNOVATION

The final level of HRM that we will consider in this chapter is the individual level. Attracting, recruiting, motivating, rewarding and developing individuals form the backbone of effective innovation management. Many companies do not recognize the strategic importance of linking people management to innovation strategy, partly because of its complexity and often because the personnel department adopts solely an administrative role. Managing human resources *strategically* means aligning people management to the innovation strategy. It has several main components, all of which influence innovation performance.[71] These are as follows:

- Recruitment and assigning jobs.
- Managing performance.
- Motivation, rewards and recognition.
- Employee development.

Recruiting and Job Assignment

Organizations that have the need and the financial resources to hire new staff have an ideal opportunity to look for people who will introduce more innovation. In a 2009 survey of senior managers, 'Ninety-two per cent of respondents consider[ed] access to talented staff to be crucial to innovation'.[72] In hiring new employees, selection criteria need to match the innovation strategy. The technology roadmap presented in Chapter 4 prompts organizations to think how their innovation strategies create needs for new competencies. A strategic approach to HRM will include a regular check on how the changes in innovation strategy create the need to build or strengthen competencies.

Innovation strategy can create needs for certain 'technical' knowledge (for example, on a particular technology, or market), or it can mean that a natural ability to drive innovation is sought. In the latter case, it is difficult to assess how innovative a particular candidate will be. Their track record, a willingness to take risks and competence at problem solving are useful indicators. The interview and selection process should be enhanced to assess the innovation capabilities of candidates. The use of psychometric tests has increased over the last ten years and specific tests have been developed to identify if an applicant is innovative. One test for example, measures adaptability, motivation towards change, work style and challenging the status quo.[73] Such tests should be used as part of the overall interviewing process but HRM specialists warn against relying on the results of tests alone.[74]

Four factors should be considered in assigning employees to particular roles: their 'technical' expertise (for example, technical or market knowledge); cross-functional team skills; their ability to champion innovative ideas; and their motivation. Technical expertise is probably the easiest to assess. The assessment of cross-functional skills and the ability to champion ideas needs to be an integral part of the appraisal and development systems, which we will discuss soon. If the appraisal system does not look at these factors, then employees will be assigned to roles without good, objective information on their capabilities being available. The earlier section on the types of innovation project teams indicated that some of these teams require particular competencies in the team members.

In job assignment, account should be taken of employees' job tenure, as it has been found that this has an influence on motivation and innovation.[75] An employee's perspective goes through three phases. First, *socialization* is the phase where an employee is new to their position and is learning their responsibilities and the supervisor's expectations, making social contacts for the role and gaining acceptance. This phase is relatively short, and for the employee it is primarily concerned with proving their competence and gaining acceptance. The next phase is called *innovation* (an unfortunately confusing label in a book about innovation management) and starts when an employee feels secure in their new position. They look for particularly challenging work and so seek to enlarge their contribution to their department's work. Hard work at this stage can enhance visibility and promotion potential. When employees work in the same position for a substantial time, they transition to *stabilization,* where their focus can move to preserving their autonomy and minimizing vulnerability. This means that their openness to innovation can drop significantly. The rate at which an employee moves between the phases depends on both their personality and contextual issues. What is pertinent from an innovation perspective is that employees who have been in their jobs for a long time tend to become less creative in their approach to problem-solving because they are more rigid in their thinking, and are committed to established processes ('we have always done it that way'). Job rotation and bringing in new team members can help counter the potential problems of job longevity (and links to the ideas about sources of creativity that we discussed in Chapter 5).

Managing Performance

Managing performance is complex and the theories that have been developed to explain *motivation* in the workplace are inconclusive, though they do provide a framework for managers to draw upon in work situations.[76] Managers also need to be aware that creative people do not necessarily generate ideas on their own accord; they need encouragement, mentoring and support.[77]

Work performance is a function of an employee's ability and motivation. Two categories of theories of motivation have developed: *content* theories and *process* theories. Content theories concentrate on the factors that motivate people. Process theories stress the process by which motivation is achieved.

Content theories include the well-known studies of Maslow and Hertzberg. Maslow's greatest insight was that individual's needs form a hierarchy (see Chapter 10), and once needs such as pay and job security are satisfied, motivation will depend on factors such as esteem (for example, status) and self-actualization (for example, advancement). Hertzberg's work essentially extends

Maslow's ideas. It divides motivating factors into *hygiene factors* (which lead to dissatisfaction if missing) and *motivators*, which when present lead to motivation and job satisfaction. The empirical evidence on these theories is inconclusive but both have been widely applied by practitioners.

Process theories look at the dynamic relationships between the variables responsible for motivation. *Equity theory* identifies the importance of employees' feelings; if they do not feel that they are being fairly treated compared with their colleagues, their motivation will drop. Objective systems for reward and recognition are therefore essential. The concept of the *psychological contract* – the two-way exchange of perceived promises and obligations between an employee and an organization[78] – is useful because it reminds organizations that the relationship with their employees is governed by mutual perceptions and not just formal contracts. *Expectancy theory* states that 'employees will direct their work effort towards behaviours that they believe will lead to desired outcomes'.[79] It stresses the importance of clear links between effort and performance, performance and rewards, and rewards and goals. Managers are responsible for clarifying these links, and showing employees how different efforts will lead to different performance, and so on (see Mini Cases 8.6 on Fischer and 8.7 on Zenith Electronics).

There are a number of points that managers can take from the above discussion. It is important to understand individuals' needs and provide the possibility of them being met. As the 'lower level' needs are met, other factors such as recognition and responsibility will be more important. The process by which

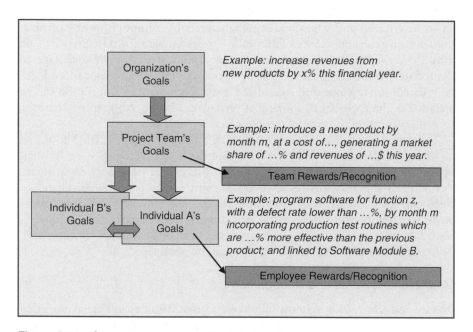

Figure 8.11   Cascading Innovation Goals to Employees

employees become more motivated depends on their perceptions of the psychological contract between them and the organization. Meeting expectations and demonstrating objectiveness are important and transparency – clarifying goals and potential rewards – is the next step.

It is useful to *cascade* the top-level innovation goals down the organization, to each and every employee. Figure 8.11 illustrates this, showing that high-level goals like revenues from new products can be linked to a project team's goals and in turn to the goals of each member of the team. In cascading goals it is important to check that the goals at each level are specific, measurable, achievable, relevant and timed (as represented by the mnemonic SMART).

At the employee level, goals also need to be linked to the work of peers, to promote teamwork. This is particularly important in fast-track breakthrough projects that require particular commitment from team members and cannot afford to have individuals focus on their personal goals to the detriment of the team's. In Figure 8.11, therefore, Individual A is tasked with not only writing a particular software module but also with ensuring that this links to Module B and incorporates manufacturing test routines. Clear links to rewards at the team and individual levels are also useful in cascading.

Goals should be clear and measurable. Table 8.5 suggests a number of possible goals that can be used to promote innovation. These include goals directly related to performance but should also cover the acquisition of new skills required.

Appraisals

There are two key aspects of appraisal from an innovation perspective: the topics to be covered and who conducts the appraisal.[80] Although most organizations perceive the importance of innovation, research has shown that few include it as a criterion in their annual appraisal systems.[81] It can be an advantage to change this, as including innovation as a criterion will certainly put more focus on it within the organization (see Mini Case 8.6 on Fischer). Innovation can be included in the appraisal by looking at reviewing actual performance versus the agreed goals, using the type of metrics given in Table 8.5.

There are several possibilities on whom to involve in the appraisal. The assessment can be conducted solely by the employee's direct manager, or by their manager's manager. Alternatively, it can be run by the personnel department, through self-appraisal, or be based on assessments by peers, subordinates or customers. A combination is also possible and the so-called *360-degree assessments* take inputs from above, peers and subordinates. Assessing an employee's contribution to innovation is not always easy and so one advantage of using 360-degree assessments is that a broader view can be obtained.

Motivation, Rewards and Recognition

Reward and recognition systems should emphasize attitudes and behaviours that support innovation; provide timely feedback from supervisors, managers and peers; encourage teamwork; and publicly signal the importance of innovation.

Mini Case 8.6

Fischer GmbH – Motivating Employees to Innovate[82]

Many companies want to become more innovative but do not effectively communicate this message to their employees. Fischer, a manufacturer of industrial fixing devices based in southern Germany, takes a different approach. The company has a tradition of innovation – it has filed hundreds of patents – and so there has always been a strong focus on R&D generating ideas for new products. However, Managing Director Klaus Fischer has attempted to extend the generation of new ideas across all functions because, he says, 'when we're not innovative across the whole company, then we haven't a chance'. Employees' contributions to innovation are assessed in annual appraisals in different ways. R&D engineers are measured on the number of patents and the speed and effectiveness with which these are converted into products. All employees are assessed on contributions to process innovation – improvements and cost reductions in manufacturing and business processes. In every appraisal a rating on a 1–5 scale is used to summarize an employee's overall contribution to innovation. Although the rating is subjective, it stimulates discussion between employees and management about innovation. The company has found that the process has been an effective catalyst in increasing overall performance.

Fischer perceives his role in promoting innovation to be central and therefore takes personal responsibility for driving the company's suggestions scheme and maintaining an effective bonus scheme linked to this.

In the HRM literature, there is strong recognition of the importance of rewards and recognition in supporting the achievement of strategic goals.[83] There are several decisions to be made concerning reward and recognition: the amount and type of reward; current performance and sort of behaviour that is desired; the type and recognition to be given; and when to inform employees of new rewards and recognition. Expectancy theory tells us that impossible goals will lead to frustration, unrewarded goals will not be taken seriously, and good performers will only be motivated by rewards that they value.[84]

The overall level of the monetary rewards available is normally driven by profitability. From this, a particular sum may be reserved for overall pay increases (for example, cost-of-living related increases) with the remaining sum available for all of the performance-related increases. In creating a focus on innovation, organizations may decide to reserve some amount for particular innovation projects and individuals that have been particularly innovative. These are, it can be noted, no different to the general types of rewards and recognition used by organizations. In shaping a culture of innovation, it is useful to launch and communicate specific schemes for promoting innovation. Here we can learn from expectancy theory and investigate the sort of recognition that good performers themselves value. The types of reward and recognition that are most normally used are listed in Table 8.6.

A key decision is which reward and recognition schemes are targeted at the individual and which should be targeted at encouraging teamwork. Individuals

Table 8.5 Employee Level Innovation Metrics

Metric	Details	Notes on Usage
Scientific publications	Number published in past x years.	• Objective measure but only applicable to R&D engineers and scientists. • Does not show the real value to the firm.
Patents	Number granted in past x years.	• Objective measure but only applicable to R&D engineers and scientists. • Does not show the real value to the firm.
Ideas generated	Suggestions submitted, etc.	• Does not show the real value to the firm. Better to use measures of the ideas implemented and the advantages they brought.
Cost savings	Transactional savings.	• Largely one-off savings.
Project goals	Specific time, quality and cost project goals that can be cascaded to the individual.	• As shown in Figure 8.10, a project's key goals should link to individuals' goals.
Process innovation	Removal of non-value adding stages from common business processes (for example, euros saved per year).	• Objective measure, easy to link to reward and recognition.
Service innovation	Enhancement of the interaction with customers during the service delivery.	• Can be linked to customer satisfaction metrics. Should cover all aspects of the service augmentation (Chapter 3).
Innovation performance rating	For example, a rating on the scale of 1 ('excellent') to 5 ('poor').	• Rating is subjective but discussion is more important than the actual rating. • See mini case on Fischer GmbH.
Teamwork	Encourages individuals to focus on achieving team or project goals.	• Is best to link the goal for individuals to be team-oriented by evaluating them directly on team goals.
Competencies gained	Helps employees focus on supporting the attainment of the organization's innovation goals and personal development (for example, developing the skills to be a heavyweight project leader).	• The Lever Fabergé company has linked employees' pay awards to the attainment of both business 'work targets' and 'personal goals'. • Useful in focusing teams on capturing the lessons learnt from projects.

are unlikely to take on unfamiliar tasks in cross-functional teamwork unless it is rewarded.[85] One of the rewards for good performance is obviously promotion. However, not every employee has the aptitude to become a good manager and so the *dual-ladder* approach recognizes that some employees can have excellent skills within their function (for example, an engineer may be an expert in particular technologies) but may not have the competences, potential or desire to develop as a manager. Dual-ladder salary schemes at large companies provide motivation for employees to develop their technical competencies.

Table 8.6 Example Rewards and Recognition for Innovation

Categories	Examples	Comments
Rewards	• Pay increase • Bonus payments • Stock options • 'Project equity' • Time and resources for 'personal projects' • Extra holiday • Company cars • Paid training • Paid education (for example, MBAs) • Promotions • Dual ladder schemes	Rewards should always be considered in light of the theories of motivation and the state of the business environment. They can have certain disadvantages. For example, stock options have little value in low-growth periods and can, when allocated to small numbers of employees, lead to equity issues. Equity theory prompts managers to consider how rewards and recognition are allocated. Peer review schemes can be very effective at both demonstrating objectivity and raising team motivation.
Recognition	• Praise from management • Publicity • Plaques and certificates • Peer recognition • What top performers themselves value (for example, development opportunities)	Content theory shows the importance of not only providing hygiene factors but also motivators, such as esteem.

The levels of most innovation rewards and recognition tend to be known *after the event*, in that they are announced after projects are finished. In some circumstances it may be beneficial to define and publish the levels of rewards available in advance. Zenith Electronics in the US decided that rewards needed to be known *before the event*, to motivate the team on a particularly challenging project (see Mini Case 8.7 on Zenith's 'Project Equity' Scheme). The Xerox Corporation has a management reward scheme dependent on company, division and individual performance.[86]

A clear link between goals and rewards is important. Such *transparency* can lead to open discussions on how goals can best be achieved and the appropriate rewards. Saab Training Systems, the Swedish defence contractor, found it useful to change the reward structure to put more emphasis on teamwork.[87] To fully support innovation, reward and recognition should not only focus on the achievement of business goals but also on encouraging individuals to increase their expertise. For example, few people have the necessary skills to manage a skunk works. Reward and recognition can be geared to encourage individuals with the necessary potential to acquire these skills and thus increase the innovation potential of the organization. The main case study for this chapter, on time:matters, demonstrates how motivating employees to be willing to take risks is an essential element of a culture of innovation.

Overall, reward and recognition systems need to be suitably maintained and sufficient management time needs to be reserved for this. A common argument from senior managers is that employees are 'expected to be innovative as part of their job' and so no additional reward or recognition is required. In such a case it is appropriate to ask the managers if they are satisfied with the current level of their employees' innovativeness. If the answer is 'no', then a change in behaviour can be accelerated by changing reward and recognition mechanisms. Figure 8.12, which came out of our consulting work with companies, is a matrix which can be useful in guiding such discussions – an organization can review its current position in the matrix and decide if it is

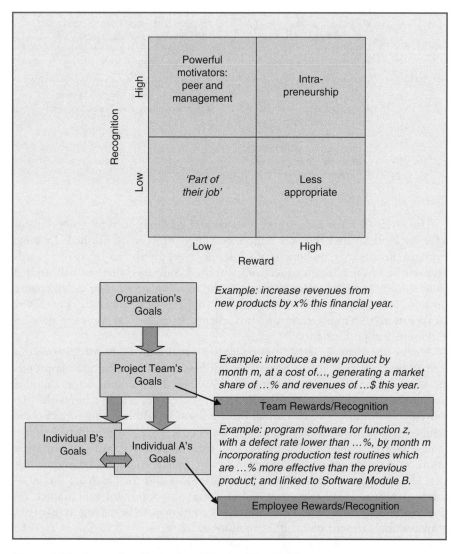

Figure 8.12   Innovation Reward and Recognition Matrix

useful to move to another quadrant in the matrix. Recognition, either from peers or management, can be a powerful motivator whereas reward without recognition is less useful.

Mini Case 8.7

Zenith Electronics – 'Project Equity' Scheme[88]

The US-based Zenith Electronics Corporation has used various approaches in providing rewards to employees involved in innovation projects. These were normally 'after the event' awards, given to teams or individuals for top performance. However, a multimillion dollar contract, which was technically risky and had a heavy penalty clause for late delivery, led Zenith to take a new approach.

It was decided to create a 'share scheme' for the project with a sum of several hundred thousand dollars reserved for rewarding the large team of over 25 dedicated members and 40 part-time members. At the start, all dedicated team members were allocated 200 shares and part-timers received 50. The initial value of the shares was zero but the successful achievement of each milestone and quality target, led to set increases in the share value, whereas each day of delay would lead to a defined loss in share value. The rules for calculating the value of shares were all defined in advance and were transparent to the team – so it was clear that, if everything went according to plan, a dedicated team member could earn upwards of $15,000 bonus. Discretionary shares were also reserved for allocation to those employees that made extraordinary contributions.

Although the scheme required careful up-front definition and explanation, it shows that in forming innovation project teams the issue of reward and recognition needs to be considered. Special projects may require special schemes. Zenith was successful at developing the high-risk technology exactly on time – it was for use in digital television – and was convinced that the adoption of a new reward and recognition scheme contributed to the achievement of all of the milestones and quality goals. Zenith has recognized the need to regularly update their reward system.

Development of Employees

To be effective innovators, employees constantly need to develop new skills. The innovation strategy should define some of the new skills that are needed in an organization and these should be apparent from the technology roadmap (Chapter 4). These requirements can then be compared with existing skills and, where gaps exist, they can be covered by hiring or employee development. Technological and specific market knowledge are clear skills that may need to be developed but cross-functional team working skills and particularly project team leadership skills also need to be constantly developed. In the service sector, the ability to design an effective service augmentation is an area where employees may need to be developed through specific training programmes.

A company's future requirements should be one driver for planning the development of employees' skills. However, of equal importance is the individual motivation – for many employees learning new skills can be hugely motivating.

SUMMARY

This chapter covered the fifth and final element of the Pentathlon – people and organization, including cultural and team issues. It stressed the strategic importance of human resources. Three levels of analysis were presented: the organization level; innovation project teams; and the employee level. Overall, the Chapter

- Explained the research on management culture and how this can be used to help develop a 'culture of innovation'.
- Summarized best practices for creating an innovative working environment, while cautioning that people management practices are context dependent and are therefore difficult to transfer.
- Described the advantages and limitations of the five main types of teams that can be used to manage innovation projects.
- Explained the steps required to form and successfully run innovation teams, including selecting team members and managing the functional interfaces.
- Covered the main aspects of managing individual employees, from their recruitment, to their appraisal, and the recognition of their performance. It also showed the complexity facing managers in their need to encourage motivation.

Illustrating the above points, this chapter's main case study is about time:matters, a company that has revolutionized 'sameday' shipments and has focused on creating the right culture to generate a constant stream of service innovation in the 'time-critical' logistics business.

This and the previous four chapters have proposed a wide range of tools and techniques for innovation management, relating to each of the elements of the Pentathlon. The management challenge is to boost innovation performance by coordinating the improvements across the elements of the Pentathlon and is the subject of the next chapter.

MANAGEMENT RECOMMENDATIONS

- Use the cultural web as a diagnosis tool and apply ideas from best practice to create a real 'culture of innovation'.
- Choose a suitable team structure for each project.
- Manage innovation project teams not only to obtain the maximum returns from projects but also to develop sufficient talent for driving such projects.
- Link innovation strategy to employee development and support this with appropriate reward systems.

RECOMMENDED READING

1. Bratton, J. and Gold, J., *Human Resource Management: Theory and Practice* (Basingstoke: Palgrave Macmillan, 2003). [Good text on HRM.]
2. Tushman, M. L. and Anderson, P. (eds), *Managing Strategic Innovation and Change* (Oxford: Oxford University Press, 1997). [Classic collection of readings on culture, leadership and innovation.]
3. Jelinek, M. and Schoonhoven, C. B., *The Innovation Marathon: Lessons from High Technology Firms* (Oxford: Basil Blackwell, 1990). [Interesting study.]

CASE STUDY
time:matters – From B to A, Sameday![89]

Before reading this case, consider the following generic innovation management issues:

*   What role does market segmentation play in service innovation?
*   How important are staff in a service operation and, when recruiting, what skills should you be looking for?
*   How can a culture of innovation be managed?
*   How can innovation be maintained in a service operation?

Spare parts logistics is a massive business worldwide. Equipment manufacturers are required to offer excellent after-sales service to their customers, as equipment failures – so-called *downtime* – can be annoying, costly or even life threatening. Therefore, for a wide range of equipment, from medical devices to turbines, rapid and 100 per cent reliable delivery of spare parts around the globe is essential.

Consider the following scenario: it is 15:48 on a Friday afternoon and the production line of your top customer in Amsterdam has stopped because your equipment has failed. The production manager has just telephoned to say that he must work '24/7 on our most critical order for 2009' and so he needs the line running again by tomorrow latest. Fortunately, the 367 kg spare part is in stock at your logistics centre in Barcelona but how can you get it from Barcelona to Amsterdam today? Call 0049-(0)800–117 117 7 and the logistics specialists from time:matters will find a solution.

THE TIME CRITICAL NICHE

The time:matters company is a spin-off from Lufthansa cargo, formed in 2002 to serve the time critical segment: through coordinated air, road and rail transportation. CEO Franz-Joseph Miller says that a separate company was necessary because, 'from 1995–2001 and as part of Lufthansa, the business grew to 8 Million Euro but there was little strategic focus on the specific needs of our target segment. We focus on speed, customized solutions, and reliability with for example "sameday" delivery in Germany and Europe. "Sameday" in our business means transport times across Europe from initial call to delivery of only 2–8 hours. Our service operations have been designed to create specific competences such as high-speed transportation through our partner networks; courier delivery when the shipment is so valuable that the customer does not

▶▶

want to let it "out of their hands"; and customized solutions. A fundamental element is our ability to give seamless tracking, door-to-door'. In 2008, over 1,072,800 time critical pieces were delivered and revenues of over EUR 60 million were generated. This covered the shipment of one-off spare parts, regular parts shipments where delivery reliability is critical, and special projects, where customized transport processes are established.

One-off spare parts can be 'seasonal'. For example, the most important time of the year for John Deere is the harvest season. However, as John Deere is one of the world's largest manufacturers of agricultural and forestry equipment, it is harvest time all the year round, as at anytime somewhere in the world John Deere products are being used for harvesting. Agricultural equipment downtime can mean that crops are lost if the weather is unstable. So, John Deere have teamed up with time:matters, which can courier urgent spare parts to the actual field where the equipment is located and thus minimize downtime. Similarly, some major airlines use what time:matters terms 'Special Speed Solutions' for the fastest airport-to-airport service to solve AOG problems ('aircraft on the ground' and unable to fly).

Client companies in the time critical niche have requirements for both urgent one-off shipments and regular shipments. Consequently, the client list for time:matters includes IT companies such as Fujitsu Technology Solutions; medical equipment suppliers such as Siemens Healthcare; InteraDent Zahntechnik (dental prostheses); and Otto GmbH (Germany's biggest mail order company). Each of these companies will have one-off problems that need to be solved and ongoing requirements (that, once recognized, can create new opportunities). For example, InteraDent may have a number of urgent shipments requiring a unique solution throughout the year but, as they produce the majority of their output of 60,000 dental prostheses per year in the Philippines, they also need regular shipments to Europe. These need to be fast and 100 per cent reliable so that dentists can provide fast treatment to their patients.

However, it is not only materials and spare parts that time:matters transports. Critical documentation is also couriered around the world. Recently, Volkswagen was conducting tests of a new vehicle and an update of the engine control software needed to be delivered urgently into the hands of the test team, which was on the move in Greece. A courier from the Frankfurt office of time:matters flew with the required CD-ROM and drove from Athens airport to meet the team and hand over the high performance software. Special shipments, where there is a need for fast delivery and careful handling of confidential or sensitive material, are typical of the problems that are solved by the time:matters special Service Centre. 'We have to react fast and so we are used to solving unique – "Logistics Lot Size 1" – problems for our customers', says Miller, 'but we also need to spot trends'.

SERVICE INNOVATION

Jörg Asbrand is Chief Operating Officer of the time:matters group and Managing Director of time:matters Spare Parts Logistics, a holding company. He says, 'it is partly our history that means that innovation is so important to us. We started by creating novel solutions to meet the needs of the time critical segment, through a network of partners. We made our name as a company that can solve almost every logistics

▸▸

problem, where fast and reliable transportation is required. Therefore, it is critical for us to innovate, so that we continue to be perceived as the leader with a unique business model'.

A number of world famous companies such as FedEx and TNT provide fast shipments and have developed their own infrastructure of aircraft, delivery agents and tracking systems, using proprietary software and scanning devices to track shipments. In this aspect, time:matters is different in that it has developed 'open architecture' software to allow it to quickly integrate its partners' systems, be it for example, those of Lufthansa, Brussels Airlines, the Deutsche Bahn (German railways), or relatively small couriers in different countries. 'We are a company with no buildings and essentially no assets' says Asbrand, 'so it is our ability to innovate and partner with other organizations that are our main assets. For example, we have negotiated with our partner airlines that we can load shipments onto their aircraft up to 10 minutes before departure; we have an exclusive contract with Deutsche Bahn and on their inter-city trains their personnel take personal care of our shipments. Then we also have a Service Innovation Group working constantly updating our service offering'.

The time:matters website identifies over ten service products including 'Sameday services' ('overnight is old news'); worldwide transportation solutions ('sameday worldwide'); 'onboard courier services'; 'charter' ('if there are no direct flights available...'); and 'emergency logistics'. A website is always an important part of any service company's branding and augmentation and time:matters have recognized this. To make their service as tangible as possible, they include a number of videos portraying actual examples of how they have solved particular logistics problems (including the urgent software delivery for Volkswagen to Greece).

CULTURE OF INNOVATION

With currently 120 employees, time:matters is proud of 'being small, non-corporate and creative' says Asbrand, 'yet we are also proud to be an extremely international company with a solid financial structure, with Lufthansa Cargo as a major shareholder'. Asbrand says, 'the creative capacity in the company is maintained by three approaches through which we "orchestrate" rather than "manage" our culture. Firstly, we hire the right people, who love working in what we call a "boutique of experts". Secondly, we promote the generation and selection of the best ideas for enhancing our service offering. Thirdly, an openness to risk and an acceptance that things can go wrong are essential if we are to spot the hidden needs of customers. We cannot as such create a demand for increased shipments – there we are dependent on our customers' own businesses. But if we can create new service products that are unique, then our customers will want to use us for all of their time critical shipments'.

A very strong emphasis is placed on hiring the right people; 'people with a "make it happen" attitude, and the personal drive and creativity to find fast solutions to unique logistics problems', Asbrand says, 'Innovation is central to us at time:matters because, without innovating regularly, what we offer will be copied by the competition. We need to be creative in two main ways. Firstly, our people need to be creative in solving customers' immediate problems. "Barcelona to Amsterdam scenarios" are common for us and our Service Centre has to deal with them minute-for-minute. Secondly, we need

▶▶

to be creative in recognizing trends in our customers' requirements and so we have the Service Innovation Group. This team gathers and selects ideas on a "survival of the fittest" philosophy, where the originator of the idea needs to show their commitment and compete for resources needed to develop their ideas into products'. One of the latest innovations from time:matters is the 'time stamp', where the shipper's IT system is notified at the exact time that a particular shipment is handed over. Whether it is an expensive spare part like a marine engine where invoicing can also be time critical, or stem cells needed for research purposes, time stamping is helping customers to better coordinate their businesses.

'Our challenge is to make sure we have the right set up and are not losing sight of innovation and growth opportunities', summarizes Asbrand. 'There are still great opportunities out there and we are 100 per cent focused on making sure that the things we are going after are successful.'

9 BOOSTING INNOVATION PERFORMANCE

> There are risks and costs to a program of action, but they are far less than the long range risks and costs of comfortable inactions.
>
> John F. Kennedy

INTRODUCTION

Managers must be proactive in attempting to master something to which most organizations aspire but which few actually achieve – continuously high levels of innovation. The Pentathlon Framework reminds us of the need to consider each of the elements of innovation management and not to focus on one area alone. In the previous five chapters we looked at the elements and presented key tools and techniques to maximize performance. However, exemplary performance in one area of the Pentathlon alone is not enough and it is necessary to 'step back' and assess an organization's level of innovation. This helps in determining priorities and choosing appropriate ways to boost performance. The five elements of the Pentathlon are not independent and so steps taken to improve, say, portfolio management will impact other areas, and vice versa. Such interactions should be managed to reinforce overall performance but the relationships between the different areas are complex and interactions cannot be predicted with certainty.

This chapter covers the main aspects of this challenge giving

- An overview of how to improve innovation performance.
- Suggestions on how to choose suitable performance measures and determine the priorities for improving innovation management.
- A discussion of the linkages between the different elements of innovation management.
- Ideas on how to improve overall performance such as developing learning loops from innovation projects and using change management techniques focused on innovation.

- A case study on an automotive supplier that has consistently achieved high levels of innovation despite its limited resources – Sidler Automotive.

PERFORMANCE IMPROVEMENT

Figure 9.1 shows a suggested process for improving innovation performance. We deliberately say 'suggested', as this flow diagram is a simplification of a methodology that is very dependent on the individual circumstances facing a company, its processes, and its culture of innovation. The diagram could leave the impression that we are being overly deterministic and the steps required are clear-cut; this is not the case. Variations on the approach and multiple iterations are likely to be necessary for any one organization to achieve significant improvements.

The diagram shows that there are three main components to improving performance, each of which will be discussed in this chapter:

- Assessing current performance. As shown in Figure 9.1, the areas for improvement can be identified using measures, the cultural web (Chapter 8) and what is called an *innovation audit.*
- Identifying priorities and linkages between the different elements of the Pentathlon.
- Implementing changes to improve performance (at both the project and organizational levels).

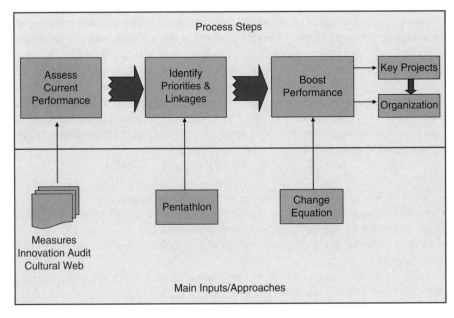

Figure 9.1 Improving Innovation Performance

ASSESSING CURRENT PERFORMANCE

In this chapter we will use the term *innovation performance*. By this, we mean the total innovation produced by an organization, in terms of the generation and commercialization of ideas for new products, new services, new or improved manufacturing or service delivery processes, *and* in terms of the underlying processes. Innovation performance is context dependent; its exact nature depends on the organization in question.

Innovation performance needs to be measured, as this is the first part of the improvement process. There are two main ways in which to determine performance. One is using quantitative performance measures. The other approach takes account of the less tangible aspects of an organization's innovation performance and uses an innovation audit.

Performance Measures

The well-known work of Robert Kaplan and David Norton of Harvard on the *Balanced Scorecard* has stressed the need for businesses to have a range of measures in addition to the classical financial ones. The measures in the balanced scorecard cover financial aspects, the customer perspective, the perspective of the efficiency of internal business processes and an innovation and learning perspective.[1] Taking a broad view, with financial and other perspectives, is similar to what we discussed in Chapter 6 – where we recommended that portfolio management should be based on a mixture of financial and non-financial approaches. Kaplan and Norton stress the importance of innovation saying 'we came to realize that innovation was a *critical* internal process' (their italics).[2]

The performance of an organization in terms of innovation is not easy to determine and our own case study research has shown that managers recognize the difficulties they have with measurement.[3] Work with their clients has also led the McKinsey consultancy company to state that measures are one of the main challenges of innovation management.[4] Recognizing that there are different types of measures is the first step in developing an appropriate measurement system.

Types of Performance Measures

Performance measurement has been studied in-depth, particularly by operations management researchers. A fundamental approach in this discipline is to view all management processes as having inputs and outputs.[5] Figure 9.2 shows this *input-output model* view of innovation. *Inputs* are the time and resources required, such as people or information technology. Innovation is largely a knowledge-based process and ideas are transformed by the work of employees into services and products that can be sold to customers. The resources required are the time and investments made, the people working on the innovation projects, information technology and can also include equipment, such as that used in service or manufacturing production and delivery processes.

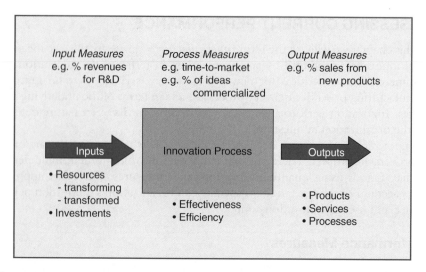

Figure 9.2   Input-Output View of the Innovation Process

Applying the input-output model to innovation helps us to recognize that there are three types of measure. *Input measures,* such as the percentage of revenues invested in R&D, are useful benchmarks but they do not gauge how effective a company is at turning R&D capacity into commercial success. *Process measures* are indicators of the efficiency of the innovation process within an organization, for instance, of the time required to bring an innovation to the market. Similarly, the percentage of ideas that are commercialized is a useful indicator of both how relevant the ideas generated are, and also how efficient the process to implement them is. *Output measures* are directly related to the commercial impact of innovations – such as revenues generated by a new service product, or cost savings through a more efficient service augmentation. Patents are a popular measure of innovation but, as noted in Chapter 2, they are not a true output measure. Inventions described in patents need to be commercialized, either by being directly applied in products, services or processes, or through licensing. The number of patents generated may be a measure of the creativity of the R&D department but not necessarily of innovation. An output measure related to patents is earnings from patent licensing (and it should be noted that Philips earns more from patents licensing than it invests in research!).

Organizations need to choose measures in each of the three categories. Using input measures alone neglects the commercial side of innovation. Taking only output measures can make an organization commercially aware but the process itself needs to be monitored, if it is to be improved. Measures of the efficiency of 'the innovation process' (that is, the various sub-processes, such as NPD and ideation, that make up the way an organization approaches innovation) are needed.

Selecting Performance Measures

Research on performance measures shows that organizations typically measure too much. Complex measurement systems can cloud priorities and so appropriate measures need to be selected. Table 9.1 gives a set of questions to determine appropriateness and can be used to determine individual measures that can be easily understood, effectively linked to strategy (and therefore support the implementation of strategy), can be trusted (because they are reliable), and are appropriate (for example, actionable).

Table 9.2 lists possible input, output and process measures for innovation, from which suitable ones should be selected. It covers the different perspectives recommended by Kaplan and Norton. Performance measures are context dependent – they should relate to an organization's business and the priorities for improvement. However, some general guidelines can be given. A range of measures should be selected that covers inputs, outputs and process (to monitor and to learn how to improve the process itself). Ratio measures are often useful, as they are easier to compare than absolute measures. An example of this would be taking the innovation rate as the number of new products ('new' is normally defined as less than three-years-old) compared with the number in the existing portfolio, rather than just the number of new products developed. Overall, the number of measures used must be appropriate because, as noted earlier, having too many measures wastes management time.

The measures given in Table 9.2 can be applied in both service and manufacturing organizations. In service, particular care should be taken to

Table 9.1 Points to Consider in Choosing Performance Measures

	Aspect	Questions to Ask about the Potential Measure
1)	Strategy	Is it directly related to the intended innovation strategy?
2)	Simplicity	Is it simple to understand (and communicate)?
3)	Action ability	Can and will it be acted upon?
4)	Appropriateness	Does it provide timely and appropriate feedback?
5)	Validity	Does it reliably measure what it is meant to?
6)	Reliability	Is it consistent, irrelevant of when or by whom the measurement was made?
7)	Clarity	Is interpretation of the measurement unambiguous?
8)	Behaviour	Will the introduction of the measure have any adverse behavioural affects?
9)	Cost-effectiveness	Is it worth the cost of collecting and analysing the data?

Source: Based on Neely, A., Richards, H., Mills, J., Platts, K. and Bourne, M., 'Designing Performance Measures: A Structured Approach', *International Journal of Operations and Production Management*, Vol. 17, No. 11 (1997), pp. 1131–1152.

Table 9.2 Example Input, Process and Output Measures

Input Measures	Process Measures	Output Measures
Financial • Per cent of revenues invested in product R&D • Per cent of revenues invested in process R&D • Per cent of revenues invested in technology acquisition • Per cent of projects delayed or cancelled due to lack of funding **Customer Perspective** • Per cent mix of projects by their strategic drivers (for example, meeting customer needs, reactions to competition; technology-driven; based on internal ideas; etc.) **Resources** • Per cent of total employees involved in innovation projects • Per cent of personnel trained in creativity and problem-solving techniques • Per cent of personnel who have worked in two or more functions • Number of ideas per source (for example, ideas from employees, ideas from customers) • Number of ideas generated per year for development into new products, services & processes • Number of ideas considered per year for new products, services and processes • Efficiency of links to external organizations • Per cent of projects delayed or cancelled because of lack of human resources	**Financial** • Average project costs • Costs of/savings through outsourcing **Process Efficiency** • Average break-even-time • Average time-to-market • Hours worked per project • Average time for a specific task (for example, initial design) • Per cent time spent on project-related tasks • Per cent time spent on non-project (administrative and support) tasks • Number of patents received/number commercialized • Per cent mix of product/process/service/business process innovation projects • Per cent usage of appropriate tools and techniques (for example, advanced market research projects; computer-aided design; computer-integrated manufacturing, and so on) • Per cent of projects that entered development and were ultimately considered commercial successes • Per cent of projects killed too late (that is after significant expenditure) • Per cent of employees actively contributing to innovation **Learning** • Per cent of projects where post-project reviews are conducted • Number of improvements to innovation processes **Specific Service Measures** • Customer contact: time and degree of intimacy • Information exchanged with the customer • Customer throughput time • Complaints: number and type • Staff satisfaction • Efficiency of innovations in products and service augmentations • Cost per customer • Profit per customer • Retention rates	**Financial** • Per cent of sales revenues from new products/enhancements • Per cent of sales revenues from new services • Per cent cost savings/revenues from process innovation • Quality improvements from process innovation • Return on innovation investment • Profitability of the new product programme • Earnings from patent licensing **Customer Perspective** • Innovation rate (number of new products compared with total number of product in the portfolio) • Number of new products compared with competitors • Number of new services compared with competitors • Number of enhancements to service augmentations • Number of process innovations (number of innovations per year compared with the total number of major processes used in operations) • Per cent mix of first-to-market, fast-follower, and me-too products • Market share growth due to new products/enhancements • Market share growth due to new services • Strike rate (ratio of orders to enquiries or quotations) • Per cent of orders delivered on time • Customer satisfaction indices

Source: Based on Goffin, K., 'Enhancing Innovation Performance', *Management Quarterly*, Part 13 (October 2001), pp. 18–26; Voss, C. A., Chiesa, V. and Coughlan, P., *Innovation – Your Move, Self-Assessment Guide and Workbook*. Department of Trade and Industry (UK) (London, 1993); Johnston, R. and Clark, G., *Service Operations Management*. Financial Times (Prentice Hall, London, 2001).

ensure that innovation performance measures adequately cover not only the service product but also the service augmentation. Table 9.2 gives measures recommended for service organizations.[6] These may also be relevant to the many manufacturing organizations that also deliver services. It should also be recognized that certain measures commonly used for innovation, such as patents and the percentage of revenues invested in R&D are less useful in service companies as benchmarking data are less likely to be available or reliable.[7]

Using Performance Measures

Measures can be used to decide whether:

- The input resources are suitable, sufficient and are efficiently used in commercializing innovations.
- The innovation process in the company is effective at producing innovations that have enough commercial impact.
- Current innovation output is strong, compared with the strongest competitors and leading companies in other fields. (Benchmarking figures from competitors are useful.)
- The innovation strategy is being successfully implemented.

Prominent visual displays of innovation data can act as powerful communication and motivation tools in organizations (for example, AXA Ireland have an 'innovation corridor' and 'innovation quadrant' – see Chapter 3 main case study).

The Innovation Audit

The fact that it is difficult to create valid and reliable measures for all aspects of innovation has led to the *innovation audit* concept. Innovations 'audits' are different to financial audits, which are based on quantitative measures of financial performance (that is, output measures of past performance). 'Measuring performance is helpful, but it's only part of the story. To learn from our past successes and failures, we need to understand how they came about'.[8] Therefore, innovation audits look at not only performance (an output measure) but also how this performance was achieved (a process measure). An innovation audit is a very useful starting point for any organization that wants to boost its performance (see Mini Case 9.1 on Evotec OAI).

The concept of an innovation audit is not new. One early audit developed in the 1980s focused on creativity and took a multifunctional perspective, with audit questions to be answered by production, marketing, R&D, personnel and so on.[10] Later audit tools have looked at all aspects of innovation management and their use has increased. New product development and innovation management consultants Arthur D. Little strongly recommend innovation audits.[11]

Mini Case 9.1

Evotec – Using an Innovation Audit[9]

Evotec is a leading provider of biological, chemical and screening services, which help pharmaceutical companies accelerate the discovery and development process, manage risk, and reduce the time and cost of bringing new drugs to the market. The company has over 600 employees, many of whom are PhD scientists, based in Hamburg and in the UK arm, which was formerly Oxford Asymmetry International (OAI). Evotec has an impressive set of clients, which reads like a 'who's who' of the chemical and pharmaceutical industries and includes BASF, GlaxoSmithKline, Pfizer and Roche.

OAI used a team of consultants to conduct an innovation audit. Interviews were held with a sample of staff, covering all functions and levels and using a comprehensive set of audit questions. The results were revealing: staff rated OAI relatively low on creativity; innovation was not perceived as sufficiently customer-led; knowledge was not optimally applied in the company; there was not enough communication between the two divisions (discovery and development); and clearer rewards and recognition were needed. Some of the management team were disappointed with the results and expressed the opinion that it did not reflect the OAI they knew and the market view that OAI was already very innovative. Nevertheless, the audit seemed to show that management and employees viewed the potential for more innovation differently and the management team quickly set about making some significant changes.

The changes included major efforts to become more creative. For example, a knowledge management system was implemented to capture and share much of the expertise of individual scientists. This made the solution of clients' problems more efficient and helped identify innovations that would most impact the customer. OAI managers also worked on both the formal and informal communication. The bringing together of the two divisions in a new building made a big impact, as did a range of new reward and recognition schemes that spurred innovation. Chief Operating Officer of Evotec, Dr Mario Polywka, sees the innovation audit as an important catalyst, 'we probably would have made a lot of the changes such as implementing a knowledge management system anyway. However, the innovation audit helped galvanize our actions. We have seen a lot of returns on the investments we have made in our people, knowledge management, and communications. What is more, our customers have also seen many tangible benefits in both the range and speed of services we offer to support drug discovery and development. For me, the biggest steps we have made are firstly that our employees now realise that being a service company involves significant technical creativity, but that also the way we do business, commercially and financially, is innovative in itself'.

At Evotec, innovation is constant and they are a world leader in a fascinating new 'technology' – zebrafish! These tiny fish are very similar genetically to humans and they can be used to testing pharmaceuticals. This development is so exciting that Evotec have created a dedicated website (www.zebrafish-screening.com). The website explains that zebrafish 'physiology, development and metabolism closely mirrors mammalian systems'. Furthermore 'exposure to compounds predominantly causes similar effects to those seen in humans. Zebrafish have the potential to accelerate and de-risk the drug discovery and development process by reducing attrition rates and lowering the development cost of producing new drugs'. Watch that website for some amazing inroads into drug testing.

Table 9.3   Example Innovation Audit Questions from the British Standard

Number	Question
1)	What types of innovation do you have in your organization?
2)	Does your organization have a procedure for developing third-generation products and services?
3)	Is this process documented?
4)	How does your enterprise use its long-term vision of the future to inform and influence present activities?
5)	What is your organization's budget for new product development?
6)	Does an innovative attitude pervade your organization?
7)	Is this innovation attitude communicated internally and externally?
8)	Does your organization have a skills audit?
9)	Is your organization involved in any alliances?
10)	What mechanism does your organization have to react fast to threats or surprises from the competition?
11)	How does your organization protect its intellectual property?
12)	How does your organization learn from failures?

The European Union has given substantial financial support for companies to have innovation audits conducted by consultants – over 760 organizations in 18 countries have benefited from this.[12] The British Standard on innovation management also emphasizes the need to audit innovation by looking at both the organizational aspects (16 questions) and product and service issues (7 questions).[13] Table 9.3 shows a number of the questions from the British Standard and it can be seen that many of them (for example, Number 6 on the 'innovative attitude') are hard to answer based on facts and so employees and managers will give their opinions. Although the answers to many of the questions are based on opinions, the range of answers from people throughout an organization (and even outside it) can help to identify the strengths and weaknesses of an organization.

Innovation audits are just as useful for the service sector as for manufacturing. A simple set of questions recommended for service companies is given in Table 9.4. This is a typical approach to make a fast assessment of innovation performance and such approaches normally use scoring, to capture perceptions in a quantitative form that can easily be summarized using descriptive statistics.

Conducting Innovation Audits

Innovation audits collect a mix of quantitative and qualitative data through survey techniques, and are normally conducted by outsiders (who are neutral) interviewing a representative sample of employees (who can remain anonymous), managers and, possibly, customers. Interpreting answers to many of the

Table 9.4   Innovation Audit Questions Recommended for the Service Sector

Number	Question
1)	Is innovation stated as part of your corporate objectives and business plan?
2)	Do you have at least two experiments or pilots of new service concepts being conducted at any one time?
3)	Do you regularly review your portfolio of service offerings to make sure that they are balanced in terms of novelty/innovation and risk?
4)	Is your objective to be the market leader by exceeding the value added of your main competitor?
5)	Does your financial reporting system reflect innovation as an investment rather than as a cost?
6)	Are you attracted by new technologies and considering how to apply them to your business?
7)	Do you provide support to staff who try out new ideas even if the ideas fail?
8)	Do you have a procedure for having staff 'mystery shop' the competition and report back?
9)	Do you provide training for staff in innovation-related skills?
10)	Do you expect to get at least 5 per cent of export revenues from innovative services?

Source: Anonymous. 'Managing Change in Your Organization', *International Trade Forum*, No. 2 (2000), pp. 26–28.

questions requires experience and so this is one reason for using an experienced outsider to conduct the audit. Other reasons for using an outsider are that they can get employees to comment candidly, and they can bring an informal element of benchmarking, by being able to compare the results with what they have seen in other organizations.

Many aspects of innovation cannot be expressed in figures and so qualitative data consisting of employees' views on performance are collected using perceptional scales. Therefore, audits gauge the innovation performance of individual organizations and data from different organizations cannot be directly compared. The cultural web discussed in Chapter 8 can be used in conjunction with an innovation audit to collect information on how the culture of an organization impacts its innovation.

In conducting an innovation audit, the aims are

- To identify an organization's strengths and weaknesses from an innovation perspective, through gaining the views of a representative sample of managers and employees.
- To collect ideas on how to make improvements.

The scope of the audit needs to be decided in advance, in terms of the number of people to be surveyed and also in terms of the breadth of questions

INNOVATION STRATEGY

- Has innovation been introduced as a fundamental part of your company philosophy and values?
- What is the role of technology in innovation?
- Does top management spend sufficient time supporting all stages of innovation?
- Are innovation goals – for new products, services and processes – defined?
- Do performance measures reflect the strategy? Are they simple, appropriate and valid?
- Is there a good balance of truly innovative projects as well as product improvements?
- Does your innovation strategy integrate all five areas of innovation management?
- Has the organization developed an 'innovation network'?

IDEAS

- Are creative ideas collected on a regular basis?
- How many ideas for new products, services and processes were developed in the past 12 months?
- Do ideas originate from all departments, often from contacts with customers (including hidden needs)?
- Are ideas quickly developed into new product/service concepts?
- Are creativity techniques and workshops used?

PRIORITIZATION

- Is there a good balance of ideas for new products, services and processes?
- Are concept reviews held regularly?
- Are choices made quickly?
- Is there a good feedback mechanism from actual product performance to ensure screening decisions
- Does the responsibility for screening decisions lie too high in the company hierarchy?
- Are appropriate tools and techniques used?

IMPLEMENTATION (NPD, etc.)

- Is this a bottleneck stage, because too many projects are attempted?
- Are best practice techniques such as simultaneous engineering applied, where appropriate?
- Is your time-to-market comparable to your competitors?
- Are manufacturing ramp-ups fast and efficient?
- Does manufacturing regularly develop new processes?
- Are project reviews effectively used?

PEOPLE AND ORGANIZATION

- Is the broad meaning and importance of innovation – new products, services and processes – understood by all employees?
- Are clear individual innovation targets set and known by all employees?
- Do human resource policies support a 'culture of innovation' through stimulating a creative, problem-solving working environment? Are organizational structures flexible and effective?
- Is innovation covered by employees' appraisals?

Figure 9.3 'Fast Innovation Audit' Questions

Source: Updated from Goffin, K. and Pfeiffer, R., *Innovation Management in UK and German Manufacturing Companies.* Anglo-German Foundation Report Series, (London, December 1999).

to be used. Normally there are two levels of audit: a simple, fast version to obtain an initial idea of strengths and weaknesses, and a version that probes more deeply. Figure 9.3 shows a 'fast' version, in which the audit questions have been grouped using the Pentathlon Framework, in order to determine in which of the five areas a company is stronger or weaker and whether output levels are sufficient. The fast audit can be conducted as a workshop with managers, where their initial ideas for improvements and their views on the cultural web can also be collected. However, considering only the views of the management team is not sufficient (and can give a biased view), and so a representative sample from the whole organization should be surveyed. This is more revealing, as individual employees will give creative ideas for improving innovation. For example, the consulting company Synectics (see Mini Case 9.2) always focuses on obtaining the views of a wide range of employees in its efforts to enhance organizations' innovation performance. Direct interviews are more effective than distributing audit questionnaires, as in the discussion, vital information about the organization's workings can emerge. A representative survey should use a more comprehensive set of questions than the fast version.

Mini Case 9.2

Synectics – Driving Clients' Innovation Products and Processes[16]

Synectics is a leading innovation management consultancy. George Prince and William J. J. Gordon, who both had extensive experience in helping companies develop new product concepts, founded the company in 1960. Fascinated by the dynamics in meetings held to develop new product ideas, Gordon and Prince taped thousands of hours of such meetings in order to study how people interacted. Analysis of the tapes showed significant differences in the flow of meetings that were successful at generating breakthrough ideas, compared with meetings that failed to do so. Using these observations, proprietary tools and techniques were developed for generating creative product ideas – including 'springboards', 'excursions', and 'itemized response'. Springboards are a way of generating thoughts that lead to new thinking. They focus on wishes, challenges to constraints on a problem, feelings, gut-level reactions, or apparently conflicting points of view. Excursions are a process to enable the power of the subconscious to be released onto a problem. The problem is put aside and thinking focused elsewhere: thinking about different worlds, objects, art and so on. Such stimuli first generate seemingly irrelevant material. Links are then 'forced back' to the original problem. Itemized response is a process for protecting ideas, which are all too easily destroyed during the process of idea evaluation. The process of itemized response focuses first on identifying the positive aspects about an idea, in order to strengthen it. Next, areas of concern with the idea are identified and answers to these sought.

The three techniques have been applied by Synectics in a diverse range of companies from both service and manufacturing. Key successes include helping Liptons turn iced tea from a summer product to a popular year-round drink, improving the logistics processes for a major shipping line Neptune Orient Lines, and even turning a struggling Gaelic football team into champions.

▸▸

Although Synectics has always been very successful in the area of creativity, it has deliberately developed a broad portfolio of services to support clients in the areas of innovation strategy, product development, marketing and critical process optimization. Trudy Lloyd is a Partner in the London office of Synectics and perceives three key issues in the management of innovation. 'Innovation is a challenge for the leaders in many organizations. The very characteristics that help them manage organizations successfully, such as decisiveness, analytical rigour, and practicality, can impact negatively on creativity. To be creative in business there is a need to suspend judgement, tolerate ambiguity and put aside practical considerations, albeit temporarily to generate a suitable stream of ideas. 'Secondly, organizations that identify breakthrough ideas select them exactly because they are new and fresh. Then they find ways to build feasibility into the idea. At Synectics we believe you cannot do the reverse...build newness into a feasible idea'.

'Finally, it's important that everyone in an organization understands their role in the innovation process'. Lloyd insists that the innovators are not just the people in the project teams who come up with new product and process ideas. 'There comes a stage when any new concept has to be operationalized and this involves everyone. Innovations present staff with challenges that are different from those of running the current business ...' says Lloyd, 'and businesses that innovate successfully have a culture where the whole organization is enthused and committed to making new initiatives work'.

A widely used innovation audit was developed by a team from London Business School (LBS) and is called a 'technical innovation audit'. It has questions covering both innovation processes (for example, concept generation; NPD; process innovation; and technology acquisition) and their 'enablers' (such as human resource practices and leadership from top management).[14] Managers are required to rate their company's performance in various areas on a scale of 1 ('poor') to 5 ('world class'). Such an audit forces managers and employees to review all aspects of their innovation management and this automatically stimulates thinking on ways of improving performance.[15] In our companion website (www.palgrave.com/business/goffin/) we give a comprehensive list of questions from a detailed review of the literature, from which relevant questions can be selected in designing an 'in-depth' innovation audit.

The cultural web and the innovation audit provide pointers on the current performance of an organization. The discussions with employees will also generate a wealth of ideas on how to improve performance. The next step is determining the priorities and considering the linkages.

PRIORITIES AND LINKAGES

Priority Areas

An innovation audit identifies the areas of the Pentathlon in which an organization is strong and those in which it is weak. Through having collected the views of a significant number of employees it becomes clear, for example, whether a broad number of sources contribute to the generation of product ideas. Similarly, employees' views on how well innovations are implemented will provide insights into how effective new product development and related processes are. A typical result would be that the implementation processes (based on Stage-Gate methodology) are very efficient but that the front end fails to generate really innovative ideas. When related back to the Pentathlon Framework, most organizations perceive they are good in 1–2 areas and need to improve in the others.

The summarized results of the audit should be fed back to the organization and management. Further workshops with management can be used to define priorities for improvement. Identifying linkages can help to generate a more effective improvement plan.

Considering Linkages

In Chapter 2 we looked at the literature on innovation and saw that it could be categorized by the level at which innovation was analysed. The numerous economic studies have looked mainly at the impact of innovation on markets and economies – the macro level. These studies should remind us that not only the linkages between the elements of the Pentathlon are important but also the linkages beyond the elements – for instance, the linkages between an organization and its external environment.

At the other end of the research spectrum, a plethora of studies have investigated the factors that influence the effectiveness of new product development. Between these two bodies of literature, there has been far less research conducted at the organizational level: 'the vast majority of previous research is project-based and lacks the general perspective of executive-level managers'.[17] However, it is this company-level perspective that is the most relevant to senior managers.

Several themes about the linkages between aspects of innovation management can be extracted from the latest literature. Table 9.5 shows how selected papers have identified these emerging themes. The mixture of academic and practitioner papers that have discussed the latest thinking on innovation management at the organizational level covers four topics:

- The type of leadership required to drive innovation.
- Creating knowledge networks inside and outside the organization.
- How idea generation needs to be integrated with new product development.
- The need to manage change to achieve innovation.

We will consider each of these in more detail.

Innovation Leadership

The role of senior managers and product champions in innovation is central. Leadership and commitment appear to be absolutely necessary to drive the successful implementation of innovation strategy.[18] Attributes of leadership in the

Table 9.5 Emerging Issues – Linkages – in Innovation Management

	Main Topics	Borins, 2001	British Standard, 1999	Calatone, et al, 1995	Chambers and Boghani 1998	Day, et al., 1994	Karol et al., 2002	Linder, 2003	McGourty et al., 1996	Sakkab, 2002	Smith, et al., 1999	Thamhain, 1990	Webber and LaBarre, 2001
1.	Innovation leadership	√	√	√					√			√	
2.	Creating knowledge networks	√	√		√	√	√	√		√			√
3.	Linking idea generation to the NPD process				√	√	√				√		
4.	Change management approach needed	√							√			√	√

context of innovation include providing a vision and a role model, instilling a culture in which innovation is visible and widely communicated[19] and rewarded[20], and having the ability to understand the multiple disciplines, processes, and projects in an organization.[21] Leadership is fundamentally important in pulling all the strands of innovation together as, 'an organization's capacity to innovate is affected far more by *those* who set the environment in which innovation is to occur and manage innovative activities than those who undertake the creative work' (our emphasis).[22] The particular attributes required to lead innovation appear to be rare and so there is a need to link innovation strategy with people development programmes that ensure the availability of entrepreneurial-thinking project managers for innovation projects.

Management leadership in the context of innovation is particularly important as both the nature of innovation and how it can be achieved is not as clear as are more developed management disciplines such as total quality management. This means that top management will need to reserve sufficient time to clearly and regularly communicate the role and goals of innovation (see Mini Case 9.3 on Cobra).

Mini Case 9.3

Cobra, Thailand – Leadership and Windsurf Boards[23]

Based in Chonburi in Thailand, Cobra International was founded in 1985 and is a manufacturer of windsurf and surfboards and a range of other items for recreational sports. Cobra's strategy has always focused on quality, technology and a strong customer orientation.

Cobra uses professional quality management techniques, focuses on quality consistency, and is the only manufacturer in the industry with ISO 9001:2000 certification. This is one of the reasons that it has become a world leader, with over 50 per cent market share today as an original equipment manufacturer (OEM) supplying the top brands. Windsurf boards must withstand tremendous loads, as top windsurfers can launch their boards up to seven meters off rolling surf. Making boards that can withstand such a buffeting requires not only good manufacturing but also an intimate knowledge of the leading technologies – fibre-reinforced composites. Cobra is constantly developing the 'combination of methodologies and materials' says Pierre Olivier Schnerb, Vice President of Technology. 'For example, Cobra Tuflite® technology applies techniques learnt from windsurfing to surfing'.

The third element of strategy has come from the employees' intimate knowledge of the sports for which they manufacture equipment. Kym Thompson, an Australian, has been a champion surfer for over 30 years. In addition, for 30 years he has been professionally pushing forward the quality standards of surfboard manufacturing as Cobra's manager of surfboard production. Many other employees are active sportspeople and bring product and design ideas into the company. Being users themselves has helped Cobra develop top designs and enabled them to build very close relationships with nearly all of the top brands.

Vorapant Chotikapanich the founder and current president thinks innovation is absolutely essential for the company's competitiveness and takes every opportunity to

▶▶

stress it. In order to stay innovative, he gives employees the power to create, experiment and decide. 'I ensure that they get adequate top management support but I also drive for hot ideas to be implemented quickly', says Chotikapanich. Additionally, he perceives organizational innovation as key, 'we are currently organized according to technology rather than industry. So, for example, the Thermo Compression Molding Division manufactures everything from windsurf boards, surfboards, wakeboards to kiteboards. It is important to apply our technical expertise across all of our products. We also supplement our own competencies with those from a network of customers, suppliers, and designers'. Encouraged by Chotikapanich, Cobra has recently used its expertise in materials and manufacturing to enter new markets. These include not only related sports equipment markets, such as kayaks and canoes, but also completely new markets such as automotive parts (using Cobra's material and process expertise).

Creating Knowledge Networks

Improving the process by which ideas are generated for all types of innovation is widely recognized as a way of gaining a competitive advantage. Ideas should come from multiple sources, both internal and increasingly external,[24,25,26,27] as unexpected links often produce the best ideas.[28] Open innovation (see Chapter 4) helps bring people together from different backgrounds and functions – generating cross-boundary ideas. (For example, external R&D can create real value, as can buying the rights of others' intellectual property[29].) Knowledge management techniques, such as systems for storing and sharing ideas can be effective.[30] The Proctor and Gamble company uses an 'Innovation Net' system to communicate ideas between employees worldwide and also has run an 'Innovation Expo' to make connections between employees from different organizations.[31] In services, employees with direct customer interaction need to be more effectively used in gathering ideas from customers.[32] DuPont is also active in looking for external sources of innovation.[33]

More connections bring the potential for more ideas but they also have an 'overhead' – managers need to find ways to manage the interfaces and sources of innovation effectively (see also Mini Case 9.4 on Fiat Iveco). Clearly, ideation is becoming more dependent on creating linkages across departmental and organizational boundaries and managers need to take a lead here.

Linking Idea Generation to NPD

Although new product development is an important part of innovation management, it is by no means the only part. From the late 1980s, there was a strong emphasis on defining effective NPD processes, many of which were based on the Stage-Gate ideas of Cooper and Kleinschmidt.[35] Nowadays, most companies have efficient product development processes and so it is hard to compete on the basis of an NPD process alone.[36,37,38] What is needed is an overall faster way of creating innovative ideas, rapidly dropping those that

---

Mini Case 9.4

Fiat Iveco – Identifying Innovation Challenges[34]

Iveco is the arm of Fiat responsible for manufacturing and marketing commercial and industrial vehicles, buses and diesel engines. Massimo Fumarola has worked as Platform Development Manager in the heavy vehicles division and as Business Development Manager in the Engine Business Unit. In both roles he has been closely involved with considering how Iveco can increase overall innovation performance. He says, 'in my opinion there are three challenges in managing innovation. The most important one has to do with the organization and there is a dilemma. On the one hand we want employees to work in structured, methodical ways to produce products in a timely, in fact a very disciplined way. On the other hand, we want people to challenge the established ways of thinking and working. This is a big problem and the only way to solve it is sometimes to take suitable people and break them out from the parent organization and give them freedom not just to act but also to think innovation'.

'Getting enough people with the right experience is something we need to work on. We have great functional specialists but not enough people that have worked in several functions and have a deep understanding of the interfaces [between functions]. Unfortunately, in this industry and other ones I talk to, not enough people want to become what I'll call "cross-functional boundary managers"'. It takes time to find, encourage and develop such people says Fumarola.

'Thirdly, it's about getting everyone involved. It's not just the voice of the customer. You also need to involve the truck operators, the suppliers, the regulatory agencies, and all the other stakeholders right from the beginning. Interfaces, not functions, generate most of the problems and we're getting more interfaces to consider. I think that the best managers of tomorrow will be the ones that can maximize innovation performance by minimizing the interface issues'.

---

are less attractive, and implementing the remaining ones quickly. Leading companies such as AlliedSignal and Alcoa in the US have focused on making such links tangible through what they have termed the 'Front-end Innovation Process'. This is based on the philosophy that, 'the faster that ideas can be evaluated and the earlier flawed ideas terminated, the more productive the pipeline becomes ...'[39] AlliedSignal and Alcoa use fast evaluation based on an integrated assessment of the technologies and market attributes of potential projects.

For managers the message is clear: ideation, portfolio management and new product development must be closely linked and in many ways it is the middle process – filtering ideas – that is the most challenging.[40]

Managing Change

To improve innovation performance requires the management of a wide range of issues, from ideas, to technologies, to culture, to organizational change. Meeting the changing needs of customers requires employees to be positively oriented towards change.[41,42] To be effective at driving change to support innovation, managers need to be effective at identifying and dealing with barriers. Barriers to innovation, particularly internal political ones, need to be effectively addressed by managers.[43] Organizational practices will need to be changed to match the strategic direction.[44] Overall, much is being written currently about the need for innovation and change management is often needed to enable companies to achieve it. Therefore, we will discuss the application of a change management technique to innovation in the next section.

In a topic as complex as innovation management, the relationships between different elements of the Pentathlon may not be obvious. But it is useful to try and predict what they might be, before launching improvement initiatives. Otherwise a common problem can arise. Anecdotal evidence shows that companies that take steps to boost the number of innovative ideas being generated within their organizations, without considering the impact on new product development, often end up pushing too many ideas into the innovation pipeline and slowing the output. Managers need to carefully consider how linkages can be turned to advantage (and researchers urgently need to investigate how companies attempt to boost innovation).

ACTIONS TO BOOST PERFORMANCE

Actions to improve innovation can be aimed at both the project and organizational levels (as shown on Figure 9.1). In our consulting work on boosting the innovation performance of organizations, we have found that it is often advantageous to focus on a key project rather than simply trying to improve processes. Taking a key project but approaching it in a different way will often create more interest in a company, and if the project can be made a big success then employees will automatically want to adopt the new approaches. In addition, the sum of the results of individual innovation projects constitutes the total output of an organization.

Change Management and Innovation

Research has shown that there are two major forms of change in organizations: either *convergent* (or *incremental*) change or *frame-breaking* change.[45] Project-to-project learning and improving processes can be seen as incremental change and so organizations that want to achieve significant improvements in innovation performance will need to do more. Market discontinuities, shifts in product life cycles and even internal company dynamics all have major consequences in the way in which a company should be organized.[46]

Performance measures, the innovation audit, and the cultural web all help to diagnose weaknesses from an innovation perspective. The tripartite approach also provides rich information on how employees perceive that innovation performance could be enhanced. Innovation has an inherent ability to excite people but managers should not underestimate the management time and energy that needs to be invested to boost innovation. In particular, changes to organizational culture require much management effort; much more than the superficial attempts usually made to manage culture.[47] Companies with a HRM function need to utilize this to support the process of change management (and Section 5.0 of the innovation audit on our companion website http://www.palgrave.com/business/goffin/includes several questions to gauge whether the HR function is playing a strategic role). Managers may need to make radical changes in the way an organization approaches innovation, in its culture, or in the way it is formally organized. Individual employees can be reluctant to change and so an organization can have an in-built inertia. Change management techniques are useful to moderate resistance to change in innovation management and there are some diagnostic and implementation tools that are essential to managers, which we will discuss.[48]

A useful way of looking at change is to consider which factors need to be considered in overcoming resistance to change. Researchers, such as Michael Tushman at Harvard, have found that different components are necessary to achieve organizational change:

- Dissatisfaction.
- A vision.
- A process for change.

Often in management situations, one of the three factors is missing and so the change cannot be achieved. Each factor is a necessary but not sufficient factor for change. A memorable 'shorthand' is to express the relationship between these factors mathematically. The three factors are linked in the *change equation* (which should be read as 'the product of D, V and P needs to exceed C')[49]:

$$DVP > C \qquad\qquad (1)$$

Where D = dissatisfaction
V = vision
P = process
C = perceived cost of change.

This equation demonstrates that there is a perceived cost to change and that the three factors must each contribute to overcoming inertia. Note also that change management experts stress that it is essential to address all three factors. If any of them is neglected, no matter how well the other two are addressed, then the change management initiative will fail. Equation 9.1 shows this in that the three factors D, V and P are multiplied and so if dissatisfaction, vision, or the process is not clear (that is equivalent to zero), then the product of all three will be zero. To demonstrate the application of the change equation to an innovation management situation, we will take an actual example.

A business division of a major international bank chose to focus on innovation three years ago. For reasons of confidentiality, we will refer to this organization as 'BankCorp'. The Managing Director (MD) of this division became interested in innovation, having read of the successes of various manufacturers in boosting their output of new products. Having decided that his organization needed to become more innovative, the dynamic MD developed the vision of an organization that would be first-to-market with new banking products. A consultant was hired to support the development and implementation of this vision. However, as discussed above, a vision is not sufficient for successful change and this was the case for BankCorp, as we will see as we discuss each of the factors of the change equation.

Perceived Cost of Change

People who resist change generally do so not just to be awkward but because they perceive – rightly or wrongly – that the change, or the process of making it, will be 'costly' for them, in that it is difficult, time-consuming, unpleasant, expensive, or any combination of these. The cost of change is perceived, and it will often be psychological: such as the fear of not being able to cope with new responsibilities; or that old skills will no longer be valued; or that their authority will be reduced. In an organization, whole departments may perceive the cost of change to be high. For example, the techniques for identifying customers' hidden needs that we discussed in depth in Chapter 5 are often seen as a threat to a department. And that department is marketing! Why? Some marketing departments' market research expertise lies only in focus groups and surveys and they perceive new techniques as a threat rather than an opportunity.

The first task in change management is to understand the perceived cost of change to all of the stakeholders involved in the moves to boost innovation. Once understood, the costs of change can be addressed – perhaps they can be reduced, or at least they can be discussed and then stakeholders may see them in a different light. If C cannot be reduced, then attention should be switched to the other side of the change equation.

Identifying Dissatisfaction

In overcoming the inertia to change inherent in every individual and organization, dissatisfaction plays a key role. The reluctance to change must be overcome by galvanizing opinion on the need for innovation. This might be obvious to managers; so obvious in fact that they cannot understand why it is not seen as a priority by everyone in the organization. Change management experts often say that a burning platform issue is required. (The term comes from the Piper Alpha oil rig disaster in the North Sea. As the platform burned, workers were forced to jump from the inferno into a sea of burning oil. Fortunately, some of the workers who made this split second decision survived.) A burning issue in change management terms is an issue that readily motivates the majority to action, even if this involves difficult decisions.

In communicating the need to become more innovative, it is useful to consider:

- Financial and market arguments.
- Customers' views on innovation. These can identify end-users frustrations and the need for all types of innovation.
- Employees' views. People in organizations that are not particularly innovative normally recognize this and become dissatisfied (consider the results of BuildCo's cultural webs discussed in Chapter 8).
- Where problems resulting from a lack of innovation affect different functions, 'shared dissatisfaction' will help overcome inertia.

Referring to the situation at BankCorp, an innovation audit was conducted by the consultant hired to support the company. In discussions with employees from across the functions and levels of the division, a high level of dissatisfaction on two points emerged. First, both employees and middle management were totally sceptical about the MD's vision as the bank had not been first-to-market with a financial product for years, and was seldom even a fast-follower ('we are a slow-follower ...' said several staff in answer to the innovation audit questions on strategy). This showed widespread employee dissatisfaction with the status quo but also that the vision of being first-to-market was unrealistic as the company did not have the appropriate capabilities. Second, the division was not fast due to its high levels of bureaucracy and slow decision-making (for example, changes to product advertising required nearly twenty sign-offs). Both these points led the top management team to work on creating a new vision.

Creating the Vision

Every innovation management programme needs a vision, which should be not only inspiring but also realistic. 'When a vision is clear, consistently articulated, and widely shared, decisions throughout the organization can be made in a more consistent, directed way', however, research shows that management often communicates only a vague vision.[50] There are several key questions to ask. What are you trying to achieve and how will this impact customers? What will more innovation mean (internally and externally)? Where could innovation make a real breakthrough for your company? Overall, the innovation vision should address some or all of the following issues:

- How customers will directly benefit from the improved products, services and processes that will result from greater innovation performance.
- How quickly innovations will be developed (Is the organization first-to-market, or a follower? Should it be faster to market?).
- The ways in which innovation will make significant improvements to an organization's competitive position.

Management at BankCorp realized that the vision they had originally decided for the innovation programme was inappropriate. Since the company had not been first-to-market in the past, and employees did not believe that this would be possible, the focus was changed to becoming a fast-follower that would learn from the first-mover's mistakes and capitalize on these. The new vision capitalized on the dissatisfaction within the organization and was quickly and widely supported by employees. For other organizations with the right capabilities, the vision of being first-mover can be appropriate (see Mini Case 9.5 on Black & Decker).

Developing the Change Process

High innovation performance does not happen overnight. Managers need to recognize that there are three key stages; moving from the *current*, via a *transition state*, to the *desired state*.[52] Individuals and organizations often enter a state of shock during change. Research has shown that being able to articulate a clear link between the current and the future state is an attribute of good leadership.[53]

The starting point of the change process is crucial. Often an innovation performance improvement programme is best linked to a particular project, the success of which should act as a signal that can fire-up the whole organization. A project that is large and very high risk should not be selected; the project chosen should present a reasonable challenge. Change management experts talk of the

---

Mini Case 9.5

Black & Decker's DeWalt – a Brand Innovation Strategy[51]

Black & Decker is famous for its power tools but it reserves a distinct brand – DeWalt – for its line of professional tools, such as drills and mitre saws. The company is well aware of the challenges of the professional market, in which the decision makers are looking for innovative, reliable and efficient tools and are not loyal to a single brand. John Schiech, president of DeWalt has adopted a first-to-market strategy and has developed the core capabilities of his organization to match this. For instance, he explains that deep customer insights are obtained by 'engineers and marketing product managers spending hours and hours on building sites talking to the guys who are trying to make their living with these tools'. Observing professionals working with power tools allows DeWalt to identify the problems and issues they face and develop products to solve these. Schiech prefers breakthrough products because 'It's only when you come with a breakthrough product that you can really change the game in terms of market share'. To be successful at breakthrough innovation, the company not only focuses on customer insights but also rapid prototyping, in the 40–50 projects that are running at any one time. The first-to-market strategy has been very successful and is tracked using what DeWalt call product vitality – the percentage of sales from products launched in the previous three years. This performance measure is typically approximately 30 per cent and some years it has even exceeded 50 per cent.

importance of looking for the 'low-hanging fruit', which are projects whose success quickly brings considerable returns.

Just as a new product development project is dependent on a product champion, so change management is dependent on an effective *change agent*. In selecting the path forward the change agent needs to be particularly careful to avoid trying to simply adopt best practice.[54] It is far better to consider the context of the organization in which change is deemed necessary and adapt ideas rather than simply adopting them. The way in which an organization can best be changed depends on identifying those in favour of change and those against. For members of both of these groups, plans should be made of making best use of allies and turning potential adversaries into allies. The change agent has a wide range of choices on how to go about change and needs to answer a number of questions. Do we need radical and fast change? Should it be organized to cascade down from senior management? Should external consultants be used to promote the changes? The answers to these questions flow into the plan for change. Performance measures should form an integral part of the change process, as they allow both challenging but realistic goals to be set and progress monitored.

The process of change at BankCorp was based on an analysis of the competencies necessary to be a fast-follower. For example, product managers were given resources and clear responsibilities to collect more competitive data and internal product development processes were streamlined. A twice-yearly 'Innovation Fair' was introduced, at which teams of employees present their ideas for more competitive products (using role-plays of sales discussions as a way of 'prototyping' product concepts). Employees appreciated the freedom to be more innovative and welcomed the changes. Middle management was initially shocked and needed to delegate many of their responsibilities (and give up their role in approvals). Known process bottlenecks, such as information technology resources were also better managed. Three years on, BankCorp has consistently achieved its target of being a fast-follower that introduces new products copied from the ideas of competitors but with sufficient differentiating factors to make them more competitive than the incumbent.

Making a Breakthrough

If an organization decides to focus on innovation then it is worth taking the time and effort to make a breakthrough in performance. Incremental improvements can help but management should set the organization's sites high. The aim should not be to just improve innovation performance but really boost it. To achieve a sustainable boost, as opposed to a short-term improvement and the generation of a few innovative ideas, all aspects of innovation management need to be considered. No single element of the Pentathlon should be considered in isolation and similarly, the organization should not be considered in isolation from its business context. Management teams must also overcome their own limitations, as 'there may be a lack of imagination that starts right at the top'.[55]

Mini Case 9.6

Magnus Schoeman – Innovation Manager[58]

What should an innovation manager do? What is their role? One person who is very well qualified to answer is Dr Magnus Schoeman, as he has managed innovation in a scientific setting, in a manufacturing company, in the public sector, and now as a consultant with Steria, the IT Services company.

Having trained as a microbiologist and conducted post-doctoral research Schoeman joined Rio Tinto Borax as a specialist on wood preservative products and coatings. In this position he gained experience of new product development, and studying for an Exec-MBA in parallel to his job, gave him the opportunity to focus on innovation management methods and learn how to address the challenge of making a Stage-Gate process faster. Then came a significant personal change; he moved to the UK's Department of Health, where he was responsible for commercializing new technologies emerging from a cluster of research institutes. 'This was a formative experience for me' he says, 'scientists in the public sector had the luxury of not needing to be focused on commercial outcomes but the barriers to innovation were just as great as in the private sector. A major blocker was the mind-set of researchers who felt that patenting inventions would stifle knowledge transfer and impede the public health agenda. In fact, a major innovation would only get support from a commercial backer if we could show that there was some degree of intellectual property rights'. Eventually, Schoeman did manage to take a number of new technologies to market – by working with the more cooperative scientists and addressing institutional issues such as reward schemes for inventors. Now with Steria, Schoeman is a consultant on process innovation and business change. Typically, he helps government departments understand how IT can deliver performance improvements. This involves working with the organizations involved and effecting behaviour change so staff members adopt 'helpful' behaviours towards new technologies.

Having experienced the public and private, manufacturing and service sectors, Schoeman has experience of managing innovation in very different contexts. He perceives there are three key lessons he has learnt. 'Firstly, I have learnt that you need to align processes and systems, such as performance appraisal mechanisms and incentive schemes, in order to support innovation', he says. The second lesson is the need to pay heed to the 'softer factors of symbolism, rituals and routines. You need to pay attention to the "red Porsche" effect as it is known in technology exploitation circles – scientists take a different view of commercialization when one of their peers has a successful invention and shows the benefits of a new car, or increased research budget!' Third, Schoeman has seen the importance of 'ensuring that the units involved in championing innovation and thought-leadership are insulated from the vagaries of the day-to-day business and do not have to follow the investment appraisal approach of the "core" business'.

In explaining the role of an innovation manager, Schoeman likes to use a metaphor from immunology. 'An innovation manager has to deal with organizational "antibodies". In any organization there are people and processes that will cause resistance to innovation and good innovation managers will find creative and fast ways of dealing with these'.

Title: Director of Innovation

Reports to: Chief Executive Officer and Management Board

Liaises closely with: Group Director of Organizational Development, Director of Quality, Chief Officers, General Managers and others.

Scope and Purpose of Job:

To establish and maintain processes of Innovation within [the XXXX Hotel Group], in order to create and sustain competitive advantage in the eyes of our principal stakeholders and support the achievement of the strategic objectives of the Company. Creating a market perception innovation and the XXXX brand are inexorably linked. Key measures and outcomes will be applied to products, services and internal processes.

Main Roles and Responsibilities:

1. To establish the Innovation architecture within the Company, applying the Pentathlon Framework (Goffin & Mitchell) or similar. This involves the following:

    a. Determining and agree the objectives/measures/outcomes of the Innovation process, linked to strategy and stakeholder expectations.
    b. Identifying gaps between stakeholder expectations and provision of products and services, taking appropriate corrective planned action.
    c. Managing the generation and prioritization of ideas through creative processes.
    d. Leading the selection of ideas and development of concepts with a management task force.
    e. Managing Innovation projects, including cross-functional teams ...

2. Understand and assess organizational culture, in order to adapt interventions to ensure their success. Contribute to the development of organization culture. Promote entrepreneurial spirit and compliance with our Innovation Guiding Principle. This involves the following:

    a. Taking the lead in communicating the need for innovation across the organization.
    b. Determining the need for training key staff in innovation management techniques. Implementing appropriate programmes.
    c. Working closely with one selected project team to ensure an early big success. Using this success story to ensure innovation thinking quickly becomes embedded throughout the organization.

3. Contribute to the selection, performance, development and recognition of individuals who will support and
   contribute to Innovation, in defined roles.
4. Apply principles of change management where necessary.
5. Evaluate the Innovation process and make continuous improvements.

Figure 9.4   Job Description for an Innovation Manager at an International Hotel Group

Some companies will turn to innovation as a solution to difficult times. This is perfectly valid and, sometimes business problems bring an urgency and therefore openness to new ways of doing things. In such conditions, though, managers will need to be particularly effective as 'one of the crucial functions of leadership is to provide guidance at precisely those times when habitual ways of doing things no longer work, or when a dramatic change in the environment requires new responses'.[56]

Boosting innovation performance is the goal of many managers with whom we come in contact. They are urgently looking for better ways to achieve this goal and this is an area where we hope that researchers will provide insights very soon. Currently, too little is known.

The Role of an Innovation Manager

Senior managers need to drive innovation but an increasingly common approach is to create a specific role: innovation manager. This is a pivotal role. One of the first companies to do this was AXA Ireland in 2000 (see main case at the end of Chapter 3) and Catherine Whelan faced the challenge of defining her role as there was no precedent. Nearly a decade later, innovation management as a subject has developed further, many companies have experience with the role, and the first certified courses for innovation managers are starting to appear. Similarly, innovation management teaching is increasingly important on MBA courses and at many universities in the USA.[57] From company to company the role varies but a key component is enabling chance and overcoming resistance (see Mini Case 9.6).

Companies like Associated Packaging, GlaxoSmithKline, Shell and Reckitt Benckiser have all advertised for innovation managers in 2009. A major luxury hotel chain has also recently decided that its future lies in becoming more innovative and their job description, for their search for a suitable internal candidate, is shown in Figure 9.4 (direct company references have been removed but otherwise unaltered).

SUMMARY

This chapter suggested a scheme for determining ways to change innovation performance, whilst stressing that individual organizations will need to find their own particular way of achieving better performance. It covered the following:

- The suggested approach with its four main steps: from assessing performance to determining actions to improve performance.
- Suggestions on how to choose suitable performance measures and conduct an innovation audit.
- A discussion of emerging evidence on the critical linkages in innovation management.
- Ideas on how to improve performance at both the project and organizational levels, including applying change management techniques to innovation.

This chapter's main case study describes a small automotive supplier, Sidler that has consistently achieved high levels of innovation despite its limited resources, through creative management of outside linkages.

MANAGEMENT RECOMMENDATIONS

- Select and use performance measures to understand and help communicate the innovation performance of your organization.
- Use an innovation audit to determine the strengths and weaknesses of your organization in innovation management. Determine the priorities.
- Develop an action plan to improve performance at both the project and organizational levels. Reserve enough top management time to take an active part in leading the implementation.
- Use change management techniques to gain acceptance for your plan.
- Be aware that there is no 'silver bullet' for improving innovation performance and it is management's responsibility to explore the best ways of achieving it in their own organizations.

RECOMMENDED READING

1. Balogun, J., Hope Hailey, V. with Johnson, G. and Scholes, K., *Exploring Strategic Change*. (London: FT Prentice Hall, 2nd Edition, 2003). [Not specifically aimed at innovation management issues but very useful coverage of change management tools and techniques.]

2. British Standard. *Design Management Systems – Part 1: Guide to Managing Innovation*. British Standard BS7000–1:1999 (London: British Standards Institution, 1999. [Interesting document based on the results of intensive workshops including managers, academics and professional associations. Somewhat deterministic in its style with a 'complete innovation management framework' but well worth consulting.]

CASE STUDY
Sidler Automotive – Open Innovation, German Style[59]

Before reading this case, consider the following generic innovation management issues:

- What role can outsourcing play in a company's innovation strategy?
- How can companies access and exploit external expert knowledge?
- What criteria should be used for selecting partners?
- How can confidentiality be managed for innovation projects involving inter-organizational collaborations?

All companies need a vision. For Sidler, a German automotive component manufacturer that is part of the Flextronics Company, it is to supply 'a Sidler component in every car world-wide'. Although it is an ambitious target, the company, which specializes in the design, development and manufacture of car interior lighting systems and interior trim, already supplies many of the major manufacturers. These include Volkswagen, Fiat and Rover, along with the American giants Ford and General Motors, and a number of the Japanese assemblers. In the competitive and technology-driven field of car interior lighting systems, Sidler is market leader in Europe and has a significant worldwide share. Sidler managers say 'innovation has to be a way of life to stay competitive. However, with limited resources we cannot do everything ourselves'.

Originally founded in 1925 to make metal parts, the company moved into the design, development and manufacture of synthetic parts – mainly interior lighting components – for the automotive industry during the 1970s. Over recent years the market for its primary product has changed significantly. Customers – car manufacturers – are no longer simply looking for a supplier to produce parts to their specifications. Instead, the market has changed to one in which complete lighting systems are designed, developed and manufactured by suppliers. Sidler employs approximately 650 people and has a turnover of over EUR 90 million, of which over 40 per cent is generated from worldwide exports.

A major part of the company's success is down to its research and development capability, in particular the development of tooling and injection moulding technology. This is used to produce interior lighting with specific surfaces, for example, rhomboid line structures, which give plastic car interior light covers the characteristics of lenses (if necessary, focusing light into particularly dark areas of a car). However, unlike many of the giants that it supplies, the company is not big enough to maintain a large in-house R&D facility. Instead, the company has developed a policy of leveraging the best knowledge available through outsourcing a significant proportion of its R&D work. This includes a whole range of approaches: using universities for specialist long-term research; technology centres in Austria and Germany for undertaking materials analysis; and establishing joint projects with other companies for developing specialist products.

'For instance', explains Herr Dr Helmut Rapp, the company's managing director, 'Our in-house technology monitoring found out that a university was working on laser holographic lenses. We need lenses, and so after assessing their initial research, we have given them a project to specifically look at whether the technology they are developing can be used in our products. If this project proves that their technology is relevant, then we will give them the task of industrialising it'.

'In fact, outsourcing is often much more efficient than trying to do everything in-house. Universities often have the equipment and the expert research staff, that most companies – including ourselves – cannot afford. They are also often looking for funding and support. Similarly, other research organizations have the staff and the dedicated processes that ensure that they can do specific jobs, such as materials testing and analysis, better and often cheaper than we could if we tried to do it in-house. Therefore, a whole range of research activities is not considered by us to be core activities. Where we can find an external source who is capable, we outsource the work', states Rapp. Other areas are regarded as absolutely core: for example, Sidler had developed advanced software to simulate the effectiveness of internal car lighting.

MANAGING RISK AND INTELLECTUAL PROPERTY

Admittedly there are risks involved with this outsourcing approach, and one that many companies fear is the loss of competencies and lack of control over intellectual property. Since Sidler understands this concern, it balances the risks by taking steps to maintain control over outsourced development.

▶▶

As Rapp notes 'when it comes to R&D for smaller companies, such as ourselves, the simple choice is between the risk of losing a lot of money if you invest in developing a technology in-house that ultimately doesn't work, or the risk of losing a bit of know-how if an outside organization develops it and it does work. Anyway, there are ways to maintain some control over the process, and what we always try to do when more than one area of research is involved – which is quite often – is that we do not bring all the experts together. We co-ordinate the development, and so in this way it is our co-ordinators who communicate with all the experts involved and pull all the possible different strands of a research project together…we actually develop the overall expertise, the competency that is most appropriate to Sidler.'

A prime example of managed outsourcing is a testing programme undertaken in cooperation between Sidler and another manufacturing company. Together, the two companies have developed a new process (not previously technically possible), which enables laser etching on pale coloured paints. However, rather than invest in in-house testing facilities, both Sidler and their partner decided to outsource the testing to a specialist paint shop and a separate laser etching business. This network of companies was used to solve the application problems, but with the work coordinated and project managed by Sidler technologists. While this meant that the external testers developed certain knowledge, it was the Sidler engineers who effectively controlled all the pieces of the jigsaw. After a two-year effort, the process was perfected and now the partners are making a 1.5 million euro investment in the special painting and laser etching process. And, because they now can offer this specific technical solution, Sidler has achieved 'sole supplier status' with a major German motor manufacturer.

In many companies, technical outsourcing is often hindered by an internal culture that refuses to accept the need for such an approach. Engineers in particular are susceptible to the desire to do all new research and development themselves, and this often permeates throughout functions and teams dedicated to research and development, where something not developed by the group is frowned upon. Sidler managers say they are not completely immune from the 'not invented here' syndrome. To ensure that this negative influence is minimized, Sidler always ensures that people know what is going on and why, and always assigns someone from R&D to oversee an outside project. So while they may not be doing the research themselves, they are actually project managing the effort.

Another problem that many companies perceive with open innovation is confidentiality. But this is not a factor as far as Sidler is concerned. This is for two reasons. One is that Sidler's research coordinators control all the pieces of the puzzle that is important to them, including the industrial application of the research. The other reason is that rapid implementation cycles do not give anyone the chance to break any confidences.

'So far we've never made confidentiality agreements', says Rapp. 'It's not worth the paperwork. You create it, you sign it and you file it. Who is really going to do the follow up? It's a waste of time. The important thing is to work with those external experts to get the problem solved, to get the process going, and then to go rapidly into industrial application with that process. You only have to be slightly in front at this stage, because within the industrial application you gain experience day by day, and it is this unique application knowledge that provides the real competitive advantage.' But such approaches mean that selecting partners is a key process.

SELECTING PARTNERS

The first step in effective use of outside research agencies is to identify opportunities. At Sidler, the internal R&D team has the brief to watch technological developments in many areas. As well as reading journals, at least one member of the team visits relevant conferences and exhibitions and reports back. If anything of interest is seen, such as a new high-pressure moulding process, this is followed up through investigations to evaluate its usefulness. This typically includes team members visiting the company or research institute that has developed the technology. If it is an existing technology and it seems applicable, then Sidler simply test it. If it is just a research idea, then the head of the R&D team will initially visit the outside organization, to instigate discussion on a possible collaboration project.

There is also the issue of finding the right outsourcing partners. According to Rapp, 'If we are looking to become part of a long term research project, it is not just a matter of finding a relevant project, as there are often a number of different organizations working along the same lines. The decision to work with an external research organization is as much about that organization's style and approach – and how they fit with our non-bureaucratic style of working – as it is about its project and competency. We also do not put too much emphasis on performance and time schedules as we recognise that these projects need time to find the answers we want'. 'Whereas', he adds, 'when we're working with companies who do all our materials testing and analysis, we are looking primarily for on-time performance and professionalism. If we send a sample out and request an answer within two days, we expect it within two days. If we get it in three weeks, that's no good.'

UNIVERSITY-BASED RESEARCH

An example of where Sidler's approach to outsourcing has helped solve one of its 'long-term' technical problems is its current work with a German university. Sidler's internal R&D team had already developed, through a combination of specialist tooling, material additives, control techniques and the usual trial and error, a special purpose machine for producing high-quality 'in-mould decorated' parts. While many companies can do in-mould decoration (the process is used extensively by the furniture trade to produce fake wood panelling and doors), Sidler is the only company who can at present meet the quality standards required by the automotive industry. As a result, the company is now building up a factory in the UK, which will start with EUR 10 million turnover, of which 80 per cent is based on orders for in-mould decorated parts for the British automotive industry.

However, the existing manufacturing process requires all parameters to be tightly controlled in order to be stable. While this means it is hard for competitors to copy, it also means that it requires very skilled operators. In looking for ways to overcome this operator dependence, the company came across a university project to create an intelligent moulding process. In this, the injection moulding machine's control system gets feedback about the pressure and temperature in the tool, and then automatically makes the necessary process changes.

'Our in-mould decoration process ideally needs a self-regulating feedback system which we do not have yet. But our internal technology watching highlighted the

▸▸

university research and having looked at the work they are doing we decided to join the project', explains Rapp.

Sidler has provided the university with moulding equipment, into which the researchers will be putting the in-tool measurement devices. Also, one member of the company's R&D team is working on the project. In return, Sidler will gain the knowledge it needs to improve its own processes and an added benefit. As Rapp concludes, 'there is now a young engineer who is doing his PhD on this project – and I know where this guy is going to work when he has finished his studies!'

10 THE FUTURE OF INNOVATION MANAGEMENT

> The commanding General is well aware that the weather forecasts are no good. However, he needs them for planning purposes.[1]

INTRODUCTION: THE INNOVATION ENVIRONMENT

In this final chapter we allow ourselves the luxury of looking forward at what the future may hold for managers and students of innovation. To provide a structure for this we first return to the first topic of Chapter 1, the drivers of innovation, and consider what trends for the future are discernible in each of the four main factors that we discussed there, namely:

- Customers
- Competition
- Technology
- The Business Environment

For each one we will indicate what we believe these developments will mean for managers and suggest the challenges they pose for the study of Innovation Management as an academic discipline.

CUSTOMERS

Customers throughout the world are generally becoming older, wealthier and more urban and these trends will affect the kind of innovation needed to serve them. In Western Europe and Japan the average age of the population is creeping steadily upwards because people are living longer and having fewer children. The same thing is happening in China as a result of the 'single child' policy.[2] Older people use more personal services (not only medical) and they have particular needs in relation to physical products.

A continuation of economic growth seems likely for many years yet, though the immediate future has been muddied by the recent financial crisis. Prospects appear particularly hopeful in India and China, a combined market of over two billion people. These markets have very different requirements to Western ones, so companies will need to 'design for culture' – taking steps to ensure that their product and service offerings are fully appropriate to local needs. Increasing wealth does not appear to satiate demand for new possessions and experiences; if it were so people in the wealthier countries would already be choosing to work shorter hours or saving, rather than spending, their money – and there is no sign of either of these. Nevertheless, as people become richer they show one very clear pattern of behaviour that has implications for the type of innovation we may expect in the future. This is highlighted by the move from agriculture to industry and then to services, a trend that, as we discussed in Chapter 1, has been observed in every major country over the past 300 years.

The underlying cause of the trend stems from what is usually known as *Maslow's hierarchy of needs*. This framework is not based on solid empirical evidence although it is intuitively appealing and frequently quoted. Maslow[3] suggested that human needs may be thought of as extending along a spectrum,

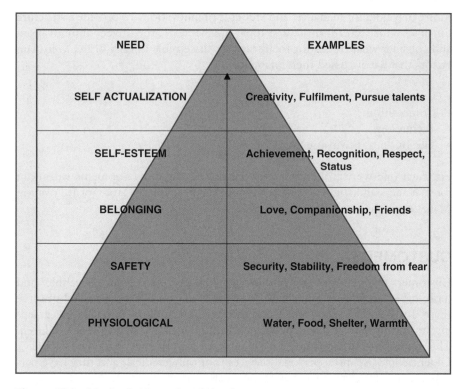

Figure 10.1 Maslow's Hierarchy of Needs

which starts from the most basic physical ones such as food, warmth and shelter and extends through social needs such as sex, love, companionship and status to more personal strivings for meaning, spirituality and self-fulfilment. Maslow's original list is shown in Figure 10.1, though it has been extended and reinterpreted many times by other authors. There is much room for discussion about exactly where a particular need fits in the hierarchy, but two aspects of the list hold broadly true. First, the most basic needs are the most urgent and until they are adequately taken care of people generally have less concern for the rest. Second, the basic needs are quite easy to define and straightforward to satisfy, while the social and self-fulfilment needs are subtle and difficult to define, and apparently insatiable.

It is also true to say that the most basic needs are to a large extent absolute in nature: one is either hungry or cold, or one is not. Social needs, such as status or well-being are often relative, in that standards move constantly according to how everybody else is doing.

It is not surprising that the proportion of the world's economy devoted to agriculture declines as productivity improves, because the demand for food (as well as the land available to grow it on) is fundamentally limited. Similarly, the other more basic needs of shelter, warmth and even mobility use relatively less and less resources as time goes on. Quite clearly much of the industrial effort and most of the service sector in the developed world are now targeted at social and personal needs that are right at the other end of the Maslow hierarchy. The effects of this on innovation are clear: although the demand for innovation in goods and services apparently has (as yet) no bound, that demand is likely to become more elusive, unstable and subject to the whims of fashion as the innovation caters to more subtle needs. As a result, there are more and more different products on the market (see Mini Case 10.1) but their lifetimes in the market are reducing dramatically. Figure 10.2 shows how the pattern of sales growth and price reduction of consumer electronics products that took 30 years for products launched in the 1970 has shortened to 8 and 4 years for more recent generations. It is this trend, incidentally, that has caused Philips, long known as a consumer electronics company, to move its business focus away from this sector towards healthcare and lighting.

Implications for Innovation Management

In such conditions companies will find it increasingly difficult to understand their customers' needs, especially their hidden needs, and will have to allocate far more resources to this aspect of market research than they are used to. Market research must embrace ethnographic-style studies and empathic design, as discussed in Chapter 5, along with more traditional methods. The application of the new methods is mostly by specialized consultancies rather than the companies involved, but this will change soon. Leading companies increasingly appreciate that understanding one's customers is a core competence, not something to be delegated to outsiders.

Mini Case 10.1

Automotive – Is the Assembly Line Bunk?

In 2004 the *Financial Times*[4] and the *New York Times* reported a proposal by Martin Leach, former head of Ford, Europe for a new approach to vehicle manufacturing. This would entirely alter the relationship between manufacturing, sales, service and the aftermarket. The concept is to assemble cars in retail parks from kits shipped in from low-cost manufacturers in India or China. By using plastic panels the company would be able to customize the vehicles to a high degree so as to be able to follow fashions and persuade customers to upgrade frequently. Crucially, the vehicles would be leased, not sold, so that returned cars could be refurbished and leased again at a reduced rate. Since there would be no second-hand market, theft would be little or no problem (why would you steal a car that cannot be resold?) so insurance would be cheap. R&D costs would also be low or zero because the product would not be differentiated by having the most up to date performance. The manufacturer would now participate in finance, spares and the rest of the aftermarket. The customer would get a new approach to vehicle ownership that emphasized customization, cost and convenience instead of performance.

This concept still has to be tested in the market place but it is an interesting example of a new approach to an established industry, offering a disruptive combination of a new business concept and an alternative value proposition.

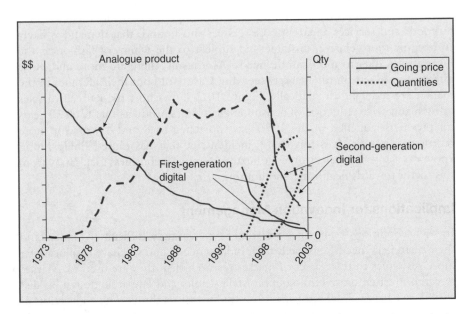

Figure 10.2   Sales growth and price decline for three consumer electronics products

Source: Adapted from Minderhout, S. and Fraser, P., 'Shifting Paradigms of Product Development in Fast and Dynamic Markets', *Reliability Engineering and System Safety*, No. 88 (2005), pp. 127–135.

The worldwide web is perceived by many as an ideal way to tap into the customer base. *Crowdsourcing*[5] as it is called is a very broad concept that involves appealing to an unorganized group of web users for ideas, solutions to problems, feedback on products and the like – not to mention software design. It can be a useful approach to understanding user needs but must be used in combination with more personal methods offering deeper analysis.

Academics have much work to do to find better ways to uncover hidden needs; and also to understand how the increasingly important influences between customers really operate in the Internet age (viral marketing). In this context we see the need for a revival of work on the diffusion of innovations, particularly Rogers' work on how the characteristics of innovations affect their diffusion (Chapter 2), to help managers to include these factors in product design.

Another need that comes from the fluidity of these markets is for more rapid and flexible product development processes because an NPD process that moves more slowly than the market changes is innately doomed to failure. So-called *agile* project management techniques are used to speed up development of software projects, as discussed in Chapter 7. Rather than defining the result and moving towards it by a single, carefully planned process, agile development homes in on the solution progressively by building and testing a series of prototypes in quick succession. The ability to make new versions very quickly was previously limited to software products but rapid prototyping and computer simulation are making the same thing possible for mechanical and electrical products. Perhaps virtual reality will make it possible for services, too. This new capability demands new ways to conceive products and services, and new ways to manage and control the development teams (see Mini Case 10.2 on Vodafone). Although there is some practitioner literature in the subject no definitive academic work has yet been done. The application to services is particularly neglected.

Mini Case 10.2

Vodafone Group Plc – Future Innovation[6]

Vodafone Group Plc provides an extensive range of mobile telecommunications services, and is the world's largest mobile telecommunications company with a staggering 300 million customers worldwide. As market leader and with such a large customer base, Vodafone has found it essential to constantly identify opportunities for technological and service innovation and this is the responsibility of Group R&D.

Group R&D consists of 7 research & development centres round the world. In Germany, Group R&D–D is officially known as Vodafone Pilotentwicklung GmbH, which has 34 permanent employees, 20 contract staff and 20 students from universities, all with a wide range of backgrounds. Their role is to analyse trends, new technologies, build future visions, monitor 'players' (organizations associated with the market), and track the business environment to derive ideas for tomorrow's competitive products and services. Their work prepares the ground for specific R&D projects by prototyping possible future products and services. To achieve this they have established a

▶▶

structured approach to identify, evaluate and utilize opportunities. This structure relies on effective use of tools and techniques, networking and communication.

Vodafone Group R&D–D uses different tools and techniques. For analysing technologies and markets, employees can choose from a range of individual methods in the 'Group R&D–D toolkit'. For example, this collection includes several scenario planning methods. No individual employee is experienced in the use of all tools and techniques but new employees are trained on the basic methods. Since the toolkit is summarized as a single-sheet mind map, it is easy to identify where alternatives to the basic methods may be appropriate and to contact experienced colleagues. Dr Christiane Hipp, who drives the Innovation process in Group R&D–D says, 'In dealing with the future we have found it better not to rely on just one or two analysis methods as most other companies do. As we have a portfolio of techniques available, this means that we can look for the best tool for the job. It also provides variety which is important in maintaining a fresh and energetic feel to our work'.

Vodafone has a philosophy of keeping individual R&D sites small, with typically around 15 to 80 permanent employees. This means that Group R&D–D employees need to communicate and network effectively with both their internal and external contacts. Torsten Herzberg, a Group R&D–D freelancer says, 'Innovation is often the result of communication between people who do not have homogeneous ideas and so we need to stimulate constant dialogue – internally and externally'. This communication takes various forms.

The Group R&D–D office in Munich is a largely open plan and was designed together with the well-known architect Prof. Gunther Henn using his 'programming concept'. In this, the architecture of the office supports the way employees work with, for example, several 'marketplaces' – open areas where all employees can meet regularly and discuss their work. In addition to doing everything to create an informal 'culture of communication', Group R&D–D has regular short meetings where employees present their work, bounce ideas around and discuss 'lessons learned' from previous projects.

Group R&D–D is also experimenting with bringing artists together with their technical employees, to help stimulate creativity. They have found that mixing artistic and technical thinking supports the creation of radically new visions and ideas for their implementation. A symbol of the use of artistic thinking is the traditional red English telephone box, which was installed in the roof garden as part of a current project, where artists and technical employees are investigating the role of 'private' areas for mobile phone calls in today's increasingly open-plan office environment.

To stimulate communication across the whole Vodafone organization, Group R&D–D organizes both internal and external marketing, including the Annual Conference. This is a two-day event where the whole of Group R&D present new ideas and innovative projects. Around 150 Chief Technology Officers and Strategy Directors from the Vodafone companies worldwide attend the conference. There are various presentation sessions and an 'Innovation Zone' with live demonstrations of the latest prototypes of new products and services. 'Piloting everything in a professional and innovative way allows visitors to understand the ideas quickly and to give constructive feedback. It requires a lot of effort but the conference has been hugely influential in optimizing communication inside Group R&D, and between Group R&D and Vodafone operations', says Eva Weber, responsible for innovation marketing and communication at Group R&D–D.

The same pressures will make the demand for new services or products more volatile and unpredictable which in turn will make all aspects of the supply chain more difficult to manage. In the fashion industry (surely the exemplar of the top end of the Maslow hierarchy), Zara have shown that great cost and sales advantages can be gained from a very short and flexible supply chain, that enables it to respond rapidly to new trends, even though it increases the cost of manufacture (see Mini Case 4.2). This allows them both to get new products into the shops very rapidly and to withdraw them if they are not successful (or have run their course) without penalty. There is a continuing need for better understanding of how to manage complex and volatile supply chains.

These trends, together with the increasing role of Open Innovation (see below), make the task of plotting an innovation strategy increasingly difficult (see Mini Case 10.3 on Innovationedge).

Mini Case 10.3

Innovationedge – Innovation Roadmapping[7]

Cheryl Perkins had over a 20-year industrial career with Kimberly-Clark, including the role of Senior Vice President and Chief Innovation Officer, from which she developed a passion for strategic innovation management. Now as President of consultancy company Innovationedge, she helps companies build their strategic capabilities and assists companies and inventors develop winning strategies, overcome barriers and bring their ideas to market. In 2006, Perkins was named as one of the 'Top 25 Champions of Innovation' by *Business Week*.

Through her extensive consultancy experience, Perkins is in constant contact with leading organizations and sees that

> Top line growth is now so urgent that real innovation is needed. Breakthrough products, services and business models are needed and not just incremental innovations. Open innovation used to be about identifying vendors, suppliers and technology scouting, whereas now it is all about creating collaborative innovation networks, with the right leaders and culture. In such networks, the combination of competencies should enable the players to develop new business models, and better experiences for the end-user with profitable solutions.

To envisage and develop such networks, Perkins works with top management teams using strategic roadmaps. However, she has enhanced the concept of roadmaps (discussed in Chapter 4) in several ways to cover the establishment of collaborative networks for open innovation. First, her roadmaps consider the full range of partners needed for open innovation (including inspired user groups:'Crowdsourcing'), and how synergies can be achieved. Second, how the cultures of the different players can be balanced to produce creative tension needs to be planned. Finally, the role of leaders in driving the change needs to be considered. 'To successfully roadmap the many opportunities and deliver your strategy with effective collaboration, you need to address competencies AND culture AND leadership. And one final thing: in today's turbulent environment, where cost saving is critical, collaborations will enable cost-savings that single organizations could never achieve in isolation. However, it will only be the leading companies that don't avoid become inwardly-focused in the current climate'.

TECHNOLOGY

Herman Kahn became famous in the 1960s for leading a think-tank that dared to debate seriously about the possibility of waging and surviving a nuclear war. He became notorious for his use of the 'megadeath' as a suitable unit for measuring casualties in a global nuclear conflict. Later he turned his attention to predicting the future of science and technology with his famous book 'The Year 2000, a framework for Speculation on the next Thirty-Three Years' written in 1967 with Anthony Wiener. In their book, Kahn and Wiener ventured a list of 'One hundred technical innovations very likely in the last third of the twentieth century'.[8] When the new millennium arrived, several commentators reviewed Kahn's predictions and tried to judge how accurate they were. Opinions varied from 15 to 50 per cent – not surprisingly perhaps as some of the predictions were rather vague. However, one report,[9] based on the views of a panel of eight experts, found that Kuhn and Wiener's predictions in one particular class were as much as 80 per cent accurate. These were the ones about (or derived directly from) developments in computers and communication. They were based on the assumption of a steady improvement in the technology of integrated circuits[10]; a trend that was already established at the time and has indeed continued relentlessly to this day. The predictions that did not have an underlying rationale of this kind were noticeably less successful – perhaps they were little more than wishful thinking. We will therefore not speculate about whether entirely new technologies may emerge but confine ourselves to trends that are already discernible.

A good place to start is with electronics and computing because a period of spectacular improvement must be approaching its end. The underlying driver of this is Moore's Law: that the number of transistors that can be fabricated on a single chip would double every 1½–2 years. This has been well borne out in practice, and the number has actually grown a million-fold since the 1960s. But it cannot go on indefinitely. The origin of the improvement has been the steady reduction in the size of the circuit elements and this is now pressing on some fundamental limits. The smallest parts of the circuits are already less than 100 atoms across; by 2020 it should be 10 atoms.[11] Moore's law may already be slowing,[12] and it seems very likely that the industry will face fundamental limits within the next decade. If so, we will see the end of the era of apparently endless cost reduction in the hardware of electronics and computing, which has made possible so much innovation in many industries: banking; financial services; audio and video recording; logistics; mobile communications; photography; and so on. When it falters, as it assuredly will, it will have a profound impact in many industries. However, the time is not quite yet, and no doubt this great summer of progress will be followed by an autumn in which we can continue to harvest benefits for some time.

Perhaps quantum computing will provide a new revolution? Perhaps; but history tells us that real revolutions in technology take time. It took over 100 years for photography to move from being a scientific curiosity to a usable product. Arguably[13] telephony took over 50 years, and radio 35. Controlled fusion power is not yet a reality more than 50 years since the first hydrogen bomb, and genetic engineering is only recently producing serious results approximately 50 years since the discovery of the structure of DNA.

Innovation in the technology of materials seems certain. Whether there will be breakthrough to room temperature superconductors is anyone's guess but the steady progress (and considerable investment) in nanotechnology will surely produce radically new materials (see Mini Case 10.4) and new opportunities. The trends in biotechnology are now well enough established for it to be clear that understanding of the way genetics shapes living things at the most fundamental level is set to accelerate rapidly. Serious impacts on the treatment of disease must follow but perhaps the greatest influence will be in engineering microbes to produce useful chemicals – including fuels – more efficiently than before.

Mini Case 10.4

The Lotus Effect – Technology Cross-Over[14]

Biologists from the University of Bonn in Germany investigated the 'lotus effect' – the apparently smooth leaves of this plant repel water and almost all dirt and grime. Microscopically, the surface of lotus leaves showed itself to have a particular undulating pattern of what looked like higher and lower 'mountains'. Nanotechnology has now enabled this surface to be mimicked and 'easy-to-clean' products are now entering the marketplace. These include coatings for bathroom ceramics, paint for walls, and coatings for surgical devices. Easy-to-clean technology promises to save not only time by minimizing the need for cleaning but also cleaning materials.

Nanotechnology and biotechnology will be revolutionary in their ways but we would doubt that their impact on the process of innovation will be as profound as the electronics and communication revolution has been. This has transformed not so much our ability to manipulate the world but our ability to manipulate knowledge itself and to communicate the results to each other. This has accelerated innovation in every part of human activity, not only in electronics, because it has affected the very material of innovation itself.

Implications for Innovation Management

Sustainability is an overriding challenge. Whenever a new product, process or service is conceived the impact it will make on the environment from cradle to grave will have to be considered and planned for. This is an extra task for managers but not one that appears to require much change to the innovation process itself.

More significantly, the rate of technical change, and the increasing speed of product development imply that whenever a new product concept takes off the performance of the competing products will catch up much more rapidly than in the past. Differentiation on the basis of product alone will become more difficult, or at least more transient, so companies must look to enhancing value through related services. Value Innovation and the related theme of Blue Ocean strategy have come to the forefront of academic discussion of recent years thanks to the work of Kim and Mauborgne[15] but there is more research to be done. In particular companies need much better tools for assessing when a change of business model offers better prospects than continued improvement of the current approach.

We have mentioned several times that economies move towards a higher proportion of services as they mature – the figure for the US is around 80 per cent. The shrunken manufacturing sector cannot provide the productivity growth for the whole economy so this is another reason why innovation in services must become an increasingly dominant theme of innovation studies. An effective equivalent of TRIZ (Chapter 5) for services would be very welcome, though it is difficult to see where the data on which to base it would come from.

COMPETITION

It is estimated[16] that by 2025 the number of people educated to graduate level will be greater than the total world population in 1900. China and India with their huge, well-educated populations, totalling more than a third of mankind, no longer provide only low-cost manufacturing but are beginning to emerge as centres of innovation in their own right. Bangalore in India has more IT professionals than the whole of Silicon Valley, and is home to Wipro, now the largest R&D services company in the world with a turnover of a billion dollars (see the main case study in Chapter 7). Fundamental research is growing rapidly in India and China[17] and although the output by no means rivals that of Western R&D laboratories these economies, based as they are on old and sophisticated civilizations, are powerful centres of innovation. The globalization of business and the spread of IT mean that they are quickly linking into world markets, just as Korea, Taiwan and others have before them.

Not only are there powerful new sources of competition, but competition itself is also becoming more efficient. Tariff barriers continue to be reduced through the expansion of trading blocks such as the EC and Mercosur. Cheaper air and sea transport help the flow of goods between countries. Perhaps most important for innovation, IT and the Internet are having a dramatic effect on the free flow of information, aided by the increasing use of English as the international language for business. The British Council recently estimated that half the world's population will speak at least basic English by 2015. These factors sharpen competition by giving customers better access than ever before to competing products and more opportunity to compare them. Well-informed customers lead to tighter competition and better products. Yet, few people can navigate confidently through the billions of pages of information available to us, and search engines are clearly only in their infancy. There is much more improvement still to come.

The lessons for innovation managers are not comforting but they are exciting. Whatever business you are in, expect more competition. It may not be local, though it will increasingly speak your language. Only those providing localized services will be exempt. But on the other hand, companies adopting open innovation will find more potential partners than ever before. Customers will be better informed, but they will also be more numerous so good companies can expect to prosper as never before. The successful companies will be those able to respond quickly to new practices and ideas, and to search constantly for new opportunities wherever they can be found.

Implications for Innovation Management

There has been much concern in the Western press about the dangers of losing our position of leadership in fundamental science and technology to the rising economies of Asia. The importance of science to technical innovation is obvious but that is not the same as saying that leadership in science is vital for innovation. In a recent book,[18] Amar Bhidé of Columbia University argues that although technical progress depends on science the basic discoveries quickly become available to all, either through publication or licensing, and most of the benefits go to the users of those discoveries and their customers. The transistor was invented at Bell Laboratories (based on original work in Germany) but Sony was the first company to use them, and it is hardly true to say that most of the benefits of the transistor have gone to Bell, nor yet to the USA. Does it matter that the computer was invented in America (or perhaps England), the Internet in Geneva or Skype in Estonia? Ultimately, it's the makers and users who benefit most.

So if excellence in fundamental science is not necessary for a country to be successful even at technical innovation, what exactly is? There really is a need for more work on understanding this fundamental and vitally important matter. A related issue, much less discussed, is how innovation operates at the personal level. Of course, the people who have the dramatic breakthroughs – Albert Einstein, Steve Jobs, Tim Berners-Lee, Francis Crick and James Watson, Bill Gates and so on – are by definition unusual people so perhaps there is no point in looking for common denominators between them. But go down a level or two and one finds a vast number of people who stand out from the rest because of their ability to do new things time and time again. Not breakthroughs necessarily, just things that have not been done before. It is well known that the best software engineers can be five or more times as productive as the average. And we know people in many other fields – chemistry, journalism, circuit design – who are far more productive than their peers. But nobody really knows why. Such large differences in performance cannot be due to innate ability alone: things such as attitude, knowledge, working methods and the right balance between theory and experiment must be involved. If we could understand this better, we should surely be able to teach it, and so to improve innovativeness at the most fundamental level.

THE BUSINESS ENVIRONMENT

The economic growth of China, India and other Asian countries and the opening up of the countries of the former USSR increases global competition but also opens up huge new business opportunities. The growing middle classes in these new markets will be purchasers of many of the goods and services already sold in developed markets. But in addition the poorer consumers, by their very numbers, provide huge new opportunities[19] that spur innovative low-cost solutions (there is even a Hindi word for such innovations: *jugaad*).[20] Many companies are finding that producing less-sophisticated versions of existing ideas can open new markets (such as Whirlpool's 'Ideale' washing machine, mentioned in Chapter 1 and the 'Jaipur Foot' (Mini Case 10.5)). The success of 'micro credit' schemes is another example. These give small loans, without collateral, to start new enterprises based on a purchase of something as small as a goat or a single mobile phone. The rates of interest are relatively high but the micro-entrepreneurs (usually women, who previously had no access to capital at all) use it very efficiently. The default rate on the loans is very low. Many *jugaad* innovations are relevant only to third world markets but many will certainly prove Disruptive in the formal sense in the richer world. Already patients from the West are flying to India for excellent and low-cost healthcare from hospitals such as Aravind

---

Mini Case 10.5

The Jaipur Foot – Indian Low-Tech[21]

What is the appropriate level of technology? This is a question that should be asked by product design teams constantly, as the customers and end-users of products and services will seldom be persuaded to adopt a higher level of technology than is appropriate. A clear example of this is the 'Jaipur Foot', which has become a household name in the war zones of the world.

Biomedical engineers have long studied the workings of the body and designed artificial limbs, some of which incorporate microprocessor control and feedback systems. Unfortunately, the demand for prostheses is heavy; a direct result of the millions of anti-personnel mines that have been laid during wars over the past 50 years. Mines are cheap and easy to produce, simple to lay and extremely difficult, dangerous and time-consuming to clear. The civilian populations in the war zones pay a heavy price and many people in countries such as Afghanistan have lost and continue to lose limbs as they return to their villages and agricultural fields following conflicts. However, these civilians do not have the money or access to the high-tech devices found in the bio-medical engineering laboratories of the West. Enter the Jaipur Foot.

It was not only the cost of conventional artificial limbs that acted against them being adopted, but it was also that their design did not fit with the lifestyle of people in Asia, where many people squat, eat and sleep on the floor. The Jaipur Foot is the solution and it is made of simple materials – rubber, wood and aluminium – which are not only readily available but also can be worked by local craftsmen. Typically it takes 45 minutes to build, lasts 5 years and costs about $30.

(main case of Chapter 2). And who will doubt that versions of Tata's low-cost car, the Nano, will be sold well beyond the borders of India?

Open Innovation

As we discussed in Chapter 4, companies are increasingly teaming up with others to find new ideas and to introduce new products to the market faster and more reliably. Instead of expecting to control all aspects of a new product, they use a network of collaborators who work with them as partners in innovation, rather than merely as subcontractors. Mini Case 10.7 shows how Philips uses intermediaries in their search for new ideas.

This has long been the pattern in industries where a dominant design has emerged (see Chapter 4). In the automotive sector, for example, manufacturers habitually source complete electronics or hydraulic systems, or even engines, from third parties who take responsibility for all aspects of design and innovation. However, the complexity of products and the need for rapid introduction has pushed many companies into collaborative ventures even when the product is still relatively immature.

Dominant design is a familiar kind of standardization that facilitates cooperative design. But another kind of standardization is well established though seldom commented on; and its scope goes far beyond the electronics industry where it resides. It derives from three sources: digitization, integration and interconnection standards. Digitization is the pervasive trend to encode all information as numbers that can be represented by sequences of zeros and ones. These signals can be stored, processed and reproduced with effectively perfect accuracy and so although digital circuits are often immensely complicated they are utterly reproducible. The manufacture of digital circuit chips is now so reliable that few companies bother to make their own; they just send the designs to a 'silicon foundry', probably on the other side of the world. Few people pause to think what an extraordinary change to manufacturing methods this is.

There are many different types of electronic function, so most pieces of electronics are still made up of many separate components. A collection of standards have evolved to govern how these parts interconnect. Using these standards an equipment maker can assemble a collection of complex components from diverse sources and be confident they will work together. The impact on equipment design has been dramatic. Much more important, though, this combination of digitization with interconnection standards is at the heart of the communications revolution. It is what allows an agent in India to handle an insurance claim from England; a salesman in Turkey to check progress of his order in the USA; the sale of an item from a supermarket in France to trigger immediate re-supply from Spain; or a traveller from China to view and then book a hotel room in Australia.

The combination of digitization, integration and interconnection standards has an effect rather like that of a dominant design in that it allows very complicated functions to be independently developed by different companies and yet linked reliably together. These can range from a keyboard or display to a complete library or logistics system.

Open innovation allows the resources of many companies to be brought together to design a new product using the most up to date of components. Such innovation can be very fast because each supplier drives its own part forward independently and brings the most up to date version to each new project.

The Dangers of Open Innovation

The danger for the lead company is that since the technical ownership and intellectual property increasingly lies with the suppliers their own contribution (the product concept and the integration of the resources to bring it into being) may prove difficult to defend. Certainly, the barriers to new entrants in such a market are much lower than in the days when large, vertically integrated manufacturers retained control of most of their product. Such a pattern has recently emerged in the mobile telephone market. In the past the industry was dominated by large vertically integrated firms such as Motorola, Ericsson and Nokia. The technology was so complicated that each company needed to have command of all aspects of the design, from the radio chips to the audio circuits. Fitting all this into a tiny, carefully styled case and then manufacturing it in high volume itself

---

Mini Case 10.6

Philips – Always Open to Outside Ideas[23]

Although open innovation has become one of the buzzwords of the moment, Philips, the Dutch-owned lighting and electronics giant has been a leader in this area for at least 16 years. Katja van der Wal is Open Innovation manager for the Consumer Lifestyle Division – which makes a range of home entertainment, personal hygiene and lighting products. Van der Wal is an expert at the practicalities of making open innovation work.

In working with outside innovators, Philips has developed novel approaches to two of the potential drawbacks of open innovation – namely, how to deal with confidentiality and intellectual property issues. In joint innovation work, Philips often needs to search for innovations that could be useful in lifestyle products. These could be promising technologies or even product solutions. However, as a large organization, Philips does not want the message to get out that it is seriously looking at a particular technology or opportunity. Therefore, confidentiality is preserved by using knowledge brokers to scout for interesting products and technologies on behalf of Philips. This is effective and it 'doesn't signal that Philips is working on this or that unmet need' says van der Wal. Working through brokers not only allows Philips to check whether an idea is sufficiently developed but it also allows them, importantly, to consider whether the other organization will be easy to work with.

For those organizations that Philips selects on the basis of their innovations and approach, it is important to establish the right relationship from the beginning. 'Before you get to legal agreements you must agree some working principles based on establishing trust and transparency between the partners' says van der Wal, 'because without this the contracts stage can become a nightmare'.

Once good relationships are established, the benefits of cooperating with outside organizations are multiple and the list of successes that Philips attributes to working with open innovation partners is impressive. For example, the Artitec shaver's innovative design resulted from working with a mobile phone manufacturer (which, in turn, applied some of the ideas to improve the ergonomics of its handsets). With Nivea, Philips has developed a novel electric shaver where skin cream can be applied to the shaving head to give a more comfortable shave. And working with Bavista connoisseur coffee company has given many ideas for the Senseo range of coffee makers. 'It is amazing what is going on outside and we always remind our R&D engineers that there are more people outside Philips who are working on the problems that interest us than there are engineers inside our company'.

required unique expertise. Now, however, the design has stabilized and all the core radio components, as well the displays, processors, cameras and so on, can be bought from suppliers who design and make modules for the whole industry. Some will even design and supply the complete product. These Original Design Manufacturers are now selling their own product directly into some markets. As a result the lead companies are reducing subcontract and concentrating some of the key design skills back in the main company so as not to lose control of the product.[22]

In the automotive field, on the other hand, the main suppliers retain major collateral assets in their assembly expertise, distribution and brand name, which are important enough to allow them to defend themselves against competition from their suppliers; though even this could be threatened by alternative business models, as Mini Case 10.1 shows, and of course by the rise of electric propulsion which will hugely simplify the design and manufacturing of vehicles (Mini Case 4.5).

In a world in which companies must collaborate with others for some of the most innovative parts of their products or services, innovation strategy becomes vital. Today's valued partners can become tomorrow's competition. Managers must be sure that they understand the sources of their competitive advantage in the long term and develop strategies to keep control of them.

Implications for Innovation Management

It's clear that much work is needed to help companies be more effective at open innovation. Some companies already seem to manage it well, but many more struggle; and those who are successful often do not know why. No coherent body of best practice has emerged and this is a major challenge for the next few years (see Mini Case 10.7 on PureInsight).

The feel from the literature and from practitioners is that the biggest difficulties lie in the difficult domains of trust and culture. As every manager

---

Mini Case 10.7

PureInsight[24]

PureInsight is a European company focused on providing busy executives with access to carefully selected, high-quality information on leading edge techniques for managing innovation. The company's portfolio of services includes regular webinars presented by experienced managers and world experts, a range of reports and seminars, plus in-company consultancy. All of these services are accessible through various levels of membership, and member organizations include leaders such as 3M, Draeger Safety, Lucent Technologies, Masterfoods and W L Gore & Associates.

PureInsight founder and managing director Klaus Schnurr has a background in engineering and product management and has been working in the consultancy sector for over 15 years. He constantly monitors the trends in the management of innovation and has seen some big changes in the past few years. 'Two years ago the interest was in managing virtual teams and IP, whereas now the focus is on the fuzzy front end', says Schnurr. 'The problem is that there are so many tools and techniques out there and everyone is saying their technique is the best. So there is confusion about what companies should adopt and concern that it is critical to get the front end right, as there is a greater need for breakthrough products'.

PureInsight maintains an enquiry database and monitors the subject of the questions they receive from members and so Schnurr is in a good position to comment on the future of innovation management. 'I see three main changes: first, the understanding of open innovation will evolve into one which is focused on developing efficient "innovation ecosystems" – strategic networks of internal and external innovation resources. Then, I also see a huge increase in interest in innovation metrics. Finally, innovation management is starting to take on a broader meaning, where it becomes a management philosophy and not just a collection of tools and techniques'.

---

knows it is difficult enough to get easy collaboration between departments within a single company who at least share certain business aims and processes. It is much more difficult between organizations which may have little in common beyond an interesting new opportunity. Difficulties often come to the surface in disputes over how to handle IPR but the underlying issues are cultural. Overly tight legal contracts can destroy the energy and creativity on which innovation depends, and yet each party must protect its own interests. Better legal frameworks are needed, and this is a challenge for practitioners and academics alike. But above all companies setting out to innovate together need effective and objective tools for understanding how their values, assumptions and ways of working differ, and how (or whether) they can be aligned enough to make joint innovation work. Academics must provide them. Indeed, the cultural issues behind innovation are themselves a fertile field for new research, for there is no doubt that the best management processes in the world can be destroyed by a poor organizational culture. Companies need tools to help them assess and understand their own culture of innovation and target improvements.

The increasingly challenging business climate points to two further areas of innovation management that cry out for new thinking. One is the whole matter of estimating the market impact of innovations. In our experience the sales forecast is invariably the weakest link in developing a business proposal for a new product. Sometimes this is because managers are reluctant to commit resources to researching a product that is only at the concept stage; but mostly it is simply because this is an immensely difficult subject. One cannot expect a precise solution but the truth is that many companies, especially small ones, often rely on little more than guesswork. This is a topic which is ripe for new insights. Good academic work could yield tools of great value to companies large and small.

A related subject is the financial modelling of projects with high levels of uncertainty. The best tool available at the moment is the decision tree linked

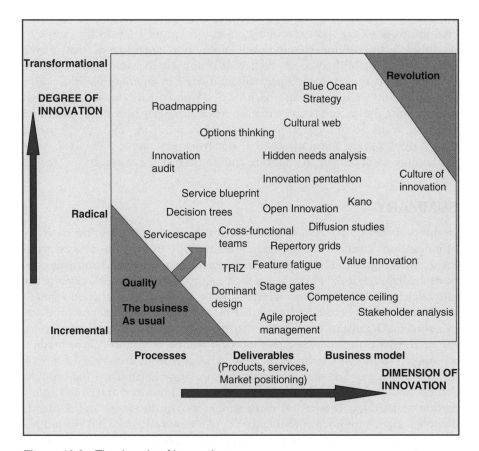

Figure 10.3 The domain of innovation

with Monte Carlo analysis but the structure of nodes, each with several discrete decisions is inappropriately rigid, and the multiple branching quickly becomes dishearteningly complex. There must be a better way.

CONCLUSION

Throughout this book we have focused on presenting tools and techniques for managing innovation, which appear from research to be both practical and reliable. In Chapter 1 we showed a diagram (Figure 1.4) in which innovation is shown as occupying the middle ground between incremental (quality) improvement and revolutionary upheaval.

The quality corner of the diagram is now very well understood as a result of years of work by academics and practitioners. There are tried and tested methods, such as Six Sigma, that are known to work. Our modest hope is that the boundary of this area of relative certainty will advance across the diagram as work goes on. Some of the tools, theories and frameworks that we have covered in this book are shown, roughly placed on Figure 10.3. In the course of time these islands of understanding will join up into larger islands, maybe even continents of established good practice. It is unlikely that innovation, with its inherent diversity and uncertainty, will lend itself to anything like the highly structured and prescriptive approach of Six Sigma quality management but over time the theory and practice of innovation management will become more coherent, more secure and more practically useful. Time will show whether we are right and, in addition, whether our own very simple framework – the Pentathlon – will remain an enduring and useful tool for managers.

SUMMARY

In this chapter we have reviewed trends for the future in the four main drivers of innovation: customers, competition, technology and the business environment. We suggest that the need and opportunities for innovation will continue unabated, but the next wave of technology will not further accelerate the rate of change. However, new services and products will be targeted at more subtle needs than before and so it will be more difficult to define products in advance. Organizations will have to be prepared to experiment more in the marketplace and to accept that demand will be more difficult to predict, so supply chains must be more flexible. And all this in a context of better-informed customer and more competitors, speaking our language and brought literally and metaphorically to our doorsteps by improved travel and information technology. Innovation management as a professional and academic discipline faces a number of challenges: better ways to understand the hidden needs of customers; faster and more responsive ways to develop products and services; new approaches to open innovation and to innovation in services; greater understanding of innovation at the personal level, and many more. There are exciting times ahead!

MANAGEMENT RECOMMENDATIONS

- Explore ways to understand your customers' hidden needs but know that this is an imperfect science.
- Be prepared to experiment with new services and products and change them as you learn.
- Expect higher levels of competition.
- Accept that more of your innovation will come from outside the organization.
- Embrace collaboration with other companies but ensure that you know and can defend your competitive position.

CASE STUDY
Hewlett-Packard BITS[25]

Before reading this case, consider the following generic innovation management issues:

- What will be the challenges in the future in managing innovation?
- Which aspects of the customer relationship are essential to a business model?
- What are the key differences between managing innovation in small and large organizations?

INNOVATION CONSULTANCY

Business Innovation and Transformation Services (BITS) is an internal consulting group serving the Hewlett-Packard Corporation (HP). BITS concentrates on sharing best practice amongst HP's business units, using knowledge transfer to improve the performance of business teams, and 'accelerating' business results.

The origins of BITS lie in the late 1980s when Hewlett-Packard began its transition from being a hardware engineering company to one that predominantly develops products based on software. The company, with its long-standing commitment to retaining employees, determined that it would be necessary to train many of its hardware-focused R&D engineers in software. A Software Initiative group was created to design training courses and improve the overall management of software projects. Meanwhile, other internal groups such as Corporate Product Marketing (responsible for product definition and market research), Corporate Quality (tasked with developing metrics and customer centred design), and Strategic Change Services (in charge of organizational design, governance, and group decision-making) were gathering and generating the approaches that later formed the basis for many of BITS's methodologies. Each of the corporate groups developed a number of company-wide programmes that focused on improving particular functional processes. In contrast, BITS was formed in 1999 to provide integrative, cross-functional services to HP's many business units.

TRUE CROSS-FUNCTIONAL THINKING

The early recognition that a cross-functional approach was essential to business performance was central in guiding the services that BITS would offer. Although engineering

▶▶

has often been a driving force within HP, the BITS team was assembled with an eye for creating a business melting pot. The 25 individuals in BITS have diverse backgrounds: including engineering PhDs, marketers, anthropologists, business analysts and medical technologists. Mike Northcott, who manages the BITS group says, 'business problems are rarely if ever singularly focused; they are not just about customers, or investments, or change management. The diversity of BITS helps us put together consulting teams that come at the problem from different angles. Furthermore, we understand the culture and language of the company's different functions'. BITS encourages business units to take a 'horizontal view' across the functions. 'You have to understand the needs of your customers through all of the interactions they have with your business, from awareness, through support, to repurchase. Only then can you develop innovations that create exceptional customer loyalty', emphasizes Northcott.

THREE TEAMS, THREE DOMAINS

Currently, BITS is active in providing business support in three domains: 'acceleration services', 'business strategy services' and 'customer strategy services'.

Acceleration services are based on the recognition that the speed at which strategic business decisions are made has a strong influence on a business unit's competitiveness. Fast but effective decision-making is supported through two types of 'event'. The first is known as 'GarageWorks' and consists of facilitated meetings with 15–30 people, designed to creatively identify breakthrough ideas or new concepts. The second type involves helping large groups quickly reach shared decisions; these are known as 'Decision Accelerators' and have 30–200 participants. In addition to running events, the acceleration services team consults on change management, corporate and business governance modelling, and team and leadership development.

Business strategy services work with HP's businesses on developing strategic plans. This team's assignments run the gamut from identifying new business opportunities and business model design, all the way through strategic portfolio analysis.

The customer strategy services team specializes in understanding the 'customer experience', uncovering latent user needs through ethnographic, empathic design, and other techniques. Their work also includes the development of value delivery systems 'maps', which help focus businesses on the operational investments that will yield the greatest returns.

Working with HP's divisions (and those of Compaq since the 2002 merger), BITS needs to not only spread innovation best practices, but also to plot the future of innovation management at HP. Focusing on the three domains will not be sufficient for much longer. Consequently, Northcott is looking at how his group needs to change. He says,

> BITS is a service operation working within what was originally a pure R&D and manufacturing company. However, HP is moving towards a services-led business model and, to remain relevant, my team needs to evolve ahead of the businesses' needs. We have to harness innovative consulting services ourselves, bring these into the company, and make them relevant to HP's problems. Unlike many external consulting services, we measure our value by our ability to improve HP's capabilities. If we don't generate extraordinary and sustaining value, then HP would be better off outsourcing our services.

▶▶

CHANGING NATURE OF INNOVATION

In developing ideas for new approaches, Northcott also works closely with William Pipkin. He is a 21-year HP veteran who now runs his own innovation management consultancy, specializing in advising start-ups how they can commercialize their technology. 'William brings the urgency and critical perspective of a small start-up into our discussions, matched with an awareness of the full implications of what he is saying for a large company like HP. Sometimes the "small company view" is painful but it certainly helps us to look at innovation differently', says Northcott.

Invention and technology have always played a leading role in innovation at HP and the garage in California where the founders set up the company is not only an icon within the firm but is also a protected historic building (hence the name GarageWorks for new business workshops). However, more than technology is needed because, 'today's latest technology is tomorrow's commodity', says Northcott, 'so we must concentrate on designing innovative business processes'. For example, although HP has a history of excellent manufacturing, outsourcing is now used extensively. Managing the interfaces between the key organizations along the value chain is where the real value can be captured. Northcott says, 'it is now a case of finding how to positively control the customer experience without having to own all the assets. It's a case of bringing customer-oriented insights into what would otherwise be standardized business processes. Like in a small company, everyone has to be engaged in customer dialogue to generate these insights'.

Pipkin and Northcott identify two main challenges for both large and small organizations that want to become more innovative. These are: expanding the skills of their employees, and understanding and meeting the transforming needs of customers.

Much has been written about pulling together the skill base required for innovative project teams. 'However, while many people are excellent at the technology, or the finance, or marketing, few if any are excellent at all three. Hardly any people have the skills needed to pull it all together and, without such people you are progressively more likely to fail', says Pipkin. Although a large company has functional expertise, Northcott perceives the need for HP to develop more individuals with 'multi-functional and entrepreneurial skills'. He thinks it is the ability to drive processes that cut across the traditional boundaries 'that are going to be critical in the future'. Pipkin identifies some major changes in the general nature of customers' needs. 'As our society continues to develop, so our needs climb up Maslow's Triangle. We are no longer hunter-gatherers. Previously, companies could focus on basic needs, but now it's all about experiential requirements; needs that are not easy to identify or satisfy', he says. Northcott has a similar view: 'it is not only getting harder to identify customers' real needs, but these are becoming more personal'. Both believe that businesses will need to deliver a consistently excellent 'experience' for customers with every interaction they have with the company. The challenge will be to identify the internal process changes that must occur to achieve this, and to do so ahead of the demand curve. As Northcott puts it, 'providing innovations to customers who will increasingly defy the rules of market segmentation is going to require radically different leadership skills'.

APPENDIX: INNOVATION AUDITING

INTRODUCTION

The following set of innovation audit questions is based on six main references, adapted to match the Pentathlon Framework. From the various sets of recommended questions available, choosing the appropriate questions for a particular context is one of the problems with innovation audits. In addition, the various sets of questions available have not been previously collated. Therefore, we provide a comprehensive set of questions on our companion website [www.palgrave.com]. In this list, we have indicated the source of each question by superscripts, referring to the numbers (below) of the references. Redundant questions have been eliminated. Italics indicate where original questions have been (slightly) modified. Questions in italics without superscript numbers are new and have been developed by the authors to cover areas such as project prioritization, where insufficient questions were previously available.

REFERENCES ON INNOVATION AUDITS

1. Anonymous, 'Managing Change in Your Organization', *International Trade Forum*, Issue 2/2000, pp. 26–28.
2. British Standard. *Design Management Systems – Part 1: Guide to Managing Innovation*. British Standard BS7000–1 (London: British Standards Institution, 1999).
3. Goffin, K. and Pfeiffer, R., *Innovation Management in UK and German Manufacturing Companies*. Anglo-German Foundation Report Series (London, December 1999).
4. Majaro, S., *The Creative Marketer* (Oxford: Butterworth-Heinemann, 1991).
5. Tidd, J., Bessant, J. and Pavitt, K., *Managing Innovation: Integrating Technological, Market and Organizational Change* (Chichester: Wiley, 2nd Edition, 2001).
6. Voss, C. A., Chiesa, V. and Coughlan, P., *Innovation – Your Move, Self-Assessment Guide and Workbook* (London: Department of Trade and Industry, 1993).

APPLYING THE INNOVATION AUDIT

Chapter 9 explains how the innovation audit can be used to better understand the innovation performance of an organization, in conjunction with other tools such as the cultural web. In using the audit, three main points must be considered:

- The results cannot be directly compared from one company to another;
- Collecting and analysing the data collected is best conducted by an external consultant with direct experience of innovation audits, rather than someone from within the organization to be audited;
- The audit needs preparation for the specific context in which it will be used.

These points need some explanation.

The questions in some innovation audits are designed to be answered on a numeric scale (for example, Majaro, 1991). However, it should be remembered that although the answers are quantitative, they are only based on managers' opinions. Therefore, we caution readers against assuming that the results can be directly compared from company to company, as the scales are not absolute. Many aspects of innovation management are too complex to allow all of the inputs, processes and innovation outputs to be represented by a single number. This means that it is difficult to 'benchmark' more than a few aspects of innovation performance, such as the revenues generated by new products, or the percentage of revenues invested in R&D. Even time-to-market figures, which apparently should be comparable, are notoriously difficult to compare reliably.

Although we present a comprehensive set of innovation audit questions on our companion website, we do not recommend that a company should attempt to apply it themselves. It is worth investing in having the audit conducted by experienced external consultants. Outsiders with the right experience are more likely to encourage employees to make a candid assessment of company performance, objectively interpret the results, draw comparisons to other organizations and support the process of boosting innovation performance. In conducting interviews, the consultants will need to gain the confidence of employees and so it is best to promise anonymity. In our own experience of conducting innovation audits, we have found that contextual issues play an important role. Therefore, the questions selected need to match the organization and the business environment being investigated.

Some questions will not be applicable to the context of the organization being investigated and will need to be dropped. For example, some of the technology management questions might not be applicable to a service sector company. Also, the number of questions needs to be manageable and the full set needs to be reduced appropriately. This is best done through a number of pilot interviews, where the external investigators learn about the organization to be audited. The audit questionnaire used should also give the interviewee adequate opportunity to suggest ways in which the innovation performance of the organization can be improved.

After the pioneering work of Majaro (the first version of his audit was published in 1988) and the widely applied audit developed by Voss et al. (1991), the area of innovation auditing has been somewhat ignored by researchers. This is certainly partly due to the difficulties of validating the effectiveness of innovation audits in complex contexts. Nonetheless, the need for innovation audits as a tool has, if anything, increased over the past few years. We have collated all the audit questions from the above-mentioned sources, in order to give a comprehensive list of questions that will cover all eventualities.

From our own experience in conducting innovation audits, we have seen that organizations have a far greater need for support in gauging performance than can be satisfied using the current tools and techniques. Much remains to be done by researchers to take this work further and develop a precise tool for practitioners.

REFERENCES AND NOTES

1 KEY ASPECTS OF INNOVATION MANAGEMENT

1. IBM, *Expanding the Innovation Horizon: The Global CEO Survey 2006*. IBM Business Consulting Services (2006), G510–6259-00.
2. Drucker, P.F., 'The Discipline of Innovation', *Harvard Business Review*, Vol. 76, No. 6 (November–December 1998), pp. 149–157.
3. Anonymous (Economist), 'A Dark Art No More' in *Something New Under the Sun: A Special Report on Innovation*, *The Economist* (13 October 2007), p. 11.
4. Hansen, M.T. and Birkinshaw, J., 'The Innovation Value Chain', *Harvard Business Review*, Vol. 85, No. 6 (June 2007), p. 122.
5. Feige, A. and Crooker, R., 'Innovationen als Medizin gegen Arbeitslosigkeit und Mittelmass', *Frankfurter Allgemeine Zeitung* (7 December 1998).
6. Taylor, E., 'Super Market', *The Wall Street Journal Europe* (Friday/Saturday/Sunday, 5–7 December 2003), p. R4.
7. www.future-store.org, accessed in January 2004 and October 2008.
8. Jordan, M. and Karp, J., 'Whirlpool Launches Affordable Washer in Brazil and China', *The Wall Street Journal Europe* (Tuesday, 9 December 2003), p. A8.
9. Nicolas, T., 'Innovation Lessons from the 1930s', www.mckinseyquarterly.com, accessed in February 2009.
10. Schumpeter, J.A., *The Theory of Economic Development* (Boston, MA: Harvard University Press, 1934).
11. Porter, M.E., *The Competitive Advantage of Nations* (London: Macmillan, 1990).
12. OECD, 'The Measurement of Scientific and Technical Activities' (Paris: OECD, 1981).
13. Priessl, B., 'Service Innovation: What Makes It Different? Empirical Evidence from Germany', in Metcalf, J.S. and Miles, I. (eds), *Innovation Systems in the Service Economy: Measurement and Case Study Analysis* (Norwell, MA: Kluwer Academic Publishers, 2000).
14. Djellal, F. and Gallouj, F., 'Innovation Surveys for Service Industries: A Review', in Thuriaux, B., Arnold, E. and Couchot, C. (eds), *Innovation and Enterprise Creation: Statistics and Indicators*. (European Communities, 2001), p. 74.
15. West, M.A. and Farr, J.L., 'Innovation at Work', in M.A. West and J.L. Farr (eds), *Innovation and Creativity at Work: Psychological and Organizational Strategies* (Chichester, England: Wiley, 1990), p. 9.
16. Pisano, G.P. and Wheelwright, S.C., 'The New Logic of High-Tech R&D', *Harvard Business Review*, Vol. 73, No. 5 (September–October 1995), pp. 93–105.
17. Case based on *cambridge-consultants.com* website accessed in June 2001 and an interview with Andrew Dobson in November 2008.
18. Sekhar, A., 'At Your Service: Your Wish Is Their Command at Les Concierges', *Asian Business*, Vol. 37, No. 5 (May 2001), pp. 48–49.
19. Chan Kim, W. and Mauborgne, R., 'Value Innovation: The Strategic Logic of High Growth', *Harvard Business Review*, Vol. 75, No. 1 (January–February 1997), pp. 103–112.

20. For a good overview of quality management see: Slack, N., Chambers, S. and Johnston, R., *Operations Management* (Harlow, UK: Pearson Education Ltd., 5th Edition, 2007).

21. Angel, R., 'Putting an Innovation Culture into Practice', *Ivey Business Journal Online* (January/February 2006), Reprint.

22. Wheelwright, S.C. and Clark, K., *Revolutionizing Product Development: Quantum Leaps in Speed, Efficiency, and Quality* (New York: The Free Press, 1992).

23. Mansfield, E., *Economics: Principles, Problems, Decisions* (New York: Norton, 5th Edition, 1986).

24. Goffin, K., 'Enhancing Innovation Performance', *Management Quarterly* (The Institute of Chartered Accountants in England and Wales, Part 13 October 2001), pp. 18–26.

25. Sakkab, N.Y., 'Connect and Develop Complements Research and Develop at P&G', *Research-Technology Management*, Vol. 45, No. 2 (March–April 2002), pp. 38–45.

26. Griffin, A. and Hauser, J.R., 'Integrating R&D and Marketing: A Review and Analysis of the Literature', *Journal of Product Innovation Management*, Vol. 13, No. 3 (May 1996), pp. 191–215.

27. Quote from: Morita, A., 'The UK Innovation Lecture' (UK: Department of Trade and Industry, 6 February 1992), Video Number INDY J1800NJ, 5/92.

28. Geroski, P., *Market Structure, Corporate Performance, and Innovative Activity* (Oxford: Clarendon Press, 1994).

29. Schumpeter, J.A., *Capitalism, Socialism and Democracy* (New York: Harper and Row, 3rd Edition, 1950).

30. Ali, A., 'Pioneering versus Incremental Innovation: Review and Research Propositions', *Journal of Product Innovation Management*, Vol. 11, No. 1 (January 1994), pp. 46–61.

31. Cowan, R. and van de Paal, G., *Innovation Policy in a Knowledge-Based Economy* (Luxembourg: European Commission, June 2000).

32. Rogers, E.M., *Diffusions of Innovations* (New York: The Free Press, 1995).

33. Rosegger, G., *The Economics of Production and Innovation* (Oxford: Butterworth-Heinemann, 3rd Edition, 1996).

34. Ali, A., 'Pioneering versus Incremental Innovation: Review and Research Propositions', *Journal of Product Innovation Management*, Vol. 11, No. 1 (January 1994), pp. 46–61.

35. Johne, F.A. and Snelson, P.A., 'Success Factors in Product Innovation: Selective Review of the Literature', *Journal of Product Innovation Management*, Vol. 5, No. 2 (June 1988), pp. 114–128.

36. Nonaka, I. and Kenney, M., 'Towards a New Theory of Innovation Management', *European Management Review* (Summer 1995), pp. 2–9.

37. Nevens, M.T., Summe, G.L. and Uttal, B., 'Commercializing Technology: What the Best Companies Do', *Harvard Business Review*, Vol. 68, No. 3 (May–June 1990), pp. 154–163.

38. Balachandra, R. and Friar, J.H., 'Factors for Success in R&D Projects and New Product Innovation: A Contextual Framework', *IEEE Trans. on Engineering Management*, Vol. 44, No. 3 (August 1997), pp. 6–287.

39. Chan Kim, W. and Mauborgne, R., 'Value Innovation: The Strategic Logic of High Growth', *Harvard Business Review*, Vol. 75, No. 1 (January–February 1997), pp. 103–112.

40. Burgelman, R.A. and Rosenbloom, R.S., 'Technology Strategy: An Evolutionary Process Perspective', in Tushman, M.L. and Anderson, P. (eds), *Managing Strategic Innovation and Change: A Collection of Readings* (New York: Oxford University Press, 1997).

41. Clark, K.B., 'What Strategy Can Do for Technology', *Harvard Business Review*, Vol. 67, No. 6 (November–December 1989), pp. 94–98.

42. Brown, J.S., 'Research That Reinvents the Corporation', *Harvard Business Review*, Vol. 69, No. 1 (January–February 1991), pp. 102–111.

43. Tushman, M.L. and Anderson, P. (eds), *Managing Strategic Innovation and Change: A Collection of Readings* (New York: Oxford University Press, 1997).

44. Jelinek, M. and Schoonhoven, C.B., *The Innovation Marathon: Lessons from High Technology Firms* (Oxford: Basil Blackwell, 1990).

45. *Ibid.*

46. Pisano, G.P. and Wheelwright, S.C., 'The New Logic of High-Tech R&D', *Harvard Business Review*, Vol. 73, No. 5 (September–October 1995), pp. 93–105.

47. Cooper, R.G. and Kleinschmidt, E.J., 'Major New Products: What Distinguishes the Winners in the Chemical Industry?', *Journal of Product Innovation Management*, Vol. 10, No. 2 (March 1993), pp. 90–111.

48. Gobelli, D.H. and Brown, D.J., 'Improving the Process of Product Innovation', *Research Technology Management*, Vol. 36, No. 2 (1993), pp. 38–44.
49. Cooper, R.G. and Kleinschmidt, E.J., 'Determinants of Timeliness in Product Development', *Journal of Product Innovation Management*, Vol. 11, No. 5 (November 1994), pp. 381–396.
50. Datar, S., Jordan, C.C., Kekre, S., Rajiv, S. and Srinivasan, K., 'Advantages of Time-Based New Product Development in a Fast-Cycle Industry', *Journal of Marketing Research*, Vol. XXXIV, No. 1 (February 1997), pp. 36–49.
51. Cooper, R.G., 'Third-Generation New Product Processes', *Journal of Product Innovation Management*, Vol. 11, No. 1 (January 1994), pp. 3–14.
52. Boag, D.A. and Rinholm, B.L., 'New Product Management Practices of Small High Technology Firms', *Journal of Product Innovation Management*, Vol. 6, No. 2 (June 1989), pp. 109–122.
53. Adler, P.S., Mandelbaum, A., Nguyen, V. and Schwerer, E., 'Getting the Most Out of Your Product Development Process', *Harvard Business Review*, Vol. 74, No. 2 (March–April 1996), pp. 4–15.
54. Bowen, H.K., Clark, K.B., Holloway, C.A. and Wheelwright, S.C., 'Make Projects the School for Leaders', *Harvard Business Review*, Vol. 72, No. 5 (September–October 1994), pp. 131–140.
55. Griffin, A., 'The Effect of Project and Process Characteristics on Product Development Cycle Time', *Journal of Marketing Research*, Vol. XXXIV, No. 1 (February 1997), pp. 24–35.
56. Lievens, A. and Moenert, R.K., 'New Service Teams as Information-Processing Systems', *Journal of Service Research*, Vol. 3, No. 1 (August 2000), pp. 46–65.
57. Cooper, R.G., 'Developing New Products On Time, In Time', *Research Technology Management*, Vol. 38, No. 5 (September–October 1995), pp. 49–57.
58. Griffin, A., 'Evaluating QFD's Use in US Firms as a Process for Developing Products', *Journal of Product Innovation Management*, Vol. 9, No. 2 (June 1992), pp. 171–187.
59. Zirger, B.J. and Hartley, J.L., 'A Conceptual Model of Product Development Cycle Time', *Journal of Engineering and Technology Management*, Vol. 11, No. 3/4 (1994), pp. 229–251.
60. Griffin, A., 'Metrics for Measuring Product Development Cycle Time', *Journal of Product Innovation Management*, Vol. 10, No. 2 (March 1993), pp. 112–125.
61. Ittner, C.D. and Larcker, D.F., 'Product Development Cycle Time and Organizational Performance', *Journal of Marketing Research*, Vol. XXXIV, No. 1 (February 1997), pp. 13–23.
62. de Brentani, U., 'Success and Failure in New Industrial Services', *Journal of Product Innovation Management*, Vol. 6, No. 4 (December 1989), pp. 239–258.
63. Hipp, C., Tether, B.S. and Miles, I., 'The Incidence and Effects of Innovation in Services: Evidence from Germany', *International Journal of Innovation Management*, Vol. 4, No. 4 (December 2000), pp. 417–453.
64. Djellal, F. and Gallouj, F., 'Innovation Surveys for Service Industries: A Review', in Thuriaux, B., Arnold, E. and Couchot, C. (eds), *Innovation and Enterprise Creation: Statistics and Indicators* (European Communities, 2001), pp. 70–76.
65. Johne, A. and Storey, C., 'New Service Development: A Review of the Literature and Annotated Bibliography', *City University Business School, Management Working Paper* B97/2 (April 1997).
66. Ramaswamy, K. and Modi, M., 'Singapore International Airlines: Service with a Smile', Thunderbird: *The American Graduate School of International Management, Case Study*.
67. Gavin, D.A., *Managing Quality: The Strategic and Competitive Edge* (New York: The Free Press, 1988).
68. Russell, R.S. and Taylor III, B.W., *Operations Management: Focusing on Quality and Competitiveness* (London, UK: Prentice-Hall International, 1998), pp. 74–75.
69. Goffin, K. and Pfeiffer, R., *Innovation Management in UK and German Manufacturing Companies* (London: Anglo-German Foundation Report Series, December 1999).
70. Jelinek, M. and Schoonhoven, C.B., *The Innovation Marathon* (Oxford: Basil Blackwell, 1990).
71. Case based on 2005 interviews with Daniel Scuka, co-founder and business manager at Wireless Watch Japan (www.wirelesswatch.jp) and John Lagerling of the DoCoMo i-mode Global Strategy Department in Tokyo; a Fujitsu technical director in 2008; company documentation on the Internet, several company reports as cited separately and: Hunter, J., Chan Kim, W. and Mauborgne, R., 'NTT DoCoMo I-mode: Value Innovation at DoCoMo', *INSEAD-EAC Case Study*, Number 303–04301 (Fontainebleau, France, 2003).
72. NTT-DoCoMo, 'DoCoMo Initiatives to Develop Energy-Efficient Mobile Phones', *NTT DoCoMo Report* (December 2002), p. 9.

73. NTT-DoCoMo, 'The Use of Cell Phones/PHS Phones in Everyday Urban Life', *NTT DoCoMo Report* (November 2000).
74. NTT-DoCoMo, 'Current Trends in Mobile Phone Usage Among Adolescents', *NTT DoCoMo Report* (March 2001).

2   INNOVATION AND ECONOMICS

1. Rosegger, G., *The Economics of Production and Innovation* (Oxford: Butterworth-Heinemann, 3rd Edition, 1996), p. 10.
2. Shionoya, Y. and Perlman, M. (eds), *Schumpeter in the History of Ideas* (USA: The University of Michigan Press, 1994).
3. Schumpeter, J. A., *The Theory of Economic Development* (Boston, MA: Harvard University Press, 1934).
4. Geroski, P. A., *Market Structure, Corporate Performance and Innovative Activity* (Oxford: Clarendon Press, 1994).
5. Chan, V., Musso, C. and Shankar, V., 'Assessing Innovation Metrics: Mckinsey Global Survey Results', *The McKinsey Quarterly*, No. 4 (November 2008).
6. Iansiti, M. and West, J., 'Technology Integration: Turning Great Research into Great Products', *Harvard Business Review*, Vol. 75, No. 3 (May–June 1997), pp. 69–79.
7. Schumpeter, J. A., *Capitalism, Socialism and Democracy* (New York: Harper & Row, 3rd Edition, 1950).
8. See for example Bound, J., Cummins, C., Griliches, Z., Hall, B. H. and Jaffe A., 'Who Does R&D and Who Patents?', in Griliches, Z. (ed.), *R&D, Patents and Productivity* (Chicago: University of Chicago Press, 1984), pp. 21–54; and Klette, T. J. and Griliches, Z., 'Empirical Patterns of Firm Growth and R&D Investment: A Quality Ladder Model Interpretation', The Institute for Fiscal Studies London, Working Paper no. 25 (1999).
9. Hanson, J. A., 'Innovation, Firm Size and Age', *Small Business Economics*, Vol. 4 (1992), pp. 37–44.
10. Wakasugi, R. and Koyata, F., 'R&D, Firm Size and Innovation Outputs: Are Japanese Firms Efficient in Product Development?', *Journal of Product Innovation Management*, Vol. 14, No. 3 (May 1997), pp. 383–392.
11. Audretsch, D. and Vivarelli, M., 'Firm Size and R&D Spillovers', *Small Business Economics*, No. 8 (1996), pp. 249–258.
12. Geroski, P. A., *Market Structure, Corporate Performance and Innovative Activity* (Oxford: Clarendon Press, 1994).
13. Cohen, W. and Klepper, S., 'A Reprise of Size and R&D', *The Economic Journal*, No. 106 (1996), pp. 925–951.
14. Brynjolfsson, E. and Kahin, B. (eds), *Understanding the Digital Economy: Data, Tools and Research* (Cambridge, MA: The MIT Press, 2000).
15. *Ibid.*
16. Gwynne, P., 'As R&D Penetrates the Service Sector, Researchers Must Fashion New Methods of Innovation Management', *Research-Technology Management*, Vol. 41, No. 5 (September–October 1998), pp. 2–4.
17. Djellal, F. and Gallouj, F., 'Innovation Surveys for Service Industries: A Review', in Thuriaux, B. Arnold, E. and Couchot, C. (eds), *Innovation and Enterprise Creation: Statistics and Indicators* (European Communities, 2001), pp. 70–76.
18. Koenig, H., Buscher, H. S. and Licht, G., 'Employment, Investment and Innovation at Firm Level', *OECD, The OECD Jobs Study – Investment Productivity and Employment* (Paris: Organisation for Economic Co-operation and Development, OECD, 1995).
19. See for example: *OECD Science, Technology and Industry Outlook 2000* (Paris: Organisation for Economic Co-operation and Development, OECD, 2000), pp. 161–183.
20. Cowan, R. and van de Paal, G., *Innovation Policy in a Knowledge-Based Economy* (Luxembourg: European Commission, Publication no. 17023, June 2000).
21. Bhide, A., *The Venturesome Economy* (Princeton, NJ: Princeton University Press, 2008).
22. Cowan, R. and van de Paal, G., *Innovation Policy in a Knowledge-Based Economy* (Luxembourg: European Commission, Publication no. 17023, June 2000).

23. Yamashina, H., 'Japanese Manufacturing Strategy – Competing with the Tigers', *Business Strategy Review*, Vol. 7, No. 2 (Summer 1996), pp. 23–36.
24. www.archi.net.au, accessed in February 2004.
25. Archibugi, D. and Iammarino, S., 'The Policy Implications of the Globalisation of Innovation', in Archibugi, D., Howells, J. and Michie J. (eds), *Innovation Policy in a Global Economy* (Cambridge: Cambridge University Press, 1999).
26. 'Innovation Policy in Europe 2001', *European Commission, Innovation Papers*, No. 17.
27. Kuntze, U., 'Research and Technology Policies and Sustainable Development – the Situation in the USA, Japan, Sweden and the Netherlands', in Meyer-Krahmer, F. (ed.), *Innovation and Sustainable Development – Lessons for Innovation Policies* (Heidelberg, Germany: Physica Verlag, 1998), pp. 187–202.
28. See for example: Roper, S., Ashcroft, B., Love, J. H., Dunlop, S., Hofmann, H. and Vogler-Ludwig, K., *Product Innovation and Development in UK, German and Irish Manufacturing* (Belfast: Northern Ireland Economic Research Centre – The Queens University of Belfast, and Glasgow: Fraser of Allander Institute – University of Strathclyde (March 1996).
29. European Commission, Luxembourg, *Entrepreneurial Innovation in Europe* (Report EUR 17051, 2003).
30. ESN, Brussels, *European Trend Chart on Innovation* (Brussels: European Commission, 2000).
31. Burda, M. and Wyplosz, C., *Macroeconomics: A European Text* (Oxford: Oxford University Press, 2001).
32. Gordon, R. J., 'Does the "New Economy" Measure up to the Great Inventions of the Past?', *Journal of Economic Perspectives*, Vol. 14, No. 4 (2000), pp. 49–74.
33. *Ibid.*
34. Burda, M. and Wyplosz, C., *Macroeconomics: A European Text* (Oxford: Oxford University Press, 2001).
35. Arena, R. and Dangel-Hagnauer, C. (eds), *The Contribution of Joseph Schumpeter to Economics* (London: Routledge, 2002).
36. McGuigan, J. R., Moyer, R. C. and Harris, F. H. D., *Managerial Economics: Applications, Strategy and Tactics* (Cincinnati, OH: South Western – Thompson Learning, 2002).
37. Grossmann, G. M. and Helpmann, E., *Innovation and Growth in the Global Economy* (The MIT Press, 1991).
38. The importance of SMEs has been identified in many publications. See, for example: Thuriaux, B., Arnold, E. and Couchot, C. (eds), *Innovation and Enterprise Creation: Statistics and Indicators* (Brussels: European Commission, 2001), Publication no. 17038.
39. Tether, B. and Massini, S., 'Employment Creation in Small Technological and Design Innovators in the UK during the 1980's', *Small Business Economics*, Vol. 11, No. 4 (1998), pp. 353–370.
40. Roper, S., Ashcroft, B., Love, J. H., Dunlop, S., Hofmann, H. and Vogler-Ludwig, K., *Product Innovation and Development in UK, German and Irish Manufacturing* (Belfast: Northern Ireland Economic Research Centre – The Queens University of Belfast, and Glasgow: Fraser of Allander Institute – University of Strathclyde (March 1996).
41. De Meyer, A. and Pycke, B., 'Falling Behind in Innovation: The 1996 Report on the European Manufacturing Futures Survey', *INSEAD Working Paper Series*, No. 96/95/TM (1996).
42. Chan, A., Go, F. M. and Pine, R., 'Service Innovation in Hong Kong: Attitudes and Practice', *Service Industries Journal*, Vol. 18, No. 2 (April 1998), pp. 112–124.
43. Ali, A., 'Pioneering versus Incremental Innovation: Review and Research Propositions', *Journal of Product Innovation Management*, Vol. 11, No. 1 (January 1994), pp. 46–61.
44. Loch, C., Stein, L. and Terwiesch, C., 'Measuring Development Performance in the Electronics Industry', *Journal of Product Innovation Management*, Vol. 13, No. 1 (January 1996), pp. 3–20.
45. Based on an MBA assignment by Dannenhauer, M. (February 2003) and information from www.extricom.de. Used with permission.
46. Ryan, B. and Gross, N. C., 'The Diffusion of Hybrid Seed Corn in Two Iowa Communities', *Rural Sociology*, Vol. 8 (1943), pp. 15–24.
47. Rogers, E. M., *Diffusion of Innovations* (New York: The Free Press, 1995).
48. *Ibid.*, Chapter 6.
49. Based on an MBA presentation prepared by Gamarci, R. (February 2003), used with permission; and the company's website, www.repsol.com.
50. *Ibid.*, Chapter 7.
51. Moore, G. A., *Crossing the Chasm* (New York: HarperBusiness, 1991).

52. *Ibid.*
53. Based on Rogers, E. M., *Diffusion of Innovations* (New York: The Free Press, 1995), chapter 1.
54. Case study based on Prahalad (ref 56), Ramesh Menon 'Aravind Eye: Infinite Vision' in *India Today* (17 March 2009), and www.aravind.org.
55. Prahalad, C.K., *The Fortune at the Bottom of the Pyramid.* (Upper Saddle River, NJ: Pearson Education, 2005).
56. *Ibid.*

3   CONTRASTING SERVICES WITH MANUFACTURING

1. Forfas, *Services Innovation in Ireland – Options for Innovation Policy.* A report commissioned by Forfas from CM International (2006), p. 10.
2. Griffin, A., Gleason, G., Preiss, R. and Shevenaugh, D., 'Best Practice for Customer Satisfaction in Manufacturing Firms', *Sloan Management Review*, Vol. 36, No. 2 (Winter 1995), pp. 87–98.
3. Djellal, F. and Gallouj, F., 'Innovation Surveys for Service Industries: A Review', in Thuriaux, B., Arnold, E. and Couchot, C. (eds), *Innovation and Enterprise Creation: Statistics and Indicators* (European Communities, 2001), pp. 77–87.
4. *Ibid.*
5. See, for example: Forfas, *Services Innovation in Ireland – Options for Innovation Policy.* A report commissioned by Gorfaas from CM International (2006) and; NESTA (UK) *Service Innovation in Services.* NESTA report NI/15 (July 2008), UK.
6. Sheram, K. and Soubbotina, T.P., *Beyond Economic Growth: Meeting the Challenges of Global Development* (New York: World Bank Publications, 2000).
7. Gwynne, P., 'As R&D Penetrates the Service Sector, Researchers Must Fashion New Methods of Innovation Management', *Research-Technology Management*, Vol. 41, No. 5 (September–October 1998), pp. 2–4.
8. Steele, J. and Murray, M.A. P., 'The Application of Structured Exploration to Develop a Culture of Innovation', Chartered Institute of Building Engineers – National Conference 2001, UK.
9. Gwynne, P., 'As R&D Penetrates the Service Sector, Researchers Must Fashion New Methods of Innovation Management', *Research-Technology Management*, Vol. 41, No. 5 (September–October 1998), pp. 2–4.
10. Chan Kim, W. and Mauborgne, R., 'Value Innovation: The Strategic Logic of High Growth', *Harvard Business Review*, Vol. 75, No. 1 (January–February 1997), pp. 103–112.
11. Goffin, K., 'Evaluating the Product Use Cycle: Design for Service and Support', in Loch, C. and Kavadias, S. (eds) *Managing Product Development,* Butterworth Heineman (Elsevier, 2007), pp. 467–493.
12. Knecht, T., Lezinski, R. and Weber, F.A., 'Making Profits after the Sale', *The McKinsey Quarterly*, No. 4 (1993), pp. 79–86.
13. Goffin, K. and New, C., 'Customer Support and New Product Development – an Exploratory Study', *International Journal of Operations & Production Management*, Vol. 21, No. 3 (2001), pp. 275–301.
14. Case based on material published on the Jura website: http://www.jura.com/
15. United Nations, *Manual on Statistics of International Trade in Services* (New York: United Nations Publications, 2002), p. 7.
16. Storey, C. and Easingwood, C.J., 'The Augmented Service Offering: A Conceptualization and Study of Its Impact on New Service Success', *Journal of Product Innovation Management*, Vol. 15, No. 4 (1998), pp. 335–351.
17. Johne, A. and Storey, C., 'New Service Development: A Review of the Literature and Annotated Bibliography', City University Business School, *Management Working Paper* B97/2 (April 1997).
18. Bitner, M. J., 'Servicescapes: The Impact of Physical Surroundings on Customers and Employees', *Journal of Marketing*, Vol. 56 (April 1992), pp. 57–71.
19. Bennett, D. J. and Bennett, J. D., 'Making the Scene', in Stone, G. and H. Farberman (eds), *Social Psychology through Symbolic Interactionism* (Waltham, MA: Ginn-Blaisdell, 1970, 2nd Edition New York: Wiley, 1981), pp. 190–196.
20. Case based on Lunsford, J. L. and Michaels, D., 'Aircraft Designers Are Masters of Illusion', *The Wall Street Journal Europe* (Monday, 25 November 2002), p. A5 and McCartney, S., 'Easing Cabin Pressure', *The Wall Street Journal Europe* (Wednesday 29 June 2005), p. A5.

21. Lunsford, J. L., 'Boeing "Dreamliner" Sets Ambitious Course', *The Wall Street Journal Europe* (Tuesday, 18 November 2003), p. A10.

22. Based partly on Russell, R. S. and Taylor III, B. W., *Operations Management: Focusing on Quality and Competitiveness* (London: Prentice-Hall International, 1998), pp. 212–215.

23. Verma, R., 'An Empirical Analysis of Management Challenges in Service Factories, Service Shops, Mass Services and Professional Services', *International Journal of Service Industry Management*, Vol. 11, No. 1 (2000), pp. 8–25.

24. Prystay, C; 'Long-Distance Learning', *The Wall Street Journal Europe*, (Tuesday July 5, 2005), pA6.

25. Based on www.dialaflight.com

26. Tether, B. and Miles, I., 'Surveying Innovation in Services – Measurement and Policy Interpretation Issues', in Thuriaux, B., Arnold, E. and Couchot, C. (eds), *Innovation and Enterprise Creation: Statistics and Indicators* (European Communities, 2001), pp. 77–87.

27. Parasuraman, A., Zeithaml, V. A. and Malhotra, A., *Journal of Service Research*, Vol. 7, No. 3 (February 2005), pp. 213–233.

28. Van Dyke, T. P., Prybutpk, V. R. and Kappelman, L. A., 'Cautions on the Use of the SERVQUAL Measure to Access the Quality of Information Systems Services', *Decision Sciences*, Vol. 30, No. 3 (Summer 1999), pp. 1–15.

29. Khan, A., 'Perceived Service Quality in the Air Freight Industry', *Ph.D. Thesis* (Cranfield School of Management, 1993).

30. Johne, A. and Storey, C., 'New Service Development: A Review of the Literature and Annotated Bibliography', City University Business School, *Management Working Paper* B97/2 (April 1997).

31. Storey, C. and Easingwood, C. J., 'The Augmented Service Offering: A Conceptualization and Study of Its Impact on New Service Success', *Journal of Product Innovation Management*, Vol. 15, No. 4 (1998), pp. 335–351.

32. Hipp, C., Tether, B. S. and Miles, I., 'The Incidence and Effects of Innovation in Services: Evidence from Germany', *International Journal of Innovation Management*, Vol. 4, No. 4 (December 2000), pp. 417–453.

33. Christensen, C. M. and Tedlow, R., 'Patterns of Disruption in Retailing', *Harvard Business Review*, Vol. 78, No. 1 (January–February 2000), pp. 42–45.

34. Lievens, A. and Moenert, R. K., 'New Service Teams as Information-Processing Systems', *Journal of Service Research*, Vol. 3, No. 1 (August 2000), pp. 46–65.

35. Rich, M., 'Hospital Design Is Tied to Health', *The Wall Street Journal Europe* (Thursday, 28 November 2002), p. A8.

36. Froehle, C. M., Roth, A. V., Chase, R. B. and Voss, C. A., 'Antecedents of New Service Development Effectiveness: An Exploratory Examination of Strategic Operations Choices', *Journal of Service Research*, Vol. 3, No. 1 (August 2000), pp. 3–17.

37. Metters, R., King-Metters, K. and Pullman, M., *Successful Service Operations Management* (Mason, OH: Thompson South-Western, 2003).

38. Tether, B. and Miles, I., 'Surveying Innovation in Services – Measurement and Policy Interpretation Issues', in Thuriaux, B., Arnold, E. and Couchot, C. (eds), *Innovation and Enterprise Creation: Statistics and Indicators* (European Communities, 2001), pp. 77–87.

39. Johne, A. and Storey, C., 'New Service Development: A Review of the Literature and Annotated Bibliography', City University Business School, *Management Working Paper* B97/2 (April 1997).

40. *Ibid.*

41. Menor, L. J., Tatikonda, M. V. and Sampson, S. E., 'New Service Development: Areas for Exploitation and Exploration', *Journal of Operations Management*, Vol. 20, No. 2 (2002), pp. 135–157.

42. Based on an unpublished case: Smart, P., Goffin, K., Jaina, J., Keliher, C. and Kwiatowski, R., 'Creating a Culture of Innovation at AXA Ireland', Cranfield School of Management 2006; company information gathered in regular interviews (between 2000–08); and from the Internet.

4   DEVELOPING AN INNOVATION STRATEGY

1. Takahashi, D., *Opening the X Box* (Roseville, CA: Prima Publishing, 2002).

2. Case based on an interview with Klaus Stemig; articles in the press such as Martens, H. 'Sprung ins Dunkle', *Der Spiegel*, no. 27, 2004, p. 97; and internal documentation from Allianz and Mondial.

3. Kano, N., Saraku, N., Takahashi, F. and Tsuji, S., 'Attractive Quality and Must-be Quality', in Hromi, J. (ed.), *The Best on Quality*, Vol. 7, ch. 10 (Milwaukee, WI: ASQC, 1996), pp. 165–186.

4. Matzler, K. and Hinterhuber, H., 'How To Make Product Development Projects More Successful by Integrating Kano's Model of Customer Satisfaction into Quality Function Deployment', *Technovation*, Vol. 18 (1998), pp. 25–38.

5. Burchill, G. W., *Concept Engineering: An Investigation of Time vs Market Orientation in Product Concept Development* (Boston, MA: MIT, 1993).

6. Information from the company's website and others.

7. 'Zara Thrives by Breaking All the Rules', *BusinessWeek* (9 October 2008).

8. Foster, R., *Innovation: The Attacker's Advantage* (New York: Summit Books, 1986).

9. Roussel, P. A., Saad, K. N. and Erickson, T. J., *Third Generation R&D. Managing the Link to Corporate Strategy* (USA: Arthur D. Little, 1991).

10. Foster, R., *Innovation: The Attacker's Advantage* (New York: Summit Books, 1986), p. 27.

11. *Ibid.*, pp. 118, 183.

12. (New York: Oxford University Press 1997), ch. 6 (Reprinted from *Business History Review*, Spring 1992).

13. Utterback, J. M., *Mastering the Dynamics of Innovation* (Boston, MA: Harvard Business School Press, 1996).

14. Abernathy, W. J. and Utterback, J., 'Patterns of Industrial Innovation', *Technology Review* (1978), pp. 40–7.

15. Rogers, E. M., *Diffusion of Innovations* (New York: The Free Press, 4th Edition, 1995), p. 8.

16. Gould, S. J., 'The Panda's Thumb of Technology', in Tushman, M. L. and Anderson, P. (eds), *Managing Strategic Innovation and Change* (New York: Oxford University Press, 1997), ch. 5 (Reprinted from *Natural History*, January 1987).

17. Nayak, P. R. and Ketteringham J. M., *Breakthroughs!* (New York: Rawson Associates, 1986).

18. Cusumano, M. A., Mylonadis, Y. and Rosenblum, R., 'Strategic Manoeuvring and Mass-Market Dynamics: The Triumph of VHS over Beta', in Tushman, M. L. and Anderson, P. (eds), *Managing Strategic Innovation and Change* (New York: Oxford University Press 1997), ch 6. (Reprinted from *Business History Review*, Spring, 1992).

19. Adapted from 'Value Innovation: The Strategic Logic of High Growth' by W. C. Kim and R. Mauborgne, *Harvard Business Review*, January–February 1997, pp. 103–112.

20. Christensen, C. M., *The Innovator's Dilemma* (Boston, MA: Harvard Business School Press, 1997).

21. Bower, J. L. and Christensen, C. M., 'Disruptive Technologies: Catching the Wave', *Harvard Business Review* (January–February 1995).

22. Christensen, C. M., *The Innovator's Dilemma* (Boston, MA: Harvard Business School Press, 1997).

23. Gilbert, C., 'The Disruption Opportunity', *Sloan Management Review* (Summer, 2003), pp. 27–32.

24. Charitou, C. D. and Markides, C. C., 'Responses to Disruptive Strategic Innovation', *Sloan Management Review* (Winter, 2003), pp. 55–63.

25. Schnaars, S. P., *Managing Imitation Strategies: How Late Entrants Seize Markets from Pioneers* (New York: Free Press, 1994).

26. Tellis, G. J. and Golder, P. N., *Will and Vision: How Latecomers Grow to Dominate Markets* (New York: McGraw-Hill, 2001).

27. See Kim, W. C. and Mauborgne, R. 'Value Innovation: The Strategic Logic of High Growth', *Harvard Business Review* (January–February 1997).

28. Kim, W. Chan and Mauborgne, R., *Blue Ocean Strategy* (Boston, MA: Harvard Business School Press, 2005).

29. *Ibid.*

30. Schoenberg, R., 'An Integrated Approach to Strategy Innovation', *European Business Journal* (2003), pp. 95–102.

31. Kim, W. Chan and Mauborgne, R., *Blue Ocean Strategy* (Boston, MA: Harvard Business School Press, 2005).

32. Anagnostopoulos, Z., Goffin, K. and Szwejczewski, M., 'Design for Supportability: Leading Edge Practices', *AFSM International – the Professional Journal*, Vol. 26, No. 3 (August 2001), pp. 50–54.

33. Mercer, M., 'Cat Launches Skid-Steers: Let the Games Begin! Caterpillar Introduces 1350 and 1500 lb Skid Steer Loaders', *Diesel Progress North American Edition*, Vol. 65, No. 3 (March 1999), p. 22.

34. *Ibid.*

35. Teece, D. J., 'Profiting from Technological Innovation: Implications for Integration, Collaboration, Licensing and Public Policy', *Research Policy*, Vol. 15 (1986), pp. 285–305.

36. Gladwell, M., *The Tipping Point* (London: Little, Brown, 2000).

37. See for example, 'A World of Work. A Survey of Outsourcing', in *The Economist* (13 November 2004).

38. Quoted in Jonash, R. S., 'Strategic Technology Leveraging: Making Outsourcing Work for You', *Research-Technology Management*, Vol. 39, No. 2 (1996), pp. 19–36.

39. Quoted in Chesbrough, H. W. and Teece, D. J., 'When Is Virtual Virtuous?', *Harvard Business Review* (January–February, 1996), pp. 65–73.

40. Chesbrough, H., *Open Innovation: The New Imperative for Creating and Profiting from Technology* (Boston, MA: Harvard University Press, 2006).

41. Quoted by Chesbrough, H., *Open Innovation: The New Imperative for Creating and Profiting from Technology* (Boston, MA: Harvard University Press, 2006).

42. Burgelman, R. A. and Valikangas, L., 'Managing Internal Corporate Venturing', *MIT Sloan Management Review* (Summer 2005), pp. 20–34.

43. McGrath, R. G., Keil, T. and Tukainen, T., 'Extracting Value from Corporate Venturing', *MIT Sloan Management Review* (Fall 2006), pp. 50–56.

44. Chatterji, D., 'Accessing External Sources of Technology', *Research-Technology Management* (March–April, 1996), pp. 48–58.

45. Nambisan, S. and Sawhney, M., 'A Buyers Guide to the Innovation Bazaar', *Harvard Business Review* (June 2007).

46. Doz, Y. and Hamel, G., 'Alliance Advantage: The Art of Creating Value through Partnerships' (Boston, MA: Harvard Business School Press, 1998).

47. Mortara, L. et al. 'Implementing Open Innovation: Cultural Issues', *ISPIM Conference*, Tours (France) (June 2008).

48. A detailed account of the venture is given in Takahashi, D. *Opening the X Box*. (Roseville, CA: Prima Publishing, 2002).

49. Takahashi, D., *Opening the X Box* (Roseville, CA: Prima Publishing, 2002).

50. *Ibid.*, p. 151.

51. Harris R. C., Insinga, R. C., Morone, J. and Werle, M. J., 'The Virtual R&D Laboratory', *Research Technology Management*, Vol. 39, No. 2 (1996), pp. 32–36.

52. Chesborough, H. W. and Teece, D. J., 'When Is Virtual Virtuous?', *Harvard Business Review* (January–February, 1996), pp. 65–73.

53. Phaal, R., Farrukh, C. J. P. and Probert, D. R., 'Strategic Roadmapping: A Workshop-Based Approach for Identifying and Exploring Innovation Issues and Opportunities', *Engineering Management Journal*, Vol. 19, No. 1 (2007), pp. 16–24.

54. McMillan, A., 'Roadmapping-Agent of Change', *Research-Technology Management* (2003), pp. 40–7.

55. Willyard, C. H. and McClees, C. W., 'Motorola's Technology Roadmap Process', *Research Management* (1987), pp. 13–19.

56. Groeneveld, P., 'Roadmapping Integrates Business and Technology', *Research-Technology Management* (1997), pp. 48–55.

57. Barker, D. and Smith, D. J. H., 'Technology Foresight Using Roadmaps', *Long Range Planning*, Vol. 28 (1995), pp. 21–28.

58. See, for example, http.//www.public.itrs.net.

59. www.foresightvehicle.org.uk.

60. Phaal, R., Farrukh, C., Mitchell, R. and Probert, D., 'Starting-Up Roadmapping Fast', *Research-Technology Management* (2003), pp. 52–28.

61. Albright, R. E. and Kappel, T. A., 'Roadmapping in the Corporation', *Research-Technology Management* (2003), pp. 31–40.

62. Van der Heijden, K., *Scenarios, The Art of Strategic Conversation* (New York: John Wiley, 1996, 2005).

63. Schwarz, P., *The Art of the Long View* (New York: Doubleday, 1991).

64. Ringland, G., *Scenario Planning. Managing for the Future* (John Wiley, Chichester, 1998).

65. According to Schwartz and Ogilvy in chapter 4 of Fahey, L. and Randall, R. (eds), *Learning from the Future* (New York: John Wiley, 1998).

66. Utterback, J. M., *Mastering the Dynamics of Innovation* (Boston, MA: Harvard Business School Press, 1996).
67. Henderson, R. M. and Clark, K. B., 'Architectural Innovation: The Reconfiguration of Existing Product Technologies and the Failure of Established Firms', *Administrative Science Quarterly*, Vol. 35 (1990), pp. 9–30.
68. Cooper, A. C. and Smith, C. G., 'How Established Firms Respond to Threatening Technologies', *Academy of Management Executive*, Vol. 6 (1992), pp. 55–70.
69. Loutfy, R. and Belkhir, L., 'Managing R&D at Xerox', *Research-Technology Management*, Vol. 44 (2001), pp. 15–24.
70. Gilbert, C., 'The Disruption Opportunity', *Sloan Management Review* (Summer, 2003), pp. 27–32.
71. Utterback, J. M., *Mastering the Dynamics of Innovation* (Boston, MA: Harvard Business School Press, 1996).

5   GENERATING CREATIVE CUSTOMER-FOCUSED IDEAS

1. Donkin, R., 'Recruitment: Men in the Empty Suits – Management Hierarchies and Concerns May be Stifling Innovation', *Financial Times* (6 December 1995), p. 202.
2. Amabile, T. M., 'How to Kill Creativity', *Harvard Business Review*, Vol. 76, No. 5 (September–October 1998), pp. 77–87.
3. Couger, J. D., *Creative Problem Solving and Opportunity Finding* (Danvers, MA: Boyd and Fraser, 1995).
4. Thomke, S. and Fujimoto, T., 'The Effect of "Front-Loading" Problem-Solving on Product Development Performance', *Journal of Product Innovation Management*, Vol. 17, No. 2 (March 2000), pp. 128–142.
5. Hargadon, A. and Sutton, R. I., 'Building an Innovation Factory', *Harvard Business Review*, Vol. 78, No. 3 (May–June 2000), p. 157.
6. Tyrrell, P., *Fertile Ground: Cultivating a Talent for Innovation.* Economist Intelligence Unit, (London, 2009), p. 6.
7. Csikszentmihalyi, M., *Creativity: Flow and the Psychology of Discovery and Invention* (New York: HarperCollins, 1996).
8. Amabile, T. M., Hadley, C. N. and Kramer, S. J., 'Creativity Under the Gun', *Harvard Business Review*, Vol. 80, No. 8 (August 2002), pp. 52–61.
9. Amabile, T. M., 'Minding the Muse', *Working Knowledge – a Quarterly Report on Research at Harvard Business School*, Vol. IV, No. 1 (1999).
10. Based on presentations by Fisher, J. H. at Cranfield School of Management in 1996 and 1997.
11. Nemeth, C. J., 'Managing Innovation: When Less Is More', *California Management Review*, Vol. 40, No. 1 (Fall 1997), pp. 59–74.
12. Hayes, N., *Managing Teams: A Strategy for Success* (London: Thompson Learning, 2002).
13. Couger, J. D., *Creative Problem Solving and Opportunity Finding* (Boyd and Fraser, 1995).
14. Tyrrell, P., *Fertile Ground: Cultivating a Talent for Innovation.* Economist Intelligence Unit (London, 2009).
15. Koestler, A., *The Act of Creation* (London: Hutchinson, 1964).
16. Ronney, E., Olfe, P. and Mazur, G. 'Gemba Research in the Japanese Cellular Phone Market' (Nokia Mobile Phones/QFD Institute, 11 May 2000). Available on the Internet.
17. *Ibid.*, p. 4.
18. Goldenberg, J. and Mazursky, D., *Creativity in Product Innovation* (Cambridge: Cambridge University Press, 2002).
19. Altshuller, G., *And Suddenly the Inventor Appeared* (Worchester, MA: Technical Innovation Center Inc, 1996).
20. Zhang, J., Chai, K-H. and Tan, K-C., 'Applying TRIZ to Service Conceptual Design: An Exploratory Study', *Creativity and Innovation Management*, Vol. 14, No. 1 (March, 2005), pp. 34–42.
21. Ambrosini, V. and Bowman, C., 'Tacit Knowledge: Some Suggestions for Operationalization', *Journal of Management Studies*, Vol. 38, No. 6 (September, 2001), pp. 811–829.
22. Case adapted from Goffin, K. and Mitchell, R. 'The Customer Holds the Key to Great Products', *Financial Times*, FT Mastering Uncertainty, (Friday, 24 March 2006), pp. 10–11.
23. Nonaka, I., 'The Knowledge-Creating Company', *Harvard Business Review*, Vol. 85, No. 7/8 (November–December, 1991), pp. 96–104.
24. Nonaka, I., Toyama, R. and Byosiere, P., 'A Theory of Organizational Knowledge Creation: Understanding the Dynamic Process of Creating Knowledge', in Dierkes, M. Berthoin Antal, A. Child, J. and

Nonaka, I. (eds), *Handbook of Organizational Learning and Knowledge* (Oxford: Oxford University Press, 2001), pp. 491–517.

25. Koners, U. and Goffin, K., 'Learning from Post-Project Reviews: A Cross-Case Analysis', *Journal of Product Innovation Management*, Vol. 24, No. 3 (May 2007), pp. 242–258.

26. Brailsford, T. W., 'Building a Knowledge Community at Hallmark Cards', *Research-Technology Management*, Vol. 44, No. 5 (September–October 2001), pp. 18–25.

27. Herstatt, C. and Sander, J. G. (eds), *Produktentwicklung mit virtuellen Communities* (Product Development with Virtual Communities) (Wiesbaden: Gabler, 2004).

28. Hargadon, A. and Sutton, R. I., 'Building an Innovation Factory', *Harvard Business Review*, Vol. 78, No. 3 (May–June 2000), pp. 157–166.

29. Saban, K., Lanasa, J., Lackman, C. and Peace, G., 'Organizational Learning: A Critical Component to New Product Development', *Journal of Product and Brand Management*, Vol. 9, No. 2 (2000), p. 101.

30. Senge, P. M., *The Fifth Discipline: The Art and Practice of the Learning Organization* (Century Business Press, 1990).

31. Balachandra, R. and Friar, J. H., 'Factors for Success in R&D Projects and New Product Innovation: A Contextual Framework', *IEEE Trans. on Engineering Management*, Vol. 44, No. 3 (August 1997), pp. 276–287.

32. Cooper, R. G. and Kleinschmidt, E. J., 'Major New Products: What Distinguishes the Winners in the Chemical Industry?', *Journal of Product Innovation Management*, Vol. 10, No. 2 (March 1993), pp. 90–111.

33. Heygate, R., 'Why Are We Bungling Process Innovation?', *The McKinsey Quarterly*, No. 2 (1996), pp. 130–141.

34. Athaide, G. A., Meyers, P. W. and Wilemon, D. L., 'Seller-Buyer Interactions during the Commercialization of Technological Process Innovations', *Journal of Product Innovation Management*, Vol. 13, No. 5 (September 1996), pp. 406–421.

35. Sandberg, K. D., 'Focus on the Benefits', *Harvard Management Communication Newsletter*, Vol. 5, No. 4 (2002), pp. 3–4.

36. Magnusson, P. R., Matthing, J. and Kristensson, P., 'Managing Service Involvement in Service Innovation: Experiments with Innovating End Users', *Journal of Service Research*, Vol. 6, No. 2 (November 2003), pp. 111–124.

37. Oppenheim, A. N., *Questionnaire Design, Interviewing and Attitude Measurement* (London: Printer, 2nd Edition, 1992).

38. Dillman, D. A., *Mail and Internet Surveys – the Tailored Design Method* (New York: John Wiley, 2nd Edition, 2002).

39. Green, P. E., Tull, D. S. and Albaum, G., *Research for Marketing Decisions* (London: Prentice-Hall International, 1988).

40. Kärkkainen, H., Piippo, P., Puumalainen, K. and Tuominen, M., 'Assessment of Hidden and Future Customer Needs in Finnish Business-to-Business Companies', *R&D Management*, Vol. 31, No. 4 (2001), pp. 391–407.

41. Goffin, K., 'Repertory Grid Technique', in Partington, D. (ed.) *Essential Skills for Management Research* (London: SAGE Publications, 2002).

42. Goffin, K., 'Understanding Customers' Views: A Practical Example of the Use of Repertory Grid Technique', *Management Research News*, Vol. 17, No. 7/8 (1994), pp. 17–28.

43. Leonard-Barton, D., *Wellsprings of Knowledge: Building and Sustaining the Sources of Innovation* (Boston, MA: Harvard Business School Press, 1995), p. 194.

44. Prahalad, C. K. *The Fortune at the Bottom of the Pyramid* (Pearson Education: Wharton School Publishing, Pennsylvania, 2005).

45. Bijapurkar, B. 'In Jugaad Land', *The Week* (31 August 2008), pp. 16–28.

46. Leonard-Barton, D. and Rayport, J. F., 'Spark Innovation through Empathic Design', *Harvard Business Review*, Vol. 75, No. 6 (November–December 1997), pp. 102–113.

47. Robson, C., *Real World Research* (Oxford: Blackwell, 1993).

48. Based discussions with Chris Towns of Clarks and: Towns, C. and Humphries, D., 'Breaking New Ground in Customer Behavioural Research: Experience from Clarks/PDD', *Product Development Management Association UK & Ireland Conference*, London, (November, 2001).

49. Burns, A., Barrett, R., Evans, S. and Johansson, C., 'Delighting Customers through Empathic Design', 6th International Product Development Management Conference (5–6 July 1999), pp. 157–171.

50. Rosier, B., 'From the Dreams of Children to the Future of Technology', *The Independent on Sunday* (UK) (15 July 2001), p. 8.

51. Herstatt, C., 'Search Fields for Radical Innovations Involving Market Research', Technical University of Hamburg-Harburg, Germany, Working Paper No. 10 (2001).

52. Koerner, B. I., 'Geeks in Toyland', *Wired* (February 2006), pp. 108–150.

53. Herstatt, C. and von Hippel E., 'Developing New Product Concepts via the Lead User Method: A Case Study in a "Low-Tech" Field', *Journal of Product Innovation Management*, Vol. 9, No. 3 (September 1992), pp. 213–221.

54. Thomke, S. and von Hippel, E., 'Customers as Innovators: A New Way to Create Value', *Harvard Business Review*, Vol. 80, No. 2 (March–April 2002), pp. 74–81.

55. Bartl, M., Ernst, H. and Fueller, J., 'Community Based Innovation – eine Methode zur Einbindung von Online Communities in den Innovationsprozess', in Herstatt, C. and Sander, J. G. (eds) *Produktentwicklung mit virtuellen Communities* (Gabler: Wiesbaden, Germany, 2004).

56. Damian, J., 'Pushing the Limits of Crowdsourcing', Business Week (Online), New York (3 March 2009).

57. Bonabeau, E., 'Decisions 2.0: The Power of Collective Intelligence', *MIT Sloan Management Review*, Vol. 50, No. 2 (Winter 2009), pp. 45–52.

58. Caroll, J. D., Green, P. E. and Charturvedi, A., *Mathematical Tools for Applied Multivariate Analysis* (Oxford: Academic Press, 1997).

59. Gustafsson, A., Herrman, A. and Huber, F., *Conjoint Measurement: Methods and Applications* (Berlin, Germany: Springer-Verlag, 2nd Edition, 2001).

60. Burda, M. and Wyplosz, C., *Macroeconomics: A European Text* (Oxford: Oxford University Press, 2001), p. 446.

61. Winograd, B. and Lu-Tien Tan, C., 'Getting Copyright Protection for Fashion', *The Wall Street Journal Europe*, (Monday, 11 September 11, 2006), p. 29.

62. UK Trade Marks Act 1994.

63. Prystay, C., 'Crocodile Battle over Chinese Turf', *The Wall Street Journal Europe* (Friday/Saturday/Sunday, 2–4 April 2004), p. A7.

64. Aeppel, T., 'Brothers of Invention', *The Wall Street Journal Europe* (Tuesday, 20 April 2004), p. A12.

65. Kingston, W., *Enforcing Small Firms' Patent Rights* (Luxembourg: European Commission, 2000).

66. *Ibid.*

67. Pisano, G. P. and Wheelwright, S. C., 'The New Logic of High-Tech R&D', *Harvard Business Review*, Vol. 73, No. 5 (September–October 1995), pp. 93–105.

68. Case based on telephone interviews with Wim Obouter and Seth Bishop. For further details of the Micro products see: www.micro-mobility.com.

69. Case based on personal interviews with senior Texas Instruments managers in April 2003 and the following published material:

70. Parks, A., Edwards, C., Reinhardt, A. and Kunii, I. M., 'Dawn of the Superchip', *Business Week*, (4 November 2002), pp. 128A–128B.

71. http://www.ti.com/corp/docs/company/index.htm

72. Texas Instruments Incorporated 2002 Annual Report

73. http://www.ti.com/corp/docs/company/2000/c00061.shtml

74. Buchanan, M., 'Make Room for More Laws, Gordon', Electronic News, (28 October 2002), p. 19.

6   SELECTING AND MANAGING AN INNOVATION PORTFOLIO

1. Szwejczewski, M., Mitchell, R. and Lemke, F., 'A Study of R&D Portfolio Management among UK Organisations', *International Journal of Management and Decision Making*, Vol. 7, No. 6 (2006), pp. 604–616.

2. Chapman Wood, R. and Hamel, G., 'The World Bank's Innovation Market', *Harvard Business Review*, Vol. 80, No. 11 (November 2002), pp. 104–112.

3. Cooper, R. G., Edgett, S. J. and Kleinschmidt, E. J., *Portfolio Management for New Products* (Cambridge, MA: Perseus Books, 2nd Edition, 2001).

4. Ryan, G. and Ryan, P., 'Capital Budgeting Practices of the Fortune 1000: How Have Things Changed?', *Journal of Business and Management* (1 October 2002), pp. 1–10.

5. Brigham, E. F. and Erhardt, M. C., *Financial Management, Theory and Practice* (Thomson Learning, 10th Edition, 2002), p. 509.

6. Brealey, R. A. and Myers, S. C., *Principles of Corporate Finance* (New York: McGraw-Hill, 1996).

7. Perdue, R., 'Valuation of R&D Projects Using Options Pricing and Decision Analysis Models', *Interfaces*, Vol. 29 (1999), pp. 57–74.

8. Dixit, A. K. and Pindyck, R. S., *Investment under Uncertainty* (Princeton, NJ: Princeton University Press, 1994), p. 109.

9. Ryan, G. and Ryan, P., 'Capital Budgeting Practices of the Fortune 1000: How Have Things Changed?', *Journal of Business and Management* (2002), pp. 1–10.

10. Brigham, E. F. and Erhardt, M. C., *Financial Management, Theory and Practice* (Thomson Learning, 10th Edition, 2002), p. 509.

11. *Ibid.*

12. Bernstein, P. L., *Against the Gods: The Remarkable Story of Risk* (New York: John Wiley, 1998).

13. Hacking, I., *The Emergence of Probability: A Philosophical Study of Early Ideas* (London: Cambridge University Press, 1975).

14. Bernstein, P. L., *Against the Gods: The Remarkable Story of Risk* (New York: John Wiley, 1998).

15. Fleming, M. C. and Nellis, J. G., *Principles of Applied Statistics* (Thomson Learning, 2000), ch. 11.

16. Antikarov, V. and Copeland, T., *Real Options: A Practitioner's Guide* (New York: Texere, 2001), p. 24.

17. Hayes, R. H. and Abernathy, W. J., 'Managing Our Way to Economic Decline', *Harvard Business Review* (July–August 1980), pp. 67–77.

18. Boer, F. P., 'Risk-Adjusted Valuation of R&D Projects', *Research-Technology Management*, Vol. 46 (September–October 2003), pp. 50–58.

19. Brealey, R. A. and Myers, S. C., *Principles of Corporate Finance* (New York: McGraw-Hill, 1996).

20. Razgaitis, R., *Dealmaking Using Real Options and Monte-Carlo Analysis* (Hoboken, NJ: John Wiley, 2003).

21. For example, 'Crystal Ball' from Decisioneering (Denver Colorado), www.crystalball.com.

22. Mitchell R., Hunt F. and Probert D., 'Valuing and Comparing Small Portfolios', to be published in Research Technology Management in March 2010.

23. From the authors' project work with the company, with permission.

24. See, for example, Angelis, D. I., 'Capturing the Option Value of R&D', *Research-Technology Management*, Vol. 43, No. 4 (2000), pp. 32–4, or Boer, F. P., 'Valuation of Technology Using "Real Options"', *Research-Technology Management*, Vol. 43, No. 4 (2000), pp. 26–30.

25. For example, two papers by T.A. Luehrman: 'Investment Opportunities as Real Options: Getting Started on the Numbers', *Harvard Business Review* (July–August 1998), pp. 51–67, and 'Strategy as a Portfolio of Real Options', *Harvard Business Review* (September–October 1998), pp. 89–99.

26. Two useful books on the subject are: Razgaitis, R., *Dealmaking Using Real Options and Monte-Carlo Analysis* (Hoboken, NJ: John Wiley, 2003) and Howell, S., Stark, A., Newton, D., Paxson, D., Cavus, M., Pereira, J. and Patel, K., *Real Options. Evaluating Corporate Investment Options in a Dynamic World* (Harlow, England: Pearson Education, 2001). See also Perdue R., 'Valuation of R&D Projects Using Options Pricing and Decision Analysis Models', *Interfaces*, Vol. 29 (1999), pp. 57–74; Boer, F. P., 'Valuation of Technology Using "Real Options"', *Research-Technology Management*, Vol. 43 (2000), pp. 26–30; and Bowman, E. H. and Moskowitz, G. T., 'Real Options Analysis and Strategic Decision Making', *Innovation Science*, Vol. 12, No. 6 (2001), pp. 772–777.

27. Luenberger, D. G., *Investment Science* (New York: Oxford University Press, 1998).

28. Perlitz, M., Peske, T. and Schrank, R., 'Real Options Valuation: The New Frontier in R&D Project Evaluation?', *R&D Management*, Vol. 29, No. 3 (1999), pp. 255–269.

29. Luenberger, D. G., *Investment Science* (New York: Oxford University Press, 1998).

30. Cooper, R. G., Edgett, S. J. and Kleinschmidt, E. J., 'Portfolio Management in New Product Development: Lessons from the Leaders – 1', *Research-Technology Management*, Vol. 40 (September–October 1997), pp. 18–29.

31. Kaplan, R. S. and Norton, D. P., *The Balanced Scorecard: Translating Strategy into Action* (Harvard: Harvard Business School Press, 1996).

32. Cooper, R. G., Edgett, S. J. and Kleinschmidt, E. J., 'Portfolio Management in New Product Development: Lessons from the Leaders – 1', *Research-Technology Management*, Vol. 40 (September–October 1997), pp. 18–29.

33. Roussel, P. A., Saad, K. N. and Erickson, T. J., *Third Generation R&D. Managing the Link to Corporate Strategy* (Arthur D. Little, 1991).

34. Quoted in Cooper, R. G., Edgett, S. J. and Kleinschmidt, E. J., *Portfolio Management for New Products* (Cambridge, MA: Perseus Books, 2nd Edition, 2001), p. 53.

35. See in particular *Ibid.*, Cooper, R. G., Edgett, S. J. and Kleinschmidt (1997) and other publications by the same authors. Also Davis, C., 'Calculated Risk. A Framework for Evaluating Product Development', *Sloan Management Review* (Summer 2000), pp. 71–77, and Davis, J., Fusfield, A., Scriven, E. and Tritle, G., 'Determining a Project's Probability of Success', *Research-Technology Management*, Vol. 44 (May–June 2001), pp. 51–57.

36. Surowiecki, J., *The Wisdom of Crowds* (London: Little, Brown, 2004), ch. 9.

37. From the authors' project work with the company, with permission.

38. Case based on visits to Agilent 2005–2007, including interviews with Werner Widmann.

39. Graves, S. B., Ringuest, J. L. and Case, R. H., 'Formulating Optimal R&D Portfolios', *Research-Technology Management*, Vol. 43, No. 3 (2000), pp. 47–51.

40. Oke, A., 'Making It Happen: How to Improve the Innovative Capability of a Service Company', *Journal of Change Management*, Vol. 2, No. 3 (2002), pp. 272–281.

41. Case based on an interview with Dr Michael Mallon in December 2004, Goffin, K., Lee-Mortimer, A. and New, C., *Managing Product Innovation for Competitive Advantage* (Haymarket Business Publications, 1999), p. 42; and Mallon, M. J., Manufacturing Technology Acquisition, unpublished PhD thesis 2002, School of Engineering, Cranfield University, UK.

42. Davis, J., Fusfield, A., Scriven, E. and Tritle, G., 'Determining a Project's Probability of Success', *Research-Technology Management*, Vol. 44 (May–June 2001), pp. 51–57.

43. Case study compiled from Sharpe, P. and Keelin, T., 'How SmithKline Beecham Makes Better Resource Allocation Decisions', *Harvard Business Review* (March–April 1998) pp. 3–10.

44. Makridakis, S., Wheelwright, S. C. and Hyndman, R. J., *Forecasting: Methods and Applications* (New York: John Wiley, 1998).

45. Case adapted with permission from Goffin, K., Lee-Mortimer, A. and New, C., *Managing Product Innovation for Competitive Advantage* (London: Haymarket Publications, 1999).

46. Cooper, R. G., Edgett, S. J. and Kleinschmidt, E. J., *Portfolio Management for New Products* (Cambridge, MA: Perseus Books, 2nd Edition, 2001).

47. Case compiled from interviews with Mark Chizlett.

7   IMPLEMENTING INNOVATIONS

1. Case based on material from Organon and an interview with Erik Hoppenbrouwer in October 2004.

2. Reinertsen, D., *Managing the Design Factory: A Product Developer's Toolkit* (New York, London: The Free Press, 1997).

3. There are many good books on project management techniques. For example, Maylor, H., *Project Management* (Harlow, UK: Pearson Education, 3rd Edition, 2003); Baguley, P., *Managing Successful Projects. A Guide for Every Manager* (London: Pitman, 1995); Reiss, G., *Project Management Demystified* (London: E. & F. N. Spon, an imprint of Chapman and Hall, 2nd Edition, 1995).

4. Nevens, T. M., Summe, G. L. and Uttal, B., 'Commercializing Technology: What the Best Companies Do', *Harvard Business Review* (May–June 1990), pp. 154–162.

5. Datar, S., Jordan, C. C., Kekre, S., Rajiv, S. and Srinivasan, K., 'Advantages of Time-Based New Product Development in a Fast-Cycle Industry', *Journal of Marketing Research*, Vol. 34, No. 1 (February 1997), pp. 36–49.

6. Smith, P. G. and Reinertsen, D. G., *Developing Products in Half the Time* (New York: Van Nostrand Reinhold, 1991), ch. 2.

7. Reinertsen, D. G., 'Whodunnit? The Search for New Product Killers', *Electronic Business* (July 1983), pp. 62–66.

8. Maylor, H., *Project Management* (Harlow, UK: Pearson Education, 3rd Edition, 2003), p. 199.

9. Adapted with permission from *Getting Results. Case Studies of Innovation in the Public Service* by Alicia Wright and Virginia de Joux (Amherst Group Ltd).

10. Maylor, H., *Project Management* (Harlow, UK: Pearson Education, 3rd Edition, 2003), p. 106

11. Highsmith, J., *Agile Project Management* (Boston, MA: Pearson Education Inc, 2004)

12. See, for example, Poppendiek, M. and Poppendiek, T., *Lean Software Development: An Agile Toolkit* (Boston, MA: Addison-Wesley, 2003) and Larmon, C., *Agile and Iterative Development: A Manager's Guide* (Boston, MA: Addison-Wesley, 2004)

13. Thomke, S., 'Enlightened Experimentation. The New Imperative for Innovation', *Harvard Business Review* (February 2001), pp. 67–75.

14. Hartman, G. C. and Lakatos, A. I., 'Assessing Technology Risk: A Case Study', *Research-Technology Management* (March–April 1998), pp. 32–38.

15. Keizer, J. A., Halman, J. I. M. and Song, M., 'From Experience: Applying the Risk Diagnosing Methodology', *Journal of Product Innovation Management,* Vol. 19 (2002), pp. 213–232.

16. Bazerman, M. H., *Judgements in Managerial Decision-Making* (New York: John Wiley, 1990).

17. Janis, I. L., *Groupthink* (Boston, MA: Houghton-Mifflin, 1972).

18. See Keizer, J. A., Halman, J. I. M. and Song, M., 'From Experience: Applying the Risk Diagnosing Methodology', *Journal of Product Innovation Management,* Vol. 19 (2002), pp. 213–232.

19. Surowiecki, J., *The Wisdom of Crowds* (London: Little, Brown, 2004).

20. Kaiser, J. A., Halman, J. I. M. and Song, M., 'From Experience: Applying the Risk Diagnosing Methodology', *Journal of Product Innovation Management,* Vol. 19 (2002), pp. 213–232.

21. See Baxter, M., *Product Design: Practical Methods for the Systematic Development of New Products* (Cheltenham: Nelson Thornes, 1999) or any of the project management texts.

22. Keizer, J. A., Halman, J. I. M. and Song, M., 'From Experience: Applying the Risk Diagnosing Methodology', *Journal of Product Innovation Management,* Vol. 19 (2002), pp. 213–232.

23. Thomke, S., 'R&D Comes to Services', *Harvard Business Review,* Vol. 81, No. 4 (2003), pp. 71–79.

24. Clausing, D., *Total Quality Development* (New York: ASME Press, 1994).

25. Cohen, L., *Quality Function Deployment* (Reading, MA: Addison-Wesley 1995).

26. Matzler, K. and Hinterhuber, H. H., 'How to Make Product Development Projects More Successful by Integrating Kano's Model of Customer Satisfaction into Quality Function Deployment', *Technovation,* Vol. 18, No. 1 (1998), pp. 25–38.

27. Clausing, D., *Total Quality Development* (New York: ASME Press, 1994), p. 133.

28. Case based on a visit to Boxer in July 2009 and an interview with Angelique Green and Julian Gwyn-Owen in December 2009.

29. Bitner, M. J., Ostrom, A. L. and Morgan, F. N. 'Service Blueprinting: A Practical Technique for Service Innovation', *California Management Review,* Vol. 50, No. 3 (Spring 2008), pp. 66–94.

30. Berry, L. L., Shankar, V., Turner Parish, J., Cadwallader, S. and Dotzal, T., 'Creating New Markets through Service Innovation', *MIT Sloan Management Review,* Vol. 47, No. 2 (Winter 2006), pp. 56–63.

31. Clark, G., Johnston, R. and Shulver, M., 'Exploiting the Service Concept for Service Design and Development', in Fitzsimmons, J. A. and Fitzsimmons, M. J (eds), *New Service Development: Creating Memorable Experiences* (Thousand Oaks, CA: Sage, 2000).

32. Bitner, M. J., Ostrom, A. L. and Morgan, F. N., 'Service Blueprinting: A Practical Technique for Service Innovation', *California Management Review,* Vol. 50, No. 3 (Spring 2008), pp. 66–94.

33. Case based on an interview with Synthiea Kaldi, conducted by K. Goffin in March 2004.

34. Design Management Systems – Part 1: Guide to Managing Innovation. British Standard BS7000–1:1999, British Standards Institution: London, 1999.

35. Wheelwright, S. C. and Clarke, K. B., *Revolutionizing Product Development* (New York: The Free Press, 1992).

36. Martin, M. J. C., *Managing Innovation and Entrepreneurship in Technology-Based Companies* (New York: John Wiley, 1994).

37. Cooper, R. G., 'Third-Generation New Product Processes', *Journal of Product Innovation Management,* Vol. 11, No. 1 (1994), pp. 3–14.

38. Cooper, R. G., 'Stage Gate Systems for New Product Success', *Marketing Management,* Vol. 1, No. 4 (1992), pp. 20–29.

39. O'Connor, P., 'From Experience: Implementing a Stage-Gate Process: A Multi Company Perspective', *Journal of Production Innovation Management,* Vol. 11, No. 3 (1994), pp. 183–200.

40. Cooper, R. G., *Winning at New Products* (Cambridge, MA: Perseus, 3rd Edition, 2001) and Cooper, R. G., 'Stage Gate Systems for New Product Success', *Marketing Management,* Vol. 1, No. 4 (1992), pp. 20–29.

41. Cooper, R. G., 'Third Generation R&D processes', *Journal of Product Innovation Management*, Vol. 11, No. 1 (1994), pp. 3–44.

42. Wheelwright, S. C. and Clark, K., *Revolutionizing Product Development: Quantum Leaps in Speed, Efficiency, and Quality* (New York: The Free Press, 1992).

43. Bowen, H. K., Clark, K. B., Hollaway, C. A. and Wheelwright, S. C., 'Development Projects: The Engine of Renewal', *Harvard Business Review*, Vol. 72, No. 5 (September–October 1994), pp. 110–119.

44. Koners, U. and Goffin, K., 'Learning from Post-Project Reviews: A Cross-Case Analysis', *Journal of Product Innovation Management*, Vol. 24, No. 3 (May 2007), pp. 242–258.

45. Schindler, M. and Gassmann, O., 'Projektabwicklung gewinnt durch wissenschaftsmanagement: Ergebnisse einer empirischen Studie die Konzernentwicklung der Schindler Aufzüge AG', *Wissenschaftsmanagement*, Vol. 1 (January–February 2000), pp. 38–45.

46. Goffin, K. and Koners, U., 'Tacit and Explicit Learning in New Product Development', accepted for publication in the *Journal of Product Innovation Management* (2009–10).

47. Gobelli, D. H. and Brown, D. J., 'Improving the Process of Product Innovation', *Research-Technology Management* (March–April, 1993), pp. 38–44.

48. Cooper, R. G., 'Overhauling the New Product Introduction Process', *Industrial Marketing Management*, Vol. 25 (1996), pp. 465–482.

49. Shapiro, A., 'Stages in the Evolution of the Product Development Process', in McGrath, M. E., (ed.) *Setting the PACE in Product Development* (Boston, MA: Butterworth-Heinemann, 1996), p. 147.

50. Fraser, P., *Managing Product Development Collaborations* (Cambridge: University of Cambridge Institute for Manufacturing, 2003).

51. McGrath, M. E., (ed.) *Setting the PACE in Product Development* (Boston, MA: Butterworth-Heinemann, 1996), ch. 10, by Amram Shapiro.

52. Wheelwright, S. C. and Clark, K., *Revolutionizing Product Development: Quantum Leaps in Speed, Efficiency, and Quality* (New York: The Free Press, 1992), p. 91.

53. Adler, P. S., Mandelbaum, A., Nguen, V. and Schwerer, E., 'Getting the Most Out of Your Product Development Process', *Harvard Business Review* (March–April, 1996), pp. 4–15.

54. Fraser, P., Farrukh, C. and Gregory, M., 'Managing Product Development Collaborations – a Process Maturity Approach', *Proc. I. Mech. E.*, Vol. 217, part B (2003), pp. 1499–1519.

55. Harrigan, K., *Managing for Joint Venture Success* (Lexington, MA: Lexington Books, 1986).

56. Fraser, P., Farrukh, C. and Gregory, M., 'Managing Product Development Collaborations – a Process Maturity Approach', *Proc. I. Mech. E.*, Vol. 217, part B (2003), pp. 1499–1519.

57. Case based on interviews with Sachin Mulay and A. Vasudevan, Wipro Technologies, Bangalore August 2008; company documentation on the Internet (www.wipro.com); and the 2006–07 and 2007–08 Annual Reports.

8   CREATING AN INNOVATIVE CULTURE

1. Bratton, J. and Gold, J., *Human Resource Management: Theory and Practice* (Basingstoke: Palgrave Macmillan, 2003), p. 485.

2. de Brentani, U. and Kleinschmidt, E., 'Corporate Culture and Commitment: Impact on Performance of International New Product Development Programs', *Journal of Product Innovation Management*, Vol. 21, No. 5 (2004), pp. 309–333.

3. Jamrog, J., Vickers, M. and Bear, D., 'Building and Sustaining a Culture That Supports Innovation', *Human Resource Planning*, Vol. 29, No. 3 (2006), pp. 9–19.

4. Soupata, L., 'Managing Culture for Competitive Advantage at United Parcel Service', *Journal of Organizational Excellence* (Summer 2001), pp. 19–26.

5. *Ibid.*, p. 19.

6. Beckhard, R. and Harris, R. T., *Organization Transitions: Managing Complex Change* (London: Addison-Wesley, 1987).

7. Schein, E. H., 'Coming to a New Awareness of Organizational Culture', *Sloan Management Review*, Vol. 25, No. 4 (1984), pp. 3–16.

8. Johnson, G. and Scholes, K., *Exploring Corporate Strategy* (Edinburgh: Pearson Education Limited, 5th Edition, 1999).

9. Schein, E. H., 'Organizational Socialization and the Profession of Management', *Sloan Management Review*, Vol. 53, No. 3 (Fall 1988), pp. 53–65.

10. Balogun, J., Hope Hailey, V. with Johnson, G. and Scholes, K., *Exploring Strategic Change* (London: Prentice Hall, 1999), p. 196.

11. Heracleous, L., 'Spinning a Brand New Cultural Web', *People Management*, Vol. 1, No. 22 (February 1995).

12. Adapted with permission from: 'The Application of a Stage-Gate Process to Developing New Markets', *Confidential MBA Thesis, Cranfield School of Management* (2001).

13. Moss Kanter, R., 'Innovation: The Classic Traps', *Harvard Business Review*, Vol. 84, No. 11 (November 2006), p. 73.

14. Houlder, V., 'Technology: Quiet Revolution', *Financial Times* (26 March 1996), p. 143.

15. Linganatham, T., 'Management of Technology and Innovation at Texas Instruments', Presentation to MBA students at Universiti Teknologi Malaysia, Kuala Lumpur (November 1997).

16. Leavy, B., 'A Leader's Guide to Creating an Innovation Culture', *Strategy & Leadership*, Vol. 33, No. 4 (2005), pp. 38–45.

17. Jelinek, M. and Schoonhoven, C. B., *The Innovation Marathon: Lessons from High Technology Firms* (Oxford: Basil Blackwell, 1990).

18. *Ibid.*, p. 203.

19. O'Reilly, C. and Tushman, M., 'Using Culture for Strategic Advantage: Promoting Innovation through Social Control', in Tushman, M. L. and Anderson, P. (eds), *Managing Strategic Innovation and Change: A Collection of Readings* (New York: Oxford University Press, 1997), pp. 200–216.

20. Zien, K. A. and Buckler, S. A., 'Dreams to Market: Crafting a Culture of Innovation', *Journal of Product Innovation Management*, Vol. 14, No. 4 (1997), pp. 274–287.

21. Howard, R., 'The CEO as Organizational Architect', in Tushman, M. L. and Anderson, P. (eds), *Managing Strategic Innovation and Change: A Collection of Readings* (New York: Oxford University Press, 1997), pp. 631–641.

22. Sakkab, N. Y., 'Connect and Develop Complements Research and Develop at P&G', *Research-Technology Management*, Vol. 45, No. 2 (March–April 2002), pp. 38–45.

23. Johne, F. A. and Snelson, P. A., 'Success Factors in Product Innovation: A Selective Review of the Literature', *Journal of Product Innovation Management*, Vol. 5, No. 2 (June 1988), pp. 114–128.

24. Lim, B. C., 'Management of Technology and Innovation at ShinEtsu', presentation to MBA students, Universiti Teknologi Malaysia, Kuala Lumpur (November 1997).

25. Hargadon, A. and Sutton, R. I., 'Building an Innovation Factory', *Harvard Business Review*, Vol. 78, No. 3 (May–June 2000), pp. 157–166.

26. Buckler, S. A. and Zien, K. A., 'The Spirituality of Innovation: Learning from Stories', *Journal of Product Innovation Management*, Vol. 13, No. 5 (September 1996), pp. 391–405.

27. Webber, A. M. and LaBarre, P., 'The Innovation Conversation', *Research-Technology Management*, Vol. 44, No. 5 (September–October 2001), pp. 9–11.

28. Szwejczewski, M., Wheatley, M. and Goffin, K., *Process Innovation in UK Manufacturing: Best Practice Makes Perfect*, Department of Trade and Industry, DTI/Pub 5468/15k/06/01/NP (London, June 2001), p. 36.

29. *Ibid.*

30. Oke, A. and Goffin, K., 'Leading Edge Knowledge Management at Oxford Asymmetry', Unpublished Teaching Case Study (Cranfield School of Management, 2001).

31. Boxall, P. and Purcell, J., *Strategy and Human Resource Management* (Basingstoke: Palgrave Macmillan, 2003).

32. Barsh, J., Capozzi, M. M. and Davidson, J., 'Leadership and Innovation', *The McKinsey Quarterly*, No. 1 (2008), pp. 37–47.

33. Drucker, P. F., *Innovation and Entrepreneurship* (Oxford: Butterworth-Heinemann, 1985).

34. Pavia, T. M., 'The Early Stages of New Product Development in Entrepreneurial High-Tech Firms', *Journal of Product Innovation Management*, Vol. 8, No. 1 (March 1991), pp. 18–31.

35. Bhide, A., 'How Entrepreneurs Craft Strategies That Work', *Harvard Business Review*, Vol. 72, No. 2 (March–April 1994), pp. 150–161.

36. Martin, M. J. C., *Managing Innovation and Entrepreneurship in Technology-Based Firms* (News York: John Wiley, 1994).

37. Drucker, P. F., *Innovation and Entrepreneurship* (Oxford: Butterworth-Heinemann, 1985).

38. Based on: Hawe, J., 'A New Style', *The Wall Street Journal Europe* (Friday/Saturday/Sunday, 26–28 September 2003), p. R2. Supplemented by information from www.qbhouse.com/singapore/index.html.

39. Amabile, T., 'Minding the Muse', *Working Knowledge – a Quarterly Report on Research at Harvard Business School*, Vol. IV, No. 1 (1999).

40. Staw, B., Sandelands, L. and Dutton, J., 'Threat-Rigidity Effects in Organizational Behaviour: A Multi-level Analysis', *Administrative Science Quarterly*, Vol. 26, No. 4 (1981), pp. 501–524.

41. Staber, U. and Sydow, J., 'Organizational Adaptive Capacity: A Structuration Perspective', *Journal of Management Inquiry*, Vol. 11, No. 4 (2002), pp. 408–425.

42. Martin, M. J. C., *Managing Innovation and Entrepreneurship in Technology-Based Firms* (New York: John Wiley, 1994).

43. Wheelwright, S. C. and Clark, K., *Revolutionizing Product Development: Quantum Leaps in Speed, Efficiency, and Quality* (New York: The Free Press, 1992).

44. Sosa, M. E. and Mihm, J., 'Organizational Design for New Product Development', in Loch, C. H. and Kavadias, S. (eds), *Handbook of New Product Development* (Oxford: Butterworth-Heinemann, 2008), pp. 165–197.

45. Anonymous, 'Face Value: The Mass Production of Ideas, and Other Possibilities', *The Economist*, Vol. 334, No. 7906 (18 March 1995), p. 111.

46. von Hippel, E., Thomke, S. and Sonnack, M., 'Creating Breakthroughs at 3M', *Harvard Business Review*, Vol. 77, No. 5 (September–October 1999), pp. 47–57.

47. Hershock, R. J., Cowman, C. D. and Peters, D., 'Action Teams That Work', *Journal of Product Innovation Management*, Vol. 11, No. 2 (March 1992), pp. 95–104.

48. Nicholson, G. C., 'Keeping Innovation Alive', *Research-Technology Management*, Vol. 41, No. 3 (May–June 1998), pp. 34–40.

49. Gwynne, P., 'Skunk Works, 1990s-Style', *Research-Technology Management*, Vol. 40, No. 4 (July–August 1997), pp. 18–23.

50. *Ibid.*

51. Chesbrough, H. W. and Teece, D. J., 'When Is Virtual Virtuous? Organizing for Innovation', *Harvard Business Review*, Vol. 74, No. 1 (January–February 1996), pp. 65–73.

52. Galvin, D. and Sucher, S., 'WingspanBank.com', *Harvard Business School Case Study*, No. 9–600-035 (July 2002).

53. O'Reilly III, C. A. and Tushman, M. L., 'The Ambidextrous Organization', *Harvard Business Review*, Vol. 82, No. 4 (April 2004), pp. 74–81.

54. Henke, J. W., Krachenberg, A. R. and Lyons, T. F., 'Cross-Functional Teams: Good Concept, Poor Implementation', *Journal of Product Innovation Management*, Vol. 10, No. 3 (June 1993), pp. 216–229.

55. *Ibid.*

56. *Ibid.*

57. Thomson. L., *Personality Type* (Boston, MA: Shambhala Publications, 1998).

58. Belbin, R. M., *Management Teams* (London: Heineman, 1981).

59. Hayes, N., *Managing Teams: A Strategy for Success* (London: Thompson Learning, 2002).

60. Tuckman, B., 'Developmental Sequence in Small Groups', *Psychological Bulletin*, Vol. 63, No. 6 (1965), pp. 384–399.

61. Souder, W. E., 'Managing Relations between R&D and Marketing in New Product Development Projects', *Journal of Product Innovation Management*, Vol. 5, No. 1 (March 1988), pp. 6–19.

62. *Ibid*, p. 10.

63. Nixon, B., 'Research and Development Performance Measurement: A Case Study', *Management Accounting Review*, Vol. 9 (September 1998), pp. 329–355.

64. Schein, E. H., 'Three Cultures of Management: The Key to Organizational Learning', *Sloan Management Review*, Vol. 71, No. 4 (Fall 1996), pp. 9–20.

65. Tsai, W., Verma, R. and Schmidt, G., 'New Service Development', in Loch, C. H. and Kavadias, S. (eds), *Handbook of New Product Development* (Oxford: Butterworth-Heinemann, 2008), pp. 495–530.

66. McDonough, E. F., 'Faster New Product Development: Investigating the Effects of Technology and Characteristics of the Project Leader and Team', *Journal of Product Innovation Management*, Vol. 10, No. 3 (June 1993), pp. 241–250.

67. Barczak, G. and Wilemon, D., 'Leadership Differences in New Product Development Teams', *Journal of Product Innovation Management*, Vol. 6, No. 4 (December 1989), pp. 259–267.

68. Cooper, R. G. and Kleinschmidt, E. J., 'Stage Gate Systems for New Product Success', *Marketing Management*, Vol. 1, No. 4 (1992), pp. 20–29.

69. Balachandra, R., Brockhoff, K. K. and Pearson, A. W., 'R&D Project Termination Decisions: Processes, Communication, and Personnel Changes', *Journal of Product Innovation Management*, Vol. 13, No. 3 (May 1996), pp. 245–256.

70. Meyers, P. W. and Wilemon, D., 'Learning in New Technology Development Teams', *Journal of Product Innovation Management*, Vol. 6, No. 2 (June 1989), pp. 79–88.

71. Balogun, J., Hope Hailey, V. with Johnson, G. and Scholes, K., *Exploring Strategic Change* (London: Prentice Hall, 1999), p. 196.

72. Tyrrell, P., *Fertile Ground: Cultivating a Talent for Innovation*. Economist Intelligence Unit (London, 2009).

73. www: opp.co.uk.

74. Bratton, J. and Gold, J., *Human Resource Management: Theory and Practice* (Basingstoke: Palgrave Macmillan, 2003), p. 485.

75. Katz, R., 'Managing Professional Careers: The Influence of Job Longevity and Group Age', in Tushman, M. L. and Anderson, P. (eds), *Managing Strategic Innovation and Change: A Collection of Readings* (New York: Oxford University Press, 1997), pp. 193–199.

76. For a good explanation of all of the theories refer to: Mullins, L. M., *Management and Organisational Behaviour* (London: Pitman Publishing, 4th Edition, 1996), pp. 497–517.

77. Cohn, J., Katzenbach, J. and Vlak, G., 'Finding and Grooming Breakthrough Innovators', *Harvard Business Review*, Vol. 86, No. 6 (November–December 2008), pp. 62–69.

78. Bratton, J. and Gold, J., *Human Resource Management: Theory and Practice* (Basingstoke: Palgrave Macmillan, 2003), p. 13.

79. *Ibid.*, p. 485.

80. Torrington, D. and Hall, L., *Personnel Management: HRM in Action*, (London: Prentice Hall, 1995).

81. Goffin, K. and Pfeiffer, R., *Innovation Management in UK and German Manufacturing Companies* (London: Anglo-German Foundation Report Series, December 1999).

82. Based on Goffin, k., and Pfeiffer, R. "Getting the Big Idea". *The Engineer*, (4th February 2000), pp. 22–23.

83. Daft, R. L., *Organization Theory and Design*, (Cincinnati, OH: South-Western College Publishing, 1998), p. 350.

84. Boxall, P. and Purcell, J., *Strategy and Human Resource Management* (Basingstoke: Palgrave Macmillan, 2003).

85. Ancona, D. G. and Caldwell, D. F., 'Making Teamwork Work: Boundary Management in Product Development Teams', in Tushman, M. L. and Anderson, P. (eds), *Managing Strategic Innovation and Change: A Collection of Readings* (New York: Oxford University Press, 1997), pp. 433–422.

86. Howard, R., 'The CEO as Organizational Architect', in Tushman, M. L. and Anderson, P. (eds), *Managing Strategic Innovation and Change: A Collection of Readings* (New York: Oxford University Press, 1997), pp. 631–641.

87. Pettigrew, A. and Fenton, E. M. (eds), *The Innovating Organization* (London: SAGE Publications, 2000), p. 251.

88. Goffin, K., Lee-Mortimer, A. and New, C., *Managing Product Innovation for Competitive Advantage* (London: Haymarket Business Publications, November 1999).

89. Case based on interviews with Jörg Asbrand and Franz-Joseph Miller in May 2009, and material from the website www.time-matters.com.

9 BOOSTING INNOVATION PERFORMANCE

1. Kaplan, R. S. and Norton, D. P., *The Balanced Scorecard – Translating Strategy into Action* (Boston, MA: Harvard Business School Press, 1996).

2. *Ibid.*, p. 97.

3. Goffin, K. and Pfeiffer, R., *Innovation Management in UK and German Manufacturing Companies* (London: Anglo-German Foundation Report Series, December 1999).

4. Holman, R., Kaas, H-W. and Keeling, D., 'The Future of Product Development', *The McKinsey Quarterly*, No. 3 (2003), pp. 28–39.

5. Slack, N., Chambers, S. and Johnston, B., *Operations Management* (London: Pitman, 4th Edition, 2003).

6. Johnston, R. and Clark, G., *Service Operations Management*. Financial Times (London: Prentice Hall, 2001).

7. Kleinknecht, A., 'Indicators of Manufacturing and Service Innovation: Their Strengths and Weaknesses', in Metcalf, J. S. and Miles, I. (eds), *Innovation Systems in the Service Economy* (Norwell, MA: Kluwer Academic Publishers, 2000), pp. 169–186.

8. Chiesa, V., Coughlan, P. and Voss, C. A., 'Development of a Technical Innovation Audit', *Journal of Product Innovation Management*, Vol. 13, No. 2 (March 1996), pp. 105–136.

9. Case based on an MBA project conducted in 2000; a visit to Evotec on 20 May 2009 with discussions with Dr Mario Polywka; and the Evotec and Zebrafish websites (www.evotec.com) and (www.zebrafish-screening.com).

10. Majaro, S., *The Creative Gap* (London: Longman, 1988).

11. Feige, A. and Crooker, R., 'Innovationen als Medizin gegen Arbeitslosigkeit und Mittelmass', *Frankfurter Allgemeine Zeitung* (7 December 1998).

12. Duhamel, M., *Promoting Innovation Management Techniques in Europe* (Luxembourg: European Commission, December 1999).

13. British Standard. *Design Management Systems – Part 1: Guide to Managing Innovation*. British Standard BS7000–1:1999 (London: British Standards Institution, 1999).

14. Chiesa, V., Coughlan, P. and Voss, C. A., 'Development of a Technical Innovation Audit', *Journal of Product Innovation Management*, Vol. 13, No. 2 (March 1996), pp. 105–136.

15. Coughlan, P. and Brady, E., 'Evolution towards Integrated Product Development in Subsidiaries of Multinational Enterprises', *International Journal of Technology Management*, Vol. 12, No. 7/8 (1996), pp. 733–747.

16. Case based on interviews with Trudy Lloyd, 2005.

17. Golder, P., 'Insights from Senior Executives about Innovation in International Markets', *Journal of Product Innovation Management*, Vol. 17, No. 5 (2000), pp. 326–340.

18. Borins, S., *The Challenge of Innovating in Government*. The PricewaterhouseCoopers Endowment for the Business of Government, Innovations in Management Series (February 2001).

19. Calantone, R. J., Vickery, S. K. and Droege, C., 'Business Performance and Strategic New Product Development Activities: An Empirical Investigation', *Journal of Product Innovation Management*, Vol. 12, No. 3 (1995), pp. 214–223.

20. McGourty, J., Tarshis, L.A. and Dominick, P., 'Managing Innovation: Lessons from World Class Organizations', *International Journal of Technology Management*, Vol. 11, No. 3/4 (1996), pp. 354–368.

21. Thamhain, H. J., 'Managing Technologically Innovative Team Efforts toward New Product Success', *Journal of Product Innovation Management*, Vol. 7, No. 1 (March 1990), pp. 5–18.

22. British Standard. *Design Management Systems – Part 1: Guide to Managing Innovation*. British Standard BS7000–1:1999 (London: British Standards Institution, 1999).

23. Case based on company documentation, an interview and personal correspondence with Cobra managers in May 2004 and January 2009.

24. Borins, S., *The Challenge of Innovating in Government*. The PricewaterhouseCoopers Endowment for the Business of Government, Innovations in Management Series (February 2001).

25. British Standard. *Design Management Systems – Part 1: Guide to Managing Innovation*. British Standard BS7000–1:1999 (London: British Standards Institution, 1999).

26. Day, G. S., Gold, B. and Kuczmarski, T. D., 'Significant Issues for the Future of Product Innovation', *Journal of Product Innovation Management*, Vol. 11, No. 1 (January 1994), pp. 69–75.

27. Linder, J. C., Jarvenpaa, S. and Davenport, T. H., 'Towards an Innovation Sourcing Strategy', *MIT Sloan Management Review*, Vol. 44, No. 4 (Summer 2003), pp. 43–49.

28. Webber, A. M. and LaBarre, P., 'The Innovation Conversation', *Research-Technology Management*, Vol. 44, No. 5 (September–October 2001), pp. 9–11.

29. Chesbrough, H. W., 'The Era of Open Innovation', *MIT Sloan Management Review*, Vol. 44, No. 3 (Spring 2003), pp. 35–41.

30. Chambers, C. A. and Boghani, A. B., 'Knowledge Management: An Engine for Innovation', *Prism* (Second Quarter 1998), pp. 31–39.

31. Sakkab, N. Y., 'Connect and Develop Complements Research and Develop at P&G', *Research-Technology Management*, Vol. 45, No. 2 (March–April 2002), pp. 38–45.

32. Anonymous. 'Managing Change in Your Organization', *International Trade Forum*, No. 2 (2000), pp. 26–28.

33. Karol, R. A., Loeser, R. C. and Tait, R. H., 'Better New Business Development at Dupont-I', *Research-Technology Management*, Vol. 45, No. 1 (January–February 2002), pp. 24–30.

34. Case based on an interview with Massimo Fumarola, conducted by K. Goffin in May 2004.

35. Cooper, R. G. and Kleinschmidt, E. J., 'Stage Gate Systems for New Product Success', *Marketing Management*, Vol. 1, No. 4 (1992), pp. 20–29.

36. Chambers, C. A. and Boghani, A. B., 'Knowledge Management: An Engine for Innovation', *Prism* (Second Quarter 1998), pp. 31–39.

37. Day, G. S., Gold, B. and Kuczmarski, T. D., 'Significant Issues for the Future of Product Innovation', *Journal of Product Innovation Management*, Vol. 11, No. 1 (January 1994), pp. 69–75.

38. Karol, R. A., Loeser, R. C. and Tait, R. H., 'Better New Business Development at Dupont-I', *Research-Technology Management*, Vol. 45, No. 1 (January–February 2002), pp. 24–30.

39. Smith, G. R., Herbein, W. C. and Morris, R. C., 'Front-End Innovation at AlliedSignal', *Research-Technology Management*, Vol. 42, No. 6 (November–December 1999), pp. 15–24.

40. Anonymous (Economist), 'A Dark Art No More', in Anonymous (Economist): Something New Under the Sun: A Special Report on Innovation, *The Economist* (13 October 2007), pp. XX.

41. Thamhain, H. J., 'Managing Technologically Innovative Team Efforts toward New Product Success', *Journal of Product Innovation Management*, Vol. 7, No. 1 (March 1990), pp. 5–18.

42. Webber, A. M. and LaBarre, P., 'The Innovation Conversation', *Research-Technology Management*, Vol. 44, No. 5 (September–October 2001), pp. 9–11.

43. Borins, S., *The Challenge of Innovating in Government*. The PricewaterhouseCoopers Endowment for the Business of Government, Innovations in Management Series (February 2001).

44. McGourty, J., Tarshis, L. A. and Dominick, P., 'Managing Innovation: Lessons from World Class Organizations', *International Journal of Technology Management*, Vol. 11, No. 3/4 (1996), pp. 354–368.

45. Tushman, M. L., Newman, W. H. and Romanelli, E., 'Convergence and Upheaval: Managing the Unsteady Pace of Organizational Evolution', in Tushman, M. L. and Anderson, P. (eds), *Managing Strategic Innovation and Change: A Collection of Readings* (New York: Oxford University Press, 1997), pp. 583–594.

46. *Ibid.*

47. Schein, E. H., 'Three Cultures of Management: The Key to Organizational Learning', *Sloan Management Review*, Vol. 71, No. 3 (Fall 1996), pp. 9–20.

48. O'Connor, P., 'From Experience: Implementing a Stage-Gate Process: A Multi-Company Perspective', *Journal of Product Innovation Management*, Vol. 11, No. 3 (1994), pp. 183–200.

49. Beckhard, R. and Harris, R. T., *Organisation Transitions: Managing Complex Change* (London: Addison Wesley, 1987).

50. Tushman, M. L. and O'Reilly III, C. A., *Winning through Innovation: A Practical Guide to Leading Organizational Change and Renewal* (Boston, MA: Harvard Business School Press, 2002), p. 49.

51. Jaruzelski, B. and DeHoff, K., 'The Customer Connection: The Global Innovation 1000', *Strategy + Business*, No. 49 (Winter 2007), pp. 69–83.

52. Tushman, M. L. and O'Reilly III, C. A., *Winning through Innovation: A Practical Guide to Leading Organizational Change and Renewal* (Boston, MA: Harvard Business School Press, 2002), p. 49.

53. Pettigrew, A. and Fenton, E. M. (eds), *The Innovating Organization* (London: SAGE Publications, 2000).

54. Balogun, J., Hope Hailey, V. with Johnson, G. and Scholes, K., *Exploring Strategic Change* (London: Prentice Hall, 1999).

55. Stalk, G. and Hout, T. M., *Competing against Time: How Time-Based Competition Is Reshaping Global Markets* (New York: The Free Press, 1990).

56. Schein, E. H., 'Coming to a New Awareness of Organizational Culture', *Sloan Management Review*, Vol. 25, No. 4 (Winter 1984), pp. 3–16.

57. Fixson, S. K., 'Teaching Innovation through Interdisciplinary Courses and Programmes in Product Design and Development: An Analysis at 16 US Schools', *Creativity and Innovation Management*, Vol. 18, No. 3 (2009), pp. 199–208.
58. Case based on an interview with Magnus Schoeman on 28 May 2009.
59. Case adapted with permission from: Goffin, K., Lee-Mortimer, A. and New, C., *Managing Product Innovation for Competitive Advantage* (London: Haymarket Publications, 1999).

10   THE FUTURE OF INNOVATION MANAGEMENT

1. Quoted by Bernstein, P. L., *Against The Gods: The Remarkable Story of Risk* (New York: John Wiley, 1998), p. 203.
2. 'A Brother for Her', *The Economist* (18 December 2004), p. 111.
3. Maslow, A. H., *Towards a Psychology of Being* (New York: Wiley, 3rd Edition, 1998).
4. Mackintosh, J., 'The Assembly Line Is Bunk Says Former Ford Executive', in *Financial Times* (20 April 2004), p. 22.
5. Howe, J., *Crowdsourcing: Why the Power of the Crowd Is Driving the Future of Business* (New York: Random House, 2008). For a somewhat more analytical take on a similar subject see: Surowiecki, J., *The Wisdom of Crowds* (London: Little, Brown, 2004).
6. Case based on 'Identifying and Tapping the Potentials of Possible Future Business via Structured Communication – Visions of Vodafone Pilotentwicklung', in Kohlgrüber, M., Schnauffer, H-G. and Jaeger, D. (eds) *Das einzigartige Unternehmen* (Berlin: Springer, 2003), company documentation and interviews with Dr Christiane Hipp, Torsten Herzberg and Eva Weber in December 2004.
7. Case based on an interview with Cheryl Perkins, President of Innovationedge on 18th December 2008.
8. Kahn, H. and Wiener, A., *The Year 2000, a Framework for Speculation on the Next Thirty-Three Years* (New York: MacMillan, 1967).
9. Albright, R. E., 'What Can Past Technology Forecasts Tell Us about the Future?', *Technological Forecasting and Social Change*, Vol. 69, No. 5 (June 2002), pp. 443–464.
10. Moore, G., 1965, 'Cramming More Components onto Integrated Circuits', *Electronics*, Vol. 38.
11. Asenov, A., 'Every Atom Counts', *IEE Electronic Systems and Software*, Vol. 2, No. 6 (2004), pp. 26–32.
12. Walko, J., 'Scaling Is Dead. Long Live Innovation!', *IEE Review*, Vol. 23 (2005).
13. There is great scope for argument over when technologies were invented and when they can be said to be fully exploited. For one view see Dussauge, P., Hart, S. and Ramanantsoa, B., *Strategic Technology Management* (Chichester: John Wiley, 1987), p. 19.
14. www.smart.com.
15. Kim, W. Chan and Mauborgne, R., *Blue Ocean Strategy* (Boston, MA: Harvard Business School Press, 2005).
16. Challenge forum, *'Weak Signals, Harsh Impacts'* (2003), www.chforum.org.
17. 'Innovative India', *The Economist* (3 April 2004), pp. 67–68.
18. Bhidé, A., *The Venturesome Economy* (Princeton, NJ: University Press, 2008).
19. Prahalad, C. K., *The Fortune at the Bottom of the Pyramid* (Pearson Education Inc 2005).
20. See 'A Snip at the Price', *The Economist* (30 May 2009), p. 74.
21. Rao, 'A Firm Footing', *Appropriate Technology*, Vol. 35, No. 4, (December 2008), pp. 61–63.
22. 'Battling for the Palm of Your Hand', *The Economist* (1 May 2004), pp. 79–81.
23. Case based on a presentation by Katja van der Wal (London, 4 December 2008).
24. Case based on an interview with Klaus Schnurr, CEO of PureInsight on 18 December 2008.
25. Case based on interviews with Mike Northcott and William Pipkin, Hewlett-Packard internal documentation, and Zell, D. M., Glassman, A. and Duron, S. A., 'Accelerating the Strategy Process: One Industry Giant's Attempt', *Proceedings of the Academy of Management Annual Meeting* (August 2004).

Index